Cambridge Studies in Music
General Editors: John Stevens and Peter le Huray

The Organ Music of J. S. Bach

III

For Lucy and Daniel

The Organ Music of J. S. Bach

III

A Background

by Peter Williams

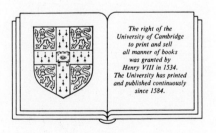

The right of the
University of Cambridge
to print and sell
all manner of books
was granted by
Henry VIII in 1534.
The University has printed
and published continuously
since 1584.

CAMBRIDGE UNIVERSITY PRESS

CAMBRIDGE

LONDON   NEW YORK   NEW ROCHELLE

MELBOURNE   SYDNEY

Published by the Press Syndicate of the University of Cambridge
The Pitt Building, Trumpington Street, Cambridge CB2 IRP
32 East 57th Street, New York, NY 10022, USA
296 Beaconsfield Parade, Middle Park, Melbourne 3206, Australia

First published 1984

Printed in Great Britain at the
University Press, Cambridge

Library of Congress catalogue card number: 77-71431

British Library Cataloguing in Publication Data

Williams, Peter, *1937 May 14* -
The organ music of J. S. Bach. - (Cambridge studies in music)
Vol. 3: A background
1. Bach, Johann Sebastian – Organ music
I. Title   II. Series
786.5'092'4   ML145.B14

ISBN 0 521 24412 9

ME

Contents

Contents

Preface

It is characteristic of the wider horizons of musical researches today that it is possible to devote to a single corpus of music three volumes of words – words if anything too densely rather than too loosely written – which not only leave open biographical–chronological questions but barely come to terms with the unique qualities of the music itself and what it is that it does to the listener. Temporarily or not, subjective approaches now seem to be out of date, and the few instances in which modern authors have tried to 'explain the meaning' of such music are not always sure to convert the sceptical and the circumspect. But in the case of J. S. Bach's works, to avoid subjective areas is not to avoid the impact of the music. On the contrary, the astonishing historical position of both the bigger preludes and the bigger fugues – comparable to which the history of music produced virtually nothing before, during or immediately after – is itself so difficult to grasp that, though nothing in such books as this opts for a description of their power and effect, it is nevertheless that power or effect which supports the writing of three volumes. A similar point could be made about the chorales and the trios: admiration for and an awareness of their musical power can now take the form not of subjective speculation but of a cool assessment of conditions and assumptions governing the composer himself.

The present volume, therefore, aims to present a background to this particular corpus of music, refining and voicing questions about the main areas in the study of it – purpose, style, instrument, performance – without wishing to convey the impression that such questions can always be answered. Not every work of Bach's is referred to individually, and readers can usually find other examples to illustrate a point being made. The confidence with which conjectures about this music are constantly expressed in words or in performance is a reflection of the music's power and of personal responses which people have been encouraged to develop, as of right, in the two centuries and more since the composer died. But in many particular respects, a crucial ignorance still affects our understanding of the music, and the sketching of a background should at least alert Those Desirous of Learning to the many details that remain uncertain. In the ways in which the background has been sketched I have tried to allow for what will presumably be learnt in the years to come. For example, if the nature of the Weimar organ should come to be better understood, or the precise details of the Leipzig services to be known, or the composer's changing habits of articulation and fingering to be more fully worked out, such new information could be 'slotted in' to what is said more generally here.

Volume III refers frequently to Volumes I and II and supposes what it says to be a supplement to many basic questions already raised in the piece-by-piece commentary in the earlier volumes. For example, the further suggestions made in Volume III about the nature and origins of the *Orgelbüchlein* need to be understood against what was said about the album in Volume II. A third volume also allows a certain number of additions and corrections to the other two, especially in the light of more recent literature (*NBA KB* etc). Moreover, I would also like to point out a detail evidently not made clear enough in those first two volumes: that many of my references to authors now known to have been incautious in some of their suppositions (in particular Keller and Klotz) were made in a spirit of irony, insofar as other evidence presented 'disproves' what they say, without my finding it necessary to say so. As to further work on this extraordinary music, it is possible to imagine a fourth volume devoted to practical issues of importance to the player: specific notes on the musical–stylistic demands and the performance details (articulation, tempo, registration etc) of the works one by one.

I wish to thank in particular the following for help and advice: Dr Alfred Dürr (Göttingen), Mr Charles Fisk (Gloucester, Mass.), Dr Klaus Hofmann (Göttingen), Professor John Hsu (Ithaca, NY), Dr Dietrich Kilian (Göttingen), Dr Yoshitake Kobayashi (Göttingen), Dr Mark Lindley (Boston, Mass.), Mr David Mather (BBC, London), Dr Hans-Joachim Schulze (Leipzig), Professor L. F. Tagliavini (Bologna), Professor Christoph Wolff (Cambridge, Mass.), M. Jean-Claude Zehnder (Basel). Once again, I owe much of the book's form and presentation to Mr Eric Van Tassel (CUP), as I owe much to the encouragement of Mrs Rosemary Dooley (CUP), Dr Peter le Huray (Cambridge) and Dr Schulze. For the completion of the book I have to thank Cornell University for the special facilities given me in the form of a Senior Fellowship at the Society for the Humanities.

April 1982   Peter Williams
Cornell University, Ithaca, NY

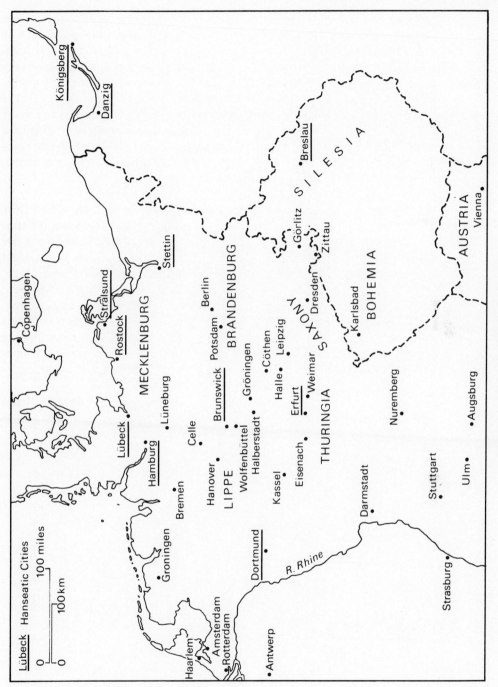

Northern Germany in the Time of J. S. Bach

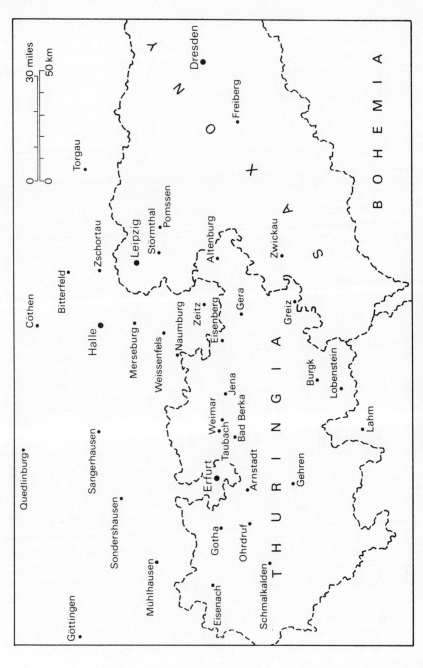

Thuringia and Saxony in the Time of J. S. Bach

The Music in Service and Recital

1. The Order of Services

While several, even many, orders of service are known from the appropriate areas of Germany between the mid seventeenth and the mid eighteenth century, two particular questions remain: What exactly were the orders at Arnstadt, Mühlhausen, Weimar, Cöthen and Leipzig, and What exactly did the organ play in them?

The general lines of both are clear. Thus at Arnstadt, the main service or *Hauptgottesdienst* (Sunday 8-10am), the Monday prayer-hour or *Betstunde*, and the midweek early service or *Frühgottesdienst* (Thursday 7-9am - Müller 1950 p37) can be assumed to have resembled the plans published in Weissenfels in 1714 and in part summarized below. Similarly, the contribution of the organ in at least the more important and traditional churches must have been of the kind summarized from the *Ordo cantionum* at Halle and served by the *Tabulatura nova* of Scheidt, both seventeenth-century (Klotz 1961 pp786-7):

1 prelude before (according to *Ordo*; nothing specified in *Tabulatura*)
2 antiphon ad introitum (ditto)
3 *alternatim* sections in Kyrie and Gloria (*Tabulatura*)
4 ditto to the Gradual hymn after Epistle (*Tabulatura*)
5 ditto to the German Creed, sung as a hymn (*Tabulatura*)
6 ditto to the Communion hymn *Jesus Christus unser Heiland* (*Tabulatura*)
7 exit, organ fantasia (*Tabulatura*)

But in neither case - order of service or supposed organ contributions - are the details certain. Thus, while fantasias were certainly included by Scheidt in his collection of organ music, just as they were by any industrious copyist of the period, the *Tabulatura* shows no specific service-plan (except in the general order of seasonal hymn - Credo - Communion), nor is it likely that before the second quarter of the eighteenth century any church service (perhaps with one or two rare exceptions) closed with any kind of organ music. The same may be true of nos. 1 and 2 above; but even in nos. 3-6, it is unclear (because custom changed at a different pace in different towns) whether in a particular instance the organ introduced the hymn with more than a few notes, accompanied the congregation as they sang, played interludes between the lines if it did accompany, played a complete verse solo in alternation with the congregation and/or the choir, or concluded a hymn (such as those preceding the sermon and closing the service) with a postlude corresponding to the prelude. Various methods can be traced during the three centuries between Luther and Mendelssohn:

no organ, hymns led by cantor or choir, themselves perhaps singing alternate verses
organ prelude and inter-verse interlude (*alternatim*) to some or all chorales, but no accompaniment of the congregation's verses
organ prelude, accompaniment of the congregation (four-part harmony, etc), interline interludes
ditto but no interludes
ditto but brief organ intonation only (i.e. no full-scale prelude)

I

While the last has been for long the most familiar method in protestant countries, the earlier methods – despite obvious practical problems resulting from them – were so customary as to make ambiguous even the clearest service-order, such as J. S. Bach's own notes on Advent services (see below). One can, however, assume that the methods were not arbitrary: for example, interline interludes as in BWV 725, 722 etc cannot have arisen until the organ accompanied the congregation's singing, and it is reasonable to interpret such interludes as in some sense 'replacing' the old *alternatim* organ solos.

Outlines of several types of service follow, from which it is possible to identify the central questions.

Some Standard Services

'Sermon Service' (*Predigtgottesdienst*)

1553 Kirchenordung
(Weismann 1956 p62)

Latin introit (*Schüler*, 'boys')
German Psalm
Sermon on the Gospel text:
   Eingangsvotum (exhortation)
   Invocation of divine grace
   Silent Lord's Prayer
   Reading of text
   Sermon
   Notices
Ten Commandments ⎫ quietly spoken
Creed   ⎬ after sermon
Lord's Prayer   ⎭
General church prayers (with collects
   on feast-days)
Lord's Prayer
Psalm or hymn
Blessing

'Early Sermon' on Sundays, with following Communion

Weissenfels Order 1714 (Advent 1)
(Blankenburg 1961 pp631–2)

Introit *musiciret* (Latin)
Ps. 19 (as a hymn)
Missa *musiciret*: Kyrie–Christe–Kyrie
Gloria in excelsis intoned from altar
Missa continues: *et in terra*
Allein Gott (hymn)
Collects
Epistle
Nun komm der Heiden Heiland (Advent
  hymn)
Gospel
Stück musiciret (cantata)
German Creed [as a hymn?]
Herr Jesu Christ, dich zu uns wend ⎫ as a
Lord's Prayer   ⎬ group
Sermon   ⎭
Stück musiciret (cantata)
Herr Gott der einig Gottes Sohn
  (Advent hymn)
Collects
Blessing
Close with *Sei Lob und Ehr* (hymn
  with amen)
Communion to follow
Allein zu dir, Herr Jesu Christ (hymn)
Consecration
Jesus Christus, unser Heiland ⎫during
O Jesu, du mein Bräutigam   ⎭Communion
Other hymns
Collects
Blessing
Christe, du Lamm Gottes (hymn)

Latin introit only on feast-days etc
(e.g. not on Advent 2); during Lent etc,
Kyrie chanted; Mass movements sung by
choir only; on feast-days, Creed in Latin at
altar before German Creed

'Afternoon Sermon' on Sundays
(*Nachmittag-Predigt am Sonntag*)

Weissenfels Order 1714 (Advent 1)
(*ibid* p632)

Deus in adjutorium intoned from altar
Response by choir, *Domine ad
   adiuvandum*
Ps. 118 (as a hymn)
Gottes Sohn ist kommen (Advent hymn)
Reading of Ps. 24
Stück musiciret
Herr Jesu Christ . . . ⎫
Sermon ⎬ as a group
Magnificat *musiciret* ⎭
Nun komm . . . (Advent hymn)
Collects
Blessing
Close with *Täglich, Herr Gott,
   dich loben wir* (last section of the
   Te Deum, as a hymn)

'Afternoon Prayer Hour' on Sundays
(*Betstunde*)

Weissenfels Order 1714
(*ibid* p633)

Intonation before the altar
Response *vom Chor* ('from quire' or
   'by choir'?)*
Psalm (as a hymn)
Hymn appropriate to Sunday Gospel
Psalm (read)
Prayers
Lord's Prayer
Hymn
Hymn
Collects
Blessing
Close (*Schlussvers*)

* In fuller services, *von der Capella* (Weissenfels
   orders of 1714) suggests the body of singers,
   Chor perhaps the place?

9am Service on Sundays
Leipzig University Church, 18th century
(Schering 1941 p103: summarized
   from *Neo Annalium Lipsiensium,
   Continuatio* II (Leipzig 1715–17) and
   Leipziger Kirchenstaat (Leipzig 1710))

Bells
Organ *praeludiret*
Allein Gott (hymn)
Organ interlude*
Hymn
Organ interlude*
Creed (German)
Sermon
Organ interlude*
Hymn appropriate to Gospel or sermon
Music on feast-days
Blessing

* according to Schering

Chief Service on Sundays
(*Hauptgottesdienst*)
Leipzig 1710, 1715

(Schering 1941 pp24–6)

Begin with Latin hymn
Praeambul on the organ ⎫
Motet or *hohe Musik* ⎬ *
Lord's Prayer (said)
Gloria intoned
Allein Gott (hymn with responses)
Collects
Epistle
(Lent & Advent: Litany and hymn)
Hymn
Gospel
Concerto (cantata, texts to be in the hands
   of the congregation)
Creed (German)
Herr Jesu Christ . . . (or *de
   tempore* hymn on ⎫
   feast-days) ⎬ as a
Sermon (from 8am to 9am) ⎬ group
Hymn relevant to sermon text ⎭

Either: more hymns until Blessing
Or: Communion hymns and motet
Blessing
Close with *de tempore* hymn on feast-days,
   or Latin hymn

* replaced by Introit and Kyrie in Lent or
   Mourning period

J. S. Bach's Notes on Services

1st Sunday in Advent, (?)1723
Note on score of BWV 61 (MS P 45)
(*Dok* 1 pp248–9)

Anordnung des GottesDienstes in Leipzig am 1 *Advent*-Sontag frühe	Order of Service in Leipzig on Advent Sunday, early
1 *Praeludiret*	Organ improvises for
2 Motetta	Motet (choir)
3 Praeludiret auf das Kyrie, so gantz musiciret wird	Organ preludes on the Kyrie, which is performed in ensemble
4 Intoniret vor dem Altar	Intonation before the altar [Gloria in excelsis and *Allein Gott*?]
5 Epistola verlesen	Epistle read [preceded by Collects?]
6 Wird die Litaney gesungen	Litany sung
7 Praelud: auf den Choral	Organ preludes for hymn of the day
8 Evangelium verlesen	Gospel read
9 Praelud. auf die HauptMusic	Organ preludes for the cantata
10 Der Glaube gesungen	Creed sung [as a hymn]
11 Die Predigt	Sermon
12 Nach der Predigt, wie gewöhnlich einige Verse aus einem Liede gesungen	After the sermon, 'as usual' some verses of a hymn sung
13 Verba Institutionis	Words of Institution [i.e. Communion]
14 Praelud. auf die Music. Und nach selbiger wechselsweise praelud. v Choräle gesungen, bis die Communion zu Ende & sic porrò	Organ preludes for the cantata; thereafter hymns and organ preludes in alternation until the Communion ends, 'and in this manner thereafter'

An almost identical service-plan (excluding the last eight words) was also entered on the score of another Advent cantata, BWV 62 (P 877), entitled as above (except *in Leipzig* omitted) and assumed to relate to Advent, 1, 1736 (*Dok* 1 p251). Whether or not the two service-orders were indeed for different occasions, the fact that the composer wrote them out suggests that they were in some way exceptional and apt for the first Sunday of the church year – perhaps in that a pair of cantatas was performed (one before the sermon, one during Communion), for the correct placing of which the organist and/or the cantor needed a plan. Although exact details of such Leipzig services are not at all clear, once one begins to look closely at each step (see Dürr 1977), it does seem that the Communion hymns were played and sung only after the second cantata. The reason why Bach's service-orders make no reference to organ music at the close of a service is unlikely to have been that the reader (the composer? a deputy? a new organist?) had no need to be told what to do (Stauffer 1980 pp196–7); one could equally well conjecture that it was because there was no question of closing with the sound of an organ. Other questions remain about the meaning of 'praeludiren' (how long? a fully fledged piece of music?), the nature of the hymns (accompanied by organ or not?), whether 'praeludiret auf' means what it seems to mean (that the improvising was on the theme of the hymn/cantata to follow?), whether the organ sounded for the Litany and Creed (before? during?), and why the other stages of the service that one might expect to see listed (hymn before sermon? one setting or other of the Agnus Dei during or after Communion?) are not mentioned.

Some Saturday Vespers Plans

General (for Luther)
(Goltzen 1956 p196)

Several Vespers psalms
Hymns as available
Lesson from New Testament (German)
Magnificat (Latin) or hymn
Lord's Prayer (silent)
Collects
Benedicamus

General (in Leipzig)
(Stiller 1970 p242)

Organ
Motet
Hymns
Sermon
Organ *praeambulo* as pastor leaves pulpit
Magnificat (German for congregation or
   Latin for choir)

Lüneburg *Kirchenordnung* 1643
(*ibid* p213)

1 or 2 psalms (Latin or German)
Catechism read
Hymns for the season (Latin or German)
Epistelpredigt (lesson and sermon)
Magnificat (Latin or German)
Collects
Benedicamus

'Musical Vespers' for Christmas 3 (cf. the
   'Afternoon Sermon' above)
Weissenfels Order 1714
(Blankenburg 1961, p633)

Intonation before the altar
Response *vom Chor* (from the quire?)
Ps. 148 (as a hymn)
Stück musiciret
Vom Himmel kam der Engel Schaar (hymn)
Music
Ps. 100 (read)
Music
Der Tag der ist so freudenreich (hymn)
Magnificat musiciret
Collects
Blessing
In dulci jubilo (hymn)

Some Special Services in Saxony

Zittau Johanniskirche
Reformation celebrations 1717, 1st day, 6.30am
(Seiffert 1917 p. xxviii)

Opens with *Es wolle uns Gott gnädig seyn* (hymn) *cum org*:
Kyrie *musiciret*, with the new organ and *Violinen*
Gloria in excelsis . . . intoniret Primarius ('intoned by first pastor')
Et in terra musicieret, with new organ and trumpets and timpani
Wir loben Gott . . . intoniret priest; choir responds *Und preisen ihn alle*

Collects sung
Coloss. 1 sung by priest (lesson)
Nun lob mein Seel den Herrn (hymn)
Dancket dem Herrn . . . intoniret priest; choir responds *Und seine Güthe*
2 Peter 1 (lesson)
Stück musiciret (cantata by J. Krieger)
Creed sung (German)
Sermon (*Primarius*)
   begins with words from Leviticus 25, v. 10
   Aria by J. Krieger, sung *cum org:*
   second *Exordio* (text) = Matthew 22, v. 21
General Confession and Prayers
   including *Vater unser* and Blessing
Herr Gott dich loben wir accompagniret by both organs, with trumpets and timpani
Preface (for Communion) sung from altar by *Primarius*
Sanctus *auf der neuen Orgel*, in a twelve-part setting
Stück musiciret (cantata by J. Krieger) during Communion
Erhalt uns Herr bey deinem Wort (hymn) *cum organ:*
Collects
Blessing

Leipzig Thomaskirche
Service on the bicentenary of Augsburg
   Confession (26 June 1730), 7am
(Schering 1941 p209)

Organ
Motet (*Lobe den Herrn, meine Seele*)
Kyrie *musiciret*
Gloria
Allein Gott (hymn)
Collects
Epistle
Gospel
Creed (Latin)
Cantata [BWV 120b]
Creed (German)
Ein feste Burg 'with organ' and
   Lord's Prayer
Sermon
Prayers
Sey Lob und Ehr (hymn)
Vers and Collect
Communion
Communion hymns
Blessing
Gott sey uns gnädig (hymn)

According to Schering, all five celebration services had a central Festival hymn 'with organ'

Freiberg Petrikirche
Opening of new organ, 1735
(Werner 1902 p70)

Herr Gott, dich loben wir (hymn)
Kyrie [choir?]
Intonation from altar: *Ehre sei Gott*
Allein Gott (hymn)
Collects and Ps. 150
Kommt Menschenkinder (hymn)
2 Chronicles 5 (lesson)
Konzert on Ps. 150, v. 6
Wir glauben all (hymn)
From the pulpit: *Lobt Gott in seinem
   Heiligtum*
After the sermon: *Konzert* on Ps. 103
Nun danket all und bringet Ehr (hymn)
Collects
Blessing
Christe, du Beistand deiner Kreuzgemeinde
   (hymn)

According to Werner, the service thus had seven congregational hymns and two choral movements

Two Services Outside Saxony and Thuringia

Osterbruch (near Hamburg), c1660–1790
Chief Sunday Service, 8am
(Mahrenholz 1960)

Intonation on the organ for:
Hymn (e.g. *Komm, Heiliger Geist*)
Kyrie (hymn, first played by organ)
Intonation from altar: *Ehre sei Gott Allein Gott* (hymn, first played by organ*)
Responses (pastor and choir)
Collects
Epistle
Chief hymn
Credo and hymn of supplication
    (e.g. *Liebster Jesu wir sind hier*),
    first played by organ*
Sermon (9am)
Prayers
Sometimes Catechism
Hymn
Prayers
Communion
Communion hymns
Blessing
Motet or music (*musizieret oder georgelt*)
Bells

* *und hernach ein Vers um den anderen gesungen und gespielt* ('and afterwards one verse sung, the other played')

Nuremberg St Lorenz, 1664, 1697
'Early Mass' (*Frühmesse*)
(Rietschel 1893 pp 68-9)

Organ prelude
Versicle for the day
Organ *moduliert*
Introit (choir)
Organ - choir (Kyrie) - organ - choir (Christe) - organ - choir (Kyrie)
Gloria (priest) - organ *moduliert* - choir (Gratias) - organ *moduliert* - choir (Quoniam)
Collect
Epistle
Organ plays (*organa pulsantur*)
Hallelujah or Tract (choir)
Gospel
Credo (priest, then choir)
Communion (exhortation, sacrament)
Organ - choir (Sanctus) - organ - choir - (Pleni) - organ - choir (Benedictus)
Vater unser (priest) & amen (choir)
Pax vobiscum (priest) & amen (choir)
Organ *moduliert* - choir (Agnus) - organ - choir (Agnus) - organ - choir (Agnus)
Organ introduces hymn
Hymn
Collect
Benedicamus (two priests)
Deo gratiam
Blessing

Some general points raised by such service-orders are:

a

On ember or penitential days (*Busstage*), the organ was usually silent. The larger churches of more traditional character preserved this custom well into the eighteenth century, so that the new organist at Zittau in 1735 was instructed to provide no organ music during Advent (i.e. after Advent Sunday?), Lent, ember and prayer days (*Buss und Beth-Tage*), or for the early services during weeks of prayer (Seiffert 1917 pp. xiv–xvi). In Leipzig during J. S. Bach's period, it seems that the organ played on the Sundays of Advent, and on Palm Sunday for the Main Service only (Stiller 1970 pp49–55). It could well be that the more integrated a part the organ took in the two chief forms of accompaniment (hymns for congregation and cantatas for the choir), the more likely it was to be heard, no doubt *piano*, on the 'silent' days. In the Catechism service later on Sunday mornings, as at Leipzig (Stiller 1970 p242) or Jena (Goltzen 1956 p212), the organ probably took no part. Schering thought that by the 1780s the organ had ceased to be silent in Advent and Lent (1941 p638), but this change may well have been earlier; though Schering is understandably often relied upon in such matters (e.g. Blindow 1957), it is not always clear with what degree of punctilio customs were observed at any one period. For example, was the organ still always silent in the period around 1700 over the five weeks before Palm Sunday, the three annual *Busstage* and the seasons of court mourning, often a month long (Schering 1926 pp14ff, 243)? In the Leipzig Nikolaikirche, the Lenten silence seems to have been relaxed only in 1780 when the Communion hymns were allowed organ accompaniment (Spitta II p97) – an interesting exception, since Communion hymns were meditative time-fillers for the congregation rather than liturgical categories.

b

On the days when organs played in the larger churches of Thuringia and Saxony – e.g. twice on Sundays and feast-days at Erfurt, plus Vespers on the previous day (Ziller 1935 pp16–18) – there is occasional evidence that some proceedings began with organ music, and the question is, From what date? It was so in 1774 at Zittau when for the service after a council election it was laid down that as soon as the council was assembled in the church the organist would begin to *praeludiren* (Seiffert 1917 p. xvii). Similarly, it was reported of J. Schneider at Leipzig in *c*1768 that he usually began the service with a regular fugue 'mit Kraft und Leben' ('with force and life', according to E. L. Gerber quoted in Stiller 1970 p66). But Gerber also praised Schneider's accompaniment to the hymns, which suggests practices different from those observed in *c*1725. Although Schering assumed that the opening line of J. S. Bach's Advent service-order for (?)1723 (see above) implied that the organist began the service with a prelude before the motet (1926 pp14ff), Bach's term 'Praeludiret' is not unambiguous: there is a great difference between playing the organ as the service begins (i.e. with choir in place, congregation assembled, etc) and playing before it begins (i.e. as the people enter). Nevertheless, Schering's interpretation is justified by a description of the Leipzig service made in 1716. According to this, proceedings at Leipzig began with the distributing of candles at 7am, whereupon the service 'began with the organ', to be followed by the motet and Kyrie, during the last verse of which the priests came from the sacristy and moved to the altar (Stiller 1970 p59). According to a source of 1710, prayers were published in order to be said privately while the organ played and the motet was sung (Schering 1926 p36); the organ played despite the dislike of it by many of the congregation (*ibid* p240).

Whether such was the custom in smaller parish churches such as Arnstadt or in court chapels such as Weimar is unknown. Even in the larger churches the organ was often less prominent than some evidence suggests. Thus at Zittau, even the special services for the Reformation Feast of 1717 began at times with hymns *sine organo* (Seiffert 1917 pp. xxix–xxxii), which makes an opening organ prelude a little unlikely. Perhaps the Erfurt, Weissenfels and Leipzig services were so systematically described in the early eighteenth century precisely because their strict orthodoxy required explanation in a period of changing customs.* Whether ortho-

---

* Certainly the court hymnbook was valid for the several residences of the duke concerned, as the title of the 1714 Weissenfels book makes clear: *Hoch-Fürstliches Sachsen-Weissenfelsisches . . . Kirchen-Buch . . . zum Gebrauch so wohl Dero Hoch-Fürstlichen Residence und den neu-erbauten Schloss-kapelle . . . in Sangerhausen* ('Church book of the Prince of Sachsen-Weissenfels, for use in his Highness's residence and in the newly built court chapel at Sangerhausen').

dox or pietist, strict or decadent, however, no churches are known with absolute certainty to have had organ music played *before* the services, i.e. as the people entered. Rather, the service proper may have begun – at least in bigger churches – with the organ as a background to prayers, its music presumably very discreet. The *Leipziger Kirchenstaat* of 1710 puts the service and its music in a broad devotional framework for Sundays (pp4–110):

5am bells
    some Latin hymns sung by the *Choralisten* in the empty church [i.e. for Christ's own devotions]
    prayers said by the people [still in their homes]
7am bells
    prayers as people prepare [now in church?]
    service begins with organ ('der Anfang des Gottesdienstes wird mit der Orgel gemacht'), during which more prayers said
    motet then sung
    [service as outlined above, p3]
    at close of Communion, priests say collects, then blessing, then final hymns; further prayers can be said at home afterwards

c

The hymns important for the organist were those between Epistle and Gospel, those either side of the sermon and those during Communion. The prominence of the Gloria hymn (*Allein Gott in der Höh'*)must have some bearing on the large number of settings by J. G. Walther, J. S. Bach and others (see Vol. II pp157-8), although it can only be guessed precisely how the settings were used – after the priest had intoned from the altar? as a prelude or as a postlude to the congregation's singing of it? That the priest or cantor intoned the hymn (i.e. sang the opening phrase?) and was then followed by an organ solo before the congregation sang is implied at Zittau in a directive of 1735 (Seiffert 1917 pp. xiv–xvi):

ingleichen vor und nach der Predigt, zu denen *intonier*ten Liedern das Orgelwerck zu spielen . . .

Immediately before and after the sermon, to play the organ to the intoned hymns . . .

It is unlikely that this refers merely to accompaniment, since elsewhere it speaks of 'playing the little organ' for (*zu*) the Te deum, i.e. in alternation; such little organs were not used for accompanying hymns. As is so often the case, the reference is ambiguous. Clearer, perhaps, is Mattheson's anecdote about the organist J. M. Rubert in Stralsund (1740 p299): improvising one day after the Credo until the preacher was in the pulpit, Rubert found him a long time coming and 'with sharp-sounding stops' launched into a fugue on the chorale line 'Der Herr wird balde kommen', continuing until the preacher appeared. Even here, however, there is a little ambiguity: obviously the organist was filling in between Credo and sermon, but was he supposed to improvise on the Credo-hymn (*Wir glauben*), or on the sermon-hymn (e.g. *Liebster Jesu*) that was to follow when the preacher was ready for the preliminaries to delivering his sermon?

Neither the nature of the organ's repertory nor the Leipzig service-orders justify the otherwise reasonable guess that organ fughettas served as the short intonations of chorales about to be sung, while the longer settings served as the longer preludes played during Communion (Klotz 1962). Yet the three and a half to four hours of the major Leipzig service (according to Stiller 1970 p40) must certainly have included more than a few merely passing interludes from the organ, and any strictures against 'too extended a preamble' even during Communion (as at the Leipzig Neukirche in 1705 – Schering 1926 p241) must be seen as a sign that the organist's contribution could get out of hand, particularly at those moments that by custom he regarded as his own. After all, in the absence of a hymnbook for general use by the congregation in the modern way, the Vopelius texts served in Leipzig as a reference only, and the organist's playing over of the melody must have been very necessary when the hymn of the day was announced. The court at Weimar seems, more straightforwardly, to have used a hymnbook (see pp15–16 below).

d

At Erfurt in 1693, the *Instruction* designated the organist's most important duty in all services as

> die Choralgesänge, wie unter den heutigen bewährtesten Organisten üblich, vorher thematice praeambulando zu tractieren und durchgehends mitzuspielen (in Ziller 1935 pp16–18).

> to play the hymns by first preambling thematically and then playing with [the singing] throughout, as is customary amongst the most approved organists of today.

But while 'preambling thematically' was time-honoured, how far were the 'organists of today' establishing new practices by 'playing with [the singing] throughout'? Since the reproval of J. S. Bach at Arnstadt almost certainly concerned his accompaniment of the hymns (see p36 below),* is it not possible that smaller town churches had their hymns accompanied by organ before the habit spread to the larger churches? While evidence has often been assembled to show that the different German provinces gradually but unevenly moved towards organ accompaniment (e.g. Rietschel 1893), and while it may well be true that chorales lost their old rhythmic variety and became more simplistic as and when organists played chords with them, precise details at Weimar and Leipzig are very uncertain. Did the organists there play harmonies below the congregational hymn verse by verse, or did they play only solo movements?

No doubt the more able or celebrated a particular choir was, the less urgent was the need for the organ to support the congregation. If at Weimar the choir, and not the aristocratic congregation, sustained the role of the hymn as the communal contribution to the music of the liturgy, there must then be a possibility that the *Orgelbüchlein* settings were usable as *alternatim* or inter-verse interludes between the choir verses, which could even have been unaccompanied.† If at Leipzig the choir supported the congregation, the organ need have played only the prelude or the prelude and inter-verse interlude – at least in theory, though presumably pitch problems will have encouraged the modern convention. But it could also be that the

---

* Only 'almost', for the possibility remains that it referred to his playing of *alternatim* interludes: too complex, too long, too short, etc.
† Whatever the purpose of the *Orgelbüchlein*, it can be assumed that the expressive settings by J. C. Vogler (appointed *Hoforganist* at Weimar in 1721) had a similar purpose, though he too published longer chorales (i.e. chorales with interludes incorporated, 1737).

variationes spoken of at Arnstadt would have been those of an organist hoping to make a musical contribution corresponding to the more varied method of singing hymns in the larger churches. As Holmes said in 1828 of the organist's performance in the Dresden Sophienkirche:

> yet as the same melody is often repeated in the service, the able variety of harmony displayed, with the impromptu moving basses or inner parts, make the skilful handling of these tunes a proof of a ready invention and profound knowledge (1828 pp209-10).

Such could be a lesser church's way of performing hymns in order to give variety to the performance – variety of the kind Praetorius had in mind when in the preface to *Urania* (1613) and elsewhere he suggested that the choir and congregation alternate verses after the organ has introduced the melody or that the organ take a verse in old *alternatim* fashion (Rietschel 1893 pp53-4). No doubt organ chords below a congregation's melody became more and more inevitable as the bass line became more and more important during the continuo period* – and as hymn melodies throughout protestant Europe settled in the treble rather than tenor part. But the old choir/organ *alternatim* method of performing (e.g.) the Te Deum at Mattins certainly remained in force in the bigger town churches such as the Leipzig Nikolaikirche (Spitta II p109).

Rietschel's survey of changing practices, from the early reformist preluding and alternating to the plain accompanying of the later eighteenth century, suggests an evolution that was gradual, but uneven and fitful. It was more advanced to treat hymns simply – for example at Lippe in 1684, when it was requested that the organ prelude be not too long and the harmonization not too complex, and that the *alternatim* verses be left out; or at Brunswick in 1709, when the organist was asked for a plain organ verse as prelude and a soft registration as accompaniment (1893 p60). This was in marked contrast to the tendency, in such churches as the Leipzig Nikolaikirche (Schering 1926 pp14-15), for the choir rather than the organ to take the lead in supporting the congregation. At Ulm in 1747, the organ preluded on the Communion hymns but did not actually accompany the congregation (Rietschel 1893 p66), and the same is assumed to have been the case with the Communion hymns at Leipzig (Schering 1926 pp16-17). But musical common sense may make one doubt how feasible it was, at so great a remove from the starker traditions of the early reformed church, for the congregation to sing a hymn unaccompanied when the organ played only before and between verses, or when the cantor had given out the hymn and the organ played only between verses (Schering 1941 p360). Schering's survey implies that only from the 1780s was the organ thought necessary to keep the congregation on correct pitch, but the theorists of that period are not clear enough for the situation to be certain. Nevertheless, more recent custom should not hide the fact that in Leipzig, and perhaps in Weimar, the hymns were introduced first by an organ prelude, intoned by the cantor, and perhaps sung unaccompanied but relieved by inter-verse interludes from the organ. On feast-days, *alternatim* may have been more in evidence (*ibid* pp58-9), whether congregation/ organ or choir/organ; and in smaller churches, the organ 'replaced' the cantor by preluding more briefly and interluding between the lines and/or between verses.†

---

* Chords on lute, organ or harpsichord were suggested in Schein's *Cantional* of 1627.
† Hence the criticism about length at Arnstadt?

The move, in the generality of churches, simultaneously away from too independent a contribution from the organ and towards its use for simple accompaniment is already clear in 1732 from C. Gerber's study of practices in Saxony (Stiller 1970 pp246–7). But perhaps Weimar, as a court chapel with a choir but hardly a 'normal' congregation, gave the organist even greater scope than in the major town churches for the varied repertory of organ chorales, from little fughettas on the first line to very long fantasias taking in the whole hymn.

e

The playing of an organ prelude before the cantata is clear from J. S. Bach's service-order for Advent 1, and it has been generally assumed that this reflects normal practice. It is not clear why Schering thought that the organist accompanying the cantata was a student (1941 p47), for there are no grounds for thinking the prelude was played by one organist (the *titulaire*), and the cantata itself by another (the student).* Petri and Türk still refer to the custom of improvising cantata preludes, and while there is no evidence that the big free preludes of J. S. Bach served for this purpose (as shown by Stauffer 1980 pp143–4) there is many a chorale that could have done so. Obviously a chorale-prelude based on a melody used in or appropriate to the following cantata would serve as prelude to the cantata, though in churches important enough to have full cantatas the organists were presumably able to improvise. In Hamburg in 1706, F. E. Niedt described cantata preludes, and in his edition of Niedt's work in 1720, Mattheson commented pertinently (1720 p102):

> der Organist alleine spielet, damit die Sänger den Ton fassen, und die Instrumentisten reinstimmen mögen . . . Solches Praeludium kann ein Organist so lange machen, als er will,* oder bis die Instrumentisten reingestimmet haben, und ihm ein Zeichen zum Aufhalten gegeben wird.
>   * [Mattheson:] Ich hätte es lieber so kurz, als immer möglich; insonderheit, wenn der Meister nicht zu Hause ist.

> the organist alone plays, so that the singer may grasp the pitch, and the instrumentalists tune . . . The organist can make such a prelude as long as he likes* or until the instrumentalists have tuned and a sign is given him to stop.
>   * [Mattheson:] I would rather it were as short as possible, particularly when the master is not at home.

It was not important for such preludes whether the cantata itself began with an overture or sinfonia of some kind. But Mattheson's remark leads to two further possibilities: Were those years (1710–20) exactly the period in which the organ's contribution generally was being reduced? and Did he make no mention of chorale melodies for such preludes because cantatas in Hamburg were themselves 'free' compositions?

f

It has often been asked whether the free preludes and fugues of J. S. Bach were ever played in church services, but much of the argument on either side will remain conjectural until the practices at Weimar – an extra-territorial court chapel – are better understood. Arguments may be basically correct though the reasoning is

---

* There is no more reason to think the copyist of the organ part was its intended player than the copyist of a violino concertino part.

faulty. Thus the absence of what might be thought suitable pieces for grand preludes and postludes in the works of the Leipzig organists Weckmann, Preisensin and Kuhnau may or may not be a good reason for thinking there was no room for such music in the Leipzig services (Schering 1926 p248). But a large number of questions arise from the presence and absence of sources. What was the situation in Weimar in 1710–20 and in Leipzig in 1725? Does the existence of preludes and fugues from Bach's Weimar years mean that they were used for the services, and if so, before, during or after? Does the absence of preludes and fugues from the Leipzig period before c1730 (?) mean that none were played by J. S. Bach, or only that preludes were formless enough not to be written down, whether played by organist or cantor? Nor are the implications obvious of Burney's information (from Mattheson) that

> Handel . . . was even more powerful upon the organ, in extempore fugues and counterpoint, than the famous Mr Kuhnau of Leipsic, who was, at this time regarded as a prodigy (Burney/Scholes 1959 1 p210).

When did Kuhnau play such music? Since so little of his exists on paper, how could it be known that he did play such music except from such reports?

Mattheson, Scheibe, Petri and Türk all refer to one or another kind of preluding and postluding; the most relevant and unambiguous is Scheibe (1745 p159):

> wenn man zum Anfange des Gottesdienstes, oder auch zum Ausgange spielet, und man dazu folglich oft sehr viel Zeit hat, etwas rechtes auszuführen, so kann auch ein Organist ganz leicht zeigen, wie weit sich seine Erfindung erstreckt, und wie geschickt er ist.

> when one plays at the beginning or the end of the service and has a good deal of time (as often happens) to play something suitable, he can quite easily show how far his inventiveness extends and how gifted he is.

To what service is Scheibe referring – to Hamburg (where he was then resident) or to Leipzig (where the book was published but where he had left no great impression of his musicianship)? Is Spitta correct to assume Leipzig (II p123)? As far as J. S. Bach is concerned, the fact that the preludes and fugues were not compiled in groups or collected with the chorale-preludes certainly suggests that they had no connection with the service. Similarly, notwithstanding the shape of *Clavierübung III* and the occasional cantata that begins with a prelude and ends with a fugue (cf. BWV 131a – see Vol. I pp5–6), there is no clear evidence that any Leipzig service began with a grand prelude and closed with a grand fugue.* Even in the 1830s, Chorley reported hearing in Dresden only 'a brief prelude on the full organ' before the 9am service in the Sophienkirche (1841 p174).

g
The organ postlude, or major piece at the end of the service, was still not usual in every church, as Spitta observed (II pp122–3), and as late as 1782 Petri referred to

---

* However, that manuscripts are often marked 'fuga sequitur' after the prelude cannot be taken as evidence that they were not separated, as has been claimed (Stauffer 1980 pp16, 181). The autograph fair copy of the Two-part Inventions closes with a 'sequitur' to the Three-part Inventions, but that can not mean 'having played the Two-part, continue immediately with the Three-part Inventions'. Besides, 'sequiturs' can be found in copies of preludes and fugues of which the pairing together has no known authority from the composer.

the exit-piece as 'usual in some towns' and implied it was not general (1782 pp297–8). Organists in the Hamburg area – where there was less likely to be an established choir even in important churches – had long played postludes, judging by F. E. Niedt's remarks in 1710 that at this point in the service certain younger players played postludes of such a kind that 'die Leute in der Kirchen bald zu tantzen angefangen hätten' ('the people would soon have begun dancing in the church': 1710 §xiii). At Quedlinburg in 1687, Werckmeister had offered to play postludes although 'they are never played'; at Dortmund in 1690, for the Christmas services the organist was instructed to dismiss the congregation by playing the organ at the close ('die Gemeinde damit dimittiren'); and at Mühlhausen in 1732 the organist was asked to play out (*ausspielen*) even during Lent. From such examples (all in Werner 1933 p113), it seems the fitful custom of playing exit-pieces was being built up, but it is rarely clear in which church and by what period they could have been heard. The purer tradition seems to have been for spoken or sung words at the close.

There is always the possibility, however, that while (e.g.) the 1717 service-orders for the Reformation celebrations at Zittau gave no indication of a postlude yet listed in detail all the hymns sung at moments when time had to be filled (Communion, Confession), they did so because postludes were outside the liturgy. What went on before the liturgy began and after it closed was of no concern to those who devised service-orders. Similarly, when the Leipzig service-orders of 1710 and 1715–17 specify that the main services on feast-days begin and end with a Latin *hymno*, it must remain questionable – because there is no actual prohibition against the organ – whether or not this means 'no organ music as prelude or postlude to the service'. Another possibility is that, as in J. S. Bach's service-order for Advent 1, it was thought unnecessary to mention the custom. It can be argued either way, though the weight of positive evidence does suggest that organ-playing at the close of services in the Leipzig area in about 1725 was not usual.

h

Saturday afternoon Vespers was listed on the rota of duties of an organist in any major church, and while terms of employment in Thuringia–Saxony suggest no particularly expansive musical event of the kind famous in one or two Hanseatic city churches, the organ nevertheless had long had a repertory of Magnificat settings written for it. In at least the major churches of Leipzig, the organ played at two kinds of Vespers: those on Sundays and feast-days, and those on the eve of Sundays and feast-days (documents in Stiller 1970 p80). Such services also included ensemble music, except during Advent, Lent and periods of mourning. The service-orders of 1710 stipulated an opening Latin or Gregorian psalm, motet, sermon and Magnificat. Further,

> wenn der Priester von der Cantzel gehet, so wird nach gemachten praeambulo auf der Orgel, das Magnificat oder Lobgesang Mariä teutsch gesungen . . . oder lateinisch musiciret (in Stiller 1970 p81).

> when the priest leaves the pulpit, then after the organ plays a prelude, the Magnificat is sung [by the congregation] in German or given ensemble performance in Latin.

Such organ interludes to fill gaps or silences in the service are the only ones to be specified, and it is open to conjecture whether the organ otherwise played its own music. (Schering supposed that after the Saturday Vespers, rehearsal for the Sunday cantata took place (Schering 1941 p27)).)

How far the sung Vespers customary in the larger churches of Leipzig, Halle, Erfurt, Zittau etc concerns Bach's organ music is uncertain, since he did not hold the post of organist in such a church. Nor is it certain whether the Leipzig organists still played *alternatim* verses of the Magnificat, such as had been composed and written down in earlier sources, including Buxtehude's. But when in his *Clavier-Kunst* published in 1713 J. H. Buttstedt included

> Fugetten, kurze Praeludia und allerhand kleine Phantasien, wie solche in katholischen Kirchen bei Choral-Aemtern und in Vespern wohl zu gebrauchen (in Ziller 1935 p133)

> fughettas, short preludes and all kinds of little fantasias, such as are to be used in catholic churches in choral Offices and in Vespers

it is not crucial to know whether 'Vespers' here meant Roman or Lutheran, since they must have been very similar from the organist's point of view in at least some areas. Short Magnificat movements of the kind familiar from Scheidemann or Pachelbel* seem not to have been needed by J. S. Bach in Arnstadt or Weimar, but the important status of the *praeambulo* between sermon and Magnificat in the Leipzig service-orders would have suited the settings BWV 733 and – for the new generation of organists – BWV 648.

---

2. Hymns, Hymnbooks and Singing

Not least in connection with the cantatas and posthumously published chorales, hymnological questions as they concern J. S. Bach – which hymnbooks did he use? for what purpose and with how much personal emphasis? – deserve a study to themselves. But particular questions also arise in connection with the organ music as composed or improvised.

Although any view of why J. S. Bach wrote organ chorales of the kind and with the particular melodies that he did will always be clouded by problems of chronology, his wide and obviously intimate acquaintance with the Lutheran heritage can often be detailed. Thus while services at Eisenach, Arnstadt and Mühlhausen very likely drew on several books† particularly for the newer seventeenth-century hymns, the situation in Weimar is more individual. On 28 February 1714 the duke decreed that the numbers of the hymns sung were to accord with those in the Weimar *Gesangbuch* (newly printed by Mumbach in 1713), and the chapel accounts for 30 March 1714 include the cost for five blackboards on which the

---

* Sources for both the Buxtehude cantus-firmus settings and the free fugal versets of Pachelbel imply that four movements were needed for each Magnificat performance; six had been the number of versets in Scheidt's *Tabulatura nova* III (Hamburg, 1624).

† Although beyond the scope of this chapter, it is often useful to ask whether a book of hymns is a 'hymnbook' in the modern sense. The collection of Luther texts made, printed in archaic type and published in the commemorative year 1717 by J. C. Olearius, pastor of Arnstadt (*Jubilirende Lieder-Freude*), looks more like a source-book (in quasi-facsimile) of Luther's hymn-texts than a congregational 'hymnbook', even though its contents list is reminiscent of that of Bach's *Orgelbüchlein*.

numbers were to be announced (Jauernig 1950 p171). This is so like modern practice that its startling originality can easily be missed – originality not only in that the numbers were to be announced in this way but that it presupposes that members of the congregation could read and had the same book to hand. Court chapels were no doubt exceptions, and the Weimar *Orgelbüchlein* (see dating in Vol. II p7) is similarly systematic. Perhaps such short preludes and/or interludes were useful precisely because the congregation used a hymnbook in the modern way, and their arrangement in the *Orgelbüchlein* corresponds to that of hymn-books – i.e. starting with Advent and closing with hymns for the dying, and collecting the non-major seasonal hymns together after the major ones (Gojowy 1972 p26).*

For the *Orgelbüchlein* as a whole (i.e. including the hymns not set by the composer) one may suppose not the 1713 Weimar book but a Thuringian hymnbook of the period *c*1650–75 to be the most relevant, supplying the repertory of hymns as the Bach family had known it for a generation or more before J. S. Bach moved to Weimar. Thus the melodies used in J. C. Bach's *44 Choralvorspiele* are all to be found in his young relation's *Orgelbüchlein*. Although the *Orgelbüchlein* belongs to the same period as the reorganization of the Weimar hymns themselves, the 1713 book – called *Gesang-Büchlein* in the preface dedicated to the duke; cf. the *Gebet-Büchlein* ('little books of prayers') printed in Weimar – is less relevant than at first it appears, not least in its listing of the hymns simply in seasons and Sundays/feast-days (i.e. not as 'Catechism' or 'general' hymns). As far as any distinction between 'seasonal' and 'occasional' hymns is concerned, the *Orgelbüchlein* has more in common with the old Thuringian books or even with (e.g.) the Dresden hymnbook of 1699 (*Geist- und Lehr-reiches Kirchen- und Hauss-Buch*).

The Duke of Weimar's decree applied to the whole dukedom, presumably in an attempt to standardize procedure in a period when more and more hymnbooks, some of a pietist cast not universally approved, were being produced. Such an attempt at standardization was a reflection of the piety and religious earnestness of Weimar under Duke Wilhelm Ernst,† often regarded today as qualities exceptional for their period (Stiller 1970 p169). J. S. Bach himself seems to have followed the 1713 edition for Weimar cantata texts, while in Leipzig he later drew on many books, not to mention his own memory (Neumann 1956). The sources for melodies in the *Orgelbüchlein* have been traced to several origins including Witt's book of 1715, a hymnbook with melodies and figured bass, called 'the best musical hymn-book I know' by Marpurg (1761 p188). But there is perhaps one particular reason why the *Orgelbüchlein* does not rely on the Weimar hymnbooks for its contents (see

---

* So too it seems did the 'yearly cycle of chorale-preludes arranged according to the church seasons' that J. G. Walther tried to get published, according to Mattheson in 1725 ('einen Jahrgang von Lieder-Praeludiis so auf die Kirchen Zeiten gerichtet ist'–pp157ff). That the final section of the *Orgelbüchlein* appears to become more arbitrary in its selection of texts was itself characteristic of hymnbooks (e.g. the *Dresdner Gesangbuch* of 1734).

† G. A. Wette (1737 p40) talks of the 'many praiseworthy things funded' by the duke ('viele löbliche Dinge gestiftet'), including the building of a new church (the Jakobikirche, on 7 November 1713, when one may imagine the *Hoforganist* to have been present), a library, a school, a kind of museum, an orphanage, a *gymnasium* and houses. The 1713 hymnbook itself does not make many new departures from that of 1708, since presumably the duke's interest did not lie in novelty; both books begin with the three Sunday hymns sung either before the service begins (*Komm, heilger Geist*) or before the sermon (*Liebster Jesu, wir sind hier* or *Herr Jesu Christ dich zu uns wend*).

below, p41); but in any case it is scarcely possible to imagine a composer not altering from time to time such details of hymns as their rhythm,* particularly since hymnbooks had different conventions for notating the ends of lines. The argument that in the *Orgelbüchlein* the composer lengthened some first and last notes in order to incorporate figuration resembling interline interludes – Ex. 1 – will remain con-

Ex. 1 'Vom Himmel hoch' (hymnbook version)

jectural, however interesting (Krey 1956), until it can be proved that the hymnbook he used conveyed the first version. Did he rely for his tunes on books, on his memory of countless performances, on local habits? Weimar was indeed more standardized than seems to have been the case in the orthodox city of Nuremberg, according to Mattheson's notes on the organist T. Volckmar, who tried to have some chorales published there:

> aber da die Melodien auch in den Kirchen einer und derselben Stadt (dergleichen in Nürnberg mit manchem Liede geschehe) verändert, gesungen würden, so wäre es, ohne besorgenden Schaden Verlegers, nicht zu wagen (1740 p386).

> but as the melodies were sung in differing versions even in the churches of one and the same town (something that happens in Nuremberg with many a hymn), it was not to be risked without anxiety lest the publisher lose by it.

Perhaps the situation in Leipzig was more uniform, since the churches there were connected in various ways. But there seem to have been common interests in the churches of Thuringia: at Erfurt, Buttstedt's organ chorales (as listed in Ziller 1935 pp43–7) correspond very closely to the repertory worked by J. S. Bach in the *Orgelbüchlein* and elsewhere, except that of Luther's seven Catechism hymns† set or listed in the *Orgelbüchlein* Buttstedt is known to have set only two. The need for particular chorale-variations too seems to have coincided, in so far as they both set *O Gott, du frommer Gott* and *Sei gegrüsset* in this manner.

One way in which particular hymnbooks (or those with melodies) are relevant to particular organ chorales has often been suggested. Luedtke, whose attempt to erect a thesis on the uses, influences and developments of the chorale was thoughtful and circumspect (*BJ* 1918), found Vopelius 1682 useful for the *Orgelbüchlein* and for the Kyries (and perhaps the Catechism hymns) of *Clavierübung III*,

---

* The very opening line of the first hymn in the *Orgelbüchlein* ('Nun komm') exists in several distinct forms, including a straight two-bar version (BWV 36), a freer one in 2½ bars (BWV 599), and a form pulled out to three bars plus a following rest (Witt's *Cantional*). Witt's rest was perhaps to allow the organist to play an interline interlude; Bach's 2½ bars strengthen the freer, Gregorian allusions of this old melody to open the *Orgelbüchlein* (see below, p275).

† *Dies sind, Mensch willt du, Wir glauben, Vater unser, Christ unser Herr, Jesus Christus unser Heiland, Gott sei gelobet.*

Crüger's *Praxis Pietatis* (1690 and 1698 editions) for 'The Eighteen', a Darmstadt book of 1699 for the Partita BWV 768, and so on. Since the Weimar *Gesangbücher* (1681, 1708, 1713) did not have melodies, perhaps at least some of the *Orgel-büchlein* were meant as harmonized tunes to correspond to them, not unlike the settings long known in some quarters for harmonized congregational chorales (e.g. Osiander 1586, Scheidt 1650).* Certainly not for some decades were hymnbooks assumed to be part of the 'equipment' for a service, and in 1745 Scheibe was still recommending that the organist keep by him one with melodies (1745 p417). The five hundred or so melodies published by Telemann in 1730 (*Fast allgemeines evangelisch–musicalisches Lieder-Buch*, Hamburg), though indifferently harmonized and untidily engraved, presumably fulfilled a need, and an increasingly pressing one.†

The more hymns were written, the more the organ accompanied congregations, the more hymns were sung in any one service, so the more necessary it became to use a hymnbook in the way now familiar. As with other details of church services, it is not always clear what the custom was in Weimar and Leipzig, particularly since those early decades of the century saw marked changes in many areas. In 1687 Werckmeister had remarked that his predecessor at Quedlinburg did not play the organ *after* the sermon (unless a party of the nobility was present for the Eucharist), nor *before* the sermon in the case of the afternoon service (Werner 1933 p91). But by 1758 Adlung counted a vast number of contributions from the organ: seventy Sundays and feast-days in the year, each with about ten chorales played by organ, each of which averaged ten verses. Perhaps Communion had always been a time when a long series of hymns was sung. But whether it had been or not, the demand for harmonizations in the later eighteenth century – plus the claim that J. S. Bach's four-part chorales were organ accompaniments (*Dok* III pp180, 341, 400) – has led to another assumption: that the accompanied congregational hymns were similar in Weimar and in Leipzig. The move towards publishing simple harmonizations in towns other than Leipzig or Weimar – e.g. C. Graupner in 1728 (Darmstadt), B. Schmid in 1748 (Nuremberg) – may justify seeing those harmonizations that follow certain Bach chorales (BWV 690 etc) as in some way working towards similar ends. Why should they be present in any source, however remote, unless the organist played them after their 'prelude'? But whether the original organist concerned was J. S. Bach or a copyist (acting on his own authority) is another question.

In Leipzig, the eight-volume Wagner hymnbook of 1697 of which J. S. Bach possessed a copy must have served – like old Gregorian *repertoria* – as a reference-source for its five thousand hymns, though for the melodies themselves Vopelius (1682) and the simpler Freylinghausen (1704 etc) could have served. The increase in the number of hymns available can be gauged from the fact that editions of the *Dresdner Gesangbuch* around 1725 contained three or four hymns for each Sunday or feast-day while the editions of around 1750 had eight to ten (Stiller 1970 p220). New hymns used by J. S. Bach in the *Christmas Oratorio* were not known in organ-

---

* Scheidt's four-part harmonizations with the melody on top (harmony to be played by organ, melody sung by congregation) rather suggest that this by now familiar way of setting out a hymn-tune was a result of organs' playing with congregations. Four parts on the organ with the melody in the tenor part (but not registered as a solo) leaves the melody barely audible.

† This book too begins with *Nun komm* and becomes less systematic.

chorale settings. There may well be in the organ chorales an inclination towards hymns useful for several Sundays, though the traditional respect in which several once-a-year hymns were held – like *Christ lag*, *Christ ist erstanden*, *Komm, heiliger Geist*, *Hilf Gott, dass mirs gelinge* – would always have led composers to set them, even if by the 1780s Türk had to warn organists to be careful with interline interludes in such unfamiliar hymns (1787 p16). The generalization that J. S. Bach's organ works belong mostly to the Weimar years and cantatas mostly to Leipzig probably 'explains' the fact that of the extant works in both categories over a third of the organ chorales use melodies not found in cantatas. Although a case can certainly be made that in various ways J. S. Bach laid on chorales an emphasis not always characteristic of his period, there are some striking omissions in the actual selection of those he did set. For example, excluding the *Schübler* transcriptions, none of the nineteen hymns of Paul Gerhardt found in cantatas appear in the organ chorales, nor do those of Melanchthon and several other major Lutheran authors (Schlueter 1954 p315). Even certain very versatile hymns – there is scarcely a Sunday not mentioned in some book in connection with *Nun lob, mein Seel* or *Wie schön leuchtet* (Gojowy 1972 p28) – seem to have been set only seldom by J. S. Bach, perhaps because of personal taste. The same goes for (e.g.) *Nun ruhen alle Wälder*, whose melodic potential was commented on by Mattheson (1739 pp121-2), and a sarabande treatment of which would have begun something like a chorale that Bach actually did set, namely 'Schmücke dich' BWV 654. Hymns for the main feasts are catered for in the Bach *oeuvre* with one or two exceptions, like Ascension (BWV 630?), though here too it is not always clear what church or province regarded what festivals as major (e.g., Stiller 1970 p245 shows relatively few communicants on Ascension Days in Leipzig). Perhaps it was because they had remained standard and had no need to be replaced by more modern hymns that the seasonal chorales in the *Orgelbüchlein* included none that were contemporary, and only four were set that dated from as late as the middle of the seventeenth century.

A general idea of the hymn's position is given by many kinds of document. Thus the Brunswick–Lüneburg church ordinance of 1657 described position and even method:

> Nach Verlesung der Epistel singe man aus den gemeinen Gesangbüchern einen deutschen Psalm oder Gesang *de tempore*. Und kann bei dergleichen Gesängen der Organist auf der Orgel die Gesänge fein langsam in Contrapuncto, wie es die Musici nennen, mit musicieren (Rietschel 1893 p59).

> After the reading of the Epistle, a German psalm or hymn for the season is to be sung out of the common hymnbooks. And with hymns of this kind the organist can play along very slowly in *counterpoint*, as the musicians call it.

How general in Saxony-Thuringia it was to have a hymnbook is unclear, but the attempt at standardization in Weimar has already been referred to. Eighty years later, there was a complaint in Leipzig:

> heute nach der in gedachter Kirche [Nikolai] gehaltenen Predigt, under der *Communion*, der *Prae-Centor* auf dem Chor, das Lied: Jesu Leiden Pein und todt, dergestallt tieff angefangen, dass die gemeinde gar nicht mitsingen können, sondern diesses schöne Lied mehr gebetet als gesungen werden müssen, mit dem Ersuchen, die nöthige Verfügung zu treffen, dass dergleichen nicht mehr geschehe . . . (*Dok* II pp285-6)

19

> today after the sermon was read in the aforesaid church [Nikolai], during the Communion, the precentor in the quire [?] gave out the hymn *Jesu Leiden, Pein und Tod* at so low a pitch that the congregation could not sing with it (although this beautiful hymn is more to be prayed than sung); it is requested that the necessary steps be taken [by J. S. Bach] so that the same does not happen again . . .

Clergy and vergers are not slow to complain about musicians, especially when it can be claimed, as Speer did in *Grund-richtiger Unterricht*, that

> das Singen ist auch ein Theil des Gottesdienstes, und andächtig gesungen ist doppelt gebetet (Speer 1697 p3).
>
> singing is also part of worship, and devotionally sung is doubly prayed.

Presumably that must always have been true, yet the tendency in hymnbooks to emphasize not simply the seasons or Catechism headings but many categories and sub-headings suggests that their authors had their own pietist leanings, or their wish to mark the repertory with their own stamp. In its 1730 edition, Freylinghausen's hymnbook (*Geistreiches Gesangbuch*, Halle, 16th edn) has no fewer than sixty such classifications, from specific seasons such as 'Of the Advent of Christ' to sub-divisions of those seasons, such as 'Of the Advent of Christ as Judge'. It also has other new categories, such as a hymn for travellers. Since in such up-to-date collections the old hymns like *Nun komm* no longer had their traditional melodies, it may be possible to see 'The Eighteen' as well as *Clavierübung III* as J. S. Bach's conscious response to fashion: perhaps an expression of loyalty to melodies often discarded elsewhere. The gesture towards orthodoxy in such collections – if that is what it is – can be paralleled in other Leipzig publications of the time, such as J. J. Gottschald's hymnbook *Theologia in Hymnis* (Leipzig 1737), whose very title suggests a classical didacticism removed from Freylinghausen and whose frontispiece (with its motto *Die Alten / sind gut zu behalten*: 'the old hymns are easy to memorize' [?]) depicts the hymn as enlivening with (or expressing in) sound the solid structure of theology and the sacraments.

---

3. Organ Chorales as Preludes

Conventions widely held during the period fail to define for us the precise contexts in which J. S. Bach composed his various kinds of organ music. With respect to improvising in the course of the service, it can only be guessed what precisely the conventions were at Arnstadt and Weimar; those at Leipzig are somewhat clearer, though here the questions are whether at this stage in his career J. S. Bach ever played at such moments and whether any of his known organ music is relevant to those moments.

The *Praeludiren* required of the Leipzig organist is clear from the composer's service-order for Advent 1 (see above, p4). In 1740, Mizler was able to summarize such 'preludes' as belonging to three particular moments (1740 pp56ff):

> for the *Choral*
>   i.e. the main hymn of the day, between Epistle and Gospel
> for the cantata or ensemble piece

for the Communion
> i.e. interspersed with several hymns sung during Communion (if a church had other hymns in the service, from this point of view they should be considered as communion hymns)

Mizler, as a Leipzig musician publishing such remarks in Leipzig, must have had in mind some reference to St Thomas's at that period, perhaps wishing to give general directives based on what was after all a city central to Lutheran orthodoxy. It is not clear, however, what precisely he is referring to when he remarks that such prelude improvisations used to be simple and the chorale melody recognizable, but that now

> bey den neuern und erst aus der Schule gekommenden Organisten ist das Vorspiel mehrentheils eine unordentliche Fantasie, oder Capriccio.

> with the newer organists barely out of school the prelude is for the most part an extraordinary fantasia or capriccio.

Such pieces were often in a ridiculous theatrical concert style, passing through all twenty-four keys before settling down to a hymn such as *Erbarm dich mein, O Herre Gott*. The cantata prelude, Mizler thinks, might admit a little more freedom, perhaps, but the Communion preludes should be majestic, serious, beautiful, cheerful within limits, giving the singers a little rest.

It is clear from Kauffmann's remarks in the preface to *Harmonische Seelenlust* (Leipzig 1733) that the practice still required explaining to some players:

> nachdem nun an den mehresten Orten gebräuchlich, dass vor jedweden Liede etwas weniges praeludiret werde, so sind diejenigen unter den Herrn Organisten dem eigentlichen Zweck am nähesten kommen, welche unter einer künstlichen Variation, Imitation oder andrer figurirten Arbeit die Melodie auf eine deutliche und vernehmliche Weise zugleich mithören lassen, indem die Gemüther allmählig praepariret werden, dass sie hernach das Lied viel andächtiger singen, als wenn man sie eine fremde Phantasie hätte hören lassen.

> since it is now customary in most places that before each hymn something brief is improvised, so those of the organists have approached closest to the real purpose of it who let the melody be heard in a clear and intelligible way in the course of an artistic variation, imitation or arrangement made in some other figural way, for then the spirits are gradually prepared towards singing the hymn afterwards much more devotionally than if one had had them listen to an unfamiliar fantasia.

Even if complaints had not become so frequent, it would be easy to imagine that such improvisations would be open to abuse. But without them, the mostly bookless congregation would be uncertain what to expect. In Breslau during the 1730s, for example, the organist introduced a system for the hymn-singing that united congregation, organ and choir (complete with brass); but before that there had been problems:

> Nach dem Eingange der Predigt steigt der Glöckner auf die Kantzel und znauselt, ohne Chor und Orgel, ein Lied nach seinem Gehirn her, dazu das Volck mit hineinblöcket (Mattheson 1740 p418).

> at that part of the service before the sermon, the sexton went up into the pulpit and 'entuned in the nose full seemly', without choir or organ, a hymn from out of his head, to which the people joined in their bleating.

Obviously Mattheson's period was one of tidying up and standardizing the procedure. In a book published in Erfurt in 1742, J. C. Voigt specified two aims – to avoid big independent organ works and to show the melody clearly:

> Es kan wohl dann und wann ein Concert gespielet werden, aber vor Chorälen und Kirchen-Musiken schickt sich solches keines weges . . . Er kan ja den Choral, welcher gesungen werden soll, zu einem devoten Präludio nach seinen eigenen Phantasien ausarbeiten, so, dass er einen ganzen oder halben Vers, wie es ihm beliebet, durch ein besonder Register vorspielet, welches viel besser lautet, als wenn Menueten, Giguen und dergleichen von irrdischgesinnten zuvor präludiret werden (Voigt 1742 pp11–12).

> from time to time a concerto [large fantasia] is played, but before chorales and cantatas such a thing is wholly inappropriate. The organist at this point can arrange the chorale that is to be sung in a devout prelude according to his own fancy, so long as he plays over a whole or half verse (as he prefers) with a solo [?] stop. This sounds better than when minuets, gigues and similar worldly pieces are improvised before the chorale.

The Erfurt organists, then, were accustomed to playing long free pieces at those moments when there would otherwise be a gap in the service. The tenor of Voigt's well-written book is to argue against abuses and to establish local practice – common aims behind such books in various protestant countries. But already in 1715 C. F. Witt found it necessary to recommend that the Thuringian organist play the hymn melody over slowly once or even twice, instead of a prelude which was open to abuse (*Cantional* preface). Perhaps the *Orgelbüchlein* was a form of such playing-over, as well as an accompaniment?

Mizler's complaints of how far taste in church music had fallen were taken up by Adlung, who criticized those players who improvised too long or did not make the melody clear enough; for him as for others in the later part of the century, *Vorspiel* meant the *Praeambulieren* before a hymn or cantata (1783 pp826, 904–5). But the difficulty in saying which works of J. S. Bach were *Vorspiele* in this sense and which were *Orgelchoräle* in other senses was one already found at the period. Some references to J. S. Bach speak of

> *freyen Vorspielen, Fugen* (free preludes, fugues)
> *Vorspiele vor Chorälen* (preludes before chorales)
> *kurze Vorspiele vor den meisten Kirchenliedern* (short preludes before most of the church hymns)

as if the categories were already clear (*Dok* III p246); in another list, E. L. Gerber attempts others terms:

> *Vorspiele über Kirchengesänge* (preludes on church hymns), i.e. *Clavierübung III*
> *Sechs dreystimmige Choralvorspiele* (six three-part [!] chorale-preludes), i.e. the *Schübler*
> *Variirte Choräle für die Orgel zu Vorspielen* (varied chorales for the organ to use as preludes), i.e. the miscellaneous settings

But in *Clavierübung III* it is difficult to imagine at least larger settings as preludes in this sense, even if J. S. Bach himself played the organ during some services and even if a case could be made for the shorter settings (fughettas) being preludes. In 1810, Gerber wrote on chorales in *AMZ*, to which the editor added a footnote which, though probably true, suggests that he too did not fully understand the old Leipzig service:

Bach selbst spielte nie Orgel, die Gemeinde zu begleiten, sondern nur, aus eigener Neigung oder Aufforderung Anderer, wenn kein Gottesdienst war. Da nahm er aller-dings oft Choräle zu Hauptgedanken seiner gelehrten Ausführung, weil sie die wür-digsten, und weil sie auch damals jedem Zuhörer vollkommen bekannt und geläufig waren, und diesem mithin dadurch ein treffliches Erleichterungsmittel geboten ward, dem Spieler, auch in den künstlichen Gewinden seines tiefen Geistes, zu folgen (*AMZ* 12 (1810) col. 433ff).

Bach himself never played the organ to accompany the congregation but only from his own inclination or at the request of others, when there was no service. Then however he often took chorales as the main ideas of his learned execution, because they were the most worthy and because at that time they were also fully known and familiar to every listener, and by these means an excellent elucidation was offered for following the player, even in the ingenious labyrinths of his profound genius.

Not only does this smack of Forkel, of course, but at most it relates only to the Leipzig period, when it is by no means certain that anybody accompanied the con-gregation. It sheds no light on the purpose of the Weimar chorale-preludes. How distinct a tradition was there in the Eisenach–Weimar area – distinct from northern conventions on the one hand and from the later, more mundane practices of Thuringia–Saxony described by Adlung and Türk on the other?

Preluding on the hymn about to be sung was common to all these situations. Niedt could equally well have been speaking of his place of birth (Jena), of employ-ment (Copenhagen) or of publication (Hamburg) when he wrote that organists

im *praeludiren* auf einen *Choral*-Gesang fein andächtig mit anmuthigen Stimmen, deutlich und vernehmlich, nicht gar zu lustig, ihre Kunst anbringen, und keine Taschenspielerey mit *Hocus Pocus* einmischen (1717 p45).

apply their artistry in preluding on a chorale very devoutly with agreeable stops, clearly and intelligibly, not too merrily, and without mixing in jugglery and hocus-pocus.

As for Hamburg, various anecdotes told by Mattheson suggest that the organist's part in the whole was not unlike that in Leipzig. For example, from a long and typical story he tells about Weckmann and Bernhard in the Hamburg Jakobikirche around the middle of the previous century (1740 pp20–1) several things can be learnt: miscellaneous ensemble pieces were performed during Communion, people walked about during sermons, the cantor jotted down on paper the keys in which he wished the organist to improvise at the various moments, the organist impro-vised before the cantata according to its mood (which would not necessarily pertain to the Sunday concerned), and the congregation had the text of the cantata in front of them. Smaller churches presumably preferred less musical independence from the organ-loft, since their services may have had a prescribed duration: at least, that is the implication behind the criticism of the twenty-year-old J. G. B. Bach at Mühlhausen in 1735 (Werner 1933 p110):

Herr Bach jun. bisher allzuviel und allzulange präludiret, mithin dadurch die zur Andacht und Gottesdienste bestimmte Zeit über die Gebühr verkürzt.

Up till now Herr Bach Jun. has been improvising far too much and far too long, so that by this means the time allocated for worship and the service is immoderately curtailed.

Mattheson rather confirms this idea when he suggests that the organist can 'regulate' the service, playing shorter preludes if the hymns are long, longer if they are short (1739 p472). Adlung cannot have been the only organist to have thought it more useful to be able to improvise preludes rather than to play from written music, since it is easier to adapt to circumstances of time, required length, etc (1783 pp830-1); perhaps it had also become general in some areas to regard the hymns sung every Sunday (Kyrie, *Allein Gott* and Credo) as requiring either a short prelude or indeed none at all (Türk 1787 p121).

It cannot be known whether in either Weimar or Leipzig one purpose of the prelude before the cantata was to enable the other instruments to tune, though Türk not only understood it as the function of this kind of prelude but warned the organist not to forget that brass instruments played at a different pitch and therefore needed other keys to be included in the prelude (1787 pp136ff).* But giving a kind of tonal organization to the service was certainly one function of the prelude. Mattheson, for example, thought the hymn-prelude useful in order to modulate from the previous piece ('Gesanges oder Stückes', 'hymn or cantata') to the next. That too seems to be the implication of (e.g.) the Leipzig Nikolaikirche service as understood by Schering (1941 p103): *Allein Gott*, followed by organ interlude, then 'another hymn', interlude, Credo, etc.

That in the period around 1700 Thuringia or the Eisenach–Erfurt region kept its own strong traditions is implied by the nature of organ chorales composed or published by Pachelbel (Erfurt, etc), J. C. Bach (Eisenach) and J. M. Bach (Gehren), and hence at times perhaps J. G. Walther and J. S. Bach. The more miniature workings of J. G. Walther would certainly have been more useful to later Thuringian organists like J. T. Krebs than (e.g.) the 'Weimar chorales' of J. S. Bach (BWV 651a etc). The earlier traditions were presumably lost for later Erfurters such as Adlung, who said that J. M. Bach's chorales 'mean little today' ('bedeuten heutiges Tages nicht viel': *Dok* III p121). When Mattheson described Walther's organ chorales as 'auf die Pachelbelsche Art, sehr nett und harmoniös' ('in the Pachelbel manner, very neat and harmonious': 1725 pp175ff) he must have been referring to shape as well as idiom. Pachelbel's and Walther's particular interest had been in a kind of chorale less familiar in the north: the chorale-fughetta or short fugue whose subject derived from the hymn to which the improvisation served as prelude – as J. H. Buttstedt (a Pachelbel student) put it, fugues in which the chorales used in the evangelical church are 'begun' ('angefangene': *Musicalische Clavier-Kunst*, Erfurt 1713). Such chorale-fughettas are like those of earlier periods but are not intended, as they were, to serve as *alternatim* versets.

Fugues and fughettas are by nature more 'objective' than the melodic chorale treatments that, in the work of Buttstedt at least, were leading to expressive and pictorial allusions – the fluttering of angels' wings in 'Vom Himmel kam der Engel Scharr', for example.† As Pachelbel's own setting of 'Vom Himmel hoch' (Walther's MS BB 22541) suggests, Christmas chorales were particularly open to more 'subjective' treatments, as the contemporary and presumably quite unconnected tastes for noëls in Paris and for pastorales in Italy also imply. How far J. S. Bach was in the vanguard among organists in shedding 'objectivity' in chorale settings will not be

---

* It is difficult to follow Türk's logic here, for by whatever name the trumpeter might call the note, and however it were notated, he would be playing the same d′ as the violins.
† In a sense anticipating those of BWV 607 (whose crotchet and semiquaver scales are very subtly composed) or BWV 701.

clear until more accurate dating of works by Buttstedt and Walther is possible, but it could be that Thuringia in general was already moving in that direction before or without Mattheson's having to suggest it. Perhaps relevant to the move towards more expressive settings is the fact that the chorale of J. S. Bach that in shape most resembles the two-verse settings of Pachelbel – namely the Whit hymn BWV 667 – keeps the *Affekt* of spiritual power in the bass-cantus-firmus section but has no Pachelbelian fugue or fughetta for the other section. That is, it is moving farther towards 'subjectivity'.

Whether the wording of their title reflects coincidence or plagiarism – like Pachelbel's, they are to be used *zum Präambulieren* – the purpose of J. C. Bach's fughettas is clear enough: they introduce one or more lines of the chorale in a series of simple fugal entries, closing with *point d'orgue* and rarely stepping outside three unintricate parts or passing beyond about thirty bars. However valid Spitta's distinctions between Pachelbel's, J. M. Bach's and J. C. Bach's work in such fughettas (i pp117–20), the type is decisive and unpretentious. Throughout, the treatment is 'objective': that is, little in the way of *Affekt* is sought, conforming more to Niedt's formulation – 'clearly and intelligibly' – than to Mattheson's taste for expressiveness. Very likely too the lost chorale collection of Pachelbel (*Choral-Fugen durchs gantze Jahr*, 1704 – *DTB* IV.i (1903) preface) was without the *Affekte* of the *Orgelbüchlein*, though apparently planned as a *repertorium* not unlike it.

Although as an inspiration for J. S. Bach's Advent and Christmas fughettas those of Pachelbel and J. C. Bach may not be more relevant than free fugues by other composers (see Vol. II p227), it is certainly striking that, just as in (e.g.) BWV 701, Pachelbel very occasionally uses a different line of the melody as a fugal answer:* Ex. 2. The maturity of idiom and technique in J. S. Bach's Advent and Christmas

Ex. 2   Pachelbel, 'Ach Herr, mich armen Sünder' (Kö 15839, copied by J. G. Walther)

Pachelbel, 'Der Herr ist mein getreuer Hirt' (Sp 1439 etc)

fughettas argues against the likelihood that they were composed while he still had connections with his uncle in Eisenach. But from Arnstadt to Leipzig, the chorale-fughetta was without doubt sufficiently familiar as a type for the composer to have consciously attempted in his own fughettas subtleties beyond anyone's improvisatory powers.

That any attempt to relate works of J. S. Bach or any other composer to very particular uses can answer many questions about their purpose, while leaving many

---

* Answering a fugal subject based on one line by a subject based on another was also known in (e.g.) J. E. Kindermann's *Harmonia Organica* (Nuremberg 1645). Was Pachelbel acknowledging a Nuremberg penchant for combinations, quodlibets, etc?

others open, is clear from two remarks of J. G. Walther. In private letters (Schüne-mann 1933 pp93, 98) he gives two reasons for writing chorales. He explains that he did not write cantatas because it was not his job:

> sondern ich habe vielmehr, als Organist, Ursache, mich auf Vorspiele über Choral-Lieder zu legen.

> but I have much more reason, organist, to apply myself to preludes on the chorales.

Thus, it would be understandable for organists who took on directorial duties as their careers progressed, such as Buxtehude, Kerll, Kuhnau and J. S. Bach, to leave behind keyboard music, which dates mostly from their earlier years (Riedel 1960 p207). On the other hand, although at the time of writing these letters Walther could not give public performances of his chorales because the organ in the Weimar Stadtkirche was out of condition and only partly playable, he still had great 'pleasure and joy' ('Vergnügen und Freude') in composing them. Organ chorales therefore had more than one purpose, as one might easily suppose – hence, perhaps, J. S. Bach's composing them while he was at Köthen (according to Adlung – *Dok* III p121) where it is assumed he can have had no occasion to play them in the service. Besides, it is clear from the title-page of Kauffmann's *Harmonische Seelenlust* (Leipzig 1733) that chorales were partly 'for the private pleasure of keyboard-lovers' ('Liebhabern des Claviers zu Private Vergnügen').

---

4. Organ Chorales as and with Interludes

In the context of organ chorales, the term 'interlude' has several particular meanings. A whole setting may serve as an interlude, not only in the general sense of 'filling a gap in the service' but as a solo contribution between verses of a sung hymn: the *alternatim* principle. Secondly, a brief interlude may be improvised in a similar position by way of quietly filling the silence rather than providing formally a movement of equal musical significance. It is not always clear which of these (full-dress *alternatim* or a short voluntary) is meant when a document refers to 'interludes': for example, Chorley's note that in 1840 in the Dresden Sophien-kirche he heard five- or six-verse psalms with interludes between the verses (1841 p175). A third kind of interlude was not between verses but between lines of a hymn: the interline interlude known in the organ settings of various composers in the late seventeenth century (e.g. Blow and Daniel Purcell in England) and familiar in the so-called 'Arnstadt chorales' of J. S. Bach (see Vol. II p255). More generally too, the interline interlude was a principle of construction behind almost all organ chorales except the *Orgelbüchlein* or fughetta types, for most chorale-preludes or chorale-fantasias or chorale-fugues proceed on the basis of episodes (interludes) between the main statements of the melody. The same point could be made about many a sung chorale with instrumental episodes in cantatas, where too the thematic material in interludes has a ritornello quality.

a

The *alternatim* practice is probably as old as organ music in the liturgy of the western catholic church, but by the end of the seventeenth century in central and northern Germany it took one or two particular forms. It is not always clear from references what precisely the organ played at such moments, but it is reasonable to suppose that the practice originated as the organ's version of what the priest or choir or *schola* or *Cantorei* was singing: organ verse between choir verses, a few bars woven around the melody or chant as theirs had been, the one gradually growing to suit the fingers as the other grew to suit the voice. That the principle still existed well into the eighteenth century is suggested from Scheibe's remark that the organist follows the key or *tonus* sung by the priest before the altar (1745 p421). In earlier organ sources, such as Scheidt's *Tabulatura* or the Lüneburg tablatures, the various chorales, Latin hymns and Te Deum and Magnificat versets suggest a similar treatment for all such movements in the service: choir (with or without congregation) sang one verse; organ replaced the next by playing the melody and some counterpoints; choir sang the next, and so on. Although the tablatures may well agree with such particular service-orders as the plans for Vespers and Mattins at the Michaeliskirche, Lüneburg (1656), the practice seems to have been widespread in the larger churches generally. And although the absence of material suggests that in some areas, perhaps Leipzig itself, the organist may have been unused to playing organ solos other than brief improvisations, the *alternatim* technique must have been very familiar in those same churches during the seventeenth century. Even villages in the neighbourhood of Leipzig, such as Pomssen in 1671, seem to have known the practice (see Werner 1933 p90).*

The *alternatim* traditions raise particular questions concerning the known organ music of J. S. Bach. For example, it is not out of the question that – in ideal circumstances at least – the longer chorales in *Clavierübung III* and 'The Eighteen' were able not only to serve as preludes to congregational hymns and as postludes to them if they occurred at moments when gaps had to be filled (e.g. after the sermon hymn), but could have been interludes between the verses, sung by choir and/or congregation as the case may be. Either of these explanations might suit the Communion hymns especially. More interesting still is the possibility that the *Orgelbüchlein* movements served as organ versets between verses sung by the choir in a court chapel of the kind in which hymns may have been more 'performed' than merely sung in parish-church manner. This idea was specifically discounted by Luedtke (1918 p26) but must remain a possibility until more is known for certain about the Weimar services and the nature of their hymns.† Certainly J. S. Bach's term *praeludiret* in the Advent 1 service-order at Leipzig in 1723 (see above, p4) could equally well indicate *alternatim* interlude or solo prelude, as Luedtke observed (1918 p6), and it cannot be regarded as certain that *alternatim* performance became rarer for chorales while remaining customary for Magnificat and Te Deum (Blume 1974 p246). Indeed, considering the non-doctrinal nature of most hymns, it is more feasible to have sung verses replaced by the organ in longer hymns than in such basic movements as the German Credo, for which some churches specifically

---

* Original church and organ of Pomssen are extant.
† Another possibility for most of the *Orgelbüchlein* chorales (that they were actual accompaniments) is discussed below, p41.

forbade the *alternatim* method (Rietschel 1893 pp36–7). But judging alone by Pachelbel's Magnificat fughettas, St Sebaldus, Nuremberg certainly kept the *alternatim* organ versets in its four weekly Vespers: little fugues by now not related to any cantus firmus.

If Leipzig could reasonably be supposed to have settled down by *c*1725 to having the free German hymns sung by the congregation, with organ prelude but perhaps without organ accompaniment, and the canticles and collects/responsories sung by priest and choir, but with organ versets, it would not contradict anything that is known for certain. Earlier on there had been various suggestions for performing the various hymns in other German cities or provinces. For example, in the preface to *Musae Sioniae* I (Wolfenbüttel 1606) Praetorius suggested various shifting blocks of sound – congregation plus organ, precentor/choir plus instruments, organ solo using two or three manuals, and so on – while another hymnbook, of 1601, spoke of the congregation's listening but not singing when choir and organ were performing hymns *alternatim*, perhaps with a solo treble (Luedtke 1918 p4). The question at Leipzig and Weimar – Did the organ ever play fully fledged interludes between the congregation's verses? – is not nearer an answer for the period around 1725 than it is for the period around 1600. In Leipzig in 1740, Mizler published some remarks that certainly imply his familiarity with major organ interludes between verses: how ridiculous it is, he wrote, when an organist

> bey dem letzten Vers, der in etlichen Minuten abgesungen wird, eine viertel, oder gar halbe Stunde allerhand Grimacen vorspielet (pp56–64)

> improvises all kinds of grimaces for a quarter and even half an hour before the last verse which is sung through in a few minutes

Presumably he would regard BWV 652 in this light, though he was referring to pieces in the 'concerto style', i.e. big free fantasias. But, as here too, there is very often doubt about what the evidence means. *Vers* may mean not the 'last verse' of a hymn but the *Schlussvers* as mentioned in some service-orders: the 'closing words' of the service (sung by the pastor), before which the organist played a solo voluntary. The provinces of Mecklenburg and Brunswick–Lüneburg, for example, gave directives in 1650 and 1709 respectively for hymn-playing (Rietschel 1893 pp62–3) which demonstrate typical puzzles: do the sources refer to *alternatim* or to accompaniment?

> wo aber Orgeln sind, soll der Organist einen Vers um den andern schlagen.

> where there are organs, however, the organist should play every other verse.

> In den Kirchen, wo Orgeln sein, sollen die Organisten, um die Melodien und den anstimmenden Gesang kund zu machen, einen Vers jedoch ohn Variation vorschlagen, auch wohl zuweilen unter dem Gesang, jedoch so gelinde, dass man das Singen der Gemeinde hören . . . kann.

> In churches where there are organs, the organists should play a verse without variation, in order to indicate the melody and pitch[?], also from time to time during the hymn, but so quietly that one can hear the singing of the congregation.

The first probably does refer to *alternatim*; if the second does not, however, it must mean that the organ was to play occasionally to keep the congregation up to pitch, with no doubt imperfect results.

The accompanying only of every alternate verse was a habit criticized by Türk (1787 p8), who neither appreciated that the practice arose originally between organ and trained choirs/priests nor thought *Vers* a suitable term, since a single line was a *Vers* and a set of them should be called a *Strophe*:

> An einigen Orten pflegen die Organisten nur eine Strophe um die Andere mitzuspielen. Woher das kommen mag, weiss ich nicht . . . klingt es sehr widrig, wenn die Orgel wider eintritt; weil binnen der Zeit gewöhnlich ein Viertel- oder Achtelton herunter gezogen worden ist.

> In some places the organists like to play only every other verse. How that arose, I do not know . . . but it sounds unpleasant when the organ comes in again because meanwhile the pitch has usually sunk a quarter or eighth of a tone.

The last point had also been made by Marpurg (1754 p89). Nor did Türk see any point in interline interludes, which he called *Zwischenpräludia*, a kind of fantasia or free improvisation: he noted

> dass die Gemeinde an einigen Orten bey jeder Strophe zB das Kyrie, Gott Vater &c inne hält. Der Organist fantasirt (order interludirt) binnen der Zeit eine Weile; alsdenn fängt der Kantor oder Vorsänger die folgende Strophe an, und die Gemeinde fällt wieder ein. Was diese Einrichtung übrigens für einen Endzwek hat, und warum man dies nur bey einigen Liedern thut, ist mir unbekannt (1787 pp135-6).

> that the congregation in some places halts at the close of each verse of (e.g.) the Kyrie. The organist improvises (or interludes) for some time; then the cantor or precentor begins the following verse and the congregation joins in again. What the idea behind this arrangement is, however, and why it is done only for certain hymns, I do not know.

The very terms in which Türk describes the procedure rather suggest that it was still known in such conservative places as Leipzig. In principle, such interluding is different from the organ solos (preludes) played between the series of Communion hymns, whose purpose – according to Mizler (1740 pp56–64) – was to give communicants time for breath and to avoid leaving the church empty of sound. For providing such 'sound', long settings such as BWV 688 or 689 would not be unsuitable (if *Clavierübung III* had a function), but for the Kyrie *alternatim* interludes as reported by Türk nothing in the Bach *oeuvre* would be suitable. Perhaps the Thomaskirche organist would have improvised them, as no doubt the Weimar organist had done in the Magnificat, Te Deum, Kyrie and Gloria.

b

From the earliest days of Lutheran chorales being written down, musical sources tended to mark either the end of each line (by incises, rests, longer note-values etc) or the start of the next line (by showing the first note (if an up-beat) shorter than the others). Incises in (e.g.) the *Geneva Psalter* indicated pauses for breath, like the rests between lines in Scheidt's *Görlitzer Tabulaturbuch* or, much later, Witt's *Cantional*; and since a line of text mostly corresponds to a musical phrase (and vice versa) such breaks or pauses or rests satisfy both musical logic and the breathing of the singer. The congregational chorale itself underwent important changes between 1530 and 1730; the plain chords in notes of equal value (so-called isometric homophony) and a melody in the treble gradually replaced the mixed rhythms, the less consistent textures and the tenor melodies of the earliest settings.* The chorales seem to have become slower, even during the eighteenth century. Assuming the demisemiquavers of BWV 715 to be eight times as fast as the chorale crotchets – a justified assumption? – the hymn itself must be very spacious indeed. Other central German sources of *c*1708–12 speak of the organ and singers performing hymns in a manner that was serious and 'moderated by devotion' ('andächtiglich gemassiget': see *Das Erbe deutscher Musik* 36 (1957) pp99–100); and in the preface to his Gotha *Cantional* of 1715, C. F. Witt suggests that the hymn be played over slowly and then sung 'also slowly' ('auch langsam'). Of course, *langsam* is very imprecise, but at much the same period Niedt tried to be more specific and recommended a tempo neither too fast (which would suggest a dance) nor too slow (which would induce sleep – 1717 p44). While it can only be conjectured what all these various terms mean, certainly they all suggest a hymn sung simply and steadily, harmonized by the organ which would play runs or other passage-work between the lines. These interludes would generally indicate the opening chord of the next line but would not be clearly derived from the melody itself.†

The first published organ interludes appear to be those in Kauffmann's *Harmonische Seelenlust* (Leipzig 1733), but J. S. Bach's (to mention no others) must be older, if the attributions to him in various unconnected manuscripts are reliable. In his preface, Kauffmann refers to the interludes as follows:

> Vors andere ist zwischen jedem Commate eine zierliche Passage zu finden, indem solche (imperfecten) Liebhaber wie sie allhier beschrieben worden, nicht eben im Stande seyn, etwas rechts dazwischen zu machen und gar stille zu halten, wäre zu schlecht.

> secondly, there is to be found in each break a decorative passage, for such inexpert amateurs as have been described here are not in a position to do anything suitable at these points; yet to remain silent would be too bad.

and claims that they had been requested 'some time ago'. It is not out of the question that the *Seelenlust* was published in Leipzig at J. S. Bach's recommendation.‡ However, it is questionable whether Kauffmann or any other organist would have expected the congregation to hold the chord while he played the interludes (Krey 1956). In any event, the filled-in gaps were becoming known by the 1730s. Scheibe, speaking of practices in Hamburg or Leipzig (it is not clear which), refers to the habit some organists had of varying the cadences in the middle of verses as well as at the end, thus implying the origin of both interline and inter-verse interludes (1745 pp418–20). He recommends that the organist hold the chord at the end of each line-cadence ('Gesangclausal'), adding the pedal at that point (! – p417) and thus presumably sustaining a chord in order to establish the pitch for the congregation.

---

* Not in a conscious desire to simplify as such but because the earliest settings necessarily supposed trained choirs in those privileged places where a single unharmonized congregational melody was not enough?

† Quite the best 'record' of such practices as they had survived into the 1820s and 1830s can be found in the opening scene of *Die Meistersinger*, and there is no reason to think that Wagner was parodying or exaggerating the nature of such performance as he heard it.

‡ See a brief report on the relevant connections in G. G. Butler, 'Leipziger Stecher in Bachs Originaldrucken', *BJ* 66 (1980) 9–26. J. G. Walther's 'Allein Gott' variations were recommended to the same Leipzig engraver in 1736 but unsuccessfully, appearing only in 1738 in Augsburg (see *Dok* II p265).

Although it must be true that such interludes, both enabling the congregation to read the next verse and dissipating the monotony of isometric chorales (Feder 1965), could have been improvised by any but the weakest organists, a few interludes were published before Türk and others described the process in detail. H. F. Quehl's variations, published in 1734 (*Der zur Beförderung göttlicher Ehre . . . musicalische Versuch*, Nuremberg), also included a pair of chorales harmonized in four to six parts and embellished with a bar or so of elementary scale-like runs between the lines. One can assume that there was a growing market for such settings. This is also the period in which slow tempos are recommended (Werner 1933 p97):

> Darum ist es nötig, dass man langsam singe (*Dresdner Gesangbuch* 1726).
>
> So it is necessary to sing slowly.
>
> Es sollen die Chorallieder auch langsam abgesungen und also dadurch der gebührlichen Andacht ein Beitrag gegeben werden (Witt *Cantional*, 1715).
>
> The choral hymns should also be sung slowly and so thereby a contribution made to seemly devotions.

By 1847, one report in Baden speaks of every syllable having four pulse-beats and the final note of each line (with a fermata) having eight to twelve, while the organist plays interludes (*ibid*). During the 1750s Adlung found that in some places the chorales were too slow, in others too fast, while at Jena J. N. Bach played without interludes, preferring to lead the congregation with a held chord (Adlung 1783 pp815, 824). In the Weissenfels court chapel Adlung heard a short chord replacing the interlude, 'like an acciaccatura' ('Vorschlag'), more than which was not allowed (*ibid* p825).*

Allowing for the sarcasm, Burney's picture of a service in Bremen Cathedral – apparently on a Monday (19 October 1772) – conveys a useful picture of Lutheran singing at that period in northwest Germany, with its details on tempo, repetitiveness, interludes, accompaniment (partial) and unison singing (the last of which he also reported in the Dresden Frauenkirche):

> . . . I found the congregation singing a dismal melody, without the organ. When this was ended, the organist gave out a hymn tune, in the true dragging style of Sternhold & Hopkins [the old metrical psalter] . . . The interludes between the line[s] of the hymn were always the same, and of the following kind: [Ex. 3]. After hearing this tune, and these interludes, repeated ten or twelve times, I went to see the town, and returning to the cathedral two hours later, I still found the people singing all in unison, and as loud as they could, the same tune, to the same accompaniment . . . (Burney/Scholes 1959 1 pp238–9)

Ex. 3

---

* That Türk (1787 p16) should still be quoting Adlung (writing in 1758) on this is witness to the reliance placed by such authors on older literary sources. Did he not himself hear many varied ways of playing interludes?

Judging by key, repetitiveness and occasion, Burney could well have been witnessing the performance of a German Te Deum: the long canticle Niedt heard often in Hamburg accompanied with organ-drums, cuckoo, star, bird-stops and so on (1717 p46) in order, no doubt, to lighten the monotony. Later in the century Türk too complained of 'brainlessly' unsuitable interludes ('hirnlos': 1787 p105), but some areas may always have resisted the interlude practice, as Potsdam is said to have done in the 1730s (Fellerer 1932 p33). Perhaps there was by nature an 'objectivity' to the interline interlude – runs and passage-work irrespective of the mood of the hymn – that offended those churches in which the congregations were anxious to be 'affected' or piously moved. Hence Adlung's suggestion in 1758 to omit interludes in sad chorales or at least to avoid fast passage-work (1783 p824).*

Complaints about the length of organ interludes become increasingly frequent but need not necessarily indicate that they got out of hand, only that fashions changed. Thus practices at Kassel in c1786 were still reported on in the *AMZ* in 1810 (*AMZ* 12 col. 437–8), and a review of J. C. Kittel's preludes in the same journal (*AMZ* 6 (1803) col. 802) thought it to their advantage that they were not as long as many of the old organ preludes – which, after all, had once been perfectly acceptable. J. S. Bach's own interludes remain consistent in length and style, and it is arguing too much from appearances to see BWV 729 as 'more integrated' than usual and BWV 732 as 'eventually homogeneous' (Geiringer 1966 p229), as if a line of actual development were traceable. Perhaps it was, but it is not clear whether when Quantz refers to interline interludes as 'stupid panpiping coloraturas' ('ungeschickten bockpfeiferhaften Coloraturen': 1752 ch.xviii) he is implying that interludes were always stupid, were getting worse, or were merely offending the new polished tastes of fashionable chamber musicians now turning away from the church.

---

5. The Duties of Organists

Werckmeister sums up the duties of organists succinctly and neatly when in the *Orgelprobe* (1698) he notes that organists should know how to deal with tuning and mechanisms that go wrong because of weather, and should be able to improvise, transpose, read *Generalbass* and play not merely bourrées and other French songs (1698 pp76–7). Contracts themselves are needed to specify the details more exactly, but Werckmeister himself was more specific in *Harmonologia musica* (1702 pp68ff), when he repeated that it was not enough for organists to play a few well-practised pieces: churches should make sure that their new organist can do the following –

> improvise a fugue on a given subject
> vary a chorale [i.e. harmonize in different ways, with some right-hand embellishments according to the nature of the text?]

* In a hymnbook published in 1780 specifically for the Lutheran congregation of Bremen Cathedral (*neues Gesangbuch der evangelisch–lutherischen Domgemeinde zu Bremen*, Bremen 1780) the preface refers to the care taken to avoid hymns 'which would be too long to be sung complete in public services' ('welches zu lang wäre, in den öffentlichen Versammlungen ganz gesungen werden zu können'). Does this suggest that the *pastor primarius*, writing the preface in 1778, was reforming abuses of the kind Burney indicated?

transpose a chorale 'durch das gantze Clavier' [i.e. into every key?]
read both figured bass and tablature
understand how to treat his instrument
satisfy an assessor practised in composition that he has musicianship

How systematically any of these subjects were dealt with by teachers is uncertain, and modern assumptions cannot be verified. The *Obituary* speaks of J. S. Bach's going to Hamburg and later to Lübeck to 'listen to' Reincken and Buxtehude ('hören', 'behorchen': *Dok* III p82); later, organists reported visiting Leipzig in 1725 and between 1729 and 1740, one 'drawing advantage from [Bach's] skill', the other 'hearing him play' (*Dok* II pp379, 380). But in none of these cases is it clear whether lessons as such were involved, and if so what they covered – though 'listening to' suggests at least a respectful master–pupil relationship. Obviously instruction of some kind is suggested by references made by Leipzig pupils, particularly when they were applying for jobs. One had the advantage of 'instruction in music' during his six years as theological student in Leipzig ('in der Music . . . Anweisung': *Dok* II p381); one who applied for a post as organist and schoolmaster claimed J. S. Bach as teacher '*in hac arte*' (*Dok* II p459); Altnickol 'learnt *Clavier* together with *Composition*' (*Dok* II pp423, 424, 466); and another (J. G. Ziegler in 1746) claimed to have learnt chorale-playing and to have been instructed

> dass ich die Lieder nicht nur so oben hin, sondern nach dem *Affect* der Wortte spiele (*Dok* II p423).

> that I should play the hymns not indifferently but according to the *Affekt* of the words.

But this last is far less clear than appears and is frequently taken today. First, it is uncertain whether *Choralspielen* means 'playing hymns' or 'playing organ chorales'; secondly, the job being sought was at the Liebfrauenkirche, Halle, a church whose consistory was well known for its interest in pietist *Affekte* and which an aspiring applicant would wish to satisfy; and thirdly, the writer's rival for the job was W. F. Bach (the successful candidate), who without Ziegler's remark would otherwise have appeared to have a unique connection with the most famous teacher of the area.

Sometimes, however, a reliable detail can be gleaned from such references, such as that some pupils learnt keyboard and organ, others composition (see e.g. *Dok* II p409), or that a pupil could be expected to be proficient at *Generalbass* (see e.g. *Dok* II p310), or that lessons could be in *Clavierspielen* (only? – J. T. Krebs*). But how pupils learnt is not described in greater detail, and such albums as the *Orgelbüchlein*, *The 48* Bk I and even the *Klavierbüchlein für W. F. Bach* are repertory collections, not planned (much less graded) methods. It is only interesting speculation to think that the preludes and fugues for organ 'were clearly involved in Bach's pedagogy' and to interpret minor differences between manuscript sources as 'small improvements . . . entered into his score . . . when he went over a prelude with a pupil' (Stauffer 1980 pp152-3). Nor are his testimonials for former pupils specific, any more than those for *Stadtpfeifer* with whom Bach had worked.

That organists learnt by travelling and visiting the acknowledged masters is clear from Mattheson's accounts in the *Ehrenpforte*, and it may have been in response to such biographies that the *Obituary* emphasized that same element of learning-by-

---

* Who may have learnt composition from Walther but *Clavierspielen* from Bach – *Dok* II p232.

observing in the career of J. S. Bach.* In addition to such autodidacticism, the *Obituary* emphasized the attention which the composer paid to old and respected German church musicians: he went to Lübeck to hear Buxtehude, Hamburg to hear Reincken. But he must have heard and learnt much more. Mattheson reported his own activities as a young organist as follows (1740 pp187ff): as a student he travelled around to play different organs (with G. F. Handel), journeyed to hear famous organists (Buxtehude in Lübeck, masters in Holland), took part in organist-trials for positions which he did not accept (including a trial of two hours in Haarlem), and as a non-professional played to visitors in Hamburg (ambassadors etc) and officiated at organist-trials (also in Hamburg). These can be paralleled – even to the ambassadors – in incidents reported of J. S. Bach's life in the *Obituary*. Furthermore, travelling had been traditional, and the *Obituary* writers must have been at least aware of the success which Handel found far from home. Mattheson frequently mentions composers' travels. One organist had come to Hamburg to hear Scheidemann, Weckmann and others because such skill was not to be heard in the court chapels, whether royal, electoral or princely (*op cit* p304), while J. Praetorius's studies with Sweelinck had been encouraged, and given some financial support, by his church president (*ibid* p306). A century or so later, a certain Silesian organist was also subsidized for his visit to J. S. Bach in Leipzig (*Dok* II p380). Perhaps J. S. Bach's leave from Arnstadt to travel to Lübeck had been regarded as a right, for it is clear from Mattheson's biographies that organists from some towns in central Germany tended to travel north for experience, while from others they went south. Thus there was a Dresden–Vienna link but scarcely a Thuringia–Vienna link.

However he learnt his art, the organist was to have a notion of his profession that changed little in the half-century after Werckmeister wrote. Thus in Leipzig in the 1730s, J. A. Scheibe (whose actual abilities are questionable) outlined similar duties, rather suggesting that few organists understood what the duties were (1745 pp413ff). The organist should

> understand *Generalbass* completely, including how to transpose and play continuo in music outside the church
>
> know all the chorales (including the *Collecten* and *Responsoria*) and how to play them, register for them, harmonize and match the words
>
> be able to improvise well ('soll er geschickt präludiren können') for which he needs to have insight and practice in composing
>
> understand organs and how to test and report on them, so that he can both keep his own in good condition and test new instruments

Compared to Werckmeister's and Scheibe's descriptions of an organist's duties, the conditions of employ known to have been presented to J. S. Bach were more specific in some respects, less in others. At Arnstadt, the appointment required certain personal qualities, specified the attendances, gave responsibility for the organ itself† and authorized payment of salary, as follows:

* The *Obituary* is also characteristic of its period in the general picture it gives of musical talent driving a small boy to withstand pressures against his studies. The child Bach had his notebook taken away; the child Handel practised secretly in an attic (Mainwaring 1760 pp5–6). Mainwaring himself remarks on the similarity between Handel's talent overcoming resistance and a story told about the mathematician Pascal as a boy.

† Evidently to the extent of entrusting the key to the organist, which he then returned on his eventual resignation (*Dok* II p27).

Demnach der hochgebohrne Unser Gnädigster Graff und Herr Herr Anthon Günther, der vier Graffen des Reiches Graff zu Schwarzburg und Hohnstein, Herr zu Arnstadt, Sondershaussen Leütenberg, Lohre und Clettenberg, Euch *Johann Sebastian Bachen* zu einem Organisten in der Neüen Kirchen annehmen und bestellen lassen, Alss sollet Höchstgedacht Ihro HochGräfflichen Gnaden zuförderst Ihr treü, Hold und gewärtig seyn, insonderheit aber Euch in Eürem anbefohlnen Ambte, Beruff, Kunstübung und Wissenschafft fleissig und treülich bezeigen in andere Händel und verrichtungen Euch nicht mengen, zu rechter Zeit an denen Sonn- und Fest- auch andern zum öffentlichen Gottes dienst bestimbten Tagen in obbesagter Neüen Kirchen bey dem Eüch anvertrauten Orgelwercke Euch einfinden, solches gebührend *tractiren*, darauff gute Acht haben, und es mit allem Fleiss verwahren, da etwas daran wandelbahr würde es bey Zeiten melden und dass nöthige *reparatur* beschehe, Errinnerung thun, Niemanden ohne vorbewust des Herrn *Superintenden*ten auf selbiges lassen und insgemein Euch bester Möglichkeit nach angelegen seyn lassen, damit Schaden verhütet, und alles in guten wessen und Ordnung erhalten werde, gestalt Ihr Euch denn auch sonsten in Eurem Leben und wandel der Gottesfurcht, Nüchterkeit und verträglichkeit zubefleissigen, böser Gesellschafft und Abhaltung Eures beruffs Euch gäntzlich zu enthalten, und übrigens in allen, wie einem Ehrliebenden Diener und Organisten gegen Gott, die Hohe Obrigkeit und vorgesetzten, gebühret, treulich zuverhalten. Dagegen sollen Euch zur Ergetzlichkeit zu Eurer Besoldung Jährlichen Funffzig Gülden und vor die Kost und wohnung dreysig thlr. gegen Eüre quittung folgender massen gereichet werden, als 25 fl. aus denen Biergelden. 25 fl. auss dem Gottes Kasten und die übrigen 30 thlr. von *Hospital*.

Urkündlich ist diese Bestallung unter dem Gräfflichen Cantzley-*Secret* und gewöhnlicher Unterschrifft wissendlich aussgefertiget.

Signatum den 9ten *Augusti* 1703.

> Gräfflich Schwarzburgische
> Verordnete *Praeses*, Räthe und
> *Assessores* des *Consistorii* zu Arnstadt.
> Mart: Volckmar Schultes.

Herrn
Herrn Johann Martin Heindorffen
HochGräfflich Schwarzburgischen
Wohlverordneten *Archivario*.
Meinem hochgeneigten Herrn
Vetter zu entsiegeln.
in Arnstadt.
(*Dok* II pp11-12)

Since the Right Honourable our Most Gracious Count and Lord, Anthon Günther, [one] of the Four Counts of the Empire, Count of Schwarzburg and Hohnstein, Lord of Arnstadt, Sondershausen, Leutenberg, Lohre and Clettenberg, has had you, Johann Sebastian Bach, accepted and appointed as an organist in the New Church, so you should keep yourself faithful, pleasant and attentive above all to His Grace, the same Noble Count, but in particular show yourself industrious and trustworthy in your recommended office, calling, artistic practice and knowledge; not to meddle in other business and affairs; to present yourself punctually at the organ entrusted to you on Sundays, feasts and other days appointed for public worship in the said New Church; to play the same properly, to take care of it and maintain it with all industry, reporting on those occasions that anything becomes unreliable and making note that a repair is necessary; to allow no one on to the same without the Superintendent's foreknowledge and generally to apply yourself according to your best abilities so that damage is avoided and everything kept in good condition and order. In respect to yourself, you are also to take pains to conduct your life in the fear of God, sobriety and good nature, preserving yourself entirely from bad society and hindrance to your calling; and in all things to keep yourself faithfully towards God, high authority and superiors, as is proper to a servant and organist loving honour. In return for this shall you be paid, for your disposal and against your receipt, a salary of 50 guilders a year and for living expenses 30 thaler [made up] in the following manner: 25 guilders from beer excise, 25 from the church chest, and the other 30 thaler from the Hospital.

In proof thereof this certificate is prepared by authority under the seal and usual signature of the Count's Chancellery.

Signed 9 August 1703.

Martin Volkmar Schulte, Count Schwarzburg's authorized *praeses*, councillor and assessor to the Consistory of Arnstadt.
To Johann Martin Heindorff, authorized archivist to the Noble Count Schwarzburg.
To be unsealed by my most gracious colleague. In Arnstadt. [?]

The well-known criticism of Bach's manner of playing at Arnstadt makes clear several details: that he travelled to Lübeck seeking experience, that he supplied a deputy in his absence, that he avoided duties in the playing of ensemble music and that he played in unacceptable styles:

Nos
Halthen Ihm vor dass er bissher in dem *Choral* viele wunderliche *variationes* gemachet, viele frembde Thone mit eingemischet, dass die Gemeinde drüber *confundi*ret worden. Er habe ins künfftige wann er ja einen *tonum peregrinum* mit einbringen wolte, selbigen auch auss-zuhalthen, und nicht zu geschwinde auf etwas anders zu fallen, oder wie er bissher im brauch gehabt, gar einen *Tonum contrarium* zu spiehlen.
. . .
Dahero er sich zu erclähren, Ob er so wohl *Figural* alss *Choral* mit den Schühlern spiehlen wolle?
. . .
[Rambach:]
Der *Organist* Bach habe bisshero etwas gar zu lang gespiehlet, nachdem ihm aber vom Herrn *Superint* deswegen anzeige beschehen, währe er gleich auf das andere *extremum* gefallen, und hätte es zu kurtz gemachet.
(*Dok* II p20)*

WE
charge him that hitherto he has been making many strange *variationes* in the *Choral* [and] mixed in with it many strange tones, so that the congregation has been confused by it. In future, should he wish to bring in a *tonus peregrinus* he is to keep to it and not too quickly light on something else, or, as he has been in the habit of doing, play even a *tonus contrarius* . . .
. . .
Therefore, he is to make it clear: will he perform figural as well choral [music] with the schoolboys?
. . .
[Rambach, prefect, on being also reproved for disorders between organist and students, immediately replies:]
The organist Bach has hitherto played really too long, but after an indication of this was given him by the Superintendent, he straightway fell into the other extreme and made it too short.

Although the scribe and/or superintendent apparently misused the musical terms,

---

* The complaint mentions only *Choral* and *Figural* music but no solo organ music as such (e.g. free preludes and postludes to the service): is this more likely to be because there was none than because the accused was allowed to do as he liked at those moments?

the tenor of the complaint is clear enough, and from the dates (consistory sat on 21 February, while the composer was probably back by 7 February or earlier), it could be that Terry is correct to see the 'many strange tones' as a result of the Lübeck visit (1933 p70). That Thuringian hymn-singing was not a natural place for too inventive an accompaniment or improvised interlude is also suggested by Witt's recommendation (in his *Cantional* of 1715) that the organist keep away from runs and 'incorrect cadences' ('unrichtige Clausuln'), the latter of which seems to refer to either chromatic turns of key or wild improvisation between lines – it is difficult to say which. Further conjectures are less convincing, however: that secular and sacred elements were being mixed in the accompaniments (Kraft 1950 p29), or that such a chorale as BWV 715 is a typical example of its composer's having heard Buxtehude's style (Klein 1976 p101), about which nothing whatsoever is known. Whether the 'strange tones' were sudden modulations, chromatic harmonizations or chords built on sevenths (as in BWV 715) it is not possible to say, and it is only speculation that such chorales date from the Arnstadt years. Since the composer was also criticized for playing at too great length, he must have been playing either preludes or interludes to the chorales beyond what was customary; the complaint certainly suggests solo organ music played at inappropriate moments. *'Variationes'* presumably refers to the embellishment of the harmonies, in left- or right-hand parts, of the kind criticized by Scheibe (1745 pp418–19), the 'frembde Thone' to chromatic passing-notes, the quickly changed *tonus peregrinus** to constant modulation (did 'Thon' mean 'note', and *'tonus'* mean 'key/mode'?) and *tonus contrarius* to a wrong key or perhaps the relative major/minor.† In any case, however, it is difficult to imagine any such characteristics as having been learnt from Buxtehude, or indeed heard in Lübeck at all.

The Mühlhausen appointment was similar in all respects to that at Arnstadt, resembling those earlier ·contracts when organists in post-Reformation times were told to stay on good terms with the cantor, play fittingly and look after the organ (Wetzel 1961 p337).

Wir bey der Keyserlich Freyen und d. h. R. St. M. sämtliche Eingepfarrete BurgerMeistere und RathsVerwandten des Kirchspiels *D. Blasij* fügen hiermit zu wissen, demnach dasige *Organist*en Stelle durch tödtlichen Hintritt Herrn *Joh. George* Ahlen weyland unseres mit Raths Freündes *vacant* und erlediget worden, solche nun zu ersetzen, haben Herrn *Joh: Sebastian Bachen* bey der *Bonifacij* Kirche zu Arnstadt bestellten *Organist*en anhero beruffen und zu Unseren *Organist*en bey obbesagter Kirche *D. Blasij* dero gestalt angenommen, dass Er zuförderst hiesigen *Magistrat* treü und hold seyn, Gemeiner Stadt Schaden weren und bestes hingegen befördern, in seiner auffgetragenen Dienst Verrichtung sich willig bezeigen und iedes mahl erfinden lassen, absonderlich die sonn- fest- und andere feiertage seine auffwarttung treüfleissig verrichten das Ihme anvertraute Orgelwerck wenigst in guten stande erhalten, die etwa befindtliche Mängel dem iedesmahl bestellten Herren Vorsteheren anzeigen und vor deren *reparatur* und *music* fleissig mit sorgen, aller guten wohlanständigen Sitten sich befleissigen auch ungeziehmende gesellschafft und verdächtige *compagnie* meiden solle, gleichwie nun obbenanter Herr *Bache* Obigen allen nach sich gemäss zu bezeigen und zu verhalten mittelst Handtschlages verpflichtet, Alss haben Ihme hergegen zu seiner Jehrlichen besoldung

---

* Presumably not a reference to the Magnificat melody?
† As a musical term, *contrarius* seems to have had its present meaning (e.g. *motu contrario* in J. G. Walther's *Praecepta*).

85 gfl an gelde

das hergebrachte *deputat* an 3 mltr Korn 2 Cl Holtz 1 buchen und 1 Eichen: oder aspen
   6 sch reissig vor die thür geführet an statt des ackers.

zureichen versprochen, und darob gegenwärttigen bestallungs Schein unter vorgedrückten
   Cantzley*secret* aussstellen lassen. Geschehen den 15 *Junij* 1707

E. b. d. K. f. u. d. h. R St M.

(*Dok* II pp24–5)

We, all the incorporated Burgomasters and Councillors of the Divi-Blasii-Kirche in the Imperial Free City of Mühlhausen let it be known with this, that the organist's position there, having been vacated and become unfilled through the passing-away of Herr Joh. George Ahle (formerly a fellow councillor of ours), in order now to fill the same [we] have called here Herr Joh. Sebastian Bach, the appointed organist of the Bonifatiuskirche at Arnstadt, and have accepted him as our organist at the said Divi-Blasii-Kirche on condition that above all he be faithful and good-natured to the Magistrate here, keep our community from harm and on the other hand promote what is best for it, show himself willing in the execution of the duties with which he is charged, and make himself available at all times, be industrious and loyal in his attendance particularly on Sundays, feasts and other holy days, keep the organ entrusted to him in good condition at the very least, indicate any fault found there to [whoever is] the appointed inspector at that time, care diligently for the repairs and *music* of the organ, strive for all good and decent morals, likewise avoiding improper society and questionable company. Now just as the said Herr Bach has shown himself in agreement with all the above, and with a handshake has undertaken to observe it, so in return have we promised to pay him a yearly salary of:

85 guilders in cash

the handed-down [=previous, not augmented] allowance of 3 measures of corn, 2 measures of wood (1 beech and 1 oak or aspen) and 6 loads of kindling brought to the door (in lieu of arable land)

and therefore we have had drawn up the present document of appointment, affixing to it the chancellery seal. Executed 15 June 1707.

Corporation of the Imperial Free and Holy Roman City of Mühlhausen

Perhaps the '*music*' of the organ meant its sound or musical quality, in particular its tuning. The fact that, though Ahle had died in December 1706, J. S. Bach's trial was not until Easter 1707 (*Dok* II pp22–3) may suggest that the organ had been left silent during Lent, whatever had been the nature of J. G. Walther's involvement there (see below, p43).

The Halle contract is more detailed, in a manner that would be expected of a large and important church. After declining the appointment, the composer claimed not to have applied for the post but only accepted an invitation to present himself for it (*Dok* I pp23–4), evidently a distinction of significance. It is known that the church then applied to G. M. Hoffmann, organist of the Neukirche, Leipzig, who also declined, whereupon G. Kirchhoff was appointed. There seems to have been no public trial in the Hamburg manner, though one document spoke of the 'usual manner of electing' the organist (*Dok* II p49).

Wir Endes unterschriebene Kirch-Väter und Achtmanne zu Unserer Lieben Frauen allhier, vor uns und unsere Nachkommen im Kirchen-*Collegio*, uhrkunden hierdurch und bekennen; dass wir dem Ehren-Vesten und Wohlgelahrten HErrn Johann *Sebastian* Bachen zum *Organi*sten bey der Kirche zu Unserer Lieben Frauen krafft dieses dergestalt bestellet, und angenommen haben, dass Er unss und unserer Kirche treu und dienstgewärtig sey, eines

Tugendhafften une *exemplar*ischen Lebens sich befleissige, zuförderst bey der ungeänderten Augspurgischen *Confession*, der *Formula Concordiae* und andern *symbol*ischen Glaubens Bekäntnüssen biss an sein Ende beständig verharre, nebst andächtigem Gehör Göttliches Wortes sich zu dieser Kirchen Altar fleissig halte, und dadurch sein Glaubens-Bekäntnüss und Christenthum der ganzen Gemeine bezeuge. Hiernächst, so viel seine ordentliche Ambts-Verrichtung *concernir*et, lieget ihm ob, 1.) alle hohe und andere einfallende Feyer- oder Fest-Tage, und deren *vigil*ien, auch alle Sonntage und Sonnabends nachmittage, ingleichen bey denen ordentlichen *Catechissmus* Predigten und bey öffentlichen *Copulatio*nen | die grosse Orgel zu Beförderung des Gottes-Dienstes nach seinem besten Fleiss und Vermögen zu schlagen, iedoch dergestalt, dass zu weilen auch die kleine Orgel und das *Regal*, zumahl an hohen Festen bey der *Choral*- und *Figural-Musique* gespielet werde. Wie er denn 2.) *ordinarie* bey hohen und andern Festen, imgleichen über den dritten Sonntag nebst dem *Cantore* und Chor-Schülern auch Stadt-*Musicis* und andern *Instrument*isten, eine bewegliche und wohl klingend-gesetzte andächtige *Musiqve* zu *exhibir*en, *extraordinarie* aber die zwey leztern hohen Feyertage nebst dem *Cantore* und Schülern, auch zuweilen mit einigen *violin*en und andern *instrument*en, kurze *Figural*-Stücke zu *musicir*en, und alles dergestalt zu *dirigir*en hat, dass dadurch die eingepfarrete Gemeine zur Andacht und Liebe zum Gehör göttliches Wortes destomehr ermuntert und angefrischet werde; vornehmlich aber hat Er 3.) nöthig die zur *Musiqve* erwehlete *textus* und *cantiones* dem HErrn Ober-*Pastori* Unserer Kirche *Tit*: HErrn *Consistorial* Rath *Doct: Heineccio*, zudessen *approbation*, in Zeiten zu *communicir*en, gestalt Er desswegen an den HErrn | *Consistorial*-Rath hiermit gewiesen wird. Ferner wird Er 4.) sich befleissigen, so wohl die ordentliche, als von denen HE. *Ministerialibus* vorgeschriebene *Choral*-Gesänge vor- und nach denen Sonn- und Fest-Tages Predigten, auch unter der *Communion, item* zur *Vesper* und *vigil*ien Zeit, langsam ohne sonderbahres *colorir*en mit vier und fünff Stimmen und dem *Principal* andächtig einzuschlagen, und mit iedem *versicul* die andern Stimmen iedesmahl abzuwechseln, auch zur *qvintaden* und Schnarr wercke, das Gedackte, wie auch die *syncopationes* und Bindungen dergestalt zu *adhibir*en, dass die eingepfarrete Gemeine die Orgel zum *Fundamente* einer guten *Harmonie* und gleichstimmigen Thones sezen, darinn andächtig singen, und dem Allerhöchsten dancken und loben möge. Wobey Ihme 5.) zugleich das grosse und kleine Orgelwerck nebst dem Kirchen-*Regal*, und andere, zur Kirchen gehörige, in einem Ihme auszustellendem *inventario specificir*te *Instrumenta* hierdurch anvertrauet, und anbefohlen werden, dass Er fleissige Obacht habe, damit die erstern an Bälgen, Stimmen, Registern und allem an|dern Zubehörungen in gutem Stande, auch rein gestimmet und ohne *dissonanz* erhalten, und, da etwas wandelbahr oder mangelhafft würde, solches alsobald dem Vorsteher, oder wenn es der Wichtigkeit, dem Kirchen-*Collegio*, zur *reparatur* und Verhütung grössern Schadens, angezeiget werde. Das auss unserm Kirchen *aerario* angeschaffete *Regal* aber, und übrige *musicali*sche *instrumenta* sollen allein zum GottesDienst in unserer Kirche gebrauchet, keinesweges aber in andre Kirchen, vielweniger zu Gastereyen ohne unsre Einwilligung verliehen, auch da etwas davon verlohren, oder durch verwahrlosung zerbrochen würde, der Schade von Ihme ersezet werden.

Vor solche seine Bemühung sollen Ihme auss der Kirchen Einkünfften, Einhundert und vierzig thlr Besoldung, imgleichen vier und zwanzig thlr. zur Wohnung und Sieben thl. 12. groschen zu Holz alljährlich gezahlet, auch vor die *Composition* der Catechissmus *Musiqve* iedesmahl 1. thl. und von ieglicher BrautMesse 1. rthlr. gegeben werden.

Wogegen Er verspricht, zeitwährender dieser Bestallung keine Neben-Bestallung anzuneh| men, sonderen die Dienste allein an dieser Kirche fleissig zuversehen, iedoch bleibet Ihme, so viel ohne deren Versäumung geschehen kan, frey, durch *information* oder sonsten *accidentia* zusuchen. Zu dessen Uhrkund haben wir diese Bestallung *in duplo* unter dem grössern Kirchen *Secret* aussfertigen lassen, eigenhändig nebst dem HE. *Organisten*, beyde *exemplaria* unterschrieben, eines davon Ihme ausgestellet, und das andre ist bey der Kirchen zur Nachricht behalten worden. So geschehen Halle den 14. *Decbr:* 1713.

The Music in Service and Recital

Andreas Ockell
Augustus Becker.

FAMatthesius *Dmpp*
Friedrich Arnold Reichhelm *mpr*
Christoph Semler *L*
Christianus Knaut Dmpp
Lt. JS Möschel *mpp.*
Johann Gotthilff Kost.

(*Dok* II pp50–1)

We, the church fathers (undersigned at the end) and Council of Eight to the Liebfrauen-kirche here, for ourselves and our successors in the church *Collegium*, make it known here-with and acknowledge: that we have appointed and accepted the worthy and well-learned Herr Johann Sebastian Bach to be organist in the Liebfrauenkirche on the strength of this, that he be faithful and attentive in the service of us and our church, devote himself to a virtuous and exemplary life, to the end of his days remain steadfast to the unaltered Augsburg Confession, the *Formula Concordiae* and other explicit confessions of faith, hold himself assiduously to the altar of this church as well as devoutly attending to the word of God, and by these means declare his confession of faith and Christianity to the whole con-gregation. In addition, so far as it concerns his regular duties, it is incumbent upon him (1) on all high holidays and feast-days and others that may occur, and on their vigils, also every Sunday and Saturday afternoon, similarly at the regular Catechism sermons [services with sermon] and public weddings, to play the great organ to the furthering of the service ac-cording to his best efforts and ability, notwithstanding that from time to time as well the little organ and the regals are played, particularly on high feast-days during the *Choral-* and *Figural-Musique*. Likewise he is (2) to present on ordinary occasions (high and other feasts, similarly every third Sunday) a moving and good-sounding piece of devotional music together with the cantor, choral students, town musicians and other players; on extra-ordinary occasions, however (the two last days of the high feasts [of Christmas, Easter and Whit?]), to perform short figural pieces together with the cantor and students), also from time to time with some violins and other instruments. And he is to direct everything in such a way that thereby the corporate congregation shall be the more refreshed and roused to the devotion and love of hearing the word of God. But in particular he must (3) notify in good time the Head Pastor of our Church, Consistorial Councillor Dr Heinecke, for his approval, of the texts and poems chosen for the ensemble music, in which respect he is herewith referred to the Consistorial Councillor. Furthermore, he is (4) to exert himself to play in a devotional manner, slowly and without exceptional decoration, in four and five parts on the Principal [alone] not only the regular chorales [*Allein Gott in der Höh'* etc] but those pre-scribed by the ministers before and after the Sunday and feast-day sermons, also those during Communion, Vespers and vigils; and to change the stops at each verse [lit. 'and with each verse to change the other stops each time'], and also to apply the Quintadena and reeds, the Gedackt as also the syncopations and suspensions, in such a way that the corporate con-gregation may suppose the organ to be the foundation of a good harmoniousness and unanimous sound, and so may sing devoutly in praise and thanks to the Most High. In con-nection with which, (5) to him are entrusted both the great and small organs, as well as the church regals and other instruments specified in an inventory to be set out for him, and he is to be urged to take great care to keep the former in good condition (as to bellows, stops, registers and all that belongs to them), also in good tune and without *dissonanz*; and if any-thing should become fragile or faulty to report it immediately to the superintendent or, if it is of importance, to the church *Collegium*, for repair and the prevention of greater damage. However, the regals (acquired by our church's funds) and other musical instruments should be used only for the service in our church – in no way to be lent to other churches, much less for entertainments, without our agreement. Moreover, should any of them be lost or broken through negligence, the damage is to be repaired by him.

For such pains, he is to be paid yearly from church funds one hundred and forty thaler, similarly twenty-four thaler for lodging, and seven thaler twelve groschen for wood, in addition each time for the composition of the Catechism music one thaler and for [the composition of?] each wedding Mass one thaler.

Against which he promises to take on no secondary appointment during the time of this appointment, but assiduously to provide his services for this church alone, although he remains free to look for incidental income by teaching or other means, as long as that can happen without his defaulting. To make this known we have had this appointment drawn up in duplicate under the great church seal, and have signed with our own hands (together with the organist) both copies, one of which is drawn up for him, the other kept in the church for the record.

This performed at Halle, 14 December 1713.

The 'great organ' was not yet completed: the old organ reported on by Praetorius (1619 pp177-8) was seriously damaged in January 1713, but in any case Contius's new organ, contracted for on 1 October 1712, was being built from Easter 1713 to Easter 1716 (David 1951 p39). Whether the 'little organ' refers to the extant instrument of 1663-4 in the east-end gallery (now called the 'Handel positive') is uncertain; but it is likely, and its high pitch suggests that *Choralmusique* means specifically the chorales played (in *Chorton*) by the *Stadtpfeifer* and organ on high feast-days. Although the directions for stop-changing, evidently expressed by a non-expert, seem to suggest accompaniments while the congregation sings (like the *Variationes* at Mühlhausen), in fact they may be oblique references to inter-verse interludes requiring variety and high professional standards, i.e. played by someone who understood 'syncopations and suspensions'. The stop-names could refer to either the 1558 or the 1713-16 organ,* the terms perhaps picked up from documents – although it is possible that what the church fathers were trying to say was merely that they required discreet accompaniments using 8' stops predominantly or even alone. The stipulation for maintenance of and responsibility for the instruments is a fuller version of that at Mühlhausen and Arnstadt, and it is possible that *Instrumenta* as a term embraced what used to be called 'Instrumenten', i.e. harpsichords.

A further possibility is raised by the Halle contract. Is the *Orgelbüchlein* in any way relevant to it? If it – or at least, the album P 283 – was begun towards the end of 1713 (see Vol. II p7), did the composer write some of the pieces to use during his presence in Halle for the election in December 1713, in response to the outlines in paragraph 4 of contract, or even with a view to satisfying what may be suggestions for discreet registration? Whether the *Orgelbüchlein* pieces were preludes, inter-verse interludes, *alternatim* verse-substitutes or compositional essays in figural harmonization, it is possible to see them as conforming to the pious *Affekt* hinted at in paragraphs 2-4, certainly in comparison with (e.g.) the northern chorale-fantasia. It is also possible (though this is of course speculative) to see the phrase 'to play in a devotional manner, slowly and without exceptional decoration, in four and five parts on the Principal [8' alone]' as peculiarly apt for the opening chorale of the *Orgelbüchlein*, 'Nun komm' BWV 599. But it would also be apt for many, perhaps almost all, of the *Orgelbüchlein* chorales, even suggesting that they were not after all preludes or interludes but actual accompaniments (or intended to be such) for the hymns as sung at Halle, i.e. slowly and expressively. (On tempo in 1715, see p30 above). If the Halle connection should ever be established without doubt, two other features of the *Orgelbüchlein* become easier to understand: the

* Was the Consistory anxious about the size and power expected of the new organ?

high pitch of some of the chorales (e.g. BWV 599 itself), suggesting an organ of lower pitch than Weimar; and the remoteness of key in other chorales (e.g. BWV 622 in E♭, BWV 639 in F minor), suggesting an organ tuned to a more modern temperament than Weimar. The Halle organ would probably have satisfied both of these conditions (see chapter 17, below). Moreover, if Weimar was not the location primarily intended for the *Orgelbüchlein*, it can be the more readily understood why its repertory does not quite tally with the Weimar hymnbooks (see p16 above).*

The terms of the Halle appointment compare fairly closely with those for Johann Krieger's successor in the Johanniskirche, Zittau in 1735, which was likewise the major church of its town (Seiffert 1917 pp. xiv–xvi). That such terms were customarily kept unchanged from organist to organist – and thus had been Krieger's in 1681 – is suggested by references in the Halle accounts: the terms offered to J. S. Bach were compared and approved item by item with those for Zachow in 1684 (*Dok* II p52), and Kirchhoff's eventual successor was offered the same contract (i.e. W. F. Bach in 1746 – *ibid* pp51–2). The Zittau terms can be summarized as follows:

1 To lead a pious life
2 services: Sunday Mattins (Te deum laudamus, small organ), regular Sunday service (ensemble music etc; chorales before and after Communion, during the Mass, before and after sermon in the afternoon services)
   Saturday afternoon Vespers
3 certain high feast-days and their eve Vespers (in the former 'to play the organ for the singing of each chorale' – 'bey Absingung iedweden Liedes das Orgel-Werck zu spielen')
4, 5 certain 'half feasts' and midweek services ('to play for the chorales intoned', i.e. by the cantor rather than full choir as on Sundays? – 'bey denen intonirten Lieder die Orgel zu spielen')
6, 7 to be on good terms with the cantor and co-operate in training singers
8 to maintain good performance with the *Stadtpfeifer* in the Sunday and feast-day music, also Saturday Vespers and weddings
9 to be responsible for the three organs and harpsichord, keeping them in good order (and no one admitted to the organs during service without special permission)†
10 to arrange the exchange of cantatas with the other town church
11 (payment)
12 not to change the church music etc without the Council's knowledge

It is not clear from this whether the chorales were accompanied and what (or at what point) the organist was to play; but the 'intonations' in the smaller midweek services rather suggest that he accompanied, with or without prelude.

* Two further speculations, progressively more conjectural, follow from this hypothesis: that work on the *Orgelbüchlein* slackened because the Halle appointment did not take place (turned down between 14 January and 19 March 1714) rather than because the composer was named *Konzertmeister* at Weimar on 2 March (he remained *Hoforganist*); and that the style of performance and registration for the *Orgelbüchlein* have to be viewed constantly with reference to the Halle terms, i.e. that the best starting-point for the organist today might well be to assume that an 8′ stop or two is all that is required for most of the settings.
† Such a clause, being part of the organist's duties as protector of the organ (cf. Halle contract above), suggests that the well-known complaint against J. S. Bach at Arnstadt (that he admitted a 'strange maiden' to the organ gallery) was aimed not at its involving a young woman but at the admission of any unauthorized (*fremd*) person.

6. Organist-Trials

In the period around 1700, the testing of organists was done with varying degrees of formality and thoroughness. At Arnstadt in 1703, the composer was appointed soon after – and perhaps as a consequence of – his testing of the new organ (*Dok* II pp10–12). At Mühlhausen, he 'played a test at Easter' in 1707, presumably in public ('auff Ostern die probe gespielet': *ibid* p23) though not perhaps in competition with others. J. G. Walther (according to a letter of 6 August 1729 to Bokemeyer) seems to have already rejected the same post because of unsatisfactory terms. At Weimar, the duke would have had him appointed without trial, public or otherwise, though the *Obituary* carefully specifies that the appointment followed on a visit the composer made to Weimar, which gave him the opportunity to be heard by the duke (*Dok* III p82).* At Leipzig, having himself performed a cantor's trial, he presumably served as examiner for organist posts under his authority (St Thomas and St Nikolai later in 1729, Neukirche May 1729); at least, he recommended the successful candidate at the Neukirche (*Dok* II p192) and had two pupils amongst the nine applicants for St Nicolai, one of whom was successful (J. Schneider, 1702-88: see Schering 1941 pp60–5). From indirect evidence he seems to have attended the trial of J. G. B. Bach at Mühlhausen in 1735, perhaps giving a theme for improvisation as he did at the Leipzig Nikolaikirche trial in 1729 (*Dok* II pp281–2, *Dok* I pp81–2; *Dok* II pp344, 365).

One of the remarks made by J. A. Scheibe, unsuccessful competitor at Leipzig in 1729, refers to a fugue as being part of the test, i.e. a fugue improvised on a theme given for that occasion (*Dok* II p344). In what sense such trials were public is not always clear. J. G. Walther, as applicant in 1707 at the less important church of Mühlhausen, later remarked on its public nature ('öffentlich-abzulegende': Mattheson 1740 p389), noting also that at the Weimar Town Church a few months later the choice among the nine (or ten) candidates was made 'privat und öffentliche' ('privately and publicly'?). Georg Böhm's phrase, when offering himself in August 1698 for public trial as prospective organist of the Johanniskirche, Lüneburg was 'ad publica specimina praestanda' ('for the presenting of samples in public' – B & H edn 6634, p. x). Mattheson himself reports on grand trials with evident enthusiasm, but the implication is that such events were a Hamburg speciality, like regular recitals on big Schnitger organs. A 'very numerous gathering' ('eine gantze zahlreiche Gemeine') heard what seems to have been the 1720 trial in which J. S. Bach may have taken part (*Dok* II pp 186–7). In 1654 at the Jakobikirche, Weckmann had been one of four candidates examined by five judges and required to play *extempore* the following (Mattheson 1740 p397):

---

* Mainwaring (1760 pp9–13) reports the Duke of Sachsen-Weissenfels hearing the young Handel play in the chapel at Weissenfels 'after the service was over', enquiring who it was, encouraging him and filling 'his pockets with money'. (The case and other parts of this organ are still extant.)

(1) a movement [fugue?] on a given theme, 'ein verkehrtes Thema primi et tertii Toni zusammen' ('a reversed theme in first and second tones together' – i.e. a double subject invertible and in contrary motion, in both tonic and dominant?)*

(2) motet accompaniment: basso continuo on two manuals

(3) basso continuo for a violin sonata

(4) settings of 'An Wasserflüssen Babylon', firstly in the 'serious manner' of J. Praetorius ('ernsthafft'), secondly as a fugue in any key (? – 'alle Töne und halbe Töne') and with many kinds of variation ('vielerley Veränderungen')

Obviously one of the conditions that often made the big German praeludia so spectacular is that the more prominent organists were virtuosos. Yet, though more modestly expressed, Werckmeister's suggestions for testing organists (quoted by Mattheson 1731 p27) also required a decided proficiency (1698 p77):

> ist bey dem *Examine* eines Organisten hoch von nöthen, dass man denselben ein *Thema* vorgebe welches er auf unterschiedliche Arth ausführe, oder man kann auch einige Lieder erwehlen, und dieselben auf gewisse Arth *variiren*, und *transponiren* lassen wobey auch in des General-Basses *Examine* muss *observi*ret werden, ob auch die *Signaturen* fein *accurat* getroffen werden.

> At the examination of an organist it is very necessary to give him a theme which he is to execute in various ways; or one can also choose some hymns and have them varied in certain ways, and transposed; here too in examining figured bass it must be observed whether the figures are dealt with very accurately.

Half a century later in Werckmeister's Quedlinburg (in 1755 – see Werner 1933 p133) the candidates at the Stiftskirche were examined in *Präludiren* (improvising), *Choralspiel* (chorale-preludes, interludes and harmonizations?), *Akkompagnement* (figured bass?) and composition (original compositions or an understanding of harmony etc?).† The 1731 trial in the Town Church at Merseburg may also indicate customs in the Weimar–Leipzig area: it took place before the magistrate, clergy and public and consisted of the following (Werner 1933 p133):

> sowohl in dem ihm vorgeschriebenen Chorale als vorgelegter Fuga wie auch in *Transpositionae*, eines ihm vorgelegten Generalbasses, ja in *Variationii*, *ligaturen* und *Syncopationibii*

> as well in the chorale prescribed for him as in the fugue on a theme presented to him, so too in transposition of a figured bass presented to him, and also in variations, suspensions and syncopations‡

---

* Perhaps this means no more than that the improvisation was based on a double subject of the kind now known from Scheidemann's G minor Praeambulum: Ex. 4.

Ex. 4

---

† It seems the unsuccessful candidate offered a good deal of money, though it is not clear whether this was as traditional as seems to have been the case in some Hanseatic cities (cf. *Dok* II p79) – hence perhaps Mattheson's story of a successful candidate 'preluding better with thalers than with his fingers', at the Hamburg Jakobikirche in 1720 (*Dok* II p187). If the post of organist was considered a guild-partnership with the church concerned – a 'master' buying a 'partnership' – then the idea of an applicant's paying for his appointment was not as improper as it is now usually taken to have been.

In the case of the big Hanseatic cities, the high price exacted by the civic authorities for appointments to the church reflects the high social status of the successful applicant (see Edler 1982 pp105–7).

‡ The last phrase, read alongside documents associated with J. S. Bach at Arnstadt and Halle, suggests that parish scribes had a conventional vocabulary for organ affairs.

The candidates were presumably to show in this way that they knew how to deal with chorales in the service, harmonize in good part-writing, etc.

No doubt the fugue themes varied in potential. Indeed, Weckmann's theme, though described in complex language, was very likely far more classical and therefore feasible than the song-like subject given the remaining candidates at the Jakobikirche, Hamburg after J. S. Bach withdrew in 1720 (theme according to Terry 1933 p133: Ex. 5). It could well be that as the century progressed, organists

Ex. 5

and their examiners tended more towards non-classical themes for improvisation, just as in other countries or in other contexts composers of the later eighteenth century adopted *stile antico* themes. Such a subject as Ex. 6, given the candidates at Bitterfeld in 1769 (Werner 1933 p133), requiring a fugal improvisation on full organ, was a wretched reversal of the coin of classicism circulating in the Mass settings of more southerly composers at that period. One of the implications behind

Ex. 6

Mattheson's demonstration of strettos and invertible countersubjects for the C major theme given to the candidates at Hamburg Cathedral in 1727 (see below) must be that such classical themes had a particular style and contrapuntal potential, as indeed they have. Whether or not Mattheson thought so himself, the nature of the theme presumably had a bearing on the way a candidate acquitted himself. Schiebe told of one candidate at the 1729 Leipzig trial preferring to play his own theme (*Dok* II p365), Mattheson of a candidate on another occasion getting hold of the theme beforehand (1731 pp32-3).

The situation was more straightforward with the chorale treatments, whether based on Latin hymns or German. According to Terry, all three were required at Hamburg: improvised fugue, accompaniment for *Helft mir Gott's Güte preisen*, and treatment of *O lux beata trinitas*. The significance of using two kinds of hymn in Hamburg might have been that the Latin required a purer, contrapuntal interlude-like style, the German a more melismatic chorale-prelude.

The two Hamburg trials reported on by Mattheson in 1731 were very likely the *ne plus ultra* of their kind and gave the examiner Mattheson scope for his particular kind of garrulity (1731 pp34-8). The first, on 14 October 1725 in the Cathedral, was as follows:

> all candidates to be shown the list of requirements, which is then placed on the music-desk of the organ.
> (1) short, free prelude, beginning in A major and ending in G minor.
> (2) the chorale *Herr Jesu Christ, du höchstes Gut* for six minutes, in particular on two manuals with independent pedal (strict three parts, no doubling of the pedal).
> (3) a well-developed fugue based on Ex. 7, introducing a countersubject (*x*). This can be up to four minutes long, but a good – not a long – fugue is wanted.

Ex. 7

(x)

(4) candidates are required to furnish evidence of skill in composition by presenting a worked-out version of this fugue within two days.

(5) accompanying with figured bass a short sung aria (one of three from a Passion by Mattheson); about four minutes.

(6) a chaconne on Ex. 8, using full organ; about six minutes.

Throughout, to play in a devotional, expressive style.

Ex. 8

The unprepossessing nature of the chaconne theme may well reflect the rather simplistic approach to ostinatos in the Hamburg repertory – cf. the one on 'Lobt Gott ihr Christen' which ends Vincent Lübeck's *Clavierübung* (Hamburg 1728). Mattheson gives the impression of recommending the winner on the grounds that he gave the correct fugal answer (1731 p36). Two years later, on 8 October 1727, another trial had to be held, in which the learned Mattheson seems by then to have required more of the candidates:

(1) a free prelude on a moderate registration for the *Rückpositiv* ('auf einem massigen Stimm-Werk'), from B minor to G major.

(2) a fugue on full organ, with independent inner parts [based on a subject close to that of the second movement of J. S. Bach's C major Violin Sonata BWV 1005]. The subject contains the first eight notes of the following chorale melody (no. 3 below); nothing complex is required of the answer; a chromatic countersubject is possible (and so a double fugue can be made of it); the main subject can be inverted in two ways; *rectus* and *contrarius* can be incorporated; strettos are possible.

(3) variations on a chorale melody (related to fugue subject); requirements as before; duration (together with no. 2) eleven to twelve minutes.

(4) aria as before (including stipulation for Pedal Untersatz 16′, manual Gedackt when suitable).

(5) from the aria subject, a full organ chaconne or Fantasie to be derived, 'such as could serve for the exit-piece' ('gleichsam zum Ausgange, dienen könne'), ten to twelve minutes long at the most.

On pp38–40 Mattheson takes the opportunity to show what can be done with the fugue theme, including treatments not all found in J. S. Bach's fugue on the subject in BWV 1005, the fair copy of which (P 967) is dated 1720. But the chromatic countersubject is close to that of BWV 1005: Ex. 9. Mattheson's use of Bach themes for both of his trials (neither with full acknowledgment – see Vol. I pp97, 119) at least suggests that the composer himself may have used them for such purposes.*

* Just as the anecdote told by J. C. Kittel – that he confounded the other competitor at the trial for the Erfurt Predigerkirche post in 1756 (on the death of Adlung) by playing the given fugue subject upside down and insisting that the other do the same – shows that improvised fugues were the conventional way, at least by then, of demonstrating mastery in music (Bal 1981 p51).

Ex. 9   Mattheson

BWV 1005.ii

7. Recitals

The various traditions of organ-playing outside the service produced a concert life of some importance in certain towns, though not those in which J. S. Bach lived. In any such concerts improvisation played a large part, and it could well have been the accounts of such things often published in Hamburg, Paris, London etc that prompted the *Obituary* and Forkel in particular to describe J. S. Bach's activities in this field, especially in the famous cities of Hamburg, Dresden and Berlin.

Regular organ concerts remained unknown outside a few contexts. Sweelinck's 'additional hour at dusk' and music 'before and after the sermon' (Curtis 1969 p7) may imply recital music for the one and service music for the other, but in any case a few Dutch churches had a tradition, going back before the Reformation, for recitals of a kind that can have little bearing on the Leipzig of 1725. The relevance of Amsterdam or Rotterdam or Haarlem lies rather in the fact that at least some of the major German Hanseatic towns as far east as Königsberg had traditions before *c*1750 of organ concerts, seasonal, weekly or even daily, with or without other music, and these may originally have followed old Dutch fashions, particularly in Lübeck and Hamburg. In Lübeck, Buxtehude's position was described in a publication of 1752 (quoted by Frotscher 1934–5 II pp437–8):

> Es soll nemlich in alten Zeiten die Bürgerschaft, ehe sie zur Börse gegangen, den löblichen Gebrauch gehabt haben, sich in der St Marien Kirche zu versammeln, da denn der Organist zu einigen Zeiten ihnen zum Vergnügen, und zur Zeit-Kürzung, etwas auf der Orgel vorgespielet hat.

> That is, it seems that in former times the citizenry had the laudable custom, before they went to the Exchange, of gathering in the Marienkirche, as then the organist played something on the organ at certain times [seasons?], for their delight and to pass the time.

Whether such traditions had been 'transmitted to North Germany by Dutch merchants' (Stauffer 1980 p148) is not yet clear, nor whether other similar cities (Königsberg, Danzig, Stralsund, Rostock) encouraged or discouraged them. Certainly nearer Holland, the strict reformist attitudes to services made organ-playing more likely outside the service than within it. For example, at Bremen in 1594

> Des Orgels ist unter dem Gesang neen Gebruck, ock by den Gadesdenst nicht, ahne allein des Sondages vor negen Uhren, wenn sich dar Volck samlet, und darnha wan Idt thor Kerken wedder uthgaeth (Blankenburg 1965 p374).

> Of the organ no use is made during the singing, and not in the service, except only on Sundays before 9am when the people are assembling and afterwards when they leave the church again.

This may well speak for general custom and, moreover, suggests that (short) recitals after the service may have been known before the closing organ postlude was. When one visitor to the Easter Fair at Leipzig in 1729 heard J. S. Bach play (*Dok* II pp196-7), it can only be guessed whether he was attempting in the Thomaskirche something comparable to the Lübeck Exchange recitals, which presumably he had himself witnessed. Since the report is unclear and not backed by newspaper notices, the former may be more likely. But an eyewitness report that J. S. Bach was not at all commonly heard outside his own house (published in 1759: *Dok* III p148) refers to his last few years only and cannot be taken as evidence that he did not play in the Thomaskirche, however likely that may be on other grounds.

A clearer and more widespread tradition was for organ music to play an important part in Vespers, particularly on Saturday afternoons. It is not always clear whether music for organ or for instruments and voices was being referred to in any given source, however. Thus Mattheson speaks of Matthias Weckmann as having the luck to hear Scheidemann in the Katharinenkirche, Hamburg (1740 p395) but it is not certain that this refers to solo organ-playing, although it is often taken to be so (e.g. Apel 1967 p581). Similarly, J. S. Bach's well-known visit to Lübeck was said by the *Obituary* to be in order 'to hear the famous organist Buxtehude' (*Dok* III p82), but it does not follow that this meant organ music during Vespers. Tunder's term for the Lübeck church concerts or *Abendmusiken* was *Abendspielen* (Stahl 1937 p6), which certainly must include instrumental and vocal music. According to Terry (1933 pp68-9), in the years around 1700 five such performances were usual, at the close of Vespers (about 4am) on the last two Sundays of Trinity and the second, third and fourth Sundays of Advent. The outline for that on Trinity 25 was:

> Sonata ariosa
> Hallelujah ('cum tubis et timpanis')
> Pss. 96 and 98
> four verses of *Allein Gott*

Presumably the first was instrumental, the second a cantata (with strings as well as brass), the third a further ensemble piece (voices and instruments), the fourth congregational; it can only be guessed what or where the organ played – perhaps interludes, postlude etc. The *Obituary* refers specifically to organ music at Vespers in recounting the occasion when J. S. Bach was in Hamburg in 1720, presumably to apply for (or to make known his availability for) the post at the Jakobikirche.* Reincken heard him play with evident delight and approval:

> und machte ihm, absonderlich über den Choral: An Wasserflüssen Babylon, welchen unser Bach, auf Verlangen der Anwesenden, aus dem Stegreife, sehr weitläuftig, fast eine halbe Stunde lang, auf verschiedene Art, so wie es ehedem die braven unter den Hamburgischen Organisten in den Sonnabends Vespern gewohnt gewesen waren, ausführete, folgendes Compliment: ich dachte, diese Kunst wäre gestorben, ich sehe aber, dass sie in Ihnen noch lebet (*Dok* III p84).

---

* Though the *Obituary* does not itself relate the concert to any such application.

and made him, particularly for the chorale 'An Wasserflüssen Babylon' (which our Bach, at the request of those present, played for almost half an hour, very fully, *extempore*, and in a variety of ways, just as formerly the better amongst the Hamburg organists were used to doing at the Saturday Vespers), the following compliment: 'I thought that this art had died, but I see it still lives in you.'

The concrete facts of this anecdote seem to be that he played the 'Babylon' melody for almost thirty minutes (apparently he was acquainted with a setting by Reincken of the same kind – *Dok* III p84),* in various ways (a set of variations or a particularly extensive chorale-fantasia?), as the better organists used to do (i.e. in several Hamburg churches?) at Saturday Vespers – but all in such a way as was by then no longer heard. The last remark could be merely mirroring regret for times past, like Mattheson's comment (perhaps equally relevant to Hamburg) on the superiority of older composers' fantasias (1739 p89). Or could it reflect the fact that organists were turning from chorale-variations or chorale-fantasias to other genres with which Reincken was out of sympathy – hence the special request for this treatment of this particular chorale?† In any case, the weaving of a long composition from one and the same theme seems to be the underlying principle of J. S. Bach's improvisations as reported by Forkel (see below) and also of Mattheson's descriptions of how to vary chorales and produce suite-like pieces from them (see chapter 8, below).

In Stralsund in 1710, Christoph Raupach began his *musikalische allusiones* (Mattheson 1740 pp587–8): the playing of 'preludes and ingenious variations' on chorales after the service on Sunday afternoons ('Präludiren . . . künstliche Variation . . . zum Ausgange'). For this, he distributed the texts amongst the listeners so that they could follow his musical mood-changing. Such mood-changing perhaps represents a coarsening of the Hanseatic chorale repertory and was characteristic of new interests in expressive music: a later manifestation of techniques used in (e.g.) Weckmann's chorales. Raupach's programmes involved particular musical techniques that Mattheson described elsewhere (see chapter 8 below) and which Mizler reprinted in Leipzig (1752 pp526–9). Such recitals as Raupach's presumably remained exceptional, at least in such a thoroughgoing form as the following suggests:

> *Trinity* 8, 1710
> Organ *Sonate*
> Temptation (*Anfechtung*): verse from 'Es ist das Heil' [see BWV 638]
> Complaint (*Klage*): with 'Ach Gott, vom Himmel sieh' darein' [see BWV 741]
> Joyful solace (*freudige Trost*): with a verse of hope from 'Es ist das Heil'

Other organists too drew audiences. According to J. G. Walther's *Lexicon* (1732 p583) Delphin Strunk, organist at Brunswick, played so well that the duke often

---

* The melody seems to have been a Hamburg favourite: the survival of Reincken's long fantasia on the theme may be an accident, but Weckmann is said also to have had to play the chorale in his trial at the Jakobikirche in 1654 (Mattheson 1740 p397) 'in a serious manner and fugally through [= in?] all diatonic and chromatic keys' ('ernsthaffte Art und fugenweise durch alle Töne und halben Töne'). Elsewhere Reincken is said to have shown his fitness to follow in the footsteps of Scheidemann at the Katharinenkirche, Hamburg by sending a copy of his setting (another setting?) to the Amsterdam musician who had questioned that fitness (Walther 1732 pp547–8).

† Or perhaps the *Obituary* authors knew the story told by Walther (1732 pp547–8) that a great musician in Amsterdam who had doubted Reincken's worthiness to follow Scheidemann 'kissed his hands out of veneration' after he had heard him play. They too needed to show that their subject was venerated by the great of the past.

came over from Wolfenbüttel 'to hear the playing at Saturday Vespers'. Perhaps such a habit was brought from Germany to London by Handel who, according to Hawkins (1853 edn II p852), 'in the afternoon was used to frequent St. Paul's church for the sake of hearing the service, and of playing on the organ after it was over'.

Pachelbel or his successor J. H. Buttstedt followed one particular convention in Erfurt (Seiffert *DTB* IV.i (1903) p. xiv, and Ziller 1935 pp16–18); their conditions of employment included the following clause:

> alljährlich und jedes Jahr besonders uf dem Festtage S. Johannis Baptistae nach geendigten Gottensdienste des nachmittags zum Andenken dieser seiner Reception und annehmung zum Organisten das gantze Orgelwerck . . . eine halbe stundenlang durchzuspielenen, und also für der gesambten Christlichen Gemeinde gleichsam eine neue Probe zu tun, wie Er sich das Jahr über in seinem Ambte gebessert habe.

> each year, and in particular on every feast-day of St John the Baptist, after the afternoon service is ended, in commemoration of his reception and appointment as organist, to play the whole organ for half an hour, and thus to give a new proof (as it were) to the whole Christian community how during the year he has improved in [the skills of] his office.

While many might find this custom laudable and worthy of imitation, two objective facts which it supplies about its own time and place should not be missed: it makes clear that Thuringia was not without organ recitals and that the organist's office included the ability to play well as a soloist.

Irregular organ concerts were no doubt more common: one example is J. S. Bach's in Hamburg. Both in its length and in the official nature of its audience (see below), the occasion seems to have been characteristic of special events. The eighteenth-century reference books tell of several such occasions, anecdotes (as in the *Obituary*) whose very interest must have lain in the fact that they were exceptional in some way. One can only guess what it was about J. C. Kerll's playing at a royal betrothal in Vienna in 1676 that led to the astonishment of all present (Sandberger *DTB* II.ii (1901) p. xxviii), but Mattheson gave some details of this or a similar occasion (1740 p136). The Emperor Leopold sent Kerll a theme which he forbore to look at before the recital; then he 'fantaisierte' (improvised) and

> machte herrliche Sachen aus seinem eigenen Kopfe; fing so dann das Thema erst mit zwo Stimmen zu tractiren an: welches den Anwesenden wunderlich vorkam. Allein bald daruf folgte ein Adagio, und hiernach die Durchführung mit dreien; nachgehends mit vier; zuletzt aber, durch Hülffe des Pedals, nicht nur mit fünf Stimmen, sondern noch mit dem Zusatze eines Gegenthematis, einer Abwechselung aus dem geraden in den ungeraden Tact, samt allen zur Doppelfuge gehörigen Kunst-Stücken . . .

> made splendid things out of his own head; then began to play the theme with [=in? against?] two parts, which struck those present as something out of the ordinary. Immediately thereafter followed an Adagio, after which the theme was worked with three parts; then four; but finally, with the help of the pedal, not only with five parts but further with the addition of a counter-theme, a change from measured into unmeasured time, together with all the artistic devices belonging to double fugue . . .

A free prelude, then, seems to have been followed by a *bicinium*, an *adagio*, a trio, a quartet, a five-part setting with pedal, a free interlude and a double fugue. That the exact order of events could be interpreted differently does not disguise the over-all picture of such concert pieces, something like the account of J. S. Bach given by Forkel (1802 ch.IV):

> Wenn Joh. Seb. Bach ausser den gottesdienstlichen Versammlungen sich an die Orgel setzte, wozu er sehr oft durch Fremde aufgefordert wurde, so wählte er sich irgend ein Thema, und führte es in allen Formen von Orgelstücken so aus, dass es stets sein Stoff blieb, wenn er auch zwey oder mehrere Stunden ununterbrochen gespielt hätte. Zuerst gebrauchte er dieses Thema zu einem Vorspiel und einer Fuge mit vollem Werk. Sodann erschien seine Kunst des Registrirens für ein Trio, ein Quatuor etc. immer über dasselbe Thema. Ferner folgte ein Choral, um dessen Melodie wiederum das erste Thema in 3 oder 4 verschiedenen Stimmen auf die mannigfaltigste Art herum spielte. Endlich wurde der Beschluss mit dem vollen Werke durch eine Fuge gemacht, worin entweder nur eine andere Bearbeitung des erstern Thema herrschte, oder noch eines oder auch nach Beschaffenheit desselben zwey andere beygemischt wurden. Diess ist eigentlich diejenige Orgelkunst, welche der alte Reinken in Hamburg schon zu seiner Zeit für ver-loren hielt . . .

> When J. S. Bach seated himself at the organ outside services, as he was often asked to do by strangers, he chose some theme or other and worked it in all the forms used for organ music, in such a way that it always remained his material, even if he played un-interruptedly for two hours or more. First he made use of the theme in a prelude and fugue, with full organ; then there appeared his art of registration for [in the form of] a trio, quartet etc, still on the same theme; then a chorale followed, around whose melody the first theme again played variously in three or four parts in the most diverse way. Finally the conclusion on full organ was made with a fugue, in which either another working of the first theme predominated, or yet another or even two others (depending on its nature) were mixed together. Such in fact was that art of organ-playing which the aged Reincken in Hamburg had thought already lost by his time . . .

Forkel is clearly speaking of an occasional recital outside (after?) the service, and a comparison with the layout of *Clavierübung III* (prelude, two- to six-part pieces, double fugue) is certainly instructive and suggestive; there does appear to be much in common between the two (Stauffer 1980 pp150–1). But it is also clear from Mat-theson's report of Kerll that such layouts – the only record of the great players of the past then available – had long been in print. Forkel knew the reports of J. S. Bach's recitals, playing skills, improvisations and contrapuntal abilities from the *Obituary* (Hamburg chorale-variations, Berlin fugues) and from letters of C. P. E. Bach (*extempore* counterpoint, the art of registration). He also knew Mattheson's reports and the general tenor of books concerned with composers recently de-ceased. His account of J. S. Bach's playing, still much quoted, could be little more than a conglomerate of these sources. The reference to Reincken no doubt bears on the *Obituary* anecdote; do such phrases as 'three or four different parts' allude to organists' examinations as described by Mattheson? Is the note about demonstra-ting 'his art of registration' an inserted gloss, drawing on what he learnt from the *Obituary* and from C. P. E. Bach? Is the reference to *Trio* and *Quatuor* even a kind of gathering-together of organ terms (in this case French) learnt from more distant sources such as Adlung and even Bedos? How does a *Choral* fit the plan – was it supposed to be derived from the original (free) subject, or is it a detail taken from Mattheson's account of examinations?

The 'two hours or more' is a less puzzling detail: the *Obituary* reports on the recital in Hamburg which took up 'mehr als 2 Stunden', and the recital in the

Frauenkirche, Dresden on 1 December 1736 was reported as lasting from 2 to 4pm (was this during Saturday Vespers? – see below). Forkel, who presumably knew only the first of these, may well have found two hours exceptional. 'Above one hour long' ('über eine Stunde lang': *Dok* II p150) was noted in the newspaper report of the recital in the Sophienkirche, Dresden in 1725. Forkel's term *Fremde* for those persuading J. S. Bach to play may at first look like a reference to visitors to St Thomas, Leipzig, but the six performances now known about took place elsewhere, in front of important people (hence the reports?):

> November (?) 1720, Hamburg Katharinenkirche
> According to the *Obituary* (*Dok* III p84) this took place in the Katharinenkirche before the magistrate and other prominent people including the organist (Reincken)

> 19 and 20 September (Thursday, Friday) 1725, Dresden Sophienkirche
> Two concerts on the Silbermann organ before the court and town musicians, consisting of organ music and 'various concertos mixed in with sweet instrumental music in all keys' ('Praeludiis und diversen Concerten mit unterlauffender Doucen Instrumental-Music in allen Tonis': *Dok* II p150)

> 14 September (Friday) 1731, Dresden Sophienkirche
> Concert at 3pm on the Silbermann organ before all the court and town musicians ('Hof-Musicorum und Virtuosen'); report of 21 September 1731 speaks of his playing 'various times . . . in the Sophienkirche and also at the court' ('zu unterschiedlichen mahlen . . . in hiesiger Sophien Kirche, auch sonsten bey Hofe': *Dok* II pp213–14)

> 1 December (Saturday) 1736, Dresden Frauenkirche
> Concert from 2 until 4pm on the new Silbermann organ (inaugurated on the previous Sunday) before Russian ambassador Keyserlingk and 'many persons of rank, and a numerous attendance of other persons and artists' ('vieler Procerum auch starcker Frequentz anderer Personen und Künstler': *Dok* II p279)

> 8 May (Monday) 1747, Potsdam Heiligegeistkirche
> Concert on the Wagner organ before a 'crowd of listeners present' ('ein Menge vorhandenen Zuhörern': *Dok* II p435)

Was the Hamburg concert a kind of *Probe* in lieu of the auditions for which Bach did not stay, being obliged to return to Köthen (*Dok* II p78)?* It seems that he was selected but declined before the formal vote, the selection no doubt having been approved by Reincken, who was one of the examiners.†

The Dresden recitals too were at least partly connected with other personal events, insofar as the 1725 Sophienkirche concerts took place a few days after the composer's first submission to the Elector concerning a dispute with the Leipzig authorities. Perhaps the second occasion in 1731 had a similar background, though in the event it may in some way have prepared the ground for W. F. Bach's appointment as Sophienkirche organist in June 1733, a position evidently approved of by his father (see *Dok* I pp71–3). In turn, the 1736 recital followed hard on the announcement of the composer's appointment as 'Electoral Saxon court composer'

---

* Bach had to journey back 'to his prince' on Saturday 23 November, having 'presented himself' on the 21st ('sich angegeben'). Perhaps he played the Saturday Vespers in the Katharinenkirche before leaving for Köthen?

† See David/Mendel p80 (not in *Dok* II). 'Sich angegeben' seems more specific than 'entered their names', and 'vote' more specific than 'choice' as translated in David/Mendel.

(19 November 1736), the appointment and the recital being linked in the journal account (*Dok* II p279). Perhaps the recital included the *Missa* (Kyrie and Gloria) settings of *Clavierübung III*, which may well have been composed by 1736; if so, the group of organ chorales would have been analogous to the *Missa* sections of the B minor Mass, also assembled by the composer in connection with his royal appointment in Dresden.* Either way, the recital demonstrated the composer's 'great ability to please on the *Clavier* and [his] special skill in composition' ('wegen seiner grossen Annehmlichkeit aufm Clavier, und besonderer Geschicklichkeit in Componiren').†

Both in 1725 and in 1731 there seems to have been more than one concert, perhaps in 1731 including chamber music in the nearby palace. Both accounts are vague, but in the first report 'Praeludiis' probably means organ improvisation, 'Concerten' ensemble pieces for voices‡ and instruments, and 'doucen Instrumental Music' chamber music not connected with the 'Praeludiis' or 'Concerten', while 'in allen Tonis' is perhaps a phrase picked up from descriptions – possibly from published poetic descriptions – of Silbermann's tuning, and is not to be taken literally. Thus the whole phrase may mean 'organ works interspersed with stylish instrumental and vocal music, in various unusual keys' or even (in paraphrase) 'organ music in one recital, instrumental and vocal music in the other, showing the versatility of the organ-tuning and the player's technique'.

In 1739 Birnbaum, perhaps on information from the composer, reported on J. S. Bach's being invited to Dresden some years previously at the invitation of 'some persons of rank' at court ('einiger Grossen': *Dok* II p348) to compete there with Louis Marchand 'on the keyboard' ('auf dem Clavier'). The Court Composer was to have been judge, but Marchand failed to turn up. The *Obituary* filled in certain details: in the year 1717, the *Concertmeister* J. B. Volumier invited Bach from Weimar to Dresden, whereupon Bach in turn wrote to Marchand offering to improvise on whatever he put before him and begging to be allowed to do the same; the meeting was to take place before a great company of high-ranking persons in the house of a distinguished minister (*Dok* III p83). This suggests the harpsichord – had Dresden no organ in fine condition until Silbermann completed the new instrument for the Sophienkirche in 1718?# But Marchand's reputation in France was certainly as an organist. According to a report of 1752 (Pirro 1901) he was a player who had no need to drum up audiences and who liked better playing to two or three *connaisseurs* than playing to the crowds who gathered to hear him on feast-days.

---

* It is certainly possible that *Clavierübung III* served both as a kind of recital programme (see above, p51) and as a kind of organ equivalent to the B minor Mass; but it also followed the make-up of hymn-books as they were developing in such orthodox centres as Leipzig. Thus, all the chorales used in *Clavierübung III* are to be found in C. G. Hofmann's *Das privilegirte vollständige und vermehrte Leipziger Gesang-Buch* of 1750, the first group (Kyrie, Gloria) as hymns for each Sunday, the second as six Catechism hymns (this group extended by Hofmann to include Litany and Absolution).

† Probably the journal did not mean specifically to indicate that the works were the player's own compositions, however likely that may be. *Annehmlichkeit* in keyboard-playing was a quality for which in 1738 Scheibe praised Handel to the disadvantage of J. S. Bach, while Birnbaum defended the Leipziger on the grounds that his *Geschicklichkeit* did not prevent his being able to move the listeners (*Dok* II pp314, 347).

‡ On the use of *Concerto* to mean 'cantata', see Vol. I pp60–1.

For example, the torn bellows of the organ in the Kreuzkirche at that period (Dähnert 1980 p78) must have meant it could not play fully.

Public inauguration of new organs is not always mentioned in the church accounts that deal with the testing and handing-over of instruments, and it cannot be assumed, as it often is, that even a large organ would always be celebrated with a recital. Silbermann's organ in Freiberg Cathedral was approved on 17 March 1714, and three days later there followed the dedication in the regular Sunday service, with special sermon and *Musik* (cantata? music with the *Stadtpfeifer*?) but no known solo organ music (Flade 1926 p55). Poems and *carmina* for new Silbermann organs were not infrequent, but the dedication services nevertheless centred on the sermon and on the mixed vocal–instrumental music, even with such fine large instruments as Zittau Johanniskirche in 1741 (*ibid* pp93–4). Similarly, the small organ of Störmthal was certainly dedicated on 2 November 1723 in a service that included Cantata 194, as is known from the autograph heading 'Concerto bey Einweihung der Orgel in Störmthal' (P 43); but whether the organ played anything more than it would have done in any village service does not appear from the accounts (*Dok* II pp127–8). Nor does it at Arnstadt in 1703, where the phrase 'zum ersten mahl schlagen' ('to play for the first time': *Dok* II p100) could indicate the usual service music of chorales and perhaps *Musik*, as could 'durch . . . Music eingeweyhet' at Halle in 1716 ('dedicated with concerted music': *Dok* II p465), or simply 'eingeweihet' at Taubach in 1710 and at Gera in 1724 (*Dok* II pp42, 143).

If such occasions were Sundays (as at both Taubach and Gera), there may have been less likelihood of a recital as such. But that organs – at least those of some importance – were frequently dedicated with one or more major pieces of music, played during or after a service, is clear from the late copy of the Toccata BWV 538 and its reference to Kassel (see Vol. I p89). The dedication of the rebuilt organ in the Martinikirche, Kassel on Sunday 21 November 1732 was described in the newspaper as 'mit einer Musicalischen harmonie inauguriret' (*Dok* II p227), which only suggests a cantata; nor is Rector Bellermann's report on Bach's pedal-playing in Kassel necessarily a reference to any 'recital' (see below, p241). But the reference in the BWV 538 copy seems conclusive, unless by then a pupil of a pupil would assume that the *Probe* (his word) was public and that the visiting examiner would indeed play a major work.

The Music and Its Composition

8. The Arts of Composing or Improvising Organ Chorales

That J. S. Bach's settings of simple melodies for organ show more traditional characteristics than those in cantatas is perhaps less a matter of chronology than of genre: the cantata was more individualistic, 'original', its very presence less a generality. Whatever their contrapuntal ingenuity, organ chorales tend to be less complex than the big cantata movements, and their having no words can be supposed to act as some kind of restricting influence on the composer. In addition, the sheer number of chorales composed and the increasing number of suggestions for their composition made in theory books would make it easier to categorize organ settings than cantata settings. In both, bright figural music produces cheerful *Affekte* whilst slow melismatic settings suit sad chorale melodies* *con affetto*, but organ music by nature has a smaller vocabulary than vocal and needs to make its point more single-mindedly. Thus the reason 'O Mensch bewein' is so much more melismatic in its organ setting than in the *St John Passion* may be that choir and orchestra together have a wider potential for what is affecting: an organ version would need to be very definite in its mood (particularly since the melody has other uses as a 'bright' Whit hymn), and melismas are one way to express it.

Despite careful work by several authors, in particular Luedtke and Dietrich, it will never become quite clear how far J. S. Bach was indebted to his various predecessors and contemporaries for two particular strands in the tapestry of his organ chorales: the expressive quality (from 'objectivity' through 'expressiveness' to 'symbolism') and certain formal shapes (the trio chorale or the ritornello-fantasia). Reasons for this difficulty lie in the uncertain chronology and in the incomplete nature of extant sources, in both cases for J. S. Bach and other composers alike. Uncertain chronology makes it doubtful, for example, whether the chorale-partitas do 'go back' in some way to Georg Böhm, as is often claimed, since Böhm lived until 1733 and the sources have not been dated precisely. A similar point may be made about other early works, such as 'Wie schön leuchtet' BWV 739 vis-à-vis Buxtehude. Incomplete sources make it doubtful even whether Böhm must be considered in relation to the chorale-partitas, in view of the activity in this field of Johann Sebastian's first father-in-law J. M. Bach, who (according to Gerber's *Lexicon*) had acquired sets with six, eight and ten variations. How many sets of chorale-variations for organ or harpsichord circulated in *c*1700 will never be known, but this very uncertainty makes it doubtful whether J. S. Bach need have been 'influenced by Böhm' or J. M. Bach or anyone else in particular.

Tracing what are called influences has been a custom in musical studies for over a century now, but in a highly active area of composition it becomes simple guesswork. For example, do the chorale-fughettas of Krieger have any bearing on J. S. Bach? Or, more generally, did the tendency towards motivic composition in Zachow,

---

* As in (e.g.) Kauffmann's *Harmonische Seelenlust* (Leipzig 1733) and the *Orgelbüchlein* (BWV 614, 622, 641).

55

or the decorative melodies of Buxtehude and Böhm, directly affect the way J. S. Bach developed? Certain details can sometimes be traced: the chorale-canons of Armsdorff may relate to Walther's later canons and hence to those of the *Orgelbüchlein*. Similarly, the gradual disappearance of the longer chorale-fantasia* no doubt bears on the fact that J. S. Bach abandoned the sectional fantasia and produced integrated ritornello settings for those long chorales which he (alone?) labelled *fantasia*. But how does it 'bear on' this? Was there ever a strong tradition of long sectional chorale-fantasias in Thuringia? Even if there was, is one to understand BWV 651a as an attempt to organize the old chorale-fantasia according to ritornello principles recently learnt from Vivaldi? Or is BWV 651a an entirely new musical shape, a new organization, barely connected with older organ settings of any kind? In this instance, only one important assertion may be made: J. S. Bach was alone in achieving, and probably in applying, such an organization. By nature, such 'organization' is difficult – impossible in the case of BWV 645–689 – to achieve except on paper, so that any 'advance' felt in the *oeuvre* of J. S. Bach has to be seen as the result of thoughtful composition away from the church service itself. It is clear that the player was expected to be able to improvise chorale-preludes (see above, chapter 5), and Werckmeister speaks disparagingly of the many organists who memorized a few pieces from written copies or played carefully practised pieces from the copy before them:

> Drum ist . . . hoch von nöthen, dass man denselben ein *Thema* vorgebe welches er auf unterschiedliche Arth aussführe, oder man kann auch einige Lieder erwehlen, und dieselben auf gewisse Arth *variiren* . . . , und transponiren lassen . . . (1698 p77)

> It is therefore very necessary that one gives [the candidate] a theme beforehand which he performs in various ways; or one can also choose some hymns and have them varied in diverse ways and transposed . . .

Perhaps Mattheson's grand trials were exceptional, a sign of the virtuoso directions that organ-playing was taking. Most organists did not need to be able to improvise long chorale-based works in several sections, though it is clear that at least some of the usual preluding was fugal or imitative.

Although they shed only a glimmer of light on J. S. Bach's practices in Arnstadt and Weimar, or on those of his assistant in Leipzig, Mattheson's suggestions for improvisation are thorough enough (1739 pp474–5). It is not clear why for such suggestions he needed to rely on an essay of C. Raupach, organist of the Stralsund Nikolaikirche, for they must have been familiar, even standard. But authors like to be able to cite other authors. Raupach suggested the following ideas, listing them 'first', 'second' as if in a set of variations:

Prayer, Penitence, Lamentation (*Butt- Buss- und Klag-Lied*)	Joy, Solace, Boldness (*Freuden- Trost- und Trotz-Lied*)
1 short theme, fugal, simple, slow	1 a strong stop or full organ for a joyful *Symphonia oder Sonatina*; if time, a *gross Sonata* with fugue (4 parts) and *simple Choral* at the close

---

* Hence Reincken's encouraging Bach to improvise such a fantasia at Hamburg in 1720 (see above, chapter 7).

2   c.f. in pedal, manual with syncopations & suspensions; in 4 parts

2   strong stop, 4 parts: little fugue on the chorale, allegro

3   *simple Choral* in rh, lh in 2 parts with suspensions, short *Tiraten, Groppi*; total = 3 parts

3   c.f. in rh, lh on second manual; total = 2 parts

4   *simple Choral* in lh, bass in ped., rh as as in no. 3, but 1 part only; total = 3 parts

4   c.f. in lh, rh with moving *contrapunctus floridus*; total = 2 parts

5   *lamento* with quiet stops on which the *simple Choral*

5   c.f. in ped., lh/rh on one manual with *Variation*; total = 3 parts

6   c.f. in lh, rh on other manual with *Variation*, adagio; 2 parts

6   c.f. in rh, bass in ped., lh on 2nd man. with *Variation*; 3 parts

7   no. 6 reversed

7   c.f. in lh, bass in ped., rh *Variation*; 3 parts

8   2 manuals in alternation: first an inventive *Fantasia* showing *Affekt* of each line (or 2–3 lines), alternating with *simple Choral* on 2nd man. (with pedal)

9   *simple Choral* in lh; rh and ped. with *Variation*; 3 parts

10   c.f. in rh; lh and ped. with *Variation*; 3 parts

The ambiguities here suggest how Raupach saw chorales. Thus nos. 6/10 and 7/9 must be different from each other in respect to what the pedal does,* and since it is three-part chorales that are concerned, the distinction between one and the other is very pertinent to J. S. Bach's settings: to which category would BWV 639, 663, 664 and 645 respectively belong? Raupach also uses both terms, '*simple Choral*' and 'cantus firmus', as if to distinguish between the chorale melody (unharmonized?) played in sung time and the chorale melody pulled out as a long-note cantus. While two or three of his categories do not seem to correspond to known works of J. S. Bach, it is at least clear from the remarks – which it is seldom so from other references – that '*Variation*' here means an interesting or inventive counterpoint, a moving line expressing the harmony that underlies the melody.

It is also clear that relating the improvisation to the meaning of the words was the purpose of the devices listed by Raupach, traditional though most of them must have been. That too seems the purpose behind the variety of treatments given the melody in such fantasias as 'Christ lag' BWV 718, where the Hallelujahs (penultimate section) are clear to anyone but where the bitterness of the 'Todesbanden' (first section) can be seen only by an imaginative player. Traditional devices such as the opening *bicinium* style of BWV 718 are by nature more 'objective' than later generations liked. Such a style could as well apply to a hymn of prayer, and indeed does so in Böhm's 'Vater unser'. Also, although in BWV 718 the jig treatment of line 6 may reflect the text at this point – *Gott loben und dankbar sein* ('praising and thanking God') – it could as well have reflected the text for the previous line – *Des wir sollen fröhlich sein* ('for this we should be joyful'). Thus while the traditional nature of the treatments at these two points – *bicinium* and jig – may not actually

---

* Adlung thought so too, it seems (1783 p829).

contradict the *Affekt* of the words, it corresponds to it only in general terms. Any claims that the traditional organ fantasia follows the chorale text (Löffler 1923) can be understood only in this very general sense.

It cannot be said with certainty how far nos. 1 and 8 in Raupach's second column correspond to any known Bach works,* to the new Hanseatic fashions of c1725, or to improvisations common in Hanseatic churches of that time. Mattheson himself seems to have seen as a model for organ settings in general Pachelbel's *Acht Choräle* (1693), with J. G. Walther a good second – a more varied composer than Raupach, he noted (1739 p476) – which rather suggests that his sources of information must have been either printed editions or personal correspondence, neither of which would have given him much acquaintance with the organ chorales of J. S. Bach. But he is certainly clear about the ideal short prelude:

> die aus freiem Sinn herfliessende kurtze Vorspiele müssen eben diejenige Leidenschafft durch den figürlichen Klang auszudrucken trachten, welcher in den Worten des zu musicirenden Stückes, oder von der Gemeine anzustimmenden Kirchenliedes angedeutet wird (1739 p472).

> the short preludes flowing from free fancy must strive to express through the figural sound that very emotion which will be signified in the words of the ensemble piece [cantata] or of the hymn in which the congregation is to join.

But for how long before 1739 had that been an aim? Since a tune may have many different texts, it was useful to show to which it was to be sung (p473); and the particular purpose of a piece is presumed to show itself in its form or *genre* (Luedtke 1918 p7) – fughetta for a hymn *prelude*, for example. But it is all too easy to assume that Mattheson is relevant to J. S. Bach; a comparison between the *Orgelbüchlein* and *Clavierübung III* suggests that Bach became less 'expressive' in the Mattheson sense, rather than more.

The same is true of technical details: Mattheson's discussion of chorale melodies treated canonically (1731) is no more than a theorist's reference to techniques familiar to the better organists over at least the century between Scheidt and the *Orgelbüchlein*. Similarly, he remarks that one 'could make all kinds of dances out of church hymns' by changing their rhythms (1739 p161), and illustrates it nicely: Ex. 10. But the sarabande rhythms of the organ chorales BWV 653 and 654 are infinitely more subtle than Mattheson could have imagined,† running through the whole texture and inviting a response from the player. The old chorale-fantasias

Ex. 10 'Herr Jesu Christ, du höchstes &c'

---

* Despite the apparently clear details which are listed. For example, does no. 2 correspond to such a fughetta as 'Gelobet seist du, Jesu Christ' BWV 697, or to something very much simpler? Does he mean to suggest anything more than what was customarily improvised in the post-Scheidtian manner?

† The fact that Mattheson's last example is at least reminiscent of the *Folia* theme may suggest that there was an ineradicable secularity in his taste. Would that explain his desire to achieve piety with pictorial *Affekt*?

would have alerted J. S. Bach to the beauties of rhythmic metamorphosis: for example, the conversion of the last line of 'Gelobet seist du' into a jig-dialogue in Buxtehude's setting BUXWV 188 (in P 802; cf. BWV 718 bb33ff), or the bewitching *louré* treatment of the third line of 'Nun komm' in Bruhns's fantasia (also in P 802). The chorales BWV 653 and 654 are in this tradition.

Perhaps it was in the very attempt to stress that organ preludes should relate to the words of the hymn rather than exploit abstract devices of musical composition in the older manner that Mattheson, Scheibe, Mizler, Adlung, Türk and others listed the ways in which organists could improvise preludes. These lists were geared to *Affekt* and, in their emphasis on accompanying the congregation, helped to produce the wretched idioms of J. C. Kittel and others of his period. In 1739 Scheibe, perhaps making up for his less than happy experiences in Leipzig, published an essay devoted to the same subject. So anxious was he that the mood of the hymn be got right that he seems to list pedal cantus firmus only as an afterthought; perhaps pedal c.f. is by nature 'objective', hence its gradual demise? He suggests that it is enough in Trio or Adagio treatments (which he preferred) if the *character* of the chorale is expressed, there being no need actually to quote from its hymn melody. Another author of the period published some remarks in 1742 (Voigt, perhaps in connection with the new Silbermann organ in Greiz) to the effect that the organist should educate the congregation as well as express the mood of each verse ('jeden versicul nach dem Affekt exprimieren': in Werner 1933 p111). But others of the period sought *Affekt* in accompanying the hymns even to the extent of using unfamiliar keys, i.e. harsh keys for harsh effects (J. B. Reimann, 1747: in Fellerer 1932 p42). Searching for *Affekt* could easily reach absurdity, a musical equivalent of the intentional fallacy. Giving a general mood decently was right but pictorializing was not, as Türk had to point out by ridiculing one organist who played

> *Meines Glaubens Licht*   the light of my belief
> *lass verlöschen nicht*   will not be extinguished

by beginning with the *organo pleno* and pushing in stops until nothing was left (1787 p27).*

Mood-playing could certainly be achieved with a far less developed musical technique (on the part of both player and composer) than a good cantus-firmus setting. The obvious musical quality of J. S. Bach's settings must have given difficulty to his later admirers. On the one hand, many of his chorales must have seemed far more difficult to play than organists were used to in the decades following his death (scarcely anyone could still play them, according to C. F. D. Schubart in 1779: *Dok* III p331); on the other hand, he was championed by such pupils as J. F. Agricola, for whom

> die Regel . . . dass der Ausdruck der Musik im Vorspiele, dem Inhalte des Liedes gemäss seyn müsse, sehr vernünftig und rechtmässig ist (*Dok* III p212).

> the rule that the musical expression in preludes must be appropriate to the contents of the hymn is very sensible and just.

If, as Agricola also implies, composing with cantus firmus is not easily conducive to this, then *Clavierübung III* can be seen as more retrospective than *Orgelbüchlein*,

---

* The point of the text, of course, was that the light was not to be extinguished, so that in any case the pictorialism was fallacious.

since by 1739 the cantus-firmus techniques had become yet more out-of-date than they had been when the *Orgelbüchlein* was assembled without them. Perhaps *Clavierübung III* was a gesture against the tastes of the time, which at least in vocal music had been well catered for by the composer, according to Mizler (1739; cf. *Dok* II p336). When J. F. Doles, a Leipzig student from 1739 to 1743, speaks of working with J. S. Bach in counterpoint but feeling the need to seek 'soft and moving melody' in the works of K. H. Graun or J. A. Hasse ('sanfte und rührende Melodie'), he may well be reflecting the composer's preoccupations over the period of *Clavierübung III* (*Dok* III p554). J. L. Krebs's interest in cantus-firmus techniques may have 'saved' his idiom from some of the pitfalls of the time, just as other pupils who entered the profession while J. S. Bach was still alive also showed good taste, judging by Mizler's remarks on J. Schneider in 1747 (*Dok* II p445). But looking broadly over the eighteenth and nineteenth centuries, one could conclude that searching for *Affekte* was probably the biggest single reason for the decline in organ music. Moreover, this searching dated from a period *before* eighteenth-century Europe can be supposed to have become so secularized as to find its best composers turning away from the organ.

Mattheson's remark on converting hymn melodies into dances (see above) is one of the few references made by any theorist to the craft of composing chorales, as distinct from the expressiveness of the end product. Though 'paraphrasing' may or may not be a very apt term, it is clearly a technique of great importance to both player and composer; and whether it is a question of converting a melody into a dance or *colouring* a few plain notes into an expressive melody, the various ways of paraphrasing a chorale must have been thought about carefully by the best composers. Whether or not the words *adagio assai* for the paraphrase setting of 'O Mensch bewein" BWV 622 are an addition and represent second thoughts on the composer's part – in order to make clear what *Affekt* he intended to convey with his decorative melismas – it can hardly be doubted what that *Affekt* is. The questions are: By 1715, did all melismatic treatment of chorale melodies suggest a languorous, sad text? Was the composer's interest in *figurae* – in this case, a melismatic melody achieved with surprisingly conventional motifs (see Vol. II p60) – more 'objective' than expressive, so that he had to use a tempo marking to clarify what the *figurae* were aiming at? And did he want to make it clear because fashions were moving towards more immediate expressiveness, or because he was himself inclined to such treatment? The fine shades of difference amongst these questions, whether or not they can ever be answered, makes one question not only how he saw the organ chorale but how he achieved his conception technically. J. S. Bach's paraphrasing techniques are often admired now, but it is probable that a contemporary in the 1730s or 1740s would have seen such ingenuity as an enemy of expressiveness.

While J. S. Bach's paraphrases are in a class by themselves, it should not be forgotten that they grew in healthy surroundings. It can be assumed that he observed two important paraphrase techniques in de Grigny's *Livre*, for example (c1713): the deriving of a fugue theme from the opening of a cantus firmus ('Pange lingua' and 'A solis ortus'*) and the paraphrasing of a complete c.f. melody as a *récit en taille* ('Pange lingua'). Whatever the date of particular chorales by Buxtehude or Böhm, the de Grigny offered any intelligent musician a fine model for a certain kind of

* The same melody as 'Christum wir sollen loben schon' – see BWV 611, 696 etc.

Ex. 11   de Grigny, 'Pange lingua'

ornamentation: Ex. 11. Though exclusive to French music with its copious vocal appoggiaturas, it is difficult to imagine that such music, whether by de Grigny or Nivers or Lebègue, had no influence on Böhm. More in the old colorist style of Scheidt were other treatments found in J. S. Bach: the lines of (e.g.) BWV 734 and 684 are in this manner, with the 'thematic' notes on strong beats. Such a treatment was *de rigueur* for the second or third variation in a chorale-partita, but in the hands of some composers, perhaps in early Bach, it led to fine free lines to which any keyboard-player can respond imaginatively: Ex. 12. The regularity of the

Ex. 12

Pachelbel, 'Wir glauben'

mature paraphrases of Bach certainly lost something of the caprice and freshness found in this Scheidtian technique at its best. Especially when, as in *Clavierübung III*, the composer seems to be paraphrasing two lines at once, the inventiveness or ingenuity is geared towards creating countersubjects. Those accompanying lines may well have been more ingeniously derived in cantatas than in organ chorales; writers today who are fond of pointing out the connection between chorale and paraphrase in Cantata 161.i – Ex. 13 – do not make it clear that the paraphrase has an identity of its own (and is melodically independent of the chorale) to a greater extent than was usual in organ settings.

Ex. 13   BWV 161.i

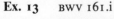

b13 Sesquialtera ad Organo

As far as melodic paraphrase is concerned, J. S. Bach's contribution consists chiefly in moving the melismas and turns of phrase away from the main beats: the beats are no longer obliged to carry the main notes of the original melody, as had been usual (e.g the Pachelbel and de Grigny examples above). Paraphrasing 'on the beat' had been so customary as even to suggest that the Arnstadt complaint arose because the composer's *variationes* were disguising the main notes. Such a prelude as Zachow's 'Vom Himmel hoch' may indicate how a chorale as a whole was played by him and performed along with the congregation: a bar or two of fugal introduction, the hymn melody (line 1) decorated, brief interlude, the hymn melody (line 2), interlude, etc: Ex. 14. If this example does reflect Zachow's own practice as a player,

Ex. 14   Zachow, 'Vom Himmel hoch'

it might encourage a similar inference about J. S. Bach and at least some movements from his chorale-variations. They too may show how hymns were accompanied in 'full-dress' performances (i.e. in large churches, on feast-days etc); it would then appear that the simple accompaniments advocated from the 1730s onwards were reactions against too 'interesting' a playing of the organ and towards merely using the organ to support the simplified hymns.*

The composer may well have set out to develop his extraordinary skill at spinning out a decorated cantus firmus into a long melody (e.g. 'Nun komm' BWV 659) because he appreciated that this was a direction in which his contemporaries were moving. Such composers as Walther drew out the ends of phrases more than any other part of the melody: Ex. 15. The inspired eloquence of BWV 659 should not disguise its origins here. Spitta credits Böhm with the 'thematic–motivic development of the melodic material' (I p203), giving as example Böhm's working of the chorale melody 'Herr Jesus Christ, dich zu uns wend": Ex. 16. Such extensions, though not strictly paraphrases, have obvious potential. But Böhm's claim to originality in this can apply only to organ music: vocal music had long known the spun-out melody, as in Buxtehude's well-known motet 'In dulci jubilo' or other simple examples (Krummacher 1978 pp78ff): Ex. 17. Organ music was presumably not as free to extend phrases in this way, for having no words meant that the link between text and notes was easily lost.

* Simplified (i.e. standardized) isometric hymns sung by a fully participating congregation from hymn-books, which by then were widely distributed.

Ex. 15

J. G. Walther, 'Aus der Tiefe rufe ich' *Vers 2* (*bicinium*)

Ex. 16

Ex. 17

(i)

A. Hammerschmidt, 'Ich hab mein Sach Gott heimgestellt'

Ich hab mein Sach Gott heim - ge - stellt, er mit mir machts, er mit mir machts,

er mit mir machts.

(ii)

W. C. Briegel, 'Erschienen ist der herrliche Tag'

Er - schie-nen, er - schie-nen, er-schie-nen ist der herr - li-che, der

herr - li - che Tag, er - schie-nen

But it is difficult to resist the view that, in any case, paraphrased melodies very easily become unrecognizable: the original chorale allusion becomes lost to the ear. If this is true of J. S. Bach's more developed paraphrases, so it is of those by the better composers among his predecessors. They seem to invite the player to search for allusions. The most familiar chorale melody, like the most familiar Gregorian *cantus*, is soon altered out of recognition as tempo or metre is changed. When melodies are paraphrased, the very strength of the new conceit is proved by its independence from the original, a point illustrated in what must be one of the best organ paraphrases outside the work of J. S. Bach, Bruhns's 'Nun komm'. Though the work was known to J. G. Walther, J. F. Agricola and J. P. Kirnberger amongst others, Bruhns's Fantasia is such that only a Bach would have seen all the thematic allusion there, for example in the *louré* section* already referred to: Ex. 18. Even in

Ex. 18

des sich wun-dert al - le Welt

Bruhns, 'Nun komm, der Heiden Heiland'

the work of J. S. Bach, there are not many imaginative strokes equal to the separated off-beat notes in the top soprano part here. Moreover, if this chorale-fantasia were a work of his or were scrutinized as closely as his are, it would surely have been claimed by now that the countersubject to this *louré* line is a quotation from 'Vom Himmel hoch': Ex. 19. Symbolists would then find it perfectly reasonable to see Advent as leading to Christmas, and therefore melodies from both as usefully combinable.

Ex. 19

da - von ich sing'n und sa - gen will.

---

* A curious remark about the Weissenfels Tremulant (see below, p128) – that it beat in 6/4 time – may refer to such music as this, i.e. gentle chorale settings.

64

A final remark on paraphrasing concerns habits of a later period. The ease with which certain composers turned even the most traditional Lutheran chorale melodies into Italianate or *galant* lines suggests that the absence of such treatment in the works of Bach shows him to have made a conscious choice against it. The kind of paraphrase in the counterthemes of the chorale BWV 650, for example (see Vol. II p122), is obviously less 'modern' than the melody in Ex. 20, which too is developed

Ex. 20

G. F. Kauffmann, 'Vom Himmel hoch'

in a ritornello manner, i.e. like BWV 650 and certain settings by J. L. Krebs, J. C. Oley and others. Whoever was responsible for the *Schübler* transcriptions, it is possible to see them as a response to fashionable styles of the day, styles more at home in the cantatas than in what J. S. Bach seems to have considered true organ music, even during his last eleven or twelve years.

9. *Affektenlehre,* Rhetoric and 'Symbolism'

Comparing the music of J. S. Bach with that of his contemporaries can lead to the impression that whatever element is being considered is one that he has taken farther, or marked more emphatically, or developed more stirringly and on more layers, than have any of the other composers. Various analytical approaches to this music are therefore made from time to time. Fashionable today, like the programmaticism of yesterday or the didacticism of the day before, is the analysis of *Affekte*, figures of musical speech, rhetoric and so-called symbolism. All appear to be justified by the complex nature of the music concerned, and all from time to time have served as the basis of revelations without which the composer's intentions have not, it seems, been understood. It is in the nature of such approaches to music that they attract much literate activity: i.e., music journals and music conferences provide space or time to those concerned with them and create the impression of an active and useful area of musical thought.

Affekt

Although J. G. Ziegler's remark on being taught by J. S. Bach to play 'according to the *Affekt* of the words' is not as wide-ranging as is often assumed today, and has to be seen in a certain context only (see above, p33), nevertheless it cannot be doubted that in his organ music, at least from the *Orgelbüchlein* onwards, the composer engaged in various kinds of textual allusion. Settings of melodies allude in some way to the words of the original chorale – evoking the same area of mood or part of the emotional spectrum (sad or happy), offering a musical parallel to the meaning of the text (timorous or vigorous, liturgical or personal), symbolizing it in some way (e.g. inversion = immersion in BWV 685), relating a key word which in itself is literal (*ten* in 'Dies sind die heil'gen zehn Gebot') or symbolic (the *fall* in 'Durch Adams Fall'). Various attempts have been made to codify areas or types of symbolism (Schering 1925 and Kloppers 1966). Subtler but still undeniable are the wider allusions: the classical liturgical orthodoxy of the Kyrie in the Lutheran Mass drawing from the composer massive classical counterpoint, although the text itself is subjective, supplicatory, pathetic (see Vol. II pp187ff). But even in such 'neutral' hymns as 'Allein Gott' (for Trinity and the Gloria), set by J. S. Bach in objective and charming counterpoint, some commentators have found textual allusions of one kind or another (see notes to BWV 662, 663). Indeed, the two problems with any approach from the more recent studies of *Affekte*, rhetoric and symbolism are (first) that commentators in this area have often drawn conclusions at variance with each other depending on the way wider fashions developed, and (secondly) that any interpretations taken beyond a certain point are by nature speculative and very often serve only to express the commentator's enthusiasm for the piece concerned.

The technical observations of early commentators on Bach do little more than express that enthusiasm, particularly for Bach the Demonstrator of how things can be done – hence Marpurg's view that the inner voices of BWV 623 'produce a mere counter-harmony' (Vol. II p64). Although in the context of his discussion of fugal techniques this remark says more than it may appear to, it is still some way from Forkel's higher flights of fancy in a book which attempts to rationalize the frequent praise of J. S. Bach uttered over the previous half-century. Forkel's was the period when literate writers became explicit in their response and attempted to re-express in words the feelings considered to be expressed by music. Already in 1805, one commentator remarked on the chorale BWV 646 in words that could belong to the next century:

> Das ängstliche Suchen der Ruhe ist meisterhaft gemalt, und der Effekt ganz wunderbar und einzig (*AMZ* 8 (1805) cols. 29–32).

> The anxious seeking for peace is painted in a masterly way, and the effect [is] very wonderful and singular.

The question is: Is it true, and if so to whom? The idea of 'painting peace' may well be characteristic of the period in general, but technically it seems barely possible to do this without assuming a gentle tempo and a legato touch. But in that case did the commentator – having inadequate comparative knowledge – misunderstand two important details of the work: that the registration rh 8′, lh 16′, pedal 4′ is unlikely to be meant literally,* and that the motif exploited in this setting (see Vol. II p115), ingenious as it is, is also conventional for the period? While his awareness of these points would not necessarily cause him to rethink his interpretation, they certainly do not of themselves either support it or justify 'a gentle tempo and a legato touch'. Perhaps it is in the nature of all such expressive interpretation that it arises from more or less inadequate awareness of the composer's context and preoccupations.†

While even a general or overall *Affekt* may often be difficult to interpret without one anachronism or another creeping in, it is clear that composers and theorists in the early eighteenth century were reaching towards a music that encouraged personal response in ways that would not always be familiar to the German composer unaware of the intricacies of the Italian *seconda prattica* of the previous century. The 'objectivity' of instrumental music had been encouraged by the conventional formality of the suite. As is clear from the *Six Sonatas*, any music that demanded a succinct, intricate form and a fully stretched contrapuntal technique continued to be free of any 'meaning' other than a generalized *Affekt*. Kuhnau implied that he saw the formal binary form of suite movements would never produce striking *affetti* when he spoke of the advantage that sonatas have over 'mere suites' ('blosse Partien'). Sonatas could have 'change of beat' and 'affects altered back and forth', no doubt aided by 'rhetorical figures' ('Veränderung des Tachtes . . . hin und wieder abgewechselten Affecten . . . oratorischen Figuren': preface to *Frische Clavier Früchte*, Leipzig 1696). But curiously, the kind of stopping-and-starting shape that he refers to – the sonata of sections and contrast, rather than the later Italian sonata evoked by BWV 525–530 – is more like the 'objective' praeludium than the ritornello prelude of his successor.

Motifs

It is clear that the composer worked very much from *figurae* which, in the cantatas, were often associated with particular words or moods; whether it is correct to interpret instrumental music (organ chorales) in accordance with such associations is another matter. If, for example, the descending chromatic fourth was necessarily associated with despondency or resistance – e.g. the bass of 'Da Jesus an dem Kreuze stund' in Scheidt's *Görlitzer Tabulaturbuch* 1650 – then it is puzzling to find it also for 'Mit Fried und Freud' in the same hymnbook. However, if the chromatic fourth is, less specifically, an expression of (device for) the negative or dark end of the spectrum, then it is puzzling to find it for 'To thee all angels cry aloud' in the Te Deum in the same book. The setting of the same hymn in BWV 725 uses both ascending and descending fourths for the verse 'O Lord, let thy mercy lighten upon

---

* That he or his readers knew little of old techniques is suggested by his explaining that the cantus firmus is played on the pedal 4' stop, in sections (i.e. one line at a time): a convention which, it seems, they would not have been familiar with.

† Similarly, periods looking for expressive interpretation can find some music more valuable than others. The defacing of one known copy of *Clavierübung III* during the later eighteenth century (source 'A 18' in *NBA* IV/4 *KB* p19) suggests that some of those who did not use J. S. Bach's later music for contrapuntal *exempla* could not find other, more expressive virtues in it: 'Zur Gemüths Ergezung' ('for the recreation of the spirit') has been crossed out for 'zur Augen Ergezung und Ohren Verletzung' ('for the recreation of the eyes and wounding of the ears').

us: as our trust is in thee', which suggests no more than that the *figura* was not inappropriate to words of faith.

If chromatic lines were appropriate to settings of chorales variously concerned with either end of the emotional spectrum, so were other motifs. Walther found falling *figurae* suitable for certain kinds of word-setting (1732 p148); the *catabasis* was

> ein harmonischer Periodus, wodurch etwas niedriges, gering- und verächtliches vorgestellt wird, z.E. 'Er ist hinunter gefahren', 'Ich bin sehr gedemüthiget' u.d.g.

> a harmonic interval [?] through which something abject, petty and contemptible is represented, e.g. 'He is put down', 'I am very humiliated' and the like.

But without text, or placed in other contexts, it is obvious that a falling figure is not necessarily graphic. In Walther's own 'Durch Adams Fall', the *bicinium* bass has conspicuous drops – Ex. 21 – but such falling basses are typical of *bicinia*, and this

Ex. 21   Walther, 'Durch Adams Fall'

one did not originate – however suitable it may have seemed to Walther – as a reference to any text. A similar point may be made about the rise at the end of a setting of the same chorale by Buxtehude (BUXWV 183): whether or not it pictures the 'ray of hope for salvation' (Apel 1967 p605), it was certainly a rising figure of the kind conventional for certain chorales. If the falling motifs in the bass of this setting, like those in the *Orgelbüchlein* setting BWV 637, do seem more allusive, BUXWV 183 even introducing chromatics at the moment corresponding to the word 'poison' (text in Vol. II p87), it must be because the text and its striking images provide a framework of allusion for motifs that are not by nature allusive. The falls in BUXWV 183 are not unlike those in BWV 605 or 606. Schweitzer, who discussed simpler motifs such as rhythmic semiquaver patterns, gradually found specific associations for them which one may not think very useful, since either they are too general to convey anything that is not already obvious, or they are so specific as to carry no conviction. But his discussion of such motifs had the benefit of directing attention to the composer's motivic method.

The chromatic fourth was one of the *passus duriusculi* listed by Christoph Bernhard in c1650 (see Vol. II p44, Vol. I p341) – the others were false relations and augmented/diminished intervals – and was like them a musical idea suitable for certain kinds of text, i.e. those that might be called 'negative'. A series of theorists from J. Burmeister (*Musica poetica*, Rostock 1606) to J. G. Walther (*Lexicon*, Leipzig 1732) listed such intervals, both melodic and harmonic, and on the basis of their listings several attempts have been made in recent years to analyse works of J. S. Bach from the theorists' viewpoint. One such essay claims that 'Durch Adams Fall' BWV 637 disregards 'all norms of regular part-writing' in the exploitation of such intervals or *figurae* (Budday 1977). Now there is no doubt that BWV 637 was for its period an exceptional *tour de force* far outstripping the conventional chromatic variation of chorale-partitas in its detail of falling bass sevenths, false relations, avoidance of conventional progressions, chromatic figurations and consecutive diminished sevenths. There is no doubt that the effect is 'negative' and that J. S. Bach and J. G. Walther knew what at least some of the theorists said. But all this amounts to no indication whatsoever that BWV 637 was composed with any regard to the theorists and their labels. Theorists are at best codifiers of musical practices beyond them as composers and often even beyond them as observers. The examples they give of texts that are suitable for such harmonies and lines are both general and obvious; they did not invent the associations and would have had nothing to offer an active composer of the ability of a Monteverdi or a Bach.

Even within the figural technique of BWV 637, and putting aside for the moment the harmonies that no theorist before Rameau could even have *described*, there are elements which an analysis would find difficult to square with the theorists. For example, the opening motif (Ex. 22) is very like the lines of a chromatic variation in a

Ex. 22   BWV 637

traditional partita. Strikingly conventional in the circumstances are the cadences at the end of each line. If BWV 637 does totally disregard the rules of part-writing because of a license granted by the theorists for such negative texts, any strong, unambiguous perfect cadence must have a purpose: it cannot be glossed over. The commentator must seek in the text some special reason why each line closes in such a way. This proves no obstacle to one committed to an *Affektenlehre* interpretation, nor very likely would the fact that each cadence is prepared early on in its line (before distant modulation estranges it), since some textual allusion can always be found.* But it does mean that if a chord or progression goes against the grain of the music (e.g. consistent perfect cadences in chromatic music), or if a chord or progression is very conventional in certain contexts (e.g. chromatic fourths in partitas), then 'meanings' become questionable since they have to be sought too deep. Only the general associations, which in BWV 637 come as much from the motion and flow as from false relations, are indisputable.

Rhetoric

Similar points can be made about a line of enquiry fashionable today, musical rhetoric. The principle here lies in both the strategy and the tactics of composition: the overall shape and the details of the material. Conventionalized rhetoric, as an art propounded by Aristotle and forming part of literate education in western culture over the following twenty centuries, offers a guide on how to shape – and how to convey the power of the shape of – various kinds of verbal material, in particular legal or political speeches. Certain areas of that western culture, such as first-century Rome and seventeenth-century Germany, produced particularly active

---

* For example, that the Fall of Adam is countered by the Redemption, that sin is conquered by firm faith, etc.

interest in the subject, leading to the publication of treatises and the dissemination of their ideas and their very terminologies.

There are bound to be similarities between the ways in which any two speeches or pieces of music of more than passing brevity are organized, since the number of formal strategies is limited. Thus each will have a beginning, middle and end, and suggestions have been made by writers in recent centuries regarding the best tactics of those sections – for example, how many ideas are contained in the 'middle', how they can be best expressed, how repetitive or dramatic they can be, how dramatic expression can be achieved so that the listener is 'moved' one way or the other. But just as during the seventeenth and eighteenth centuries certain German theorists applied such generalizations more particularly and 'explained' music in such ways, so more recently German and other writers have restated what those theorists said and organized it into a more or less systematic scheme (e.g. G. J. Buelow, 'Rhetoric and Music', *The New Grove*). Such generalities as that after the impact of 'Renaissance humanism . . . every educated man was a skilled rhetorician. This universal development had a profound impact on composers' attitudes to text-bound music' (*ibid*) have in turn led to studies of the shape of particular pieces. More recently still, the note-by-note make-up of various pieces has been examined with a view to labelling the events in terms of musical 'figures of speech', and whole collections have been explained in terms of the rules of rhetoric laid out by (e.g.) Quintilian (thus U. Kirkendale on the *Musical Offering* in *JAMS* 33 (1980) 88-141). Such examinations often have an elegance of their own.

The question is, however, not so much Are they relevant? as Do they actually say anything? If a writer (whether an ancient theorist of rhetoric or a more recent musical theorist) explains a point – for example, that a brief pause can heighten the impact of a statement – and if a contemporary composer from the same cultural background introduces a sudden melodic rest that heightens the impact of the melody, what conclusion is to be drawn?

(*a*) that the composer merely belongs to the same 'cultural background' as the theorist and somehow absorbed the same ways of thought;

(*b*) that both composer and theorist belonged to a cultural tradition without which neither would have known or been able to discover that rests heighten impact;

(*c*) that the composer needed to read such a theorist in order to know how to make this effect;

(*d*) that listeners (including those today) must read such a theorist if they are to grasp what effect the composer was aiming at;

(*e*) that the theorist needed to have experience of such an effect (from an actual piece of music) in order to give such advice – i.e., his theory comes after the event;

(*f*) that the theorist who labels such a rhetorical device *tmesis* has achieved anything relevant to the piece of music?

Of these, *b* and *c* are obviously absurd, while *a* is too general to be useful; *d*, *e* and *f* can be considered together since they offer the only positive outcome – namely, that rhetorical analysis, on a large or small scale, has no usefulness except as a means of alerting the reader to a detail in the composition to which he may not before have given sufficient weight. For example, a player who understands the idea of a rhetorical rest will be more aware of what the piece's notation tells him; he will thus pause 'rhetorically'. Labelling it *tmesis* has as much relevance, neither more nor less, as labelling words in a line of blank verse *simile* or *metaphor* etc; the poet needs no theorist to label his figures of speech, which are so basic to language that as a principle they belong to no particular period or culture.

Reasoning in this way it is impossible to agree with such conclusions as the following, however well backed by examples which, as any rhetorician knows, do not prove but only illustrate:

> While neither Mattheson nor any other Baroque theorist would have applied these *rhetorical prescriptions* rigidly to every musical composition, it is clear that such concepts not only *aided composers* to a varying degree but were self-evident to them as routine techniques in the compositional process . . . only now is it beginning to be understood how much Western art music *depended on* rhetorical concepts at least until the beginning of the 19th century (Buelow, *op cit*, italics mine).

Whatever may be true of composers so totally without creative ability that they depend on a theorist to aid them in their work – and it is possible to imagine composition being so learnt in certain circumstances – I do not believe that any case has been made for the relevance of 'rules of rhetoric' to the music of J. S. Bach except in the general sense under (*d*), (*e*) and (*f*) above. Mattheson himself betrays the weakness of any such approach. With reference to musical *dialogues* and the inherent drama of word-setting in such music, he remarks:

> Dass auch die Orgeln mit verschiedenen Clavieren, auf gewisse Weise solche Gespräche nachahmen können, ist eine recht artige Anmerckung im Waltherischen Wörter-Buche. Es gibt uns solche Vorstellung einen neuen Beweis, dass die Klang-Rede auch auf Instrumenten zu Hause gehöret, und sehr vernehmlich gemacht werden kan (1739 p220).

> That also the organ with several manuals can in a certain manner imitate such discourses is a very pretty observation in Walther's Dictionary. Such a notion gives us a new proof that rhetoric is also at home with instruments and can be made very intelligible.

It is inconceivable that after three centuries of making organs with two manuals it required a dictionary to inform musicians that those manuals could be used in apposition to each other or, as we might say, 'used to rhetorical effect'. If by 'intelligible' Mattheson means to imply that instruments can convey a particular text or kind of text, then the music concerned would be merely analogous (a quasi-transcription of an actual dialogue) rather than rhetorical in its own right.

But in any case, it is by no means certain that Mattheson intended to convey anything so profound as so many modern studies imply when they draw parallels between music and rhetoric. For example, of the organist Raupach he remarked that he was

> in der rhetorisch–musikalischen Schreibe-Art sehr angefeuret worden, auch die Dichtkunst mit der Setzkunst gewisser massen zu verbinden (1740 pp283ff).

> very much fired by the rhetorical–musical way of writing, even to combining in some degree the art of poetry with the art of music.

Now this appears to be connecting Raupach with the subtleties of music-as-rhetoric. Moreover, it seems that he was well read in the theorists (Speer, Printz,

Falck, Quirsfeld), had made great use of the music of many composers (including Kuhnau (whose prefaces he would have known), Krieger, Buxtehude, Pachelbel, Corelli and Froberger) and had used his time in Hamburg well (composing, playing organs, visiting the opera and concerts, etc).* In other words, he was a well-read, well-experienced musician. Yet it is clear from Mattheson's other account of Raupach (1739 pp474-5) that what such study and research led to was no subtle blending of the arts of music and rhetoric – whatever that would be – but nothing more than simple mood-painting, of a kind that might easily lead to absurd pictorialism, even if it did not in Raupach's own improvisations.

If music's parallels with the spoken word are exaggerated or simplified, 'rhetorical' can become merely another word for 'programmatic';† if they serve to make simple analogies between music and words, they remain mere analogies offering no real illumination on either. It could therefore be claimed that a rhetorical analysis of the G minor Fantasia BWV 542 produces certain parallels between a piece of music and a speech but that those parallels, though perhaps of some interest in themselves, in no way clarify how the composer's mind worked and, if anything, cloud the issues even further by appearing to offer guidelines.

Symbolisms

Dürr observed that while the inverting of melodies in a group of Weimar cantatas (BWV 31, 165, 185, 163) was no doubt to be explained from the symbolism of the text,‡ the movements concerned seem all to have been composed within a few weeks of each other (1951 p156). This serves as a healthy reminder that though various features in a piece of music may be open to interpretation outside the notes themselves, they are not incontrovertibly associated with the effect or allusion discovered but are rather the result of the composer's own musical preoccupations at the time. He might use canon to act as a musical allusion (e.g. *imitatio Christi*); he might use it as a pun to refer to the text (e.g. *canon* = law): either way, it acts as a musical reminder – a kind of aural *nota bene* – which does not necessarily have to be given by the composer, which is in itself ambiguous and unspecific, and which accords with his own technical ability or interests as a composer. For example, the canons of the *Orgelbüchlein* can all be seen as symbolizing *imitatio Christi* only if the chorale texts are arbitrarily seen as emphasizing an appropriate sentiment; conversely, other texts equally open to such interpretation have not been so interpreted by the composer (e.g. 'Lob sei' BWV 602 or 'Jesu, meine Freude' BWV 610). Moreover, in view of the musical tradition of setting certain chorale melodies canonically, one would have to ask whether the canon in (e.g.) BWV 600 did have any other significance – i.e., did it mirror anything more than 'objective' convention?

---

* Such a catalogue must surely give some idea of what J. S. Bach experienced in his visits to Hamburg, Lübeck etc?

† It should not be forgotten that Kuhnau, who used the phrase 'oratorische Figuren' in the preface to *Frische Clavier Früchte* (Leipzig 1696), also worked his compositional techniques, which were not profound, towards programmatic ends in his keyboard music, particularly the 'Biblical Sonatas' (see below, pp91ff). Was the interest in 'oratorical figures' a sign (even a consequence) of the undeveloped state of native German literature of the period, compared to that in England, France, Italy etc?

‡ E.g., motifs descend in BWV 185.i for the first line of the following text, ascend for the second:
Barmherziges Herze der ewigen Liebe   Compassionate heart of eternal love
errege, bewege mein Herze durch dich . . .   Inspire and stir my heart through you . . .

Programmatic elements themselves are usually clear enough: for example, in J. N. Hanff's 'Ein feste Burg' (Walther's MS Den Haag 4 G 14) there is little problem in seeing successively the coloratura figures ('bulwark and weapon'), the energetic rhythms ('the old wicked enemy') and the big figurations ('great power') as offering musical versions of the verbal images. After all, these verbal images were themselves already pictorial. The same would be true for using certain intervals (such as the minor seconds decorating the melody 'Weinen, Klagen') and for using certain tone-colours (the massive pedal *pleno* for the reference to the devil in Gronau's setting of 'Ein feste Burg'). To augment the graphic effectiveness, it was possible to supply listeners with a text to read as the organist played; this was done with C. Raupach's improvisations (Mattheson 1740 pp287ff – see chapter 8 above). However, it is obvious that musical elements such as intervals, figurations and registrations do not of themselves denote specific phenomena; equally, only a small range of readily understood phenomena – images to be paralleled in the music – can be expressed graphically in musical terms in such a way as to leave the listener certain how he is to interpret it. Thus, while it is not out of the question that Hanff's 'Auf meinen lieben Gott' achieves a more gentle style than one might expect for such a text because it is responding to particular words of questioning and hope (according to Frotscher 1934–51 p453), such interpretation is by nature less certain. More difficult still is the case of music which apparently does not aim at allusiveness: is it correct to see Böhm's extraordinarily contrasted settings of 'Vater unser' as 'not symbolic' (*ibid* 1 p463) simply because the three treatments have no obvious graphic qualities? Given the old-fashioned nature of the organ sound in Lüneburg, the conventional rigour of *canto fermo in basso* settings, and the forthright nature of rh *Rückpositiv* coloratura chorales, is it not quite as possible that Böhm was wishing to convey a strong, confident interpretation of the Lord's Prayer?

The *genre* or type of chorale-setting does not necessarily bring with it a mood or *scopus*. Even from Raupach's suggestions for chorales, it is clear that *canto fermo in basso* can in itself serve for either happy or sad texts. Perhaps a slow fugue is, as he implies, suitable for a sad chorale rather than a happy one; but it is difficult to see how *kleine Fugen* are suitable only for happy texts. Even if he thought so, there would be no reason for forcing such an interpretation on J. S. Bach's Advent/ Christmas fughettas. For one thing, it should be remembered that almost every moment in the church year can be treated in more than one way: Advent can be subdued or exuberant, depending on local tradition, on the degree of Lutheran orthodoxy observed in a given church, and on the composer's own view of the ultimate purpose of incarnation. Only at times will individual details, such as the 'joyful' virtuoso figuration in Buttstedt's Advent/Christmas chorales, convey what that view was. Other musical details are often less certain – for example, why the sudden chromatic line at b105 of Bruhns's Advent chorale 'Nun komm'? Was Bruhns alluding to the text? Is he inviting the player to ponder or form his own view? Or is there a strictly musical reason for it – i.e., because the section does not end in the key in which it began, does it require a strong gesture to 'justify' it?

In the case of less graphic, more abstractly symbolic interpretations, the problems are compounded. The 'cross motif' is a celebrated example of a symbol supposedly operating even when the music has no text, 'wider significances' serving as a reason for it. Three objections can be raised to this: there is little evidence to suggest that such symbols did operate; there is no 'symbolism' involved in those other figures which are very typical of organ music but which in cantatas are associated with particular notions;* and it should be clear, as it is not, where such 'symbolism' passes to mere pictorialism. 'Mere pictorialism' would be the sort of thing Türk complained of when he wrote that one organist used to play with his two hands crossed at the text 'am Kreuze gestorben' ('died on the cross'), imagining that the notes worked through the eye to the listener (1787 p25). Accordingly, whether or not the 'totality of God' is symbolized in the octave motifs of the central movements of the B minor Mass (Ex. 23), it is never going to be demonstrable that the

Ex. 23

Tu   so - lus   sanc - tus

falling octaves at the end of the D major Fugue BWV 532 bear the same symbolism. This remains true even though the commonsense reasons against symbolic interpretation here (that there are no words, that it is too early a work for occult symbolism, and that its close follows the conventions of praeludia) could no doubt all be countered by a committed commentator, one by one. For example, the absence of any words or chorale melodies underlying the Four Duets in *Clavierübung III* has been no unsurmountable problem for symbolists (see Vol. I pp322–3).

Yet if wordless organ music is to have a particular symbolic significance conveyable to the listener/player, it surely has to be unambiguous, however subtle. For the octave drop at the end of BWV 532 to be symbolizing the 'totality of God', too many factual assumptions would have to be made – for example, that J. S. Bach already indulged in occultism of this kind at an early period. For the Four Duets to be symbolizing the four elements, too many corollaries would have to be satisfactorily explained (e.g. that for J. S. Bach the four elements were so closely involved in the Catechism and Mass that he found it useful to refer to them). But were they and did he? And what justifies making the assumption that the nature of the four elements could be paralleled in musical terms? For the E flat Prelude and Fugue to be symbolizing, alluding to, reminding the listener of, or giving a parallel in musical terms to the three-in-one dogma of the Trinity is much more feasible, since threeness and unity are indeed easily transferable to the experience-in-time that music is. There can be three themes or sections, and they can be integrated or combined as one, in one sense or another. Indeed, viewed in this light, it is difficult to see how any mode of thought other than music *can* express or illustrate the dogma of the Trinity.

Key characteristics

That tuning systems gave keys their different effects is clear from details of temperaments and from what theorists said as they argued for and against equal temperament. Some, such as Heinichen and Marpurg, resisted the idea that keys should

---

* E.g., the crown motif of Cantata 71, 'Gott ist mein König', is a very keyboard-like motif scattered profusely through all the organ works without any possible allusion to crowned kings.

preserve distinct character; versatility was more important. The writer who is now viewed as the most instructive in describing key characteristics is Mattheson, who published a list in 1713 (pp232–51), and such close agreement has been found between his descriptions and the music of J. S. Bach that some have thought it possible the composer knew the book (Wustmann *BJ* 1911 pp6off). The key characteristics have also been particularly applied to Bach's organ works (Kloppers 1966 pp132–6). Some of Mattheson's salient adjectives are as follows:

C major	freche Eigenschaft . . . Freude
	has a bold quality . . . joy
C minor	lieblicher . . . auch trister . . . Gelindigkeit
	gentler . . . also sadder . . . mildness
D major	scharff . . . eigensinnig . . . kriegerischen . . . delicat
	sharp . . . headstrong . . . warlike . . . delicate
D minor	*devotes*, ruhiges . . . angenehmes . . . Gemüths-Ruhe . . . fliessendes
	devout, peaceful . . . pleasant . . . peace of mind . . . flowing
Eb major	viel pathetisches . . . ernsthaften . . . plaintiven
	much feeling . . . serious . . . plaintive
E major	verzweifelungsvolle . . . Traurigkeit . . . leidendes
	despairing sadness . . . suffering
E minor	sehr pensif . . . etwas hurtiges aber nicht lustig
	very pensive . . . perhaps somewhat agile but not gay
F major	ist capable . . . zu exprimiren: Grossmuth, Standhaftigkeit, Liebe
	can express generosity, resoluteness, love
F minor	gelinde . . . schwere . . . hülflose Melancholie . . . Herzens-Angst
	gentle . . . heavy . . . unavailing melancholy . . . heartache
F♯ minor	Betrübnis . . . misanthropisches
	affliction . . . misanthropic
G major	viel insinuantes . . . sowohl zu serieusen als munteren Dingen
	much of the insinuating [?] . . . for serious as for cheerful things
G minor	allerschöneste Ton . . . Ernsthaftigkeit . . . muntere Lieblichkeit
	most beautiful of all keys . . . serious . . . cheerful gentleness
A major	klagenden und traurigen Passionen . . . brilliret auch
	plaintive and sad passions . . . also shines
A minor	klagend . . . gelassen
	plaintive . . . passive
B major	sehr divertissant . . . prächtig
	very entertaining . . . brilliant
B minor	unlustig . . . melancholisch
	cheerless . . . melancholy

The authority afforded to Mattheson by scholars today leads to many absurdities. Irrespective of agreements or disagreements with particular pieces by J. S. Bach – the original keys of some of which are far from certain – it is clear from the further descriptions of A minor and C minor as 'sleep-inducing' that Mattheson is speaking of keys suitable for (or found in) aria texts in opera or chamber cantata. The idea that a composer would 'follow' or even have more than a passing interest in such descriptions for any other music – and perhaps not even a passing interest, unless it was because he had no way of learning about Italian arias except from books – is baseless. In Leipzig in the 1730s Mizler was pointing out that only generalities could be uttered on key characteristics: majors were cheerful, sharp and jolly, minors were demure, pleasant and sad ('munter, scharff und lustig . . .

sittsam, angenehm und traurig': 1736 pp33–4). 'One should go no farther', he said: any key can be sad or jolly, depending on the skill of the composer. Mattheson's volubility and didacticism – qualities which in his case rarely betray more than a looking-in from the outside on the mysteries of good composition – can be too easily seized upon by pedants of any period.*

Numerology

In the search for layers of significance in the complex music of J. S. Bach, a further area has opened up over the last half-century: number-counting with a view to discovering number symbolisms. Like the other areas of study described in this chapter, this resembles an ever-widening arc radiating from the pinpoint of a hint originating in the Bach period. In this instance, there are two such 'hints' found in the music itself. The first is not a matter of symbolism but of architecture: the number of bars in (e.g.) the C minor Prelude BWV 546 suggests clear proportions (see Vol. I p148):

24 - 24 - 48 - 24 - 24 bars

or, put another way (as in Meyer 1979 p59):

A (4 bars) + B (8) + C (12)
D (24)
A (4) + (17) + (8) + D (7) + C (12)
D (23)
A (4) + B (8) + C (12)
where A:B:C = 1:2:3
and where all D sections together = $A + B + C$ sections together†

Few pieces are quite so symmetrical as this; but the underlying principle is neither rare nor implausible. The second 'hint' is more a matter of symbolism: the number of movements, bars, entries, parts, notes in a theme, notes in an interval, repetitions of a word, or notes in the continuo allude to something outside the music, such as some particular word. Such numbers can be allegorical: eleven entries in a chorus concerned with faithful disciples, three themes in a movement 'dedicated' to the Trinity. They can also be semantic: seven 'stands for' the Creation, twelve for the Church. Numbers can also be cabbalistic: A = 1, B = 2 etc., so that B + A + C + H = 14 and J + S + B + A + C + H = 41. Numerical symmetry may itself be seen as symbolic of 'the life of the church and of the Christian' (Stiller 1970 p210), and it is clear that there were traditions in Lutheran theology for number-counting on various levels (e.g in the Olearius Bible commentary owned by J. S. Bach), as indeed numbers are obviously significant in many Bible stories. While the pursuit of such ideas reaches its highest flights in the case of Bach's vocal music, both organ chorales and free pieces sometimes offer suitable material for such interpretations, particularly those in *Clavierübung III* and the *Art of Fugue*. Like other arcane approaches, it has a seductive pseudo-scientificism to it.

The types of number allusion (allegorical, semantic and cabbalistic) offer results

---

* Burney's poor opinion of Mattheson both as theorist and as composer (see *An Account of the Musical Performances . . . in Commemoration of Handel*, London 1785, pp*6–*7) is illustrated in part by the report that Mattheson arranged the notes in one of his own pieces to portray the rainbow. This must have been a late flowering of such eye-music as cross motifs, ever an interest of minor talents.
† For Meyer, bars 70–8 = A_2 and bars 78–85 = B.

that are variously uncertain. Thus allegory is the simplest, for example in the Ten Commandments settings:

> *a* ten *diatonic* entries in BWV 635 (see Vol. II p84)
> *b* 2 × 10 bars in BWV 635 (i.e. twice as long as it should be – but the cantus firmus is also in double-length notes)
> *c* ten sections in BWV 678 (see Vol. II p202)
> *d* ten phrases in the cantus firmus of BWV 678
> *e* ten fugal entries in BWV 679
> *f* theme encompassing ten semitones in BWV 679

But here too there are differing degrees of plausibility. Thus *a* is specious, *d* is not strictly correct, *a*, *c* and *f* are barely audible, *b* is special pleading, and so on. However, it must be acknowledged that 'inaudibility' is not a reason to think a composer did not have a certain detail in mind: the three flats of the E flat Prelude and Fugue BWV 552 are strictly inaudible and exist only on paper, but they can be conjectured as part of the symbolism just as well as can the three themes or three sections or $3 \times 3 \times 3$ movements in *Clavierübung III* as a whole. Notation is, in its own way, as perceptual as what it notates.

Yet it is only right to recognize that some number allegories are more likely to be valid than others. For example, while the three-in-one nature of the Trinity can be unambiguously alluded to by a fugue in three sections (see above, p74), difficulties arise when the allusion is followed through on a more abstruse level. Thus the equal status of the three Persons as described in the Athanasian Creed has been taken to be expressed in, or to be the cause of (it is unclear which), the numbers of bars in relation to the numbers of contrapuntal parts in the E flat Fugue (U. Siegele *MuK* 51 (1981) p8):

first fugue	36 bars (9×4),	5 parts
second fugue	45 bars (9×5),	4 parts
third fugue	36 bars (9×4),	5 parts

Further observations on the equality in status and time of the three Persons can be made as one ponders the 'unity of the main theme and the trinity of its forms' in this fugue. But if any such approach is to offer more than a sterile speculation, it has to be shown that any practical musician would regard the number of bars as being of the same order of musical significance as the number of parts in any given composition, that bar-numbers have any significance other than notational, and (if they do) that the symmetry in BWV 522.ii is more 'symbolic' than that of BWV 546.ii as described above.

It seems to be no problem for those writers today who enthusiastically count bars that what they seem to be demonstrating implies two undemonstrable hypotheses about the way J. S. Bach composed: that in the act of composing he was governed by the need to calculate bars from the point of view not of musical phraseology but of extra-musical allegory, and that he was undeterred by the fact that what he was doing remained obscure, unexplained and (even to the buyer of a published work) totally unexplicit. Although such hypotheses cannot be proved or disproved, it is to be recognized that lurking behind them is a form of biographical speculation different only in kind, not in principle, from the speculations about composers' lives and beliefs found in countless popular biographies.

The 'semantic' numbers, being less concrete, are even more difficult to invoke in the organ music of J. S. Bach, though from Werckmeister it is clear that a practising organist and expert would see the lower numbers as emblems or tokens of platonic and Christian truths: the three of the Trinity, intervallic ratios and the harmony of the spheres (1:2, 2:3, 3:4), the 'resting number' 7 (days of creation). For some musicians today more to the point are the 'cabbalistic' numbers, especially for works that are puzzling in various other respects, such as the chorale BWV 668 (see Vol. II p172).* While the 14 of B + A + C + H has sent searchers looking ever since Smend publicized the idea in *J. S. Bach: Kirchenkantaten* I–VI (Berlin 1947–9), only indirect evidence has been found to support such activities, quite apart from confusion over what exactly ought to be counted (is a tied note counted as one or two, etc?). If J. S. Bach was indeed signalling the number 14 in the 'deathbed chorale', he will have been engaged in an occupation of which we have no confirmed report and one which would very likely never have been suspected if the true history of this piece were known.

The indirect evidence, however, is certainly suggestive, and demonstrating that cabbalistic activities were in principle foreign and inimical to strict Lutheran traditions (as in U. Meyer *MuK* 51 (1981) 15–19) no more proves that J. S. Bach never indulged in such things than conjectural examples prove that he did. But it is important to recognize the different kinds of claim in numerological interpretations. Thus it is beyond question that in the *Canonic Variations* (manuscript version, BWV 769a) Vars. I, II and V add up to the same number of bars as the variations they frame (83 bars). But what does this suggest about the different order of movements as published? – that the engraver got it wrong, that the composer had carefully calculated a symmetry he was willing to forgo, that other numerical significances are operating, etc? Cabbalistics are yet more uncertain. In this example, what is the significance of the number 83? – that it spells ANNA MAGDALENA, and if so why, and in any case why *twice* 83? Demonstrating such numbers says nothing certain about the intentions of a composer or even a theorist. For example, Kuhnau left a cabbalistic riddle in the preface to the 'Biblical Sonatas' (Leipzig 1700) in which the letters of a certain composer's name are expressed in what he calls algebraic form (A = 1, B = 2 etc); yet this has nothing to do with the sonatas themselves. Wide though his examination of musical grammar, aesthetics and rhetoric is in this preface, he does not link letter codes with the number of notes or bars of music.

Much the same point can be made about the numerology of Werckmeister or, at the other end of the Bach period, the mathematical calculations (logarithms) in the organ treatises of G. A. Sorge, another member of Mizler's society: neither need have any implications that pertain to music itself. Nevertheless, fancied connections between particular number theories and particualr pieces of music are often made today. One such example is the recently claimed connection between a posthumous treatise of Werckmeister (*Paradoxal-Discourse*, 1707) and the Passacaglia BWV 582 (Kee 1982), according to which the clearly felt but elusive architecture of that unique work depends on or is paralleled by – it is unclear which – certain elements in that treatise, as follows:

* Meyer (1979 p62) reports on one attempt to apply psalm numbers to both versions of BWV 668: the incomplete BWV 668 has 374 notes (= 17 × 22, the 'crucifixion psalm'); the complete BWV 668a has 453 (= 3 × 151). No doubt someone removed the continuation-sheet of BWV 668 to make this possible?

The Passacaglia 'is based on' the Lord's Prayer ('Vater unser') as treated in Werckmeister's book. The two themes themselves begin in a similar way, and the Passacaglia's variations can be interpreted as expressing the sentiments* of the prayer, clause by clause.

The Passacaglia 'is based on' the simple numbers (*Radical-Zahlen*) 1, 2, 3, 4, 5, 6, 8, as described by Werckmeister. These are the numbers corresponding to the overtone series C c g c' e' c'' and are to be seen as symbols of the Christian tenets outlined in the Lord's Prayer (1 = God the Father and Creator, 2 = the Son in harmony but separate, 3 = the Holy Ghost, 4 = Heaven, 5 = mankind, 6 = the world etc from which mankind is saved, 8 = complete harmony). Each group of variations in the Passacaglia except the first begins with successive notes of this series (c for that beginning in b32, g in b48 etc), and each group can be interpreted as conveying the symbolic nature of the figures as described by Werckmeister.

The strategy as well as the tactics of the Passacaglia spring from a response* to Werckmeister's treatise. Thus the key is C (minor for 'sad'), the theme begins with the second and third harmonic and ends with the first, there are 21 statements (the sum of 1 to 6, the symbolic 3 × 7), there are seven groups of variations corresponding to the seven simple numbers, the fugue follows as doxology to the Lord's Prayer ('for ever and ever, Amen'), and its subject, countersubjects and entries (*repetitiones*) have specific rhetorical functions.*

The main problem with such an interpretation, as it was with the programmatic interpretations of yesterday, is that it is the result of a private revelation convincing only to those in a similar state of grace. Now it is quite clear that J. S. Bach was aware of at least some of Werckmeister's writings (see chapter 17 below), and that the period immediately after 1707 was not only one in which he and Werckmeister's pupil J. G. Walther (see his *Praecepta* of 1708) may have shared interests in aspects of musical theory but also one in which the Passacaglia may well have been composed. Moreover, Werckmeister must have been voicing many sentiments common to believers, and one can often find echoes of his remarks elsewhere – for example, compare a remark in his preface to the same treatise with the couplet on the title-page of the *Orgelbüchlein*:

> es werden nur diese unsere guthertzige Gedancken (wie dann ein jeder Christ schuldig ist) dem Nechsten in gebührendem *Respect* vorgestellet, und wäre zu wünschen, dass ein jeder Mensch seinem Neben-Christen mit seinem *Talento* dienete . . . (1707 p7)

> these kind thoughts of mine are simply offered – as each Christian is bound to do – to my neighbour in proper respect, and it is to be wished that every man might serve his fellow Christian with talent . . .

> Dem Höchsten Gott allein zu Ehren / Dem Nechsten, draus sich zu belehren.

> For the highest God alone Honour,
> For my neighbour, that he may instruct himself from it.

But in the absence of more copious documentation concerned with the composer's development, parallels can be pressed home only as matters of conjecture, particularly when (as here) in the piece of music as now known there is no explicit

---

* These are not Kee's words, and it is not clear what precisely is being claimed. It is also characteristic of Werckmeister that he too ultimately leaves vague what point it is he is making. What does 'is' mean in the statement '4 is an angelic or divine number' ('die Zahl 4 ist eine Engel oder Göttliche Zahl': p119)? Is he saying that the Lord's Prayer originated as an *exemplum* of number symbolism?

reference whatsoever to a symbolism that was very explicitly outlined in the supposed theoretical source. Are we to think that J. S. Bach had the *Paradoxal-Discourse* before him, or that, being intimately familiar with such symbolisms already, he was demonstrating ideas then current? Why should he need Werckmeister for such ideas, when he certainly needed no theorist to demonstrate the potential of composition by *figurae*? Even if he knew and took an interest in such symbolism, is not our tracing specific details of the kind merely a confusion of thought with action, equalizing *teorica* and *prattica* in a manner quite inappropriate to the Lutheran organist?

Symbol-tracing seems also to have to be selective. Because both the Lord's Prayer (a kind of outline) and the basic numbers (1 to 6) are so elementary, parallels with either are infinitely extensible. Can the numbers not be applied to (e.g.) the harmonies of the C major Prelude, *The 48* Bk 1, or to the figural repertory of the *Orgelbüchlein*? Do the numbers not have other symbolisms that need to be 'explained'? – where, for example, in the Passacaglia is the 'virginity' of the number 7, as listed by Werckmeister (p95)? Or did the composer have to ignore 7 (though of course not sevenths) because astronomers gave reasons why it will 'not harmonize with other harmonic numbers' (*ibid*)? Even in this one treatise, Werckmeister indicates other symbols or analogies (it is not clear which), such as that between incorrect temperament and false Christianity: could this idea too not be found to be an organizing principle of the Passacaglia, a work which passes from unisons in the minor to a massive seven-part major chord?

Symbol-tracing leads often – perhaps always, when important music is considered – to specious reasoning. For example, the resemblances between the Passacaglia theme and the first line (only!) of 'Vater unser' are by no means incontrovertible. Not only are the intervals of both so elemental as to produce 'similarities' that need have no significance whatever, but the continuation of both would then have to be irrelevant – whereas the second half of the Passacaglia theme has as interesting an 'origin' as the first, insofar as it is almost as close to one theme of Raison as the first half is to another (see Vol. I p256). In any case, C minor would be a strange key for 'Vater unser', a chorale associated with D minor or the dorian mode as Walther calls it (1708, 1955 edn p171).* Similarly specious is the identifying of Werckmeister's overtone-notes as those first heard at the beginning of each group of variations; not only would this be a circular argument, but in the case of (e.g.) the fifth group of variations (Var. 13 beginning at b104), it is not e♭' (the 'fifth note') but c' that begins it – the slur makes this quite clear (see below, Ex. 97). Then, although it may be useful to show that the Fugue is a particularly fitting close to the Passacaglia because its theme makes repeated entries, it is a major leap to suppose that J. S. Bach had to learn this from the rhetoricians' notion of *anaphora*.† For one thing, since Walther himself illustrates the figure *anaphora* by referring to chaconnes (1732 p34), it seems arbitrary to invoke it for a fugue that follows a passacaglia. Nor is much purpose served by quoting a sixteenth-century theorist on the worthiness of fugue (Kee 1982 p241) when *fuga* then meant something rather different, i.e. motivic imitation of the kind found frequently in the Passacaglia, but not in its Fugue.

* The well-known C minor settings by Scheidemann in Bärenreiter edn 5481 were transposed from D minor for that edition.

† *Anaphora*: 'the repetition of the same word or phrase in several successive clauses' (*OED*).

Symbol-tracing can lead to far-fetched pictorialism. For example, to see the opening unison statement of the theme of the Passacaglia as alluding to the personified 'Unity' and 'Origin' of the Lord's Prayer ('Our Father . . .') is unnecessary in view of the old convention, already made clear by J. S. Bach in the B flat Capriccio BWV 992, of first playing over a chaconne bass *tasto solo* perhaps even when figured. Indeed, the true achievement of the Passacaglia, viz. a work of stature based on certain conventions but surpassing them all in its sustained and cumulative sense of organization, could be obscured by any attempt to find the inspiration behind it outside music itself and in treatises concerned with (e.g.) number theology. Both chaconne and fugue forms originated as small-scale attempts to create continuity, and obviously J. S. Bach could have seen both of them as a challenge to his ability to create sustained music. Much the same could be said of his treatment of other forms – binary suite movements, *ABA* arias, concerto or cantata ritornello form, etc.

Dealing at length with one particular hypothesis is necessary first because the major works of J. S. Bach do appear so isolated and the mystery of their power so unfathomable that any way of looking at them deserves attention, and secondly because the seeking of significances in what are called symbolisms (and drawing on contemporary theorists to illustrate the points made) has become fashionable and is likely to remain so for some time. Even between the writing and printing of these words other essays will appear, for the field is vast and the seeds of conjecture prolific. But those wishing to believe that the approach leads to useful and verifiable conclusions should be aware of two duties falling on them: that they have the onus of proof, and that they are obliged to make clear what precisely they are claiming for a theory or a theory book and its supposed impact on the composer.

---

10. *Figurenlehre* as a Background to Composition

The obvious inferiority of such keyboard music as Kuhnau's, Zachow's and J. G. Walther's to that of J. S. Bach has naturally had the effect of deflecting attention away from the Thuringian–Saxon styles to the more imaginative and whimsical composers of Lüneburg, Lübeck and Hamburg. Although the northern composers did influence J. S. Bach at times, their obvious superiority as composers seems to have persuaded commentators and players that those more local to him, more a part of his routine context, are less important rather than more. While the present chapter aims at redressing the balance in this respect, it makes no contrary claim that J. S. Bach was 'most influenced' by the local styles of J. C. Bach, Pachelbel and Walther; rather, it is an attempt to reconstruct some salient features of their musical thinking, regardless of how 'influential' it may have been.

To define influences accurately requires great care. Clearly the shape or 'formal principles' behind (say) the chorale BWV 735 are like those of chorales by other composers, such as J. G. Walther's 'Es spricht der Unweisen Mund wohl'; the grander scale of BWV 735/735a may reflect several other influences, though there is a vigour and drama (in the closing *point d'orgue* of the version BWV 735) that are unmatched in *any* settings other than the expansive but disjunct northern chorale-fantasia. At certain moments, however, Walther and Bach treat the situation very similarly, e.g. at the final notes of each pedal cantus-firmus phrase: Ex. 24. The true significance of this is not merely that the phrase-ends are similar but that for both composers the musical interest of the harmonization above pedal c.f. lies in its figuration.

Ex. 24   J. G. Walther, 'Es spricht der Unweisen Mund wohl' (MSS Kö 15839, Den Haag 4 G 14)

BWV 735a (MSS include Kö 15839 and Den Haag 4 G 14)

That Walther's harmony is rarely if ever so well reasoned should not disguise the identity of approach between the two composers. He too worked in several styles which are now spoken of as if they had been J. S. Bach's special province, such as the *stile antico*, several salient characteristics of which were present in (e.g.) 'Es wol uns Gott gnädig sein' or 'Herr Gott, dich loben wir', presumably long before *Clavierübung III*. But their particular use of *figurae* or note-patterns may suggest ways in which J. S. Bach developed. In Ex. 25, (i) is by Walther, (ii) by the young

Ex. 25   **(i)** Walther, 'Lobt Gott, ihr Christen' (*Vers* 5)

(ii) BWV 735a

J. S. Bach, whereas the opposite might have been expected. It is particularly in the figural inventiveness of the *Orgelbüchlein* that its composer went beyond Walther, just as into the 1740s he kept an interest in devising his own original *figurae* (see Vol. I pp152–3). Both at Weimar and Leipzig, such note-patterns played an important part. Similarities between the two composers' *figurae* do not imply chronology: whether Ex. 26 (i) or 26 (ii) came first, or whether either composer

Ex. 26   **(i)** J. G. Walther, 'Wir Christenleut' (*Vers 2*)

(ii) BWV 535

knew the other piece, is not known. Moreover, so far neither composition shows any particular 'organic growth' or 'hidden energy'; BWV 535 could proceed as statically as the Walther piece, and only from bar 3 does it 'grow'. It would seem strange that Walther should use such motifs more 'statically' than Bach if he already knew BWV 535; but such could after all be the sign of inferior ability. Similarly – since all three pieces were copied into P 802 – the *bicinium* characteristics in Walther's 'Schmücke dich' *Vers* 3 might have 'followed' those in BWV 767.ii and 768.ii just as easily as the other way round.

While composition through note-patterns arising from a 'doctrine of figures' (*Figurenlehre*) has too long a history in both Italian vocal music and German instrumental music to be easily summarized, it can be said that for J. G. Walther, in his *Praecepta* of 1708, such figures could be quickly listed and demonstrated as a means a composer has of 'filling in' long notes or of setting a text appropriately. Such advice would be useful to the young Prince Johann Ernst learning with such a book. From other sources, notably Bernhard, Printz and Walther's *Lexicon*, the names of some such *figurae* can be found, though neither theorists' terminology nor treatment should be valued at more than their worth. More to the point is the coinciding of time and place: at Weimar in 1708 Walther prepares a music textbook three or four months before his relation J. S. Bach comes to take office as organist to the court to which the young prince belongs. Whatever one imagines the musical relationship of Walther and Bach to have been in the ensuing years, it can be reasonably guessed that both composers aimed at creating music from basic note-patterns of this kind. This would be so even though they were to develop along different formal paths: Walther remaining with sectional praeludia, Bach moving on to the ritornello shapes of the new generation of Italian composers.

It is likely that in 1713 both Walther and Bach presented the fruits of what might be called figural activity: the first in a publication of two sets of chorale-variations (the print now lost but reported on by Mattheson – see Seiffert 1906 p. xxiii), the second in the initial phase of the *Orgelbüchlein*. Whether there was any connection between the two events cannot be known. While Walther's variations are generally similar to those of Froberger, Pachelbel, Buttstedt, Böhm and others, it is the use of certain *figurae* that throws light on the two Weimar composers: both develop a certain pattern in each movement.* For Walther, the *figurae* remain naïve and decorative: Ex. 27. Even in those settings in which the dactyl or *suspirans* remains conventional, Bach gives his harmony a certain urgency: Ex. 28. 'Urgency' is dif-

Ex. 27   J. G. Walther, 'Meinen Jesum lass ich nicht'
          (i) *Vers* 2

          (ii) *Vers* 3

Ex. 28   BWV 627 (*Vers* 1)
          b1

          BWV 627 (*Vers* 3)
          b40

* According to Mattheson (1740 p389), the variations of Walther's two chorales were called 'preludes' ('Vorspielen'), which would agree with the title-page of Walther's 1738 publication of variations on 'Allein Gott' (*VIII Vorspielen*). Does this suggest that at least in certain parish churches, so-called partitas were series of settings to be used as the player or pastor wished: any of the variations serving as prelude and chosen according to taste or the sense of the text (which could vary), or in a regular order (Var. 1, then Var. 2 the next time the hymn was sung, etc)? If so was this usage characteristic of devotional Jesus-hymns in smaller parish churches, as distinct from practices in major churches, court chapels etc?

ficult to define but can be seen as coming from an avoidance of the obvious or, equally, from using in a new way conventions known to every composer of chorale-variations. The best example of the latter can be seen in his treatment of the chromatic fourth: common property amongst composers of partitas and double fugues.* Walther's Var. 6 of 'Jesu, meine Freude' is well managed (Ex. 29), but it

Ex. 29   J. G. Walther, 'Jesu, meine Freude' Var. 6

cannot be doubted that the chromatic fourth in BWV 767 Partita VIII and in 'Das alte Jahr' BWV 614 is of a different order. Not only is it more ingeniously exploited, but in BWV 614 it surprises both whenever it appears (stretto in inner voices) and whenever it does not (less often in pedal than is possible). Yet 'avoiding the obvious' can itself be difficult to define. There is a lot of unobvious harmony in BWV 767.viii, to such an extent that few progressions are without surprise; BWV 614 is on a higher plane, perhaps because the chromaticism is not constant, less full yet always producing new progressions which the ear has time to grasp. It is less assertive than BWV 767. Similarly, urgency in harmony is often provided by the movement and inner logic of one of the simplest effects: the perfect cadence, as in the first phrase of BWV 627 *Vers* 3 above. There is no urgency whatever in Walther's perfect cadence in Ex. 27 (i): on the contrary, the repetitive *figura* helps to trivialize the progression even further.

Similarities of background and intent between J. G. Walther and J. S. Bach have often led to the finding of direct similarities between their music (e.g. Senn 1964), but how reciprocal this was, or who had priority in a given technique, can only be guessed. Walther's *stile antico* settings are a case in point: do they suggest that it was a style that already occupied both Weimar organists in the 1710s? In the case of the two late published sets of variations on Advent/Christmas hymns – Walther's *Vorspiele . . . Wie soll ich dich empfangen* (Augsburg *c*1745) and Bach's *Vom Himmel hoch* (Leipzig 1747/8) – is there any significance in the fact that Walther too closes his set with a *point d'orgue* after attempting to combine chorale lines?

Other formal similarities between works may not be justified by the sources: thus the plan of Walther's 'Allein zu dir' may look like a simplified version of the way J. S. Bach extemporized, according to Forkel:

1 hymn harmonized with moving parts and interline interludes
2 two-part *variatio*
3 three-part *variatio*
4 four-part fugue in *stile antico*

---

* See Vol. I pp5–6. That the chromatic fourth was natural to fugues with more than one subject is already suggested by its appearance in the *fuga quadruplici* in Part I of Scheidt's *Tabulatura nova* (Hamburg 1624). Like other themes found in complex fugues of that and earlier periods – e.g. the hexachord – the chromatic fourth could serve as main theme or gradually emerge as countersubject to another; but it seems to have kept this versatility longer than the hexachord.

but the sources do not justify this plan (Seiffert 1906 p. xxix), nor is Forkel to be trusted too literally (see above, p51). But which came first, Ex. 30 (i) or 30 (ii)?

Ex. 30   **(i)** J. G. Walther, 'Allein Gott' (*Vers* 4)

(ii) BWV 656

Walther's was published in 1738 (*Harmonisches Denck- und Danckmahl*, Augsburg), but the several verses of the partita appeared in the Walther manuscripts presumably at much the same period when BWV 656a (the so-called Weimar version of BWV 656) appeared in the same sources. There is a similar closeness between themes derived from the melody 'Herr Jesu Christ, dich zu uns wend' – compare the trio BWV 655a (known to Walther) with Ex. 31, or Ex. 32 with BWV 632 (see Vol. II p141). Such thematic similarities are far less important than the probability that the two composers were thinking on the same lines, both working with *figurae*, attempting to create music from conventional patterns. Similarities of this

Ex. 31   J. G. Walther, 'Herr Jesu Christ, dich zu uns wend', *Variatio* 5

Ex. 32   Walther, 'Herr Jesu Christ', *Variatio* 6

kind bring out differences: in BWV 656 the fugal answer is coloured, and from b2 onwards the whole verse is characterized by a perpetual quaver motion that constantly adapts patterns springing from the motif labelled *x* in Ex. 30 (ii), whereas Walther's quaver motifs are neither so constant nor so adaptable (Ex. 33). Given

Ex. 33

Bach's facility at such adaptation, it looks as if his idea in each *versus* of BWV 656 is to play with such patterns as Walther might have used but to do so more pliably and with a better sense of interesting diatonic harmony.*

That could well be the conclusion drawn from any comparison between Walther's nearly three hundred chorale-settings and those of Bach as far as their bar-by-bar composition is concerned. Although he seems to have made no collection using either the type of chorale found in the *Orgelbüchlein* or its seasonal plan, Walther certainly knew the interlude-less harmonization of a melody, based on one or two motifs.† Similarly, though many are constructed of an 'objective' counterpoint, certain chorales aim at producing from the *figurae* particular moods polarized at the happy/sad extremes. Thus Walther's setting of the same hymn as in BWV 609 – Ex. 34 – can be seen to follow the same shape and to achieve the same

Ex. 34   J. G. Walther, 'Lobt Gott, ihr Christen'

positive mood, here conveyed by the pattern *x*, which is its composer's own invention and is not to be found in the textbooks. In fact, the difference in achievement between the two composers makes it undemonstrable who composed which chorale first. The same goes for such techniques as canon and paraphrase. Some of Walther's Christmas canons seem merely to acknowledge an interest in them which he shared with J. S. Bach, but his double canons on 'Puer natus in Bethlehem',

---

* Which means, in practice, with more use of dissonance arising from accented passing-notes.
† His writing-in of rests at the end of lines (points at which J. S. Bach writes a long note) might sometimes disguise the fact that certain chorales are without interludes, in the *Orgelbüchlein* manner. The fact that (as in Ex. 34) Walther did not use end-of-line ⌒ signs in places where they appear in the *Orgelbüchlein* may be further evidence that J. S. Bach intended no actual pause there.

though less sustained than in Bach's 'In dulci jubilo' BWV 608 (where drone harmony makes a double canon easier), suggest a particular interest in weaving fine lines around the canonic melodies: Ex. 35. Whether Walther's settings of

Ex. 35   J. G. Walther, 'Puer natus in Bethlehem' (*Vers 2*)

'Erschienen ist der herrliche Tag' are only partially canonic because BWV 629 had already shown the ideal way, or whether BWV 629 was written in response to Walther's attempts, is not known. Similar points may be made about paraphrases. Running semiquaver colorations as in Vars. 3 and 4 of the partitas BWV 766, 767, 768 can easily be found in Walther (and elsewhere), and both composers began to paraphrase in such a way that the melody notes did not always fall on main beats. This is rarer in Walther than in Bach, and it could well have been the *bicinium* that evoked Walther's most imaginative paraphrases; whether this is true or not, both may have worked on such things during Bach's early Weimar years, the younger never resting with an easily achieved effect or relaxing the creative effort.

The composers who were older contemporaries of·the Pachelbel–Zachow genera-tion were still much in the tradition of composing with superficial note-pattern decorations; and although (as Froberger shows) conventional figuration can achieve originality in the hands of a master, the *figurae* of Walther and Bach take the interest in note-patterns a stage further. Superficial decoration becomes more expressive. Zachow's chromatic variation on 'Jesu, meine Freude' (Ex. 36) applies

Ex. 36   Zachow, 'Jesu, meine Freude'

the chromatic fourth more than Walther's quoted above (Ex. 29), and in such cases 'more' seems to mean 'less discriminately' and therefore less expressively: formula rather than feeling. Zachow and Pachelbel reserve *figurae* for variations of this kind, and the Zachow chorale-preludes known from Walther's copies are not so clearly based on carefully worked-out *figurae*.

When a setting is given a strong character by a composer who exploits the note-patterns imaginatively, the music begins to resemble the Bach idiom more closely:

Ex. 37   G. F. Kauffmann, 'Allein zu dir, Herr Jesu Christ' (Leipzig 1733)

Ex. 37. But single-mindedness in the pursuit of a *figura* is characteristic of neither Walther nor J. S. Bach, and of Bach less than Walther (see Vol. II for comments on BWV 693 and 721). Exploiting *figurae* imaginatively is not a matter of endless sequential repetition of the kind that produces the picture of the trembling Israelites in Kuhnau's first sonata (Ex. 38). Such treatment would be difficult to ascribe to J. S.

Ex. 38   Kuhnau, *Musikalische Vorstellung* (Leipzig 1700)

Bach after the Weimar period (cf. BWV 721): in addition to its single-mindedness, its expressive quality has a programmatic element in which the listener becomes no more than an interested spectator. A point is reached in music at which the listener merely observes the greater or lesser skill of the composer and stands back from it; this must often be the case with various composers' clever use of the chromatic fourth. It may well be that the *Orgelbüchlein* on the whole consciously avoids or underplays the chromatic fourth. Considering the number of opportunities for melancholy chorale-settings in that collection, and the ease with which composers used chromatic fourths in penitential settings (e.g. Telemann's 'Ach Gott vom Himmel sieh' darein', *c*1740), they remain curiously unprominent in the album.*

   It is equally difficult to involve the listener in joyful music. The cheerfulness of Telemann's 'Nun danket alle Gott' (*c*1740) may be clear enough, like comparable *bicinia* by Kauffmann: Ex. 39. But in any music that applies such simple and excessively jolly motifs there is an unelevated quality acceptable only insofar as it has melodic interest. Simple *bicinia* in which the right hand has the figuration and

* A similar point could be made about the chromatic fourth in the *Art of Fugue*, considering the key (D minor) and the convenience of the *figura* as a countersubject. It looks as if the composer avoided the easier conventions.

Ex. 39   Telemann, 'Nun danket alle Gott'

the left the cantus firmus became popular in the middle of the eighteenth century (J. L. Krebs, *Clavierübung*, *c*1745), perhaps because it was thought that melodiousness could be gained from the free and wide tessitura possible in the right hand: Ex. 40. The effectiveness of such treatment is a late salute to *Figurenlehre*, but it is of a kind not found in J. S. Bach. Similarly, another Bach pupil, J. C. Kittel,

Ex. 40   Telemann, 'Herr Jesu Christ, dich zu uns wend"

published in his *Der angehende praktische Organist* (Erfurt 1803–8) a catalogue of harmonic and other treatments for chorales, chorale-preludes and free works using many of the *figurae* which he and other late pupils presumably found realized at their best in the *Orgelbüchlein*. It is certainly possible that its composer did use the *Orgelbüchlein* for purposes of teaching improvised and/or written harmony by at least the 1740s – when its sensitive treatment of chorales, originally inspired by conditions in Weimar and perhaps in Halle, was likely to appeal very widely, Kittel only occasionally achieves a four-part harmony that even approaches a comparable mastery, e.g. Ex. 41. While his limited skill is responsible for the scarcity of good examples, it is also true that the more formal or neutral elements in *Orgel-*

Ex. 41   J. C. Kittel, *Der angehende praktische Organist* II pp28, 95

büchlein settings – e.g. the pedal mostly entering at once beneath the melody, which then follows without breaks between the lines – were not followed by Kittel or pointed out as a good method. Perhaps those elements had not been impressed on him, and he saw such settings instead as offering examples of how to harmonize with *figurae*?

11. Italian Influences

Kuhnau, writing in the preface to *Frische Clavier Früchte* (Leipzig 1696), said that many who have once breathed the air of France or Italy will esteem local produce less and quite miss the fact that German fields also yield fruit unavailable elsewhere. Less fancifully, however, he remarks on his new pieces called *sonatas* –

> Womit ich will zu verstehen geben, dass ich auff allerhand *Inventiones* und Veränderungen bin bedacht gewesen, worinne sonsten die so genannten Suonaten vor den blossen *Parti*en einen Vorzug haben sollen. Denn, dass ich der artigen Veränderung des *Tact*es, und der hin und wieder abgewechselten *Affecten* geschweige, so wird man unterschiedene *formale Fugen* antreffen . . .

> by which I wish it to be understood that I have been intent on all kinds of inventions and varieties, in which, besides, the so-called sonatas are said to have an advantage over mere suites. For, without mentioning the agreeable variety of beat, and the affects changed here and there, one will come across various formal fugues . . .

That is to say, the sonata is composed with more freedom than the suite, more individually conceived, with a succession of different movements (various metres and tempos) and a consequent increase in variety of *affetto*. Such remarks, originating and published in Leipzig, are likely to have been much more characteristic of views surrounding the young Bach than what are vaguely called today 'French and Italian influences'.

To take one example: in overall shape and in many details, the D major Sonata BWV 963 is so close to (e.g.) the third of Kuhnau's *Frische Clavier Früchte* that the influence cannot be doubted.* Whoever the composer of BWV 963 was, he too had but two basic methods for sustaining a movement: the first was to write a fugue (which has its own way of sustaining musical logic),† the second to cast a non-fugal movement in a kind of chaconne-ritornello shape. In turn, this second would gradually produce the characteristics of a fully fledged ritornello movement: the returning theme, the returning episodes and the developed material that passes through keys with a more or less marked sense of involvement. Though no doubt primitively, the Sonata BWV 963 does suggest the ways a maturing composer could begin to conceive of true sustained form: the biggest problem in the early eighteenth century for the thinking composer, and one solved uniquely well in J. S. Bach's big organ preludes. That these were quite unlike anything before, during or after does not hide their origins as a gifted composer's response to 'the biggest problem in the early eighteenth century'. Precisely what the Italian influence of the better-known kind (the Vivaldi concerto) could add to the basic ideas underlying Kuhnau's *Früchte* and BWV 963 is difficult to say two and a half centuries later: it can only have been a matter of degree. With or without Vivaldi, would not the ritornello principles outlined in BWV 963 naturally be more fully developed fifteen or twenty years after Kuhnau's *Früchte*? Binary forms,‡ the *ABA* aria and the *recitativo secco* and *stromentato* all underwent similar refinement at the hands of J. S. Bach, even if (unlike Handel) he was slow to develop without the benefit of sojourns in Italy.

Unfortunately, because the dates of the organ and harpsichord works are so very uncertain, it is still quite out of the question to build a picture of J. S. Bach's maturing experience with ritornello form. One certain landmark is that by the end of 1716 the cantatas show that he had totally mastered and turned to his own use the ritornello forms, the *ABA* aria and the recitative.# Gestures towards the last two can be seen over the previous years. If the Sonata BWV 963 does belong – like the Corelli Fugue BWV 579, written by the same copyist in what is now P 804 – to the Arnstadt–Mühlhausen period, then one can imagine not a gradual move but a sudden lurch towards the cantata ritornello movements brought about by the influence of Vivaldi in the period around 1714. That Forkel saw this to be the case (see Vol. I p286, with respect to the concertos) is no evidence, but it is borne out by

---

* Spitta too (I pp239–41) saw the similarities between BWV 963 and Kuhnau, comparing the former with the latter's programmatic music ('Biblical Sonatas' or *Musicalische Vorstellung*, Leipzig 1700).

† Fugue for Kuhnau was like ground bass for Purcell: the set form made it possible – one may even believe it was the only way to make it possible – for the composer to keep up momentum and a feeling of shape.

‡ The conventions behind the widely received binary form of suite movements (a criticism of which is implied by Kuhnau's remarks above) also have degrees of sophistication, of course. Whoever the composer of the little D minor Prelude BWV 539.i was, he could not have made the piece (as it now stands) into a binary movement with two repeated sections because, although it has a theoretical binary shape (see Vol. I p98), it ignores two important conventions: the first half would be longer than the second, and the first half takes too long to settle in the dominant.

Such a cantata as BWV 161 gives the impression of providing a 'catalogue' of musical devices, forms, genres etc with great confidence and flair, its movements giving carefully planned *exempla* of what could be done.

considering first how older composers of the Kuhnau generation and secondly how contemporary composers not so affected by Vivaldi managed to sustain a movement beyond a few minutes long.

So far as extant works suggest, older central German composers such as Kuhnau, Zachow and Pachelbel were basically outside the traditions of northern praeludia and chorale-fantasias, which is ironic in that such music is wonderfully full of the very oratorical figures ('oratorische Figuren') mentioned elsewhere in the preface to Kuhnau's *Früchte*. One can imagine that J. S. Bach would gradually turn from these sonata-like praeludia, as the weight and sustained quality of his own pieces in this mould (such as BWV 549 or 532) developed into more massively constructed preludes and fugues. No doubt the great, unique ritornello movements like the C minor Prelude BWV 546.i could have been composed only by someone familiar with Italian concertos, but their 'weight and sustained quality' seem already to have been emerging in BWV 531 or even 551, which may owe as much to the approach outlined by Kuhnau as to the praeludia of Bruhns or Buxtehude.

Amongst contemporary composers, J. G. Walther is particularly important in view of his concerto-transcriptions – nearly eighty of them, according to his note in Mattheson's *Ehrenpforte* (1740). He even published a 'Concerto' for organ in 1741, with five movements one of which was cast in a lively *ABA* shape (with *B* derived from *A*) and labelled 'ritornello'. But quality aside, it is clear that Walther was taking as his model not Vivaldi but one of the older composers (Torelli?) familiar from his many transcriptions of their concertos: it is as if Vivaldi's Op III or the Brandenburg Concertos did not exist. Similarly, Walther's free preludes for organ make no attempt at any formal organization more advanced than, say, BWV 531. In short, although he picked up many an Italianate detail – turns of phrase, echo-like repeats down an octave, violin figuration and counterpoint – Walther's connection with the Italian concerto did not lead to even the palest imitation of (e.g.) BWV 546.i, as far as extant sources show.

J. S. Bach's experience of making organ transcriptions of Vivaldi's concertos affected his composition much more deeply and widely, certainly well beyond the organ music itself. It could well be that the impression the concertos made on him outside organ music is still not fully grasped today, despite the attempts made by Forkel to describe it (see Vol. I pp284–9) and the generalized comments in more recent studies. For example, although claims are made that the solo cadenza in the Fifth Brandenburg Concerto is unprecedented, there is already in the first movement of the transcribed Concerto in C BWV 594 a cadenza built on the same principles:

> it is a very long final solo episode (rather than a 'cadenza' in the classical sense)
> it begins and ends without any cadential break
> the style is measured not free
> a *perpetuum mobile* includes thematic interest
> there is a leaning towards pedal points in general

The very intensity of texture and harmonic drive in the Fifth Brandenburg is itself Vivaldian in origin.

Knowing a composer's music does not lead necessarily to being influenced by it. That is clear in the case of Bach's 'persistent' admiration for Froberger ('jederzeit', according to Adlung: *Dok* III p124),* whose identifiable influence on the young or the mature Bach is very inconspicuous. In the case of Italian influences in general, it is important to identify several very distinct musical styles, and the tracing of such lines as Palestrina/Fux, Frescobaldi/Froberger, Carissimi/Kerll, Froberger/ Buxtehude, Froberger/Strunck would produce a picture of the several contrapuntal idioms against which the young Bach was no doubt brought up. Handel too, according to Mainwaring (1760 p14), had been exposed to such styles early on in his life:

> [Zachow's] next care was to cultivate his imagination, and form his taste. He had a large collection of Italian as well as German music; he shewed him the different styles of different nations ... and ... frequently gave him subjects to work, and made him copy, and play, and compose in his stead.

But the status of both Zachow and the Liebfrauenkirche, Halle was well above any with which J. S. Bach came into contact before his move to Lüneburg, where the repertory of vocal music laid considerable emphasis on Italian composers, not least Monteverdi and Carissimi (Blume 1968); Mainwaring himself says that Handel had 'more exercise, and more experience than usually falls to the share of any learner at his years' (1760 pp14-15). In any case, newer Italian styles seem to have been circulated without hindrance: already in 1700 Böhm was writing miniature arias based on the continuo-ritornello idea familiar in the *bicinia* of J. S. Bach's Chorale-variations (see *DTÖ* LXV p44 etc). But any study of Italian influences on J. S. Bach or any other composer cannot be thought of simply in terms of 'form' or even of melody. It can be guessed that a composer is at least as likely to be taken with inventive harmonies, however fleeting – for example, the sequences over the *point d'orgue* in Vivaldi's concerto transcribed for organ (BWV 596.iii bb61-6), or the bleak chromatic lines over the *point d'orgue* that closes the slow movement of the Vivaldi Concerto in C BWV 594. The *point d'orgue* harmonies, simple but striking, at the close of the Canzona BWV 588 bb162-5 show that their composer had an ear for such nuances.

From the point of view of keyboard music there seems little point in looking back beyond Froberger, though his counterpoint too seems to have been influenced by particular composers (e.g. Gentili's *Solfeggiamenti et Ricercaria*, Rome 1642). Buttstedt's canzonas with variant fugues or Strunck's Viennese ricercars can be related to Froberger, quite apart from Germany's widespread and vivid interest in Italian music (traced in Riedel 1968). It can only be conjecture – and a doubtful conjecture – to view Buxtehude's G minor Praeludium BUXWV 150 as a specific Frescobaldi imitation (Riedel 1960 p204). More puzzling are the Corelli-like moments in Buxtehude, such as the running bass in the interlude of the G minor Praeludium BUXWV 149. Whether or not they can actually be credited to Corelli

---

* Perhaps J. S. Bach owned a copy of Froberger's *Toccate* of 1693 (Kobayashi 1973 pp69-70, 76). There are striking similarities among the 1754 *Obituary*'s list of the composers copied by the young Bach from his brother's forbidden notebook (Froberger, Kerll, Pachelbel – *Dok* III p81), those admired by Quantz in 1752 (Froberger, Pachelbel, Reincken, Buxtehude, Bruhns 'and some others' – *Dok* III p20), the list of composers whom C. P. E. Bach told Forkel his father admired (Froberger, Kerll, Pachelbel, Frescobaldi, J. K. F. Fischer, Strunck, Buxtehude, Reincken, Bruhns, Böhm and 'some old French masters' – *Dok* III p288), those included in Handel's notebook of 1698 (Froberger, Kerll, Strunck, Zachow, Krieger, Ebner and Alberti (J. F. Alberti?) – W. Coxe, *Anecdotes of George Frederick Handel and John Christopher Smith*, London 1799, p6) and those included in one fascicle of the manuscript Lpz MB 51 (Buxtehude, Pachelbel, Kerll, Merula, Frescobaldi, Froberger and others – *DTÖ* IV.i (1897) p121).

himself, such lines must certainly have been very much up to date and, judging by Kuhnau's attempt at the same thing in *Frische Clavier Früchte*, not easy to reproduce. J. S. Bach too seems to have adopted Italianate figures soon after he learnt them, for example in the cantatas composed in or soon after 1714 (Dürr 1951 p168). Specific Italian counterpoint remained an active force in the composer's vocabulary, as is often strikingly clear in the Six Sonatas. For example, the finale of the C major Sonata BWV 529 has characteristics of both melody and part-writing very close to the fugue of Corelli's Violin Sonata Op V no. 3, a work probably by then half a century old.*

Keeping up to date may not have been particularly important to organists in the early eighteenth century. Walther's and J. S. Bach's activity in transcribing new concertos seems to have arisen out of the young Prince's interests at Weimar (Schulze 1972), but generally it was older Italian music that was more eagerly collected and copied, e.g. Frescobaldi by Buxtehude, or Battiferri by Zelenka and W. F. Bach (Riedel 1960 pp55–6). Of course, the skill of the old Italian contrapuntists was a prime influence on composers exploiting the *stile antico* in the 1730s, but an equally strong influence on the younger J. S. Bach was probably exerted by the motivic *tour de force* of a more 'popular' piece in Frescobaldi's *Fiori musicali* (1635), the Bergamasca. As a more modern counterpoint playing ingeniously with certain melodic *figurae*, it must have sparked off in the practical organist of Weimar a lively interest in motifs and their versatility.

Another characteristic Italian counterpoint is that of the seventeenth-century string fugue, not only the Corelli movement taken into BWV 579 but the unknown Legrenzi work behind the C minor Fugue BWV 574/574a. Various guesses can be made about Legrenzi's original. First, was it a trio? If J. S. Bach added a fourth part, it is possible to see the obtrusive changes of harmony in bb77 and 89 as arising from the added part being dropped at that point. Secondly, if it was a trio, was it for violin, viola da gamba and basso continuo? The dialogue in b99, to which a part has been added, suggests some such texture, even if the original key was not C minor. Thirdly, if some of the counterpoint is owed to Legrenzi (as in BWV 579 it is to Corelli), one can assume that such passages as the Buxtehude-like sixths in b100 (without pedal point in BWV 574, with it in BWV 574a) were the contributions, so to speak, of the German Lutheran organist setting out to create a praeludium-like piece of organ music, something with wider allusions (cf. the sixths in the D major Praeludium BWV 532.i bb5–9).

It would be in the nature of such instrumental counterpoint to do things the vocal *stile antico* of the sixteenth century would not, though still remaining within the general *ambiance* of classical rules. The very presence of a triple-time section in a canzona (such as BWV 588) must have been the result of organists experimenting with an idiom outside its usual framework in old vocal music and yet still largely obeying its rules. For example, in BWV 588 at b104 it is unclear how long the treble a′ should be, precisely because in the pure Palestrina idiom the final note of a phrase is at least twice as long as the beat. But how feasible is that in triple time? Should a final be one, two or three beats long? Is triple time one in a bar or three?

---

* Another particularly Corellian moment is the rondeau-chaconne (third movement) of the Fantasia in G major BWV 571: its ostinato bass, key, modulations, imitation, and position after a prelude may all suggest more than a chance resemblance to Corelli's *sonata da camera* Op III no. 12. Whether or not the Corellian flavour in BWV 571 makes it more likely to be an authentic work of J. S. Bach (an early and somewhat Italianate experiment?) is an open question.

Nevertheless, it is the Vivaldi concerto in particular that is assumed to have changed J. S. Bach's life. Circulating in central Germany from about 1712, copies of Vivaldi were brought to Weimar in 1713 (perhaps along with the copy of *Fiori musicali* signed by J. S. Bach in 1714), and although the Weimar vice-kapellmeister had been to Venice in 1702-3 (Schulze 1972 p8), the impact of Vivaldi had not then been so evident (see Vol. I pp283–90). No doubt because of its catholic and aristocratic cosmopolitanism, Dresden became a centre for such works: the Sächsische Landesbibliothek now holds the Torelli concertos transcribed by Walther (though presumably not the actual copies he used?) and to this day has the largest Vivaldi collection outside Italy (see Eller 1961). The city's musicians were markedly Italophile – not only Zelenka but J. G. Harrer, later Leipzig cantor, whose library included Masses and other music from Palestrina to Fux (Schering 1941 p336). The extent to which J. S. Bach was familiar with music by other Venetian composers can be surmised from J. G. Walther's extant organ transcriptions of Venetian concertos (all before *c*1725?) and from Bach's choosing Albinoni's violin sonatas for figured-bass work with his pupil Gerber. The 'Italian influence', then, has many facets: classical counterpoint, chamber-music themes (fugue subjects, running bass lines) and Vivaldian concerto forms, in particular the partially recapitulated ritornello form of (e.g.) BWV 593.i.

If the influence of (in particular) Vivaldi on J. S. Bach was so great that only under such influence was he able to compose sustained and structured music (see Vol. I pp286–7), are we to understand that as a unique reaction? What is the significance of the fact that J. G. Walther seems to have been more inclined to the multi-sectional concerto of the older type? Did Kuhnau feel no interest in imitating the Torelli concerto which Pisendel brought to Leipzig in 1709 (Schering 1926 p342)? Did Bach already know some Torelli by 1709 when Pisendel is said to have visited him in Weimar (*Dok* III p189)? Was no one able to assimilate Italian forms – or, rather, the potential of Italian forms, often imperfectly realized by Vivaldi himself – as skilfully as was J. S. Bach when he wrote, as early as 1715, a cantata with an Italian prelude (BWV 31)? Yet such 'assimilation' is more than a matter of copying or personalizing set forms. It is surely correct to see the mature organ ritornello movements – the preludes BWV 544, 546, 548 – as having 'melodic material which reflects vocal practice' (Stauffer 1980 p69) and to see such massive movements as being generally the fruits of experience in writing cantata ritornellos. They cannot be merely the consequence of contemplating Italian concertos. The composer seems to have been ever at pains to develop an idea or notion beyond its origins even in his own work – a constant originality springing from intimate knowledge of the details of style. This is true of the small details. For example, the Neapolitan sixth is put to three astonishingly varied uses in Cantata 4, the Passacaglia BWV 582 and the Toccata BWV 564.ii: in the first, an expressive cadence for the prelude; in the second, a dramatic pause in the fugue; in the third, a sweet melodic formula for an Adagio. No Italian composer could or would have been more inventive with this chord. On the other hand, in the interests of closely imitating Italian styles, J. S. Bach would also imitate the simpler, more elementary details, avoiding any personal 'inventiveness' of this kind. For example, the simple cadence

$$\text{I}^5_3 \quad \text{I}^6_3 \quad \text{V}^4_2 \quad \text{V}^5_3 \quad \text{I}^5_3$$

at the end of the first episode in the G major Sonata (BWV 530.i, bb49–53, 97–101) is certainly to be seen as characteristically Vivaldian.

   If such a detail is open to such variety, how much more difficult it is to trace the roots of the grand formal plan for a movement. The opening of the C minor Prelude BWV 546 is often likened to a cantata dialogue: but where in the cantatas are there such massive dialogue-chords on a *point d'orgue*, which (at least in its *sostenuto* forms) is usually reserved in cantatas for quiet moments? Although the Brandenburg Concertos and many a cantata first movement may have a shape similar on paper to such organ preludes, no ear could hear them as related, beyond the element of variety-within-repetition that J. S. Bach saw as a natural means of sustaining a movement.

12. French Influences

The *Obituary* says that while the young Bach was in Lüneburg he travelled to Hamburg to hear Reincken* and also had the opportunity of hearing the Duke of Celle's *Capelle*, which consisted mostly of Frenchmen (*Dok* III p82). Both experiences must have introduced him to music of marked style, in each case very different from what he was used to – the one in keyboard-playing, the other in string-playing. Indeed, how far this 'French influence' included keyboard music is open to doubt, whatever may have been true a decade later. The *Obituary*'s claim that at the time of the Lüneburg–Celle visits the 'French taste . . . in that country was something then entirely new' ('Frantzösischen Geschmacke . . . in dasigen Landen, zu der Zeit was Ganz Neues war') is no doubt a simplification, but the impact of that taste on Bach can scarcely be questioned. It is important for playing much of J. S. Bach's keyboard music that the Celle court had French musicians and was not merely an importer of French music: playing methods were as crucial as actual repertory.† As Mainwaring pointed out in connection with Handel, the Italian style of performance 'cannot be marked, or written, or even described' (1760 p43); nor, on the other hand, could the Italians easily understand French playing styles (particularly in the *ouverture* – hence Handel's need to demonstrate it to none other than Corelli: *ibid* p57).

   Just as local contemporaries of J. S. Bach were familiar with the several kinds of Italian music – old counterpoint, later chamber sonatas, recent concertos – so his

---

* The anecdote of the young Bach finding a ducat in a fish-head also illustrated the desire to learn: with his new-found fortune, the boy was able to make another pilgrimage to Reincken (*Dok* III p424).

† If, as is likely, J. S. Bach first got to know Italian concertos from scores (manuscript or printed), is it possible that his understanding of the brilliant Italian style of string-playing – without the benefit of hearing good imported players, such as Roger North was able to describe (with an evident sense of their unusualness) in London at much the same period – was so deficient as to cause him to misjudge the tempos of the concertos? BWV 593 and 594 have to be played much less fast than string-players familiar with Italian manners would then or now assume. Similarly, does the opening 2/4 signature of the Italian Concerto for Harpsichord also lead to a far less *allegro* character than is usual today, one more in line with his notion of an Italian first movement?
   The *Obituary* speaks of Bach's taking 'a very lively tempo' ('im Zeitmaasse . . . sehr lebhaft': *Dok* III p87), but this is not specific enough to be helpful here. The authors seem to be speaking of his conducting ensemble music, presumably in the later Leipzig period and perhaps in a manner more forthright than *galant* composers were used to.

knowledge of certain French music was in no way isolated. Not only did French harpsichord suites form an important part of the Krebs–Walther manuscript P 801 (see also *Dok* II p193), of the earlier Möller MS (five suites by Lebègue) and even of the Andreas-Bach-Buch (Marchand suite, date of insertion still uncertain),* but J. G. Walther copied Boyvin's first and second *Livres d'Orgue* (1689, 1699) and probably even de Grigny as well (Riedel 1960 p56). That French organ idioms did not affect the German composers more than they did was probably due not so much to differences in liturgical requirements – after all, the *tierce en taille* manner could have flavoured many a German chorale-prelude perfectly well, as BWV 663 suggests – as to a German rejection of French taste, hinted at by Adlung (see last footnote) and made clear in the *Obituary's* account of the abandoned Bach–Marchand improvisation contest in Dresden in 1717.† From their report in the *Obituary* it seems that C. P. E. Bach and/or Agricola doubted

> ob aber *Marchands* Müsetten für die Christnacht, deren Erfindung und Ausführung ihm in Paris den meisten Ruhm zu Wege gebracht haben soll, gegen Bachs vielfache Fugen vor Kennern würden haben Stand halten können (*Dok* III p84)

> whether however Marchand's musettes for Christmas Eve, the composition and performance of which are said to have brought him most of his fame in Paris, would have been able to hold their own in the opinion of connoisseurs against Bach's multiple fugues . . .

The sarcasm raises some interesting questions and ignores others. Why should Marchand gain his reputation from playing noëls when his earlier music was so accomplished? Were French composers not also capable of producing good counterpoint in organ music? If that was the case, why was it an 'even greater honour' for J. S. Bach to conquer Marchand than to be offered the fine position in Halle not long before (*Dok* III p83)? Were there already in 1717 *Kenner* so appreciative of German counterpoint (uniquely well wrought as it may have been) as to win them away from French rhetoric? Were the authors of the *Obituary* aware of what remarks on Marchand had recently been published in Paris (cited in Pirro 1901)? –

> Titon du Tillet (1739)
> Marchand a été le plus grand organiste qu'il y ait jamais eu pour le toucher, et que ses mains ont toujours fourni à tout ce que son beau génie produisoit.

> Marchand was the greatest organist there ever was with respect to playing; his hands were always able to realize everything his fine genius [in composition? improvisation?] produced.

> Daquin (1752)
> génie vif et soutenu, des tournures de chant que lui seul connaissoit . . . Couperin moins brillant, moins égal, moins favorisé de la nature, avait plus d'Art . . .

---

* No doubt this was one of the two suites that Adlung heard J. S. Bach play from copies owned by Adlung, who had 'liked them only once, namely when [Bach] played them to me' (*Dok* III p125). It was de Grigny's and Du Mage's *Livres d'Orgue* that Birnbaum referred to in 1738 when he defended J. S. Bach against Scheibe's criticism of his ornately written-out embellishments (*Dok* II p304).

† Dresden's French ties then were as strong as its Italian ones later. J. B. Volumier, who invited Bach to Dresden for the contest, according to the *Obituary*, was *Konzertmeister*, and Mattheson noted that J. F. Alberti (1642–1710) had 'gained richly' in composition and keyboard-playing from lessons taken there with Albrici, recently returned from France – lessons, moreover, 'from first principles' ('belohnte ihm . . . reichlich dafür . . . von neuem': 1740 pp6–7).

lively and sustained genius, turns of melodic phrase that only he knew . . . [François] Couperin, less brilliant, less even, less favoured by nature, had more art . . .

Perhaps the *Obituary* authors knew too that Marchand was offered a position in Dresden in 1717–18 and that he had won exceptional fame as a *claveciniste*. Certainly it would not be the only occasion on which the *Obituary* was written with an eye to statements published about other composers in the previous decade or so, statements that coloured its own remarks. In any case, the new self-awareness of 'Germany' in the early eighteenth century must also have meant a sensitivity to the characteristics of other, older cultures. This is implied by the remarks of Kuhnau paraphrased at the beginning of chapter 11 above, and by the scorn with which the young Handel is reputed to have regarded Italian music (contemporary chamber sonatas?) before he ever visited Italy and heard it played there (Mainwaring 1760 p40).

The decay of French keyboard taste generally by the 1740s presumably justified or prompted the anti-Marchand sarcasm, but in any case the evident appreciation of French harpsichord music from about 1700* until well after J. S. Bach's death is unlikely to have been matched by admiration for French organ music. The harpsichord Ouverture in F major BWV 820 seems (assuming it to be authentic) to belong to that scanning by Bach of many styles and genres to which the Andreas-Bach-Buch bears witness (see Vol. I pp254–5); but there is no comparable organ piece, only subtle hints of such details as French textures in certain works (BWV 562, 572). Closer aping of the *forms* of French organ music would have had no clear aim; the service had no call for them. Study, however, was a different matter. While J. S. Bach's admiration for Couperin, claimed in Leipzig in 1768 (*Dok* III p199), was presumably with respect to his harpsichord music and perhaps to his playing method (*L'Art de toucher*), the Berlin copyist of the manuscript Am.B.529 (J. F. Agricola?) must have been fulfilling some need when he copied organ music by Lebègue, Boyvin, Corrette and even Marchand: music by then quite out of date in France itself. Besides, the *Obituary*'s sarcasm may have been badly aimed: the musette-noël may well be more characteristic of other popular composers such as P. Dandrieu, whose frequently reprinted album *Noëls* (Paris c1700?) included a canonic *muzette* on 'Puer nobis nascitur'.

Spitta's attempt to describe characteristic moments in Böhm's Praeludium in G minor for harpsichord (Andreas-Bach-Buch) as possessing both 'bittersweet harmonies of which only the German soul is capable' and also 'a gracefulness then possessed only by the French' (Spitta I p206) is understandable. A work so imaginative, so idiomatically conceived for its instrument and so individual in character is difficult to credit to a provincial mind that has sustained no direct influence by music outside its province.† But what is 'French gracefulness'? The shape of the work (prelude–adagio–fugue–postlude) is closer to German praeludia than to the occasional prelude–fugue–postlude of earlier composers such as Louis Couperin, and its figuration has the simplicity and drive typical of south German composers

* Earlier in Dresden, perhaps, and wherever it was that Pachelbel had introduced the *ouverture* style on the harpsichord, according to Mattheson (1740 p247).
† The fact that most of Böhm's keyboard music is now known because it exists in manuscripts which contain music by J. S. Bach (e.g. Walther manuscripts) raises questions, some of which were asked by Geiringer 1966 p13: Did Walther receive them through Bach? Did Bach get to know Böhm's written music through Walther? Is the situation as described merely an accident of sources?

whose manner is more Italian than French. The most French element is the shape and ornamentation of Böhm's fugue theme (cf. Nivers, de Grigny), as it is with the first fugue of J. S. Bach's Capriccio in B flat BWV 992 (a very Böhmian movement). Although an ornamented notation should not be trusted necessarily to indicate style, it is one of the means a composer has of making his allusions explicit.* But 'gracefulness' cannot be judged from notation, since with similar ornaments and a sensitive idea of touch many a movement by Kuhnau or J. K. F. Fischer could achieve 'gracefulness' without the presence of French figuration or harmony. It is striking that the ornament tables in the Andreas-Bach-Buch, the Möller MS and the *Klavierbüchlein für W. F. Bach* are French (see below, p226), but ornament tables are easy to understand compared to the characteristic notation of the old free preludes perfected by the French composers. It could well be that those preludes prefacing Lebègue's suites were omitted in the Möller MS because they were not understood.†

It seems from a remark made by a Bach pupil in 1713 that Prince Johann Ernst was expected to bring back to Weimar from Holland French overtures as well as Italian concertos (*Dok* III pp648–9). This may explain why the church year 1714–15 saw both a cantata with an Italian prelude (BWV 31) and a pair of cantatas with French overtures (BWV 61, 152) and may have something to do with the composer's copying of de Grigny (*Dok* III p634).‡ Though the scoring of BWV 31 is scarcely Vivaldian or the shape of BWV 61 close to de Grigny, the juxtaposition is striking: ritornello shape in the former (complete with figural details such as opening and closing octaves, short invertible imitations etc), prelude and fugue in the latter (with such French characteristics as dotted rhythms# and a triple-time stretto-fugue). However, in BWV 61 the 'Frenchness' is already modified insofar as the dotted prelude has as its bass the chorale cantus firmus; and the fugue too is sung. On the other hand, subtly French is the way that certain details have been composed. For example, the fugue subject of BWV 61.i is exposed stretto with some Lullian thirds◊ – Ex. 42(i) – whereas a 'German' answer would have entered later – Ex. 42(ii). The sinuous derivation of the fugue subject from the second line of the chorale melody is itself perhaps a salute to de Grigny's fugue subjects drawn from Gregorian hymns, for *Nun komm der Heiden Heiland* too is a Gregorian hymn.

But without pursuing French elements in all the keyboard works attributed to

---

* Using the fiddle clef (g′ on the second line) for the right hand, as in the sources for the *Pièce d'orgue* BWV 572 (including Walther's copy in P 801 – for him an exceptional notation), is also probably meant to be a stylistic allusion. A similar point can be made about the use of a 4/2 signature to indicate *stile antico* counterpoint. Especially for a lesser composer like Kauffmann, an allusion to a particular style of composition is easier to achieve with details of notation than in the music itself.

† An omission already noticed in *BJ* 9 (1912) p59.

‡ That dotted rhythms implied a piece 'in the so-called French style' was still clear to a reviewer of BWV 681 in *AMZ* 8 (1805) col. 31.

Perhaps the Prince brought back with him a copy of the 1700 print of de Grigny's *Livre*. It is clear (from M.-C. Alain, 'Réflexions sur le livre d'orgue de Nicholas de Grigny d'après la copie de J. S. Bach' in *L'Orgue à notre époque*, ed. D. Mackey (Montreal 1981) 91–105) first that the print was J. S. Bach's source, and secondly that he understood the musical and notational character of such French *livres*, correcting obvious errors, observing the ornaments faithfully, etc. But the date of this copy is still not established; it must lie between 1708 and 1714, earlier perhaps than the 'c1713' sometimes suggested (e.g. *Dok* III p634)?

◊ Parallel thirds in 3/4 metre are also alluding to a particular style in the little 'Trio' section of the chaconne used to demonstrate praeludium form in Niedt's *Musicalische Handleitung* (1721 edn, pp122–30).

Ex. 42   **(i)** BWV 61.i

(ii)

the young J. S. Bach, it is clear that the composer of the harpsichord Ouverture in F major BWV 820 had caught many details of French orchestral suites. From the way the opening dotted prelude remains in the dominant for the fugue (when it could have reverted to the tonic), as in Ex. 43; from the fugue subject itself, its scurrying development and emphatic close; from the nature of the operatic *entrée* that follows; from details in the minuet and trio (the last clearly for two oboes and bassoon); and from the ballet-like succinctness of the gigue, it would not be difficult even to suppose it a transcription of a kind then becoming popular.

Ex. 43   BWV 820.i

Such examples serve to suggest that 'French elements' are a more subtle affair than ornaments or dotted rhythms, and suggest that however French certain details in the organ works BWV 562 or 572 may be, the *texture* of BWV 633 and 634 or the *harmonies* of BWV 552.i (from b64) and 548.ii (from b160) are quite as allusive. As the notes in Vol. I suggest, style-imitation in such pieces is a matter of more than merely adopting externals – the sort of thing implied by Telemann's remark to Mattheson that he dressed up 'in an Italian coat' (i.e. in the form of an Adagio or Allegro) some Polish music that had impressed him (1740 p360). It is difficult to imagine J. S. Bach 'dressing up' anything in the style of something else: Telemann's remark smacks of the glibness that is ineradicable from his music. It is not mere 'dressing up' to ornament the chorales BWV 691 and 753 in such a way as to take in so many of the d'Anglebert-like embellishments listed in the *table* of the album which includes them (*Klavierbüchlein für W. F. Bach*), nor was it 'dressing up' when the young W. F. Bach wrote a praeludium in the same album imitating the French style of such composers as Gaspard LeRoux (see *NBA* v/5 p66). Perhaps Telemann's French overtures, and the interest in such things aroused at Eisenach by at least 1708 (Engel 1966 p17), were more worthy of him. The paucity of sources makes it difficult to guess how 'elevated' the other *ouvertures* composed in Thuringia were, such as Stölzel's in Gotha from c1719 onwards; and this whole area of German music-making deserves closer study.

The shortage of sources also makes it difficult to understand the dissemination of those crucial details of musical composition that make up style: the remaining in the dominant in Ex. 43 is one such detail. Another is the five-part texture divided between hands and feet as 2:2:1. This is often now associated specifically with de Grigny, especially when it is in 6/4 time. The five parts in Lully's *ouvertures* seem here to be distributed specifically for organ. But if the disposition of five parts in 6/4 is in principle imitating de Grigny, how can it be found so well realized in the third section of the 'Nun komm, der Heiden Heiland' of Nikolaus Bruhns, who died before de Grigny's *Livre* was published?*

It looks as if the intense interest of German composers in the music of other countries – perhaps precisely the factor that helped German music to become the dominating force it later became – is still not fully understood today, at least as it affected the period 1690–1715; the forms that influence took have not even been fully described or catalogued. In the case of J. S. Bach, it could well be that in addition to actual themes and forms taken from foreign composers for new, carefully conceived compositions (Raison, Legrenzi, Albinoni, Corelli) there were also *types* of theme consciously taken or imitated: de Grigny for the Fantasia BWV 562 and the chorale BWV 634, Frescobaldi for the Canzona BWV 588, Corelli for the *Allabreve* BWV 589. These are to be seen as analogous to the theme-type borrowed from the more native (or rather naturalized) traditions, such as sectional praeludia in the Toccata BWV 566. How far all of these date from the same period in the composer's output (was the de Grigny idiom adopted later than the others?) can only be conjectured.

---

13. Niedt's and Mattheson's Praeludia

As far as organ chorales are concerned, it is clear from Mattheson's praise of Pachelbel's *Choräle zum Praeambulieren* (Erfurt 1693) and J. G. Walther's chorales that he did not regard music which had originated in Thuringia as unsuitable for Hamburg, and that the directions he gave for harpsichordists' *Fantasiren* were not for local consumption only (1739 p476). Nor do the reports of organists' trials in Hamburg disagree with what seems to have been required, broadly speaking, of central German organists. Yet the directions he and F. E. Niedt gave for organ praeludia carry no hint of the symphonic preludes-with-fugues achieved by J. S. Bach.

In the *Capellmeister*, Mattheson briefly lists the kinds of music that may go into the making of *Fantasiren*, including *intonatio* (full chords, perhaps some broken),

---

* Conjectural answers to that question can easily be offered. But perhaps of all the composers admired by J. S. Bach it is Bruhns the scantiness of whose musical remains are to be regretted the most. The lost works of his *oeuvre* must have held many hints of the paths to be taken by his young contemporary.

arpeggio, arioso, adagio, passaggi (demisemiquaver runs divided between the hands), fugue, chaconne, *capricci* ('the more wonderful and extraordinary, the better') and 'a kind of accompaniment' (i.e. figured-bass-like harmonies or full chords on the beat). Such treatments are suitable for organ or harpsichord, and it is possible to find examples of them in such works as BWV 531, 532, 533, 549, 550, 551, 564 etc. Not the least interesting item in Mattheson's list is the last: the plain chords of the kind found at characteristic moments in (e.g.) Buxtehude's Praeludium in F sharp minor, which look like a plain continuo realization. *Präludiren* and *Fuge* are 'the highest practical peak in music' ('der höchste praktische Gipffel in der Music') and require a skilful man (1739 pp478–9).

Agreeing with Mattheson's later remark that such pieces have several sections none of which should be too long, Niedt's *Musicalische Handleitung* gave directions for 'the curious'* in which successive techniques are described (2nd edn by Mattheson (1721) pp117–30). The Praeludium is founded on the bass line shown in Ex. 44. He suggests that this outlined prelude be introduced by one or another of the passages in Ex. 45. Mattheson, however, said later that he preferred to end with a run than to begin with one (1739 p478) – which might be relevant to the close of final sections in the C major praeludia BWV 531 (end of a prelude) and 564 (end of a fugue).† Niedt's movement would then begin with a descending run, followed by held chords; as a written-out version shows (Niedt/Mattheson *op cit* p122), the run

Ex. 44   (Niedt/Mattheson 1721 pp119–20)

Ex. 45

* 'Lehrbegierigen' (cf. the title dated 1722 for Bk I of *The 48* in P 415: '. . . zum Nutzen und Gebrauch der Lehr-begierigen').
† It may even suggest either that copyists had no authority for adding final chords, short or long, in such movements (which ought to end without the chords but with a downward run of the kind Mattheson refers to) or that the composer of these movements was making his own interpretation of an old (improvised) convention.

is meant to end on a single note before the next section follows with chords, as in BWV 533.i (b5), 564.i (b5), 566.i (b4) and 572.i (b29). The direction of the run may change, as may the figuration (Ex. 46). Elsewhere, Mattheson quotes the openings of two Froberger pieces in the *Fantasiren* style (since the older composers took greater pains in such styles than did those of c1739) and notes that they are played

Ex. 46

con discrezione 'so that one need not be tied to the beat at all' ('dass man an den Tact gar nicht binden dürffte': 1739 p89). The very regularity of motif in such openings as BWV 536 or 566 seems to require a regularity of pulse; it is equally in style to treat (e.g.) the opening of BWV 531 or 551 rather freely until the motifs are confirmed by repetition or sequence.

The *gute Meister* who made use of such opening gestures, and whose written works should be studied, according to Niedt (*op cit* pp120–1), seem however to be the Hamburgers. Extant works of J. S. Bach have a periodicity (BWV 536, 550) or motivic rhetoric (BWV 564) or imitation (BWV 551) not touched on by Niedt: the opening of BWV 551, for instance, resembles the last of Niedt's ideas (Ex. 46) but is given a two-handed sequential treatment that goes farther than comparable Hamburg openings. At this point in his description of praeludia, Niedt addresses himself to the pedal, criticizing the 'wretched habit' ('übele Gewohnheit') of constantly registering it with 16′ stops and over-using it in continuo playing. He refers neither to *points d'orgue* during opening preludes (BWV 533, 536 etc) nor to pedal solos, whether opening (BWV 531, 549) or following the first section (BWV 550, 564). Niedt then gives the complete prelude, changing the value of his bass notes to suit the flow ('the more unforced and natural the better' – 'desto besser . . . je ungezwungener und natürlicher': p122), including a fifteen-variation *ciacona* (which can be made longer) and closing with a short *Final* or coda. While the result may have rather less musical interest than most German praeludia from Froberger onwards, it does indicate the outlines of a sectional movement from which it is possible to see J. S. Bach as gradually moving – not necessarily because the Italian ritornello shape was 'the only answer' but because those Niedtian outlines had already had to grow beyond recognition in order to incorporate into one movement such widely different material as that of (e.g.) the A minor Prelude BWV 543.i.

Earlier composers were of course closer to Niedt's model, not only in Hamburg. Amongst others, Kuhnau (Leipzig) and Krieger (Zittau) left praeludia which so exhausted the currency as to make any good composer look for his own.* Ex. 47 shows the beginning of two C major examples. Before a composer could produce a work like the A minor Prelude BWV 543.i he would have to know of better possibilities than the extant praeludia of Kuhnau, Krieger or Niedt could supply. Nevertheless, it is possible to see behind the new, regular theme at b36 of the A minor Prelude (built on *x* in Ex. 48(i)) the change of texture, mood and direction that Niedt aimed at in b6 of his model (Ex. 48(ii)). Figuration more like Niedt's will be

---

* However, Kuhnau's progressions in Ex. 47(i) anticipate another C major prelude – Bk II of *The 48* – so much as to make it clear that the younger composer kept alive earlier associations of key.

Ex. 47

(i) J. Kuhnau, Praeludium (opening movement of *Clavierübung I*, Leipzig 1689)

(ii) J. Krieger, Praeludium (16th movement of *Anmuthige Clavier-Übung*, Nuremberg 1699)

found at a comparable point in the C minor Praeludium BWV 549 (at bb12ff). Similarly, the opening manual (and hence pedal) solo of BWV 543.i is built on a *passaggio* figure which is not unlike one which Mattheson used to show how three-part harmony could be conveyed by imaginative motifs (1739 pp354–5); Ex. 49. Various features of the opening of BWV 543 therefore could be seen as part of a tradition, however the knowledgeable player may enthuse over its no doubt infinitely greater musicianship. Moreover, awareness of tradition not only brings out the originality of working in BWV 543.i but makes it easier to see the attempt made in the G major Prelude BWV 541.i to develop the idea a step further: the same opening flourish as in Niedt and the more homophonic subsequent material. But now the 'subsequent material' is a fully fledged ritornello movement as original as it is sophisticated, belying its apparent simplicity (like another G major prelude, the first movement of the Harpsichord Partita no. 5). The next step would be therefore to drop the opening flourish, do without pedal points and avoid sectionality altogether, a line of development shown as follows:

Niedt – BWV 551 – BWV 543 – BWV 541 – BWV 552

Ex. 48

(i) BWV 543.i

(ii) Niedt/Mattheson 1721 pp122–3

Ex. 49

last 2 ½ bars editorial

Niedt's praeludium (prelude–chaconne–postlude) uses for its set form a chaconne rather than a fugue. While this seems an unfamiliar feature, it could well be that ostinato movements were more widely heard in praeludia than the few well-known examples* suggest. For one thing, a chaconne is much easier to improvise than a fugue. Ideally in a written piece both could be present; moreover, it certainly looks as if BWV 571 and 569 (whoever composed them) convey the tradition of 'modified chaconnes', i.e. ostinato movements that do not strictly follow the principle of constant repetition. The final work in J. Krieger's *Anmuthige Clavier-Übung* (Nuremberg 1699) has several features found both in J. S. Bach and in the Niedt/Mattheson conception of praeludia:

> opening pedal solo (cf. BWV 531 in particular)
> long held chords (Niedt)
> two passages of figuration between the chords (Niedt; BWV 565)
> *chaconne en rondeau* (not so called)
> fugue following without break (cf. BWV 550 etc)†

* E.g. Buxtehude's C major Praeludium BUXWV 137.
† This is another detail suggesting that the early works of J. S. Bach were given a misleading notation by the copyists. Should (e.g.) BWV 531.i end without a full chord and without a long break before the fugue (see below, chapter 26)? Do not copyists' fermatas at the end of BWV 549.i merely mark the close of the section, without implying *tenuto*?

Of these, the *chaconne en rondeau* was the one that found no place in J. S. Bach's maturer praeludia for any instrument. Moreover, the distinctly French flavour of German organ chaconnes of the Krieger/Muffat kind (see Vol. I p229) is not pronounced in either BWV 571 or BWV 569, rather suggesting that northern passacaglias, such as were copied in the Andreas-Bach-Buch, were needed to lead J. S. Bach into his extraordinary experiment with organ ostinato (see notes to BWV 582 in Vol. I).

A further detail of Krieger's praeludium (entitled 'Toccata mit dem Pedal aus C') suggests how the composer conceived such movements as BWV 531.i and 549.i: although their *points d'orgue* might suggest older toccata traditions, in fact as a series of decorated and spun-out harmonies they relay a distinctly different tradition. After his pedal *point d'orgue*, Krieger writes his harmonies plain, characteristically separated at times by little figures: Ex. 50. The little figures are exactly of

Ex. 50   Krieger, Toccata mit dem Pedal

the kind woven into more continuous music in J. S. Bach's praeludia – but not necessarily with great imagination, for only the hectic motion of bars 29–34 in the C major Prelude BWV 531.i makes the passage superior to Krieger's held chords.

---

14. Influences on the Preludes and Fugues: Further Remarks

The relative ease with which organists can now find editions of organ music *c*1700 and read comparative studies tracing what are called 'influences' makes it possible for them to form their own views on what J. S. Bach learnt from his predecessors and what can be credited to his own imagination. Such comparisons, however, can slip out of focus: the net is often cast too wide. Volume I gives hints as to musical influences on J. S. Bach, and yet it is all too easy to find influences which were either not there or which are secondary to more elusive factors. Books tend to rely on written sources only. In the case of Buxtehude, for example, it is often claimed that the toccatas in several sections, with metamorphosed fugue subjects, spring from the older traditions of Frescobaldi and Froberger. So they might, as to technique of subject-metamorphosis; but a bigger factor in their make-up, as to both shape and detail, must have been the kind of large organs for which they were written, organs whose chests had equal immediacy for the listener, scattering sounds from different directions (upper and lower chests, chair organs, pedal-towers), all based on bright, sharp colours that caused the player to use the stops and manuals inventively, not least with a sense of rhetorical silence and reverberant rests.

Other than the composers said by C. P. E. Bach to have been 'liked and studied' by his father* one needs to bear in mind only those keyboard composers working in his area who, though presumably less admired, did compose and even at times publish keyboard works that must have been known to him: J. G. Walther, J. C. Bach (1642–1703), Buttstedt, Zachow, Kirchhoff, Lübeck, Telemann and Kauff-mann.† To simplify the situation, it can be seen that the crucial comparisons to make are general and wide comparisons with a particular number of older composers of marked ability, and more specific and occasional comparisons with a certain few older or younger composers of lesser ability. A further point is that some of the composers admired by J. S. Bach were themselves working with the style of others he admired. As has been pointed out (Riedel 1960 p183), many north German fugue and toccata motifs resemble those in Froberger toccatas and even Frescobaldi *capricci*: that is, some composers admired by J. S. Bach were already under the influence of others he admired.

It is clear to any observer that the organ, harpsichord, vocal and instrumental works of J. S. Bach represent approaches to fugue-writing far in advance of most previous work done in such genres. How far such changes are due to the composer's extraordinary ability in writing counterpoint and how far to more general notions (such as that musical power ought to be sustained and form to be well organized) is a subject large enough for a study of its own (e.g. Bullivant 1959). Comparisons are rarely as instructive as they may appear to be. Thus while it is true that certain details in fugue subjects may be traced elsewhere – leaping-octave patterns in Buxtehude, Bruhns or Böhm; such patterns as Ex. 51 in Buxtehude; repeated notes

Ex. 51

in Reincken, Bruhns, Buxtehude or Lübeck (Krey 1956 pp169ff) – more subtle and important details can be easily missed or, if noticed, are traceable elsewhere only with the greatest difficulty. What, for instance, is the significance of the fact that many Bach fugues in C major have a final entry in the top part? Why do some fugues have their first and second answers tonal (BWV 533, 531), others their first but not their second (BWV 536, 566.ii, 566.iv)? In the case of the two fugues in the Toccata BWV 566, is it significant that both expositions are very regular – answers appearing after the same number of bars each time – but the number of bars differs

* Froberger, Kerll, Pachelbel, Frescobaldi, J. K. F. Fischer, Strunck, Buxtehude, Reincken, Bruhns, Böhm and 'some old French masters' (*Dok* III p288).

† Telemann was listed by C. P. E. Bach not only as one of the composers admired by J. S. Bach in his later years but as one with whom his father 'was often together' in his early years (*Dok* III p289). None of the more recent composers contributed directly to the repertory of traditional organ music (Fux, Caldara, Handel, Keiser, Hasse, J. G. Graun, C. H. Graun, Telemann, Zelenka, Benda and those 'especially admired in Berlin and Dresden').

(4-bar phrases for BWV 566.iv, 4½-bar phrases for BWV 566.ii)? What would it signify? – the composer's constant wish to vary what he does, to give each piece a series of individual characteristics? How are we to understand the astonishing D major Fugue BWV 532? – as the composer's conscious response to contemporary fugue form, giving it a subject not so very different from those of Buttstedt's fugues but altogether more 'controlled'; then developing it into and through more keys than usual (at least, in written-down fugues) and so producing a long ritornello movement stamped with uniqueness? Is it possible that in such a way he achieved fully fledged ritornello movements before he had heard Italian concertos? Are we to see (e.g.) the only partially accompanied pedal entries in this fugue as an experiment, a device perhaps taken from elsewhere but now elevated into a distinct feature? What are we to think of the fact that the D major Fugue has no final cadence, perfect or plagal? – that this too was an 'experiment', a sign of J. S. Bach's 'constant wish to vary what he does'? Despite Spitta's attempt to look at such works with a view to grasping the originality of their achievement, it is probable that we are barely able yet to grasp the significance of each of the composer's gestures towards rethinking the conventions as he found them, especially in the case of the early praeludia and in particular their fugues.

The attempts often made by written commentaries (including this one) to label or describe characteristics go only a certain way to help the musician grasp the composer's intentions. For example, any description of the C minor Fugue BWV 537.ii that speaks of its ricercar-like arch form, its violin-like subject (repeated notes) and its song-like *melos* is alerting the musician to develop some thoughts of his own but cannot be said to do much else. On the other hand, it will be found that technical observations – for example, that Bach subjects are more firmly in a key and more sharply contrasted in tonic and dominant than Buxtehude's (Pauly 1964 pp154ff), or that his 'motoric' fugues show him to have been a follower of Reincken more than of Buxtehude (Riedel 1960 p191) – can help to pin down just where the composer seems to have made his own contribution. So can negative observations, such as that he made no use of the fast repeated-note subject found in Pachelbel, Buttstedt, Kuhnau and others. It could well be the case too that the decidedly French flavour of the rhythm of the second fugue in the E major Toccata (BWV 566.iv, the dotted-note variant) was not fully appreciated by the composer himself, insofar as the complexity of his semiquaver figuration is bound to produce a tempo too sluggish for this 'French flavour' to be fully realized. Often one can only guess whether he invented for himself such details as 'dotted-note variants' or took the idea from German canzona-writers who likewise may not have appreciated the French flavour of such rhythms. Some of the comparisons most likely to have been fruitful – in particular with Bruhns, the product of whose influence on J. S. Bach was surely far greater than a pedal scale or two in BWV 532 – cannot now be made.

One problem with negative observations is that they result from inadequate sources. Thus the idea that the C major Toccata from J. Krieger's *Anmuthige Clavier-Übung*, published in Nuremberg (1699) but presumably composed in Zittau, is 'perhaps the only fully developed toccata composed in central Germany before J. S. Bach' (Apel 1967 p648) is so difficult to confirm that it can be discounted. Since praeludia like BWV 531 or 549, or Niedt's directions for composing or improvising such pieces, can be seen in some respects as developments either from Krieger's Toccata or from something very like it, there is all the more reason to suppose it to belong to a type familiar at the period. Perhaps it was familiar to (e.g.) Kuhnau, whose extant organ music is scanty but is based on not dissimilar exploitation of *passaggi*, pedal solos and big chords. Links joining Erfurt (Pachelbel), Halle (Zachow), Leipzig (Kuhnau) and Zittau (Krieger) are likely to have been strong even if they are rarely recorded, and it may well be that traditions of coupling modest preludes with fugues were current in such areas. If this was so, the prelude-and-fugue pair would not have had much to do either with the full-dress northern praeludia or with the southern prelude-and-fugue miniatures (Kerll 1686, Murschhauser 1698, Fischer *c*1702 etc). In any case, the conversion of the praeludium into the prelude-and-fugue – if one can really speak in such terms any longer* – is also implied in a handful of works whose short codas do not amount to full postludes (Böhm, J. C. Bach). Such short codas must represent one common practice, as no doubt the separately copied movements of some major works of J. S. Bach (BWV 532, 539, 540, 542, 546 etc) represent another.

That big multi-limbed preludes remained totally unknown, except in a few essays by Bach pupils, is suggested in particular by Walther's extant praeludia, which, in addition to their paucity of melodic and harmonic interest, show very little sign of ritornello influence even in the two works published after *Clavierübung III* (*Concerto* and *Preludio con Fuga*, both Augsburg *c*1741). Both have several sections in which some salute is made to Italian details (two-manual phrases like a ritornello theme etc), but neither has a formal grasp beyond that of Krieger's Toccata. The sectionality of the *Concerto* is like that of earlier Italian concertos less continuous and sustained than Vivaldi's. Three manuscript praeludia of Walther (all in BB 22541) follow the prelude-and-fugue plan but rely entirely on a succession of old praeludia figurations (including tonic then dominant *points d'orgue*) or, in the C major *Preludio*, meander with old figurations. Such figurations can often be found elsewhere (e.g. the D major Fugue BWV 532.ii) but, more significantly, suggest that the C major Prelude BWV 545 (or 545a) was a response by the composer to such traditions. Was the prelude of BWV 545a an organized, well-constructed, more carefully textured and more melodically inspired version of such music as Ex. 52?

Arguing that it is a sign of his 'musical development' that J. S. Bach dropped the old multi-section praeludia and worked towards major monothematic movements in intricate form, and claiming that he did so out of a growing sense of musical rhetoric (Kloppers 1966 p221), can lead the player to assume a chronology that is not borne out by other factors – e.g., that BWV 540.i belongs to the 'latest period'. This is a problem with many attempts to trace the composer's development. Since BWV 551 and 565 are by no means undoubtedly the work of J. S. Bach, it is question-begging to call BWV 551 'Buxtehudian' in its five sections, or to see in the three sections of BWV 565 the influence of J. Speth's *Ars magna* (Augsburg 1693 – see Krey 1956 pp102ff). Even when the music is undoubtedly the work of J. S. Bach, technical observations can lead to unwarranted chronological conclusions – for

---

* Pauly (1964 p106) speaks of Buxtehude 'purifying' the fugue of toccata elements in his later works, but there seems yet no reason to see any such tendency (even if it existed) as a matter of chronology.

Ex. 52   J. G. Walther

example, that the fugues in BWV 550, 545, 538 and 542 may be equally mature (i.e. roughly contemporary) because each has entries in four new keys, while 'earlier works' and 'the maturest works' (which 'rely on formal complexity') have entries in fewer keys. Similarly, while it is a point of interest that it was from trio sonatas that J. S. Bach seems to have taken his Italian fugue themes (Corelli, Legrenzi, Albinoni – see Braun 1972), it is difficult to justify in detail the idea that the D minor Toccata BWV 538 owes its simple prelude-and-fugue shape to J. S. Bach's encounter with Italian masters (Geiringer 1966 p217). In the case of the early works, relating particular influences to particular periods is severely difficult. Does BWV 719 show in its fugal fore-imitation the influence of J. C. Bach, or is it indeed more likely to have been a work of J. C. Bach? If the musical quality of BWV 741 is justly admired (e.g. Naumann *BG* 40 p. xlvii), it is quite irrelevant to ask 'to whom else could its cantus-firmus stretto in the pedal be attributed?' (Keller, in Peters IX preface) when that stretto is quite conventional and lay within the ability of many composers from Weckmann onwards.

The student of J. S. Bach must often be struck by the individual and independent character he gave to the different *genres* in which he worked – types of melody, harmony, form or texture so often belong to one *genre* and no other – yet his achievements in one can sometimes be understood only after comparison with another. For example, the permutation fugue of the Passacaglia BWV 582 can immediately be seen (if it is compared with the permutation fugue in the early Cantata 131 of 1707 – see Vol. I p5) to have been conceived in keyboard terms, and this not merely because of the way its texture has been created but because its overall shape includes episodes. That these episodes or interludes become progressively longer may also illustrate the composer's sense of keyboard form. Conversely, the development of choral permutation fugues suggests that the composer saw them as requiring (or providing the opportunity for) further concentration of what might be called permutability (BWV 71, 182). The neat and systematic layout of the fugue in Cantata 182 (1714) is particularly striking:

1, 2, 3, 4 = four themes; T = tonic, D = dominant

```
S   1  2  3  4  1  2  3  4  ⎫
A      1  2  3  4  1  2  3  4 ⎬
T         1  2  3  4  1  2  3  ⎬  section A of an ABA movement
B            1  2  3  4  1  2  ⎭
    T  D  T  D  T  D  T  D  T
```

Such 'permutability' was more thoroughgoing than was ever hinted either by the relevant theorists (Werckmeister, Walther, Marpurg – see Dahlhaus 1949 p106) or by keyboard composers themselves. Indeed, before the last decade of his life J. S. Bach seems to have been concerned with a less learned organ counterpoint than he would have found in the *antico* ricercars and *capricci* of one particular composer he admired (N. A. Strunck), whose sheer variety of treatment in combining themes, metamorphosing themes and producing complete triple fugues may have been rather isolated, despite frequent traces of antique flavours in Krieger, Zachow or J. S. Bach (BWV 540.ii). Perhaps the permutation fugue of BWV 182.i, a succinct section in a *da capo* movement, is also be seen as part of another interest on the composer's part: how to handle a long movement proportionally. Certainly the Italianate Sonatas BWV 525–530 show a tendency in this direction:

first movements of	BWV 527	48, 64 and 48 bars
	BWV 529	50, 54 and 51 bars
	BWV 530	20, 140 and 20 bars
finale of	BWV 525	32 and 32 bars

But there seems little reason to see this as a quasi-Italian element, since other works could be viewed in a similar light – such as BWV 540.i (176 + 176 bars plus coda), 541 (82 bars in prelude, 83 in fugue), 574 (fugal sections 37 + 33 + 34 bars), 566 (two fugal sections 88 + 95 bars).*

---

15. *Bicinia*

Though not at first glance one of the major musical categories for J. S. Bach – and though the term is not certainly known to have been used by him – the *bicinium* raises some interesting musical questions, since it is a species of music particularly close in manner to its Italian origins, more so even than the big preludes along ritornello lines. Scheidt's *Tabulatura nova* in particular helped to establish it as a form or technique, and the remarks on BWV 711 in Vol. II suggest composers who produced characteristic effects so similar to J. S. Bach's (see Vol. II pp248–9) that modern writers have found 'an amazing similarity' between (e.g.) BWV 768 Var. 1 and a *bicinium* of J. B. Bach (1676–1749: *NBA* IV/5–6 *KB* p182). From its sources BWV 711 appears to be a separate setting, but *bicinia* also occur as the first variations of three 'partitas' (BWV 766, 767, 768), and two others begin the sectional fantasias of longer organ chorales, BWV 718 and (less clearly) 720.

J. G. Walther's *Lexicon (1732)* defines the term *bicinium* simply as 'a two-part song' ('ein zwey-stimmiges Lied'), but in the preface to *Harmonische Seelenlust*

---

* Not that bar-counting is a reliable method of understanding proportions, particularly when applied to free works. But effective proportions can certainly be conveyed to the listener, who will feel (e.g.) that the final section of BWV 565 is only half as long as the opening.

(Leipzig 1733) G. F. Kauffmann seems to recommend two-part organ chorales as being particularly able to awaken the listener to 'a special attention' ('eine besondere Attention'). Kauffmann's registration aims at a forthright contrast between the two parts, e.g. Cornett or Sesquialtera (rh) against reed + flue 16' (lh),* such as indeed awakens attention in any listener. The *bicinia* with which some of his composite settings begin have a running bass, sometimes derived from the chorale melody but still in principle much like Scheidt's simple, continuous lines. During the late seventeenth century, however, the Italian continuo aria coloured the development of the *bicinium* and gave it some characteristic turns of melody in both bass and treble, as it did some other kinds of contemporary music, such as solo sections in English church anthems *c*1710. Kauffmann also implies that two *bicinium* parts can convey the effect of 'missing voices' ('mangelnden Stimmen'), which no doubt is why *bicinium* basses tend to be busy with broken chords. As Burney wrote of the *bicinium*-like continuo arias in Handel's *Il Pastor Fido* (1712), they

> are only accompanied by a violoncello in the old cantata style; but Handel always contrives to make this single accompaniment interesting without overwhelming the voice part, or depriving it of attention. (C. Burney, *A General History of Music* II (London 1789) p682).

While the leaping lines and broken chords of BWV 711 are more like those of Kauffmann – except that they are melodiously and inventively accomplished – and while the opening *bicinia* of BWV 718 and 720 are too short to develop their own shape, the three *bicinia* of BWV 766, 767 and 768 show specific traits of the Italian aria. The basic material of the bass line itself (whether derived from the chorale melody or not) is not unlike the theme of the aria by Marcello taken as a model by Mattheson in his *Vollkommener Capellmeister* and described in such a way as to demonstrate the rhetorical nature of musical development (1739 pp237–9): Ex. 53.

Ex. 53

(Mattheson)

BWV 768 Var. 1

(Very similar themes and motifs are also worked out in more than one Bach cantata – e.g. the opening movement of BWV 163, 1725?) While Mattheson's analysis, and even its underlying implication that drawing parallels between speech and music is a valid occupation, can have no bearing on BWV 768, it is clear that J. S. Bach knew the characteristics of the musical *genre* he was imitating. One such characteristic is the ostinato-like returns of the bass theme (including a final complete restatement);† another is the cello-like character of the bass line in such

---

* The Bärenreiter edition of P. Pidoux (no. 1924: Kassel 1967) does not give all the original registrations.
† Spitta's note that this structure was known to Böhm (1 p208) may suggest to some readers that Böhm was composing such pieces before J. S. Bach – a common assumption that has not been justified. Forkel says that Bach was already composing chorale-variations at Arnstadt (1802 ch.ix), i.e. thirty years before Böhm died.

partita movements as BWV 766 Var. 1 (not entirely unlike the 'obbligato' middle line of 'Ich ruf' zu dir' BWV 639). Any such bass line looks more mature – i.e. more up-to-date Italian – than those in the early cantatas: Ex. 54. The dropping figure *x*

Ex. 54   BWV 71.vi (1708)

BWV 766 Var. 1

was one used by other *bicinium*-composers such as J. G. Walther (see Ex. 21); it is also found in the left-hand parts of BWV 718 and 720, less obviously in BWV 711. Although the *bicinium*-bass opening of BWV 718 may seem more bassoon-like, there is no clear demarcation between cello and bassoon in the continuo arias: Ex. 55.

Ex. 55   BWV 718

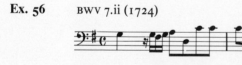

The right-hand part (with the chorale melody) is highly decorated, and in each of the partita examples begins with a short phrase that breaks off only to begin again and then extend itself further – features typical of the Italian aria as understood too by (e.g.) Böhm in his *bicinium* on 'Vater unser' or more simply by J. G. Walther in 'Schmücke dich' *Vers* 2 (both in P 802). Compare any of the *bicinia* of BWV 766, 767 and 768 with the Leipzig aria in Ex. 56. Such restating of the opening phrase is

Ex. 56   BWV 7.ii (1724)

not itself characteristic of J. S. Bach's earliest continuo arias, e.g. Cantata 106.iii (1707?), nor of the simpler *bicinia* of (e.g.) Walther. In addition, all three Bach *bicinia* make further breaks in the melody and extend the phrase-ends of each chorale line, producing a right-hand melismatic melody that is obviously akin to Italian arias. This too is found in simple form in Walther's 'Schmücke dich' but more fully and imaginatively in Böhm's 'Vater unser'. Already in his early Italian arias, Handel reacted to convention by denying his melodies simple periods, square phrases and too easily achieved cadences. But in any catalogue of J. S. Bach's paraphrase techniques, the spinning-out of (e.g.) the final phrase in BWV 768 Var. 1 (Ex. 57) would have an important place. The organist's right hand is freer than any

Ex. 57

BWV 768 Var. 1

voice (or instrument) in such melismas, underlining intrinsic differences between vocal/instrumental and organ works of Bach even in a form or genre common to them both. Details of certain cantata arias might suggest that the organ *bicinium* influenced the aria rather than vice versa. Thus, in Cantata 44.iv the continuous *bicinium* bass is derived from the tenor chorale sung against it in the Kauffmann manner, while the chorale melody itself is sung in four simple strains without aria-like development: Ex. 58. Such a cantata aria is therefore 'imitating' the older kind

Ex. 58   BWV 44.iv

of organ *bicinium*. A more significant example is the Handelian continuo aria which uses 'a rhythmically generated and contrapuntal accompanying figure' (unlike A. Scarlatti, whose opening bass themes give way to simpler harmonic basses) and is 'true to the Hamburg school' (Harris 1980 pp480–1). No doubt Handel did acquire this technique 'in Germany' (Halle? Hamburg?), but very likely from the organ *bicinium* tradition rather than from the imported Italian aria.

The Music and Its Organ

16. The 'Bach Organ'

Defining the 'Bach Organ' and even pointing out that it cannot be defined have become twentieth-century habits. But the question seems not to have exercised earlier players until Schweitzer, writing in the period of the organ's nadir (1908), noted that for J. S. Bach's music the Walcker instruments of 1860–75 were better than the organs of his (Schweitzer's) day, and implied that the organs of Silbermann (was he thinking of Andreas? Gottfried? Johann Andreas?) were better still. Yet earlier in the nineteenth century, particularly in England and France, it was precisely to play the music of J. S. Bach that organs were rebuilt with pedals and adequate second manuals. Although the biographers Forkel, Hilgenfeldt, Bitter and Spitta became progressively more detailed about the organs he played, wider claims were not made except indirectly. By drawing particular attention to the Schnitger organ in the Katharinenkirche, Hamburg, Hilgenfeldt implied that it was very appropriate (1850 p50), while Bitter described the 'restoration of the Bach organ' in Arnstadt by Hesse & Meissner in 1864–78 without betraying any sense that its sixty stops and detached console were irrelevant to J. S. Bach (1881 IV pp48–52). The 1927 Freiberg conference (Tagung für deutsche Orgelkunst) raised the matter in connection with G. Silbermann (see Löffler 1928); and while in 1948 Keller was still claiming that Silbermann was best for what he called the 'Leipzig works' (p13), the technical limitations of Silbermann's organs were soon pointed out by Frotscher (1935). Over the years several organs with which J. S. Bach had some personal connection have successively been seen as ideal – Halle Liebfrauenkirche (Löffler 1928), Naumburg (Dähnert 1970), Hamburg Katharinen- and/or Jakobikirche (*passim*) and Silbermann's project for the Leipzig Paulinerkirche (Klotz 1980) – but for none of them should too many claims be made.

   Although a detail in favour of Silbermann is that the more reliable of his extant and contemporary organs in Saxony are 'some of the most beautiful organs ever made' (Williams 1980 p114), the earliest surviving documents that connect composer and builder stress the differences between them. J. S. Bach's music in unusual keys meant that the best keyboard instruments were unusable

> wegen ihrer unreinen Stimmung . . . selbst die schönen Silbermannischen Orgeln waren falsch gestimmt (Petri 1782 p100).

> on account of their impure tuning . . . even the beautiful Silbermann organs were tuned false [i.e. in a too-unequal temperament].

Writing as a Berliner editing the book of an Erfurter, J. F. Agricola implied that the Saxon organs of Silbermann were not unreservedly admired by 'real connoisseurs', by whom he seems to have meant J. S. Bach (Dähnert 1970 p23):

> An seinen Orgeln, finden ächte Orgelkenner weiter nichts zu tadeln, als: die *allzueinförmige Disposition*, welche blos aus einer übertriebenen Behutsamkeit, nichts von

Stimmen zu wagen, wovon er nicht ganz gewiss versichert war, dass ihm nichts daran missrathen würde, herrührte; ferner die *allzueigensinnige Temperatur*, und endlich die *allzuschwachen* Mixturen und Cimbeln, wegen welcher seine Werke, zumal für grosse Kirchen, nicht Schärfe und durchschneidendes Wesen genug haben (Adlung 1768 I p212).

in his organs, real connoisseurs find nothing further to complain of than: the all-too-uniform stoplists, which arise merely from an excessive caution in not risking stops of which he was not completely certain (so that nothing in them would miscarry for him); then the all-too-individual temperament; and finally the all-too-weak mixtures and cimbels, because of which his organs, especially those for large churches, do not have enough sharpness and penetrating character.

It is difficult to see why Silbermann's uniform stoplists should be reprehensible unless Agricola is referring to his not making 32′ principals and reeds and to what may have been a reluctance to make the soft string stops or the colourful flute stops that were increasingly popular in Thuringia between 1700 and 1750. As for the weak mixtures, Agricola must have in mind the absence of shrill brilliance, for though Silbermann's cimbels duplicate in part the mixtures they are certainly not deficient in power. If these views really do belong to J. S. Bach, it seems he did not understand that to some extent Silbermann's *pleno* mixtures produce the colour of a French *plein jeu* rather than the power of a German *tutti*. But Adlung's and Agricola's taste for 'Schärfe' (including tierce-ranks in mixtures, avoided by both Silbermann and Hildebrandt) may have been responsible for opinions of the kind quoted above. (Concerning tuning problems, see chapter 21.) Kuhnau himself implied that Wender, the builder of the Arnstadt organ, used the same tuning as Silbermann: neither builder wished to understand Neidhardt's equal temperament, since church music did not need the remote keys even though (according to Mattheson – 1725 p235) they were just bearable in the temperaments they did use. Hildebrandt's adoption of the Neidhardt tuning at Naumburg in 1746 (Dähnert 1962 pp115–16) may reflect the late date as much as the wishes of J. S. Bach, who in any case can be presumed to have changed or at least modified his opinions by the time Agricola knew him.

In the following pages the 'Bach Organ' is examined from four particular approaches, none of which is self-contained: stoplists, the composer's organ reports, registration and *organo pleno*. Only the most careful fieldwork will suggest what the Thuringian organ of 1715 (the crucial Bach organ type) was like and how it was registered. The situation of Hamburg in 1715 or of Saxony in 1740 is much clearer, and it is an irony that the organ of one of the most important of all repertories (J. S. Bach's Weimar organ music) is so little understood. But many Thuringian organs of the earlier eighteenth century do exist in good enough condition to give an idea of their nature and of the influence they must have exercised on the composer. How far Lüneburg, Lübeck and Hamburg introduced him to new ideas, or to what extent he thought of the later organ at Naumburg as incorporating some of the ideas he had picked up in northern Germany (see below), can only be conjectured when the nature of those Thuringian organs is understood. In the first place, they were deeper organs than those of Hamburg, Groningen, Paris, Milan etc; by 1700, organ cases from Berlin to Vienna were losing the shallow box-like construction characteristic of older organs and built for immediacy of sound, quick response in tall gothic churches, and independence between departments – independence both in the way they were used and in their tonal nature. Secondly, the pedal-chest was normally placed at the back of the organ, against the wall, and relied on a fundamental tone of the kind desirable in a period and region that favoured bass-orientated hymn harmonizations. The Thuringian organs almost always contained an open wood Violone 16' (sometimes 8'), and the wooden Posaune generally showed a striking uniformity from organ to organ. Thirdly, the stoplist almost always provides at least one example of a soft string stop: this was the period (in other places on the Berlin–Vienna axis) of Dulcianas 4' and 8'. The variously named string stops (and later the overblowing flute stops) of Thuringia are always narrow or small-scaled open stops providing softer contrasts (even semi-choruses) for the flexible requirements of local music (quiet preludes/interludes, soft hymn accompaniments). Fourthly, the action was usually suspended to the manuals with pallet-box to the front, so that rear reeds were less important in the immediacy of sound, did not receive wind directly and indeed were altogether absent from many a *Hauptwerk*. Carillons – a row of interlocking bells played by hammers tripped from the upper half of the upper manual – were general by at least 1725. Also, Adlung suggests that the Thuringian keyboards for manual and pedal had dimensions greater than those on other organs, hence perhaps the particular avidity with which they were rebuilt from the mid eighteenth century on. In any case, efforts to attain some degree of uniformity in Thuringia by about 1725 are illustrated by what must be the first organ-builder's schedule or sales brochure, issued by J. G. Schröter in Erfurt in 1723 (*MGG* 'Schröter, Johann Georg'.) Few extant instruments give a total picture of the sound and the mechanical characteristics of the Thuringian organ, but the largely unaltered thirty-stop organ of Elsleben near Erfurt (completed in 1750 by F. Volkland – see Adlung 1768 1 p216) can still serve as an example of an organ type particularly relevant to J. S. Bach.

Arnstadt, Neue Kirche (Bonifatiuskirche)

J. F. Wender, contract 17 October 1699; tested end of June or beginning of July 1703 by J. S. Bach, who subsequently became organist (*Dok* II pp10–12).

Original position (David 1951 p23): in west-end gallery above two other galleries. Extant: console *en fenêtre* (in town museum), case-front and at least seven ranks, marked + (extant pedalboard not original?).

m = metal; t = 50% tin; t^* = 87.5% tin; wd = wood

Contract (Müller 1950 p32): 800 reichsthaler including woodwork

Oberwerk		'Brustwerk und Positiv'		Seiten Basse oder Pedal	
Principal t^*	8	Principal t^*	4	Principal t^* (case)	8
+ Viola da Gamba t	8	+ Stillgedacktes m	8	Sub Bass wd	16
+ Quinte dene m	8 [= 16?]	Spitzflöte m	[4?]	Posaunen Basse wd	16
+ Grossgedacktes m	8	Quinte	3	Cornet Basse [m?]	2
Offene Quinte m	6	Sesquialtere doppelt m			
+ Octave m	4	+ Nachthorn m	4		
Mixtur m	8 [! IV]	Mixtur m	III[IV]		
+ Gemshorn m	8				
Cympel doppelt	[III]				
Trompete m	8				

Tremulant [listed as *Ow* stop, but to whole organ?]
Cymbelstern

Contract compass: manuals CD–c''' (48 keys), pedal CD–c'd' (25); D = a 'sharp' key (see below)
Couplers: *Bw/Ow* (shove-coupler?), *Ow/P* (wind-coupler, i.e. double pallets?)

Doubts about the precise stoplist as played by J. S. Bach in 1703 arise from discrepancies between the signed contract and the extant, albeit damaged, stop labels (now stuck to stop-knobs, not placed above or below*). Clarifications were attempted by Terry (1929 pp349–50), Emery (1972) and Klotz (1975 p379); Spitta (1 pp218–221) adds further alternatives. The biggest difficulty concerns the Quintatön (8' stopped = 16' tone, necessary in view of proposed Quinte 6'?) and Cornet 2' (replaced by Violon 16' on the console, but the original location would have allowed no room for such pipes – see Harmon 1971 p348). Further: the mixture-ranks above are as specified at the console, the Cymbelstern is replaced by two *Glockenaccord* (*Ow* and *Bw*? = tuned bells already there in 1703?), and there is a *Hohlflaët* 8F von g–d' (treble *Bw* stop? incomplete pedal stop? does g–d' mean g–d''''?). Various writers claim that the extant Octave 4' is that of the *Ow* or of the *Bw*. Perhaps the Quintadena 8' was a *Bw* stop, as became conventional in this area later in the century?

    NB: the order of stops in the contract may reflect order of ranks on the chests. The division of the *Bw* on either side of a central panel (now altered) suggests that this was to allow the *Ow* to have suspended action (without squares), as was conventional in the area. Such action remained conventional, though the chest-plan at Arnstadt – halved pedal-chests to the front, either side of the side-work or *Bw* – was not; in principle, this must be considered an antique feature. Chest layout probably followed the pipe arrangement of the case, with both *Ow* and *Bw* pallet-boxes to the front of the organ, corresponding to the impost-level (another antique feature). The Violon 16', probably of very small scale, may have been placed at the back, with or without the (full-length?) Posaune; the increasingly frequent placing of pedal-chests to the back of the organ, where space was less critical, is itself a result of desiring more *Gravität*. On the present case-front, one *Ow* tower and both pedal towers have Cymbelstern designs. On the present console, the *Ow* keys protrude from the case-front, the *Bw* not at all; the keyboard is symmetrical (like some later harpsichords with FF–f''' compass), i.e. natural-sharp-natural-natural. . . at either end. This would make the 'D' key play C and the 'D♯' play D, without an actual D♯ (though the contract does not say this). But it has not been conclusively shown that the 'extant Arnstadt keyboards' (including the pedals) have anything to do with the organ known to J. S. Bach in 1703, typical though they certainly are of Thuringia in the early or mid eighteenth century.

    Though much larger, the Eisenach Georgenkirche (rebuilt 1696–1707) was more northern in its stoplist, with a *Hw* suited to a big town church:

16.8.8.8.6.4.4.3.III.VI.III.8

Unlike Ohrdruf (rebuilt 1690–1706), neither Eisenach nor Arnstadt had a *Rückpositiv*, and both were displayed high and wide against the west-end wall, opposite the altar. The divided Arnstadt *Brustwerk* (a technique followed throughout the eighteenth century in the Eisenach–Brunswick region) was paralleled on a larger scale at Eisenach, with its *Hw*, *Bw* and two pairs of side chests, upper and lower. In neither organ were manual reeds prominent, but both had low chorus Quint and important Sesquialteras (three at Eisenach). Wender's contracted pedal of 8.16.16.2 seems to have been replaced by a heavier pedal department, though this is not certain; either way, the eventual Eisenach pedal (1707?) reflected the repertory more likely in a larger church:

16.32.16.16.8.8.4.4.1.V.32.16.8.2

* Therefore the labels, however old they may be, are almost certainly not in the 1703 positions.

Ohrdruf was altogether more traditional than Arnstadt, with almost no colour stops in the contracts of 1688 and 1690 (Lux 1926 pp154-5):

Hw 8.16.8.4.3.2.IV.II.8
Rp 4.8.3.2.1.Sesq
Ped 16.16.8.III.16.2
Four octaves [CD-c''''?]

But the two choruses, pedal solo stops and Sesquialtera would make the repertory from Scheidt to Pachelbel possible. Lüneburg Michaeliskirche was far more old-fashioned until its rebuild in 1705-8 as a full-sized Hamburg organ (43 stops divided between three manuals and pedal – Niedt/Mattheson p191); the organ presumably known to J. S. Bach in 1700-2 had one big chest shared by *Hw* and *Ped* in Dutch and/or north German style and a *Bw* like those common across northern Europe in *c*1625 (David 1951 p80):

Hw/Ped 16.*16*.8.4.*2*. *2*.II.IV. *8*.*2*
Rp 8.8.8.8.4.3.2.1½.IV-v.4
Bw 2.2.II.III-IV.8

Probably the pedal had the italicized ranks as well as a valve to the Principal 16′ and/or total chorus: this would have allowed the young Bach a very versatile pedal. Sangerhausen, when J. S. Bach applied for the post there in 1702, had a smaller but not dissimilar organ of 1603/1697, no doubt the 'expression of a different sense of style' from the Hildebrandt organ that later replaced it, probably on the composer's recommendation (Dähnert 1962 p61).

The Arnstadt organ must have been suitable for two good *pleni*, Sesquialtera solo, various soft colours including three or four characteristic 8′ registrations, *pleno* bass and various continuo accompaniments. The two sets of bells played triads of (e.g.) C major (as Werckmeister seems to recommend, 1698 p38) and presumably were used for a special effect on feast-days (Mattheson 1713 p261); the Tremulant may or may not have illustrated Mattheson's description of a 'held note without a *trillo*'.* Less well suited to this organ would be works requiring more equal choruses, various solo colours (reeds, Larigot etc), tenor or alto cantus firmus in either manual or (more importantly) in pedal, and (should they have been required) brilliant manual lines for trios. The *Obituary* says of Arnstadt:

> Hier zeigte er eigentlich die ersten Früchte seines Fleisses in der Kunst des Orgel-spielens, und in der Composition, welche er grössentheils nur durch das Betrachten der Wercke der damaligen berühmten und gründlichen Componisten und angewandtes eigenes Nachsinnen erlernet hatte. In der Orgelkunst nahm er sich Bruhnsens, Reinkens, Buxtehudens und einer guter französischer Organisten ihre Werke zu Mustern. Hier in Arnstadt bewog ihn einsmals ein besonderer starker Trieb, den er hatte, so viel von guten organisten, als ihm möglich war, zu hören, dass er, und zwar zu Fusse, eine Reise nach Lübeck antrat, um den dasigen berühmten Organisten an der Marienkirche Diedrich Buxtehuden, zu behorchen (*Dok* III p82).

> Here he really showed the first fruits of his industry in the art of organ-playing and in composition, which he had learnt to a large extent only from contemplating the works of solid composers who were famous at the time, and from applying his own study. In

---

* 'something like what a voice does at certain times, when it holds a note without a *trillo*' ('wie etwan eine Stimme zu gewissen Zeiten thut, wenn sie etwas ohne Trillo aushält': *ibid*). This suggests a gentle wavering as distinct from the strong vibrato applied from time to time by the singer.

the art of the organ he took the works of Bruhns, Reincken, Buxtehude and some good French organists as models. Here in Arnstadt he was moved on one occasion by such an especially strong desire to hear as many good organists as he could that he set out on a journey – walking all the way, in fact – to Lübeck in order to listen to the famous organist of the Marienkirche there, Dietrich Buxtehude.

If J. S. Bach got to know Buxtehude's larger instrument in the Marienkirche, it is the more striking that he did not ask for more manual reeds at Mühlhausen, particular in the *Rp*.* Perhaps there was no question of its being totally rebuilt or enlarged in a radical manner.

It was on the occasion of the consistory's complaint over his four-month absence from Arnstadt that J. S. Bach was also criticized for certain of his musical practices (see above, p36). How far these faults reflected practices heard in Lübeck cannot be known, nor whether such chorales as BWV 715 actually do convey Buxtehude's method of accompaniment, despite assertions of this kind still often made.

Mühlhausen, Blasiuskirche (Divi Blasii)

Organ originally of 1687–91, rebuilt by J. F. Wender 1708–9 after report by J. S. Bach (before 21 February 1708 – see below, pp141–4).

Original position (David 1951 p29): in second west-end gallery.

Stoplist in Adlung 1768 I pp260–1.

Ober- und Hauptwerk (II)		*Rückpositiv* (I)	
Principal	8	Gedackt	8
Oktave	4	Salcional	4
Oktave	2	Spitzflöte	2
Cymbel	II	Sesquialtera	
Mixtur (50% tin #)	IV	Principal	4
Violdigamba	8	Quintatön	8
Gedackt	4	Quintflöte	[1⅓] (Dähnert 1970)
Quinte (*Nassat)	3	Oktave	2
Fagott von C bis c′	16†	Cymbel	III
Quintatön	16		
Sesquialtera	II	(*Rp* stops behind organist's back)	
Brustwerk (III)		*Basslade*	
Principal	2	Untersatz	32
Mixtur	III	Principal	16
Schallmey	8	Subbass	16
Quinte (*3)	1⅓	Oktave	8
Terz	1⅗	Oktave	4
Flöte	4	Mixtur	IV
Stillgedackt	8	Posaune	16
		Cornetbass	2
		Rohrflötenbass	1

\# Wender's report (*Dok* I p154)
* J. S. Bach's report

Tremulant throughout ('durch alle 3 Claviere' according to Adlung)
Cymbelstern, Pauke, Calcantenwecker (star, drum [beating pipes], blower's signal)
six bellows (four to manuals, two to pedal)

Compass: CD–d′–d‴ (26, 50 notes); keys of ivory (Wender's report)
Couplers: *Bw/Hw, Rp/Hw, Hw/P*
† in Adlung, 'Von C bis c̄′ (*sic*)

* The Marienkirche reeds were *Hw* 16.8.8, *Rp* 16.8.8.8, *Bw* 8.8, *Ped* 32.16.16.8.8.2 (Niedt/Mattheson 1721 pp189–90).

Doubts about the stoplist of the organ as it was in J. S. Bach's period or soon afterwards (it was completed after his move to Weimar) arise from the absence of documentation between Wender's report of 22 February 1708 and Adlung (1768). David (1951 pp86–7) suggests the following: Violdigamba was a Gemshorn before the rebuild (but this could be only a change of name); the Fagott was a Trompete 8′ (perhaps narrow-scaled); the Cymbelstern was a Glockenspiel, planned but not made (in 1742 J. C. Voigt said it had been projected ('angegeben') by J. S. Bach but that he had left for Weimar before it was finished – *Dok* II p405); the *Bw/Hw* was new (perhaps with wire-couplers as suggested by Werckmeister 1698 p38). Klotz, arguing from music which supposedly dates from the Mühlhausen years, suggests a complete compass of C–d′c‴ (1950 pp193), but there is no reason to think that Aldung's compass is not that of 1708: Zavarsky (1975) suggests that the Pauke and Cymbelstern, as they were not mentioned by J. S. Bach, either were added later or were not of significance to him.*

NB: the order of stops in at least the *Hw* as given by Adlung probably reflects the order at the keyboards (two columns, *l* down from Principal 8′ *r* down from Violdigamba). The distribution of the bellows is as recommended by Werckmeister. The Sesquialtera seems to have been 17.19, according to Zavarsky (1975), but there is no clear evidence for this.

The stoplist looks like a somewhat smaller version of Werckmeister's model 'disposition for a large organ' (1698 p50):

Ow   16.16.8.8.8.8.8.6.4.3.2.1⅗.VI.16.8
Rp   8.8.4.4.4.3.3.2.1⅗.IV.8.4
Bw   4.8.8.4.4.3.2.2.1.1⅗.III.8
Ped 16.32.16.8.8.4.2.1.1.IV.16.8.2
2 Tremulants, Zimbelstern, Pauke

It is certainly possible, on the basis of his known report, to see J. S. Bach as having been influenced by or at least acquainted with J. C. Bach's 'improvement plan' ('Verbesserungsstück') at Eisenach Georgenkirche (1696 – see Löffler 1928), for the elder Bach also required 32′ pedal stop (with its own wind – see J. S. Bach's report, p142 below), large Posaune scale, a Fagott 16′, Viola da gamba, Sesquialtera and Glockenspiel. What these Glockenspiels were used for can only be a matter of conjecture, but Eisenach, Mühlhausen and Weimar each had one projected. Zavarsky (1975) also sees as characteristic of the period and area the 'dark tone' resulting from a wide Quinte (Nassat) and from the thickening Sesquialteras (cf. the three tierces of Werckmeister, above). Coupling all three manuals may also have been a new taste; might it even have been required for the passage in the chorale BWV 720 from b20? Insofar as their later organ in the Marienkirche, Mühlhausen (1734–8) had some of the same effects as those implied by J. S. Bach in his report,† J. F. Wender and his son may well have been influenced by the composer. Perhaps there was resistance at the Marienkirche to giving the contract to the Wenders, since J. S. Bach seems to have recommended Hildebrandt (*Dok* I p80) and since J. F. Wender's work at Divi Blasii in 1710 had not been satisfactory. Spitta thought Wender 'not a solid worker' (I p218), but Kuhnau had singled him out with Silbermann as a particularly good builder (in Mattheson 1725 pp234–5). J. G. Walther said it was

---

* If the Zimbelstern was not an important stop to J. S. Bach, he must have been exceptional, coming as he did between (e.g.) L. Compenius (who recommended three at Erfurt Predigerkirche in 1650, all 24 bells of which could be pulled 'zur vollen Musik': Bal 1981 p58) and Adlung (who liked the bells to be tuned to a triad).

† The fact that the Marienkirche had as its only solo reed a Sordino or 'muted Trumpet' (Adlung 1768 I p259) may indirectly suggest that J. S. Bach's Schalemoy at Divi Blasii was of the same kind.

Wender who advised him to apply for the post at Mühlhausen early in 1707 (Spitta I p332).

For further comments on the organ as projected by J. S. Bach, see chapter 17. Some implications are unclear: Was the Nassat stopped or semi-stopped? Was the Sesquialtera merely a Tierce and did it therefore need the $2\frac{1}{3}'$, or did the Nassat have a place in the *pleno*? For the Viola and Salicional, does 'admirabel concordiren' (see p141) mean they were combined by means of coupler or they 'went well together' in two-manual play? If so, at octave pitch? Does 'thoroughly tuned' suggest that the old temperament remained? Does the Gedackt's 'zur Music accordiret' suggest that it had to fit the pitch of instruments and was thus at lower pitch than the other stops? Why should the *Bw/Hw* coupler be necessary – for the *Bw* reed and Mixtur to be in the *pleno* or for *Hw* Nassat versus *Bw* Terz combinations?* Was the Glockenspiel not made, or was it merely not mentioned by Adlung/Albrecht (perhaps because it was out of order)? Was it a pedal stop?

Compared with Arnstadt, the Mühlhausen project must have had more variety in continuo work and in the scoring of cantus-firmus music (bass, tenor, alto and soprano in the pedal, soprano and tenor in the *Bw*, soprano in all three manuals). The position of its stop-knobs may suggest that the *Rp* was set up for a movement without change of stops and mostly as a secondary chorus. The *Hw* in particular is very colourful: 16' reed, two different flute colours, Sesquialtera, string stop, principals with or without Cymbel. The pedal has two distinct choruses, with one flute only, and no auxiliary 16' or 8' ranks such as were added in a later renovation reported in Adlung. The string colours may have served for continuo work as well as for the preludizing moments in the service, but without a Trumpet the Pauke must have been limited to thunder effects only. That some kind of Sesquialtera was associated with chorale melodies is clear from much earlier contracts (e.g. 'zum Choralspielen' at the Erfurt Predigerkirche in 1647: Ziller 1935 p25) and from such ensemble pieces as the Weimar cantata BWV 161.

Weimar, Schlosskapelle

Organ originally of 1658 (L. Compenius, contract 15 December 1657), repaired and partially rebuilt 1707–8, 1713–14 (H. N. Trebs, contract 29 June 1712), 1719–20 (precise dates and extent of work done at each stage are as yet unclarified; a forthcoming *BJ* article is to be devoted to the Weimar organ).

Original position (Jauernig 1950 pp60–8): in third gallery above altar-pulpit, recessed in a chamber (with its own roof) away from gallery balustrade; moved to the back of that gallery in 1707–8 rebuild. Compenius gave the option of a *Rückpositiv* (Schneider 1937 pp73–4), but the second manual seems to have been a 'side positive' (see comment on the Arnstadt organ, p120 above).

Stoplist as described in 1737 (David 1951 pp29–33, 88):

Ober Clavier		Unter Clavier		Pedal	
+ Principal *t*	8	Principal *t*	8	Gross Untersatz *wd*	32
+ Quintadena *m*	16	Viol di Gamba *m*	8	Sub-Bass *wd*	16
+ Gemsshorn *m*	8	+ Gedackt *m*	8	Posaun Bass *wd*	16
Grobgedackt *m*	8	+ Trompete *m*	8	Violon Bass *wd*	16
Quintadena *m*	4	Klein Gedackt *m*	4	Principal Bass *m*	8

* Since the *Bw* Quint was an open tin rank in the front.

Octava *m*	4	Octava *m*	4	Trompete Bass *m*	8
Mixtur *m*	VI	+ Wald-Flöthe *m*	2	Cornett Bass *m*	4
+ Cymbel *m*	III	Sesquialtera	IV	

Glocken Spiel und
   Spiel-Register dazu
   ('with stop-knob')

aus 3 und 2 Fuss
(= 12.15.17.19?)

+ Compenius stops (Schneider 1937 p75)

Tremulant *Hw*, Tremulant *Uw*
Cymbelstern

Compass: probably the CD–d'e'–c''' of the Compenius organ (but see below)
Couplers: *Hw/P*, *Uw/Hw*
Pitch: see below

Doubts about the precise stoplist as played by J. S. Bach arise from uncertainty about the contents of the organ in 1708 and about the nature of the repair work (particularly 1719–20), and from the absence of a stoplist earlier than the 1730s (two sources: David *op cit*); moreover, the new organ begun in *c*1756 and described in Adlung 1768 1 p282 appears to have been virtually identical to that in 1737 (except for its low pitch or *Kammerton*?). Compenius's project was as follows:

Hw and *Ped*   8.16.8.4.8.4.3.2.IV–V. II (or III)
Ped chest   16.16.16.2
Rp   4.8.8.4.2.II.8.4
Bw   4.2.16.4

Cymbelsterns, Vogelgesang, Trummel, tremulant (throughout), 2 Sperrventils
Compass: with D♯, F♯ and C♯, also 'toppelten dis und gis' (i.e. keys for d♯'/eb', d''/eb'' and g♯'/ab', g♯''/ab''?)
Ivory keys, four bellows, metal alloy of 9:6 lead:tin

It is assumed (e.g. Klotz 1975 p326) that the *Rp* was not in fact built, but it is always possible that the removal away to the back of the gallery in 1707–8 included the discarding of a chair organ, and even that the registrations in the D minor Concerto BWV 596 reflect uncertainty as to what the much worked-on organ was eventually to contain.

The *compass* is equally uncertain: there is no later reference to split sharps, and the 29 bells bought from Nuremberg on 6 October 1712 and a further 12 on 22 May 1713 (cf. Schulze 1972) complicate the calculations further. Were the 29 for the pedal, and if so what compass (C–e' complete; CD–f')? Were the 12 bought to replace some of these, or was there a total of 41; and if the latter, for what compass?

The *pitch* has often been claimed, in literature from Spitta onwards, to have been high (3 semitones above *Kammerton*), but if the *Orgelbüchlein* melodies were composed at sung pitch, it can not have been much above a' = 440Hz. On the other hand, the report of eight choirboys singing chorales (Jauernig 1950 p71) may suggest that they, rather than the congregation, needed to be accommodated and may have found a higher pitch appropriate; in any case, there may well be no purpose in looking at the *Orgelbüchlein* for signs of the Weimar pitch, since it may have been begun with reference to another church (see p41 above). For cantatas, Weimar seems to have had a positive organ (Trebs was paid for 'eine Positiv Bank' ('a bench for the positive'?) on 7 March 1712: Terry 1933 p97).

The *stoplist* as recorded may well be the result of the major work done in 1719–20 (110 reichsthaler – Jauernig 1950 p74); it is difficult to see how the organ chamber as implied by the sources (with its tinplate-lined* roof shaped out of the main cupola – *ibid* p66) could hold such a pedal department, or how its modest front as recorded in the well-known painting (*Dok* IV p93) could include such a second manual, with Principal 8' etc.

Elucidation of the Weimar organ and its history during J. S. Bach's tenure is particularly important in view of the claim made in the *Obituary*, and not contradicted by any sources known today, that

---

* Cf. the composer's report of the Halle organ (below, p146).

> hier hat er auch die meisten seiner Orgelstücke gesetzt (*Dok* III p83).
>
> here he also composed most of his organ works.

Moreover, the great amount of rebuilding that took place while he was organist may well reflect another aspect of the post he held at Weimar: as the *Obituary* put it,

> Das Wohlgefallen seiner gnädigen Herrschaft an seinem Spielen, feuerte ihn an, alles mögliche in der Kunst die Orgel zu handhaben, zu versuchen (*ibid* pp82–3).
>
> The satisfaction of his gracious Lordship with his playing fired him to try everything possible in the art of handling the organ.

Besides,

> In Weymar hat er nicht weniger verschiedene brafe Organisten gezogen (*ibid* p83).
>
> In Weimar he no less brought out several fine organists.

That he composed so much music here, had the opportunity to direct various organ repairs, and influenced several important organists (J. G. Walther, J. T. Krebs, J. C. Vogler) makes the Weimar instrument the single most important Bach organ.

J. G. Walther's organ in the Town Church at Weimar (C. Junge, 1685) was more old-fashioned in important respects (Wette 1737 pp256–62):

> *Hw* 8.16.8.8.8.4.3.2.IV.III.8
> *Rp* 4.8.8.4.4.4.2.1.II.III
> *Ped* 16.16.8.2 (3 reeds)
>
> Tremulant to each manual
> *Hw/P*, *Rp/P* couplers (plus manual shove-coupler?)
> Zimbelstern to *Rp*
> Six bellows

Here were still the colourful *Positif* 4′ ranks and the restricted pedal of a previous period. In comparison, the castle organ had some unusual features: the scope for 8.4 combinations was far wider, the bass line stronger; there seem not to have been high chorus ranks but two manual choruses of very distinct character. It certainly looks as if Bach kept or consolidated the idea of a *plein jeu / grand jeu* relationship (Klotz 1975 p387):

> *plein jeu* *Hw* 8.4.VI.III
> *grand jeu* *Pos* 8.4.Sesq.Tromp

Such an arrangement would be encouraged by a court-chapel organ having two wide tiers in a single case high above the altar, rather than a vertically designed structure complete with separate chair organ. How far such choruses coloured performance is conjectural (see chapter 18), but the distant effect of the organ placed in a top (third) gallery, and in a chamber back from the front of the gallery, would obviously contribute a certain sound quality to (e.g.) 8.4 registrations in the *Orgelbüchlein*. The two flute choruses (16.8.4 and 8.4.2) must have appeared to hover at the top of the tall narrow chapel.

Very little either of heavy, obtrusive organ sound or of the tinkling baroquery fashionable during our own period would have been possible at Weimar. The emphasis seems rather to have been on wide-ranging colours and combinations, more perhaps for solo interlude and/or background music as required in a court chapel than for the range of accompaniments necessary in a parish church, where the organ was placed so much nearer most of the congregation.* But from the Untersatz 32′ to the Cymbel III, one could imagine the full coupled *tutti* as being adequate for the room – indeed, 'incomparable' was one expression used ('unvergleichlich' – Wette 1737 pp174–6). How far it accompanied the courtly congregation in communal singing, however, is uncertain. Nor can its connection with the contemporary organ music be assumed *tout court*. The chorale BWV 620 may suggest that its compass included pedal C$\sharp$ – but only if it can be proved both that J. S. Bach always composed with an eye to available compass, and that P 283 was not so written merely for the sake of clarity but was intended literally (i.e., that the pedal did not play an octave higher with 16′ and 32′ stops). The Concerto in D minor BWV 596 seems to avoid d‴, but if that was for the sake of the Weimar organ, what can its *Rp* registration mean?

J. G. Walther (1732, under 'Trebs') said that H. N. Trebs became privileged court builder in 1712 and built sixteen organs in that capacity, in addition to the Jakobikirche, Weimar. In a testimonial written for him in 1711, J. S. Bach praised his industry and conscientiousness (*Dok* I p156). Whether Bach drafted the stoplist for the little Trebs organ in Taubach which he inspected in 1710 is not known (though it is often supposed that he did); but the provision of pedal flute and manual tierce suggests priorities (Jauernig 1950 p83):

> *Manual* 4.8.8.3.2.1⅗.1.III
> *Ped* Subbass 16(*wd*).Waldflöte 2(*m*).Principal 8(*wd*)
> Tremulant, Zimbelstern, Coupler

In *c*1742 Trebs and Bach collaborated on the organ for Bad Berka, according to a later note (*Dok* II p406):

> *Hw* 8.16.8.8.8.4.4.3.3.2.v.Sesq.8
> *Bw* 4.8.8.4.3.2.2.1⅗ .III
> *Ped* 8.16.4.16.8.4
> *Hw/P* (and *Bw/Hw* shove-coupler?)

Solo pedal reed and tierce ranks were now filled out with other stops, but there were no strings or *plein/grand jeu* contrasts of the Weimar kind. Bad Berka was altogether more conventional, reflecting †he requirements of a normal parish church.

That court chapels had a distinctive type of organ is also suggested by the instru-

---

* Lutheran castle chapels and their organs deserve separate study, not least as the requirements of both must have been more specialized than those of parish churches. From Torgau Schlosskirche onwards (dedicated by Luther on 5 October 1544), the small rectangular shape of such chapels emphasized the focal points: pulpit to one side (usually left?), altar at one end, organ in the gallery at the other, font conspicuous. The shape varied (Stuttgart 1553–60, Stettin 1570–7), but at Schmalkalden (1590) a conception arose that was important for developments in Thuringia: altar, pulpit and organ were arranged in one vertical line facing the congregation. The organ was placed high and held back discreetly from the gallery front (as also at Eisenberg, Schütz's chapel in Dresden, Bach's chapel in Weimar, etc). The chapels of Weimar, Eisenberg and Weissenfels changed the proportions by having a much greater height, thus removing the organ music further.

ments at Weissenfels (where J. S. Bach visited in 1713 etc – see *Dok* IV p413) and Eisenberg, in Thuringia (no known visit):

Weissenfels (Werner 1911 pp126–7; early-18th-century comments)
C. Förner (Leipzig), 1673
Hw   8.16.8.8.4.3.2.Sesq.IV. 16.8
Bw   4.8.8.4.3.2.Sesq.III.8.4
Ped 8.16.4.3.2.IV.16.8.2
Tremulant 'gentle and adjusted to a precise 6/4 beat' ('leise und gerade auf 6/4 Takt gerichtet')
CD-f'-c''' (or pedal CD-d'e'f'?)
Sensitive action, 'like a well-quilled spinet'
3 spring-chests (*Bw* rather than *Rp* because of continuo requirements in a court chapel? *Bw* placed on floor of organ)
Reeds 'very durable and constant'; many longer pipes mitred; 3 bellows of special design so capacious that they can play for 180 bars, such as a Credo of three verses

Eisenberg (Adlung 1768 1 p215)
J. Donat (Zwickau), repaired in 1732 by H. G. Trost
Hw   8.16.8.8.8.4.4.4.3.VI
Bw   4.8.4.4.2.1⅓.8
Ped 8.16.16.8
Tremulant

Weissenfels is the organ with the famous pedal compass reaching f', a 'superfluous' note in Adlung's opinion but not in J. F. Agricola's (Adlung 1768 II p27):

Zu gewissen Arten von Pedalstücken ist es vielmehr sehr gut.

On the contrary, for certain kinds of pedal pieces it is very good.

Both instruments are extremely decorous: Weissenfels swinging high in the west gallery, compelled by architectural or acoustical priorities to be as high as possible under the barrel-vaulted ceiling (hence the mitred pipes of Subbass and 16' reed?), Eisenberg in the back of the gallery above the altar-pulpit. Though Trost may be responsible for some of the 8' colour at Eisenberg, the four 4' flutes and Regal recall the style of older court chapels (e.g. Gotha: five regals in a 15-stop *Brustwerk*). The variety at Weissenfels was greater than at Weimar, but it had neither the pedal weight nor the *plein/grand jeu* contrast.

Several of the assumptions made about the Weissenfels organ by Werner in 1911 (pp128–30) are not so clearly backed by evidence as was then thought: that the 'west'-end organ was separated from the choir at the 'east' end (for cantatas? chorales? motets?), that the organ accompanied the hymns (sung by choir? court congregation? both?), that it played the chorales *alternatim* with the choir (but this is quite possible and might indeed suggest west–east stereophony), that the organist always played at the beginning of services as the ducal party was making its entrance. However, it does seem that the duke's birthday celebrations began with an hour's organ music in the court chapel (before the town procession etc), and that the organist played a group of suitable chorales (Werner 1911 pp55, 130), presumably in the form of chorale-variations in Dutch manner. Similarly, there seems to be no doubt that the organ was silent on *Buss-* and *Bettage*.

Leipzig, Paulinerkirche (Universitätskirche)

J. Scheibe, contract 11 May 1711, completed 4 November 1716; advisers D. Vetter and A. H. Casparini; tested by J. S. Bach,* report signed 17 December 1717.

Original position: in west-end gallery (incorporated parts of old organ in south gallery). Church destroyed *c*1968 for buildings of the Karl-Marx-Universität.

Stoplist from 1718 (*Dok* I p167): 2926 taler (Dähnert 1980 pp183–4)

Hauptwerk (II)		*Brustwerk* (III)		*Hinter-Wercke, als ein Echo* (I)	
Gross-Principal *t*	16	Principal *t*	8	Lieblich getackt	8
Gross-Quinta-Tön	16	Viol di Gamb ('naturell')	8	Quinta-Tön	8
Klein Principal	8	Grob getackt (wide)	8	Fleute douce	4
Schalmo	8	Octav	4	Quinta decima	4
Fleute Allemande	8	Rohr-Flöte	4	Decima nona	3
Gems-Horn	8	Octav	2	Holl-Flöte	2
Octav	4	Nassat	3	Viola	2
Quinta	3	Sedecima	I	Vigesima nona	1½
Quint-Nassat	3	Schweitzer-Pfeiffe	I	Weit-Pfeiffe	I
Octavina	2	Largo [Larigot]		Mixtur	III
Wald-Flöte	2	Mixtur	III	Helle Cymbal	II
Gross Mixtur	V–VI	Helle Cymbal	II	Sertin	8
Cornetti	III				
Zinck (flue?)	II				

Pedal					
large chest		*small Bw pedal-chest*		*large side-chests*	
Gross Principal *t*	16	Gross hell-Quinten-Bass	6	Gross Principal-Bass *t*	16
Gross-Quinta-Tön	16	(case-front)		Sub-Bas	16
Octav	8	Jubal	8	Posaune	16
Octav	4	Nacht-Horn	4	Trompete	8
Quint	3	Octav	2	Holl-Flöten	I
Mixtur	V–VI			Mixtur	IV

Sperrventils to *Hw*, *Bw*, side-pedal, Zimbelstern, *Hinterwerk*
Blower's signal

Compass: unknown
Coupler: *Bw/Hw*

The *Dresdner MS* (Smets 1931, no. 76) lists some stops differently: *Bw* Gedackt of wood, *Hw* Schalmo = Chalumeau, *HiW* Mixtur IV not III, *Ped* Nachthorn 8' not 4', Mixtur VI not IV (one Mixtur only); and it describes one Principal 16' only (*Hw* Principal 16' and Quintatön 16' playable by pedal). Its author describes some stops as follows, after a visit in 1736:
Chalumeau (stopped reed, very soft and gentle, imitating the instrument)
Fleute Allemande (narrow-scaled open wood, sharply voiced, imitating the traverso)
Weite Pfeiffe (open metal, very wide, sharply voiced, also called *Glöcklein-Thon*)
Sertin (stopped reed, called muted trumpet on account of sharp voicing and blaring tone ('Blättern'))
Largo (wide-scaled 1⅓' metal open, almost a *Glöcklein-Thon*)
Schweitzer pfeiffe (very narrow open pipes, sharply voiced) [i.e. overblowing]
Jubal (Principal-scale, rather dull-voiced ('stumpff'), less sharp than Principal)
Grosse Hell Quinte (wide-scaled, with a rather high cut-up, therefore very loud and reverberant).
For the arrangement of the stop-knobs at the console, see *Dok* IV p163; for J. A. Scheibe's comments on the organ see Mattheson's *Ehrenpforte* (1740) p311; and for Silbermann's scheme of 1710 see Flade 1926 p50.

---

* He seems to have been the fourth choice (*Dok* II p69): Kuhnau, G. F. Kauffmann of Halle, and E. Lindner of Freiberg had already been asked.

It is possible to conclude from J. S. Bach's report (see chapter 17) either that it was a very fine organ (Schering 1941 p112) or that it was mediocre (Flade 1926 p50).* The scope is immediately much greater than most organs of the area, but it does not rival the completeness of Lübeck Marienkirche. The echo organ obviously had a different purpose from the Lübeck/Hamburg *Oberwerk*. Neither manual reeds nor strings feature prominently, and though either the Cornetti or Zinck must have resembled a Sesquialtera, Tierces are also discreet. The array of small flutes suggests Scheibe's loyalty to the past, though he was not alone in this: see the famous and not dissimilar organ of Görlitz (E. Casparini, 1697–1703), with which indeed the Paulinerkirche stoplist has not a little in common. The organ rather suggests a lack of focus: for what kind of music was it built, other than *pleno* pieces, and interludes using a variety of stop-combinations?

The Augustinerkirche, Erfurt (inspected by J. S. Bach in 1716: *Dok* I pp161–3), was more in the Thuringian tradition (string stops, Sesquialteras, heavy pedal) but also had various arrays of flutes including the imitative side-blown pipes increasingly typical of the future organs of its maker J. G. Schröter and others. More important still was the large organ of Halle Liebfrauenkirche (inspected by J. S. Bach in 1716 – see chapter 17): its stoplist, given by Adlung and by Marpurg (1758 pp512–13), was thought by Hess (1774 p116) to be impossible to improve upon:

C. Cuncius, 1712–16
  Hw (I)   16.16.8.8.8.6.4.4.3.2.2.1⅗.VI.IV.16.8
  Ow (II)   8.16.8.8.4.4.4.3.2.2.1.1⅗.V.III.16.8
  Bw (III) 4.8.8.4.4.3.3.2.2.1.1⅗.IV.II.8.4
  Ped   16.32.16.8.8.6.4.4.3.2.1.VII.IV.32.16.8.4.2
Adlung 1768 I pp239–40: Zimbelstern
Serauky 1939 pp481–3:
  3 couplers, 3 Tremulants, compass of CD–c′–c‴
  Hw Gedackt 'strongly voiced'
    Rauschpfeiffe 19.24, Mixtur 22.26.33.36
  Bw Gedackt 'gentle for cantatas' ('lieblich zur Music')
    Mixtur 26.29.33.36
  Ow Mixtur 22.24.26.29.33.36
  Ped 32′ alone, on a separate chest
    Mixtur 19.22.24.26.29

Neither *Ow* nor *Bw* quite corresponds to an older *Rückpositiv*, nor are string stops prominent (one 8′ only); but the rest includes most of the flute, reed and mutation ranks then customary. A somewhat smaller number of stops was distributed over four manuals in the Hamburg Katharinenkirche organ (renovated 1669–74) so evidently admired by J. S. Bach. Of reeds in general, Agricola reported that

> der seel. Kapellmeister Bach war ein grosser Freund davon: der musste doch wol wissen, was und wie darauf gespielet werden könne (Adlung 1768 I p66).

> the late Kapellmeister Bach was a great friend of them; he just had to know what could be played on them, and how.

---

* Perhaps the fullness of J. S. Bach's report (especially when compared with those at Erfurt and Naumburg) suggests that he had written it in some kind of deference to Kuhnau, who may well have been an adviser to the university and whose taste for detailed reports is shown in the one he prepared for the Halle organ (see chapter 17).

This rather suggests that Agricola understood (from hearsay only) that the composer searched out combinations for particular kinds of music – not *grands jeux* so much as solo colours (reeds plus mutations?), pedal cantus firmi, reed choruses and dialogues etc. Judging by Werckmeister's praise of Schnitger's reeds and regals in the Johanniskirche, Magdeburg (1698 p66), the central Germans admired the Hanseatic reeds more than their own stoplists suggest. Of the Hamburg Katharinenkirche organ, where Reincken had had the two 32′ stops in the early 1670s (Fock 1974 pp45–6) and was still organist on the occasion of J. S. Bach's visits in *c*1701 (?) and 1720, Agricola said that

> Hr. J. S. Bach in Leipzig, welcher sich einsmals 2 Stunden lang auf diesem, wie er sagte, in allen Stücken vortrefflichen Werke hat hören lassen, konnte die Schönheit und Verschiedenheit des Klanges dieser Rohrwerke nicht genug rühmen (Adlung 1768 1 p187).

> Herr Bach in Leipzig, who once played in public for two hours on this organ – excellent in all its parts, he said – could not praise enough the beauty and variety of the sound of these reeds.

In drawing attention to reed stops Agricola may well reflect the taste of J. S. Bach, as too he might when he remarks of *Rückpositiv* and reeds that the French liked both (*ibid* p289).

In number of stops, the matching among the three manuals at Halle was also characteristic of the area.* Hamburg was less balanced in this respect, showing much more clearly that each department, in its location and make-up, was a kind of separate organ with its own job. The amorphous equality of manuals on the big organs from *c*1715 onwards is itself a sign of loss of purpose. Halle, with its one wide case, aimed to present a huge array of varieties and combinations, not quite duplicating from manual to manual but without doubt offering similar effects from one to the other. But that it did not give the organist the same kind of idiomatic potential as an older organ – and no doubt was losing that special quality of sound that seems to have died with old tunings – is suggested not least by the gradual disappearance in the music itself of the most idiomatic genres, i.e. the chorale-fantasia and praeludium. Halle would scarcely have served for such pieces: far more suitable for it would have been the new large-scale ritornello preludes (with or without manual-change, which on such organs provided optional variety rather than essential dialogue) and the expressive chorale-prelude. Either way, such hall-churches give an unimaginable 'bloom' to any sound made in them.

Leipzig, Thomaskirche (two organs)

From at least the *Obituary* onwards, when it was reported that J. S. Bach frequently regretted never having a fine organ at his constant disposal, the Thomaskirche organs have been criticized.† Yet the stoplists of the two organs are not at all with-

* This is also characteristic of Silbermann's two-manual organs.
† One could certainly conjecture that had the composer taken the job at the Jakobikirche, Hamburg he would have placed a greater emphasis on organ music in the 1720s than appears to have been the case. The dominating physical presence itself of Schnitger's large organ in a rather modest church speaks for its importance in such Hanseatic town churches. Even Bach's calling himself *director musices* at Leipzig might reflect the Hanseatic organist's use of this term to put himself on an equal footing with the court Kapellmeister (see Edler 1982 pp87–8).

out potential in their old-fashioned character, and the renovation they both under-went a year or two before J. S. Bach's cantorate, with regular attention paid them over the following years, cannot have left them useless.

Old organ (pre-1525?) rebuilt: major work in 1720–2 (J. Scheibe), 1730 (J. Scheibe), 1747, etc; broken up in 1772 ('gar alt', 'very old').

Original position: rear of second west-end gallery (above town councillors' gallery), with *Rp* at gallery-front. The gallery also contained, as well as the choir, two fixed platforms for the string-and wind-players (Stiehl 1971 p73).

Stoplist as in 1722 (Schering 1926 p108; Dähnert 1980 pp184–6)

Oberwerk		Rückpositiv		Brustwerk	
Principal	16	Principal	8	Grobgedackt	8
Principal	8	Quintadena	8	Principal	4
Quintadena	16[8?]	Lieblich Gedackt	8	Nachthorn	4
Octava	4	Klein Gedackt	4	Nasat	3
Quinta	3	Traversa	4	Gemshorn	2
Super Octava	2	Violin	2	Zimbel	II
Spiel-Pfeiffe	8	Rauschquinte	II	Sesquialtera	
Sesquialtera	II	Mixtur	IV	Regal	8
Mixtur	VI/VIII–X	Spitzflöt	4	Geigenregal	4
		Schallflöt	I		
		Krumbhorn	16		
		Trommet	8		

		Pedal	
Tremulant			
Vogelgesang		Subbass *m*	16
Zimbelstern		Posaunenbass*	16
Sperrventil to every chest		Trommetenbass*	8
10 bellows		Schallmeyenbass*	4
		Cornet*	2

* resonators of metal ('ver-
zinnten Blech': Dähnert
op cit)

Compass: unknown

Couplers: unknown, but Praetorius's description of the old organ (1619 p180) said Principal 16′ playable also by *Ped* and couplers 'to both manuals' (i.e. *Bw/Ow, Rp/Ow*?) as well as *Rp/Ped*.

Doubts about the stoplist concern individual stops: perhaps the *Ow* Quintadena was 8′ (i.e. a very narrow Gedackt), the *Rp* probably got its Sesquialtera in 1722, and perhaps the *Rp* Principal was 4′ not 8′. However, none of these suggestions is confirmed by a report made *c*1700 (Schrammek 1975).

Scheibe's report of 27 February 1730 speaks of the organ as being 'newly tempered' ('von neuen temperiret'), which seems to suggest more than mere adjustment in the course of cleaning work undertaken during that period; the report speaks also of a 'thorough revoicing throughout the organ' ('eine Hauptstimmung durch das gantze Werk'), including the Posaune 16′, which

> etwas zu schwach ist und nicht wohl durchdringet, als ist es nöthig, dass in der Kirche, so viel es seyn kann, verstärket werde (B. F. Richter *BJ* 5 (1908) p53).

> is somewhat too weak and does not really penetrate, so it is necessary that it be made as strong-sounding in the church as it can be.

Temperament and voicing were therefore worked on under the responsibility of J. S. Bach. Since the organ parts in Bach's Leipzig cantatas had to be notated and played a tone lower to allow for the organ's high pitch, at least one rank (*Bw* Grobgedackt? *Rp* Lieblich Gedackt?) must have been tuned to equal temperament; Scheibe's remark may suggest that all the organ was so tempered. As for the pitch itself, Kirnberger noted in 1769 that

Zu Leipzig stehen die Orgeln, die zu Herrn J. S. Bachs [Zeit] vorhanden waren, ganz gewiss alle im Chortone (*Dok* III p204).

In Leipzig the organs available in J. S. Bach's time were certainly all in *Chorton*.

Further major work done in 1747 (Spitta II pp870–2) suggests that the organ needed periodic attention beyond minor repairs, and the set of cantatas of 1726 which require *organo obbligato* seems not to have been developed further.

Small organ enlarged by H. Compenius (1630) and repaired by J. Scheibe (1720–1) and Z. Hildebrandt (from 1727?); broken up by Scheibe 1740–1.

Original position: before 1639 on west wall near large organ, removed then to east wall above arch leading into quire, in special gallery facing west.

Stoplist (Dähnert 1980 p186)

Oberwerk		Brust		Rückpositiv	
Principal	8	Trichterregal	8	Principal	4
Gedackt	8	Sifflöt	1	Lieblich Gedackt	8
Quintatön	8	Spitzflöte	2	Hohlflöte	4
Octave	4			Nasat	3
Rauschquinte	12.15	*Pedal*		Octave	2
Mixtur	IV/V/VI/VII–X	Subbass *wd*	16	Sesquialtera	II
Cymbel	II	Fagott	16	Dulcian	8
		Trompete	8	Trompete	8

Tremulant, Zimbelstern, Sperrventil to each chest, 6 bellows

Doubts about the stoplist concern the organ's original position (since the church is conversely orientated, was the first 'west' position in fact the liturgical east wall?) and the number of manuals (a report of c1700 speaks of the large organ having three but gives no details of the small organ – Schrammek 1975). Perhaps the *Brust* (*sic*: not *Brustwerk* etc) was played by *Oberwerk* keys.

Despite frequent assertions today, it is uncertain how playable the small organ was for the performances of the *St Matthew Passion*, or whether it did take the cantus firmus in 'O Lamm Gottes' and 'O Mensch bewein'; but Hildebrandt's work on it may indicate a particular need for the organ.

The main manual of each organ gave several *plena*, both *Rückpositiven* gave much old-fashioned variety, both *Brustwerke* served continuo purposes well (the little organ still reflecting the German practice of having a wind band in the gallery), and on both organs it was possible to have pedal playing the cantus firmus in the bass or the tenor. Moreover, the bigger organ must have found a dialogue of two manuals perfectly feasible. Providing it was thoroughly playable, this organ offered the important choruses that had been traditional, without satisfying the taste for string stops nurtured in Thuringia. It was the kind of organ that had been normal before the new fashions for lifelike flutes and up-to-date reeds or for big single-case organs came about.

Agricola, one of the *Obituary* authors, remarks on an advantage the Leipzig Thomaskirche and Nikolaikirche organs had: that, as in Schnitger's organ in the Berlin Nikolaikirche, the manuals protruded from the front of the organ (so that the lower-manual keys and the front half of the length of the upper-manual keys were clear of the case), which facilitated pedal-playing (Adlung 1768 II p24). Unless they protruded, or unless the pedalboard was placed further back into the organ, it was not possible to sit upright, and as Adlung said, 'Wer recht auf dem Pedale spielen will, muss ganz gerade sitzen' ('he who wants to play on the pedal correctly must sit completely straight'). This basic idea may well have originated with J. S. Bach and in particular from the rebuilds at the hands of Scheibe. Either way, it suggests a newer approach to pedal-playing, one presumably more versatile and 'easy'.

The somewhat larger organ of the Nikolaikirche had a similar character and made possible every registration known, with whatever authenticity, in Bach sources. It is possible that, especially because in the 1730s and 1740s its maintenance was in the hands of Hildebrandt (Dähnert 1962 pp80–1), it was better admired by the composer than that of the Thomaskirche. Although there was a 4' Viola (Salicional?), it still had none of the myriad flute and other effects described in Adlung (1768 I pp229–30) for the organ of the Johanniskirche, Gera, which was 'examined, approved and inaugurated' by J. S. Bach in 1724 (*Dok* II p143); e.g.

> *Hw* new Vox humana (double rank, one flue, one reed)
> Tierce Mixture (C 15.19.22.24.26.29, repeating at c')
> *Ow* Gedackt of cherrywood (turned?), languid and lip lined with tin
> Flöte douce (double rank, one open metal, one open cherrywood)
> Tierce Mixture (C 15.19.22.24)
> *Bw* Nachthorn 'voiced in the treble like a harp' ('obenaus wie eine Harfe intonirt')
> Dolkanflöte with two mouths
> Tierce Mixtur (C 22.24.26)
> *Ped* the Violdigamba 16' 'gives three notes on each key' ('Jeder Clavis giebt 3 Töne an'): i.e., either each pipe had three strong partials (16' 8' 5⅓'?), or there were three pipes (Löffler 1928 p127 suggests 16' 8' 2⅔')

It is not known whether such fashionable inventions are implied by the phrase 'arranged according to the manner of today' used for the rebuild of the old 32' organ in Kassel Martinikirche by the Thüringers J. F. Stertzing and N. Becker in 1732 (Bernsdorff-Engelbrecht pp122–3). It seems that in his report on this organ J. S. Bach may have required that some work be done on the bellows (David 1951 pp59–60). Hildebrandt, whom Bach unsuccessfully recommended for the rebuild of the organ in Mühlhausen Marienkirche when his son J. G. B. Bach went as organist there in 1735 (*Dok* II pp257–8), kept novelties to discreet proportions. So did H. G. Herbst for the still intact organ at Lahm, opened with the church in 1732, played by J. L. Bach (a Weimar pupil: *Dok* II p64) and based on two good choruses, a pedal of 8.16.16.12.8.4.v.32.16.8, and a generally rough tone but with two of the by then customary new colours: Viola 8' and Flaut-traversière 4'.* But H. G. Trost's organ at Altenburg, said to have been praised by J. S. Bach (*Dok* II pp368–9, 372), had several new effects of the kind shown at Gera above (Dähnert 1980 pp19–25):

> Viola da gamba: narrow cylindrical
> Vugara 8': wood, rectangular cross-section
> *Ped* 16 and 8' ranks of wood with tin-lined mouth
> Posaune 32': leathered and rounded shallot
> temperament: can be used 'in allen Modis musicis' but B major and D♯ major have a 'somewhat tolerable hardness' ('einige, doch noch erleidliche Härtigkeit')

The organist, a predecessor of J. L. Krebs, had requested the *Hw* Viola as well as a complete *Hw* flute array at 16', 8', 4' and 2' (Löffler 1932). Trost himself gave in-

---

* Recent claims that this is a 'Bach organ' are not unjustified, and its roughness is useful in counteracting the suavity of the much-restored Schnitgers and Silbermanns.

dications for use of the stops (see below, p159), and Agricola praised the combination of 8.8.8.8 auxiliary stops as well as the effect of a bowed-string sound given by the Flaut travers 16′ in running basses (Marpurg 1758 pp497, 505) – an effect also claimed by J. F. Walther (1727) for the combination of *Ped* principal 16′ + Gemshorn 8′ in J. Wagner's organ in the Berlin Garnisonkirche.

Such were the characteristics of organs in up-to-date castle chapels, and it seems that Trost's parish-church organs were more conventional. The most conventionalized organs of J. S. Bach's acquaintance during the Leipzig period were without doubt those of G. Silbermann, which had virtually no novelties except what could be provided by incomparable voicing, perfect action (in weight, keyfall and keylength) and logically planned stoplists.

Dresden, Frauenkirche

G. Silbermann, 1732–6 (destroyed February 1945).

Position: in gallery above altar and pulpit, high in the 'quire' off a central dome.

Stoplist (Dähnert 1953 p206):

Hauptwerk		Oberwerk		Brustwerk	
Principal	16	Principal	8	Principal	4
Cornet	IV	Gedackt	8	Gedackt	8
Octava	4	Quintaden	16	Rohrflöte	4
Spitzflöte	4	Quintaden	8	Nasat	3
Octava	2	Octava	4	Octava	2
Fagott	16	Flöte [Rohr?]	4	Gemshorn	2
Trompete	8	Nasat	3	Quinta	1⅓
Octavprincipal	8	Octava	2	Sifflöt	1
Viol di Gamba	8	Sesquialtera		Mixtur	III
Rohrflöte	8	Mixtur	IV	Chalumeau	8
Quinta	3	Vox humana	8		
Tertia	1⅗			*Pedal*	
Mixtur	IV			Principalbass	16
Cimbel	III			Clarinbass	4
				Mixturbass	VI
				Octavbass	4
				Gross Untersatz	32
				Posaunenbass	16
				Trompetenbass	8
				Octavbass	8

Kammerton
Compass: C–c′–d‴

For the order of stop-knobs at the console, see Flade 1926 p132. The stoplist resembles Freiberg Petrikirche (*Hw*) and both Zittau and Dresden Hofkirche (*Ped*). For J. S. Bach's 'recital' here, see chapter 7.

The celebrity of the church (begun in 1727) and its circular plan drew attention to this organ, and W. F. Bach, organist of the Sophienkirche, referred in a poem to its 'natural' Vox humana, its Cornet 'sharply penetrating with sweetness' ('mit Anmuth scharff durchdringend') and the *Gravität* of its Fagotto (David 1951 pp61–2). But its volume of sound may not have been great, bearing in mind the criticisms quoted at the beginning of this chapter, as well as reactions to the larger Silbermann in the Hofkirche:

But the reverberation in the building is so great, that the organ, though most cleverly played by Herr Klengel, and a thorough Silbermann in its silver-sweet tones, did not assert its superiority over its kinsman I had just been hearing [Sophienkirche] (Chorley 1841 pp178–9).

That so many Bach pupils worked in or competed for posts in churches with Silbermann organs cannot be taken as evidence that the composer thought such instruments ideal for his music; their stop-palette was very different from those of Leipzig or Thuringia, and even for the modestly scaled pieces in the *Orgelbüchlein* neither Silbermann's tuning nor his compass was convenient.* Like the relatively frenchified Dresden harpsichords made by the Gräbner family, such instruments contribute a rather foreign colour and bespeak catholic Dresden more than orthodox Leipzig.

Zschortau, village church

J. Scheibe, 1744–6; remodelled in 1870 (second manual etc).

Extant organ in the west gallery (case open at top).

Stoplist (Dähnert 1980 pp285–6)

Principal *t*◇	8	*Pedal*		
Mixtur (1⅓') *m*	III	+ pulldowns to manual		
+ Super Octava *m*	1	Posaune *wd*	16	
Octava *m*	2	Subbass *wd*	16	
Quinta (stopped) *m*	3			
Gedackt *wd*	4	Tremulant, blower's signal		
+ Fleut travers *wd*	4	Compass: CD–c'–c'''		
Octava *m*	4	Pitch: about semitone above a' = 440Hz		
Gedackt *wd*	8			
+ Viola di Gamba†	8	Mixtur C 19.22.26, c 15.19.22, c' 12.15.19		
+ Quinta Thön *wd*	16			

◇ lowest 4 *wd*, rest *t*
† lowest 11 *wd*, rest *m*
+ added above contract (according to J. S. Bach's report, *Dok* I pp168–9)
Pedal mechanism as Silbermann's

For J. S. Bach's report, see p153 below. The comparable Hildebrandt organ at Störmthal (examined by Bach 1723) had had a more Silbermann-like stoplist:

Man 8.8.8.4.4.3.2.1⅗.1⅓.1.III. Cornet(III)
Ped 16.16
Hw/P, Tremulant
Compass: CD–c'–c''; pitch about semitone above a' = 440Hz

Since both organs are extant and in part reliable, it seems that Hildebrandt's voicing was more in the Silbermann mould of even, forceful sweetness. Hilde-

---

* Though it should not be overlooked that only c' pedal is required for such published works as BWV 552 and 769, as well as for the Passacaglia BWV 582 etc. Indeed, it is open to argument how far the short pedal compass usual with Silbermann (i.e. up to c' only) is a reason for seeing his organs as unsuited to the music of J. S. Bach. This compass confirms what might already have been suspected, i.e. merely that Saxon village organists did not play the Six Sonatas or the maturer preludes and fugues, and that the city organists of Dresden or Freiberg did not draw on the *Orgelbüchlein* in their services.

brandt and J. S. Bach together also reported on Scheibe's organ in the Leipzig Johanniskirche (1742), an instrument which received a particularly severe examination according to several references (see *Dok* III p192). Zschortau may have been more modern in its flute and gamba stops, but it seems (as it has no Tierceranks or high flutes) to have been designed more for playing restrained interludes than interestingly registered chorale-preludes. The village organs of Saxony kept closer to the Silbermann/Hildebrandt plan at Störmthal.

Naumburg, Wenzelskirche

Z. Hildebrandt, 1743–6; remodelled 1842, 1915 (cone-chests), 1932–3 (electric action).

Extant organ in the third west-end gallery (case by Z. Thayssner 1695–1705).

Stoplist (Adlung 1768 I pp263ff; Dähnert 1962 pp95–102)

Hauptwerk		*Rückpositiv*		*Oberwerk*	
Principal *t*	16	Principal *t*	8	Bordun *wd*, *m* from c	16
Quintatön *m*	16	Quintatön *m*	8	Principal *t*	8
Bombart *wd*, *m* from c	16	Violdigamba *t*	8‡	Holhflöte *m* [Rohr]	8 +
Oktave *m*	8	Rohrflöte *m*	8	Vox humana	8 #
Spitzflöte* *m*	8	Prästant *t*	4	Gemshorn *m*	4
Gedackt *m*	8	Fugara *t*	4‡	Prästant *t*	4
Trompete *t*	8	Rohrflöte *m*	4	Quinte *t*	3
Oktave *t*	4	Nasat *m*	3	Oktave *t*	2
Spitzflöte* *m*	4	Oktave *t*	2	Waldflöte *m*	2
Quinte *t*	3	Rauschpfeife *t*	II	Quinte *t*	1⅓
Weitpfeife *t*	2	Cumbel *t*	V	Scharf *t*	V
Oktave *t*	2	Fagott *m*	16	Sifflöte *t*	1
Cornet *t*	IV			Terz *t*	1⅗
Mixtur *t*	VI–VII–VIII†			Unda maris (a–c''') *t*	8
Sesquialtera *t*	III				

Pedal		
Posaunenbass *wd*	32	
Principal *t*	16	
Violonbass *wd*	16 =	
Subbas *wd*	16	
Posaunenbass *wd*	16	
Violon *m*	8 =	Tremulant *Rp* only
Oktave *t*	8	4 Sperrventils
Trompete *t*	8	Zimbelstern
Oktave *t*	4	7 bellows (4 manual bellows producing 36 *Grad*, 3 pedal bellows
Clarino *t*	4	producing 40 *Grad*), 10 × 5 Schuh
Nachthorn *m*	2 +	*Hw/P* Windkoppel (Hildebrandt's draft; not in Adlung) ◊
Mixtur [*t*]	VII	Manual shove-couplers (*Rp/Hw*, *Ow/Hw*)

Compass: C–e′–e′′′

Details of stops: * 'Spill- oder Spitzflöte'
 † VII throughout in completed organ
 ◊ stop-knob for coupler (i.e. not permanent)
 ‡ narrow, of tin, somewhat conical (inverted)
 # 'part tin, part brass', i.e. tin resonators (double conical)
 + wide scale
 = conical

For J. S. Bach's report, see chapter 17. It seems from a reference in his testimonial for Altnickol, who applied for the post of organist in 1748, that J. S. Bach was consulted for the rebuild of this organ in addition to examining it on completion (*Dok*

I ppi12–13). His recommendations for the organ have been conjectured to be as follows (Dähnert 1962 pp95–102 and 1970 pp26–8):

> Hildebrandt as builder, then living in Leipzig
> the *Rückpositiv* kept and rebuilt
> stoplist as a whole
> particular stops (Quintadena 16′ rather than Bourdon 16′, the 32′ reed, cylindrical Fagott, double-conical Vox humana, string stops and wide-scaled stops in both *Hw* and *Rp*, the multi-rank Sesquialtera, the big Mixtures, the high pedal stops)
> the temperament (Neidhardt)

Against these conjectures, however, there seems little to associate the composer either with the *Rückpositiv* (since the 1695–1705 case as a whole was kept) or with its stoplist (no Tierce colour, sparse mutations, few solo effects), much less with the stoplist as a whole which was not particularly generous in reeds. Similarly, that Hildebrandt kept the difference in scaling between departments may well derive from Silbermann's habits and from practices made familiar in the famous Görlitz organ, but such a difference was recommended before that (even in organs with *Rückpositiven*) by Werckmeister (1698 p53).

Nevertheless, it is clear that the Naumburg organ offers on each manual a wide range of 8.4 combinations and 8′ colour, not least the Unda maris; and both the flute and other colour combinations have their own pedal stops. Like other big organs of its period, Naumburg strove to be individual in its emphases, while the fanciful effects of those other organs normally had at least their fancifulness in common. Perhaps all the works of J. S. Bach would have been playable on it: the *Schübler Chorales* with their generalized registrations, the earlier works with their gaps allowing changes of stops, the praeludia or chorales *in organo pleno*, works with two choruses, the *Orgelbüchlein* with its more intimate palette. No *grand/plein jeu* contrast is possible, however, nor do such comprehensive instruments permit the true intimacy of the Six Sonatas or the startling immediacy of tone typical of older organs. From the present state of the organ it is not possible to conjecture how its musical quality compares with Silbermann's.

But the quality of J. Wagner's organs, such as the one which the composer played in the Potsdam Heiligegeistkirche in May 1747, is clear from other extant examples. Alas, acquaintance with Wagner's fine instruments came too late in the composer's life for them to have influenced him,* but their strong personality must have been obvious: somewhat frenchified reeds not unlike Silbermann's (perhaps doubled in the treble or blown with the higher wind from the pedal bellows?), strong Cornet (also used in the *pleno*, according to J. F. Walther 1727), faultless action (both manuals with *mécanique suspendu*) and a discreet number of new stops. Visits to Dresden, Berlin and even Naumburg may well have left the composer displeased with the Leipzig organs.

---

* Forkel (1802 ch.II) said that J. S. Bach played all the organs in Potsdam, presumably including Wagner's 33-stop instrument in the Garnisonkirche; perhaps the newspaper report of 1747 referred only to the organ of the Heiligegeistkirche (*Dok* II pp434–5) because the king's father had given it?

17. J. S. Bach's Organ Reports

C. P. E. Bach's picture of his father as one who learnt by assiduous observation, practical as well as intellectual, is clear to see from comments on his knowledge of organs:

> er kannte auch den Bau der Orgeln aus dem Grunde . . . Aller dieser Orgelwissenschaft ungeachtet, hat es ihm, wie er oftmals zu bedauren pflegte, doch nie so gut werden können, eine recht grosse und recht schöne Orgel zu seinem beständigen Gebrauche gegenwärtig zu haben . . . (*Dok* III p88)
> Noch nie hat jemand so scharf u. doch dabey aufrichtig Orgelproben übernommen. Den ganzen Orgelbau verstand er im höchsten Grade . . . (*ibid* p284)
> . . . hat er das arrangement des Orchesters kennen gelernt. Diese Erfahrung, nebst einer natürlichen guten Kenntnis der Bauart, in wie ferne sie dem Klange nützlich ist, wozu seine besonderen Einsichten in die guten Anlagen einer Orgel, Eintheilung der Register und *Placi*rung derselben ebenfals das Ihrige beygetragen haben, hat er gut zu nutzen gewusst (*ibid* pp288–9).

> he also knew the construction of organs thoroughly . . . Irrespective of all this knowledge of organs, it never could turn out so well for him – as he often used to regret – that he had at hand a really big and really fine organ·for his constant use . . .
> Never has anyone undertaken organ-testing so severely and yet at the same time so fairly; organ-building as a whole he understood in the highest degree . . .
> He also learnt the placement of the orchestra. He knew how to profit well from this experience, together with a naturally good knowledge of architecture as far as it contributes to sound, to which his special insights into the good layout of an organ, dispersal of the stops and placing of the same also contributed its share.

As his knowledge of architecture was 'natural', so it was of acoustics and even of organs. There is no report of how J. S. Bach came by his knowledge early and thoroughly enough to have advised at Mühlhausen so soon in his career, though several organs with which he must have been connected were involved in major repairs of one kind or another between 1695 and 1705. Perhaps he did learn keyboard-playing with his brother in Ohrdruf, as the *Obituary* said (*Dok* III p81), but it is not known from documents how he acquired what is usually thought of as a 'profound knowledge' of organ-building (Blume 1968). Perhaps J. C. Bach's scheme for the Eisenach Georgenkirche rebuild of 1696–1707 influenced the composer's ideas for Mühlhausen (Kwasnik 1966 p222); but the unsatisfactory nature of the work itself (requiring much repair, according to Adlung 1768 I pp214–15) may well have been instructive, as must have been the long-drawn-out work at his brother's instrument in Ohrdruf from 1690 to 1706 (reported on by Pachelbel in 1693 – David 1951 pp12–14) and at the new organ at Arnstadt of 1699–1703 (tested and inaugurated by J. S. Bach – *Dok* II pp10–11). Perhaps too he was aware that certain elements in the old organ of the Michaeliskirche, Lüneburg were being felt to be out of date at the time (including its position in the north gallery? – hence the report made in 1705 by the builder M. Dropa, which advised moving it to the west end (David 1951 pp14–16)). No doubt he learnt too from contact with his predecessor at Weimar, Johannes Effler (Jauernig 1950 p70), who was known as an organ adviser and had put in hand new work on the Weimar organ in the years before J. S. Bach's appointment; the same Effler had been responsible for the rebuilding of the Town Church organ in Weimar, not without much trouble (Wette 1737 pp257ff).*

A further influence on the young Bach must have been written sources, in particular the revised *Orgelprobe* published by Andreas Werckmeister in 1698: a book far more specific and helpful than sources recommended by Werckmeister himself (such as J. P. Bendeler's *Organopoeia* of c1690). No conclusion can be drawn from the absence of any known reference to the book in J. S. Bach's library, since little is known about his books on musical theory particularly during the early period. Only from a brief note in a letter is it known that J. G. Walther owned a copy of the *Orgelprobe*;† but Werckmeister's writings must have been particularly influential in his native Thuringia, not least because of his position as 'Royal Prussian Inspector of All Organs in the Principality of Halberstadt' (Walther 1732 p648). Although the original *Orgelprobe* of 1681 was itself indebted to C. Förner (Leipzig), Werckmeister became the best-known authority – never systematically organizing his material, perhaps, but succeeding (through the amount of material he published) in eclipsing Förner's *Vollkommener Bericht* (Berlin 1684). His booklet on the rebuilt organ of Gröningen (Werckmeister 1705) also rehearses many of the issues in a clear way.

The several reports on organs made by J. S. Bach, from Mühlhausen 1708 to Naumburg 1746, are readily available, have been often commented upon and have been mostly translated into English (David/Mendel).‡ Two particular areas can be usefully explored: relating them to the writings of Werckmeister (see Williams 1982), and drawing from them hints about the composer's view in particular. In the following documents, agreements with Werckmeister's terminology and emphases are noted. Though his terms were not particularly new and expressed little more than commonsense approaches to organs, later references to Werckmeister suggest that his influence must have been paramount, and it is likely that testers used him as a guide. Nor is there any reason to think J. S. Bach unusual in this. In c1746, the organist of the Naumburg Wenzelskirche complained of Silbermann and Bach's approval of the new organ with many phrases close to Werckmeister's. It is difficult to see how the following could be coincidence:

> und wenn man mit vollen Griffen offte *repetir*et, so spielen die Bälge und fallen schleinigst nieder . . . (1746 in *Dok* II p429)

> wenn . . . mit vollen Griffen offte *repetir*et wird . . . so spielen die Bälge und fallen hastig nieder . . . (Werckmeister 1698 pp27–8)

---

* An evocative picture of the changing attitude to organs in central Germany c1675 is given by the story of the new organ in the Town Church, Weimar (see above, p126). It seems from Wette that the old organ had very heavy pipes and that it was placed high on the west wall near to the choir gallery; Effler, finding fault with it, had a new one installed, now in the gallery front and made of much lighter pipes. So an old organ of the swallow-nest type, with thick lead pipes, gave way to a choir-gallery organ of new type.

† In addition to Praetorius, Boxberg (Görlitz 1704), Buliowski (*Brevis de emendatione organi*, Strasbourg 1680) and the 'Pulsnitzische Orgel-Beschreibung' – Schünemann 1933 pp101–2.

‡ Some of the technical details are not quite satisfactorily translated in David/Mendel, however.

when one repeats full chords a great deal, the bellows perform thus [= jerkily] and collapse quickly . . .

The oddity of it is that one would imagine organists themselves to be experts in musical matters of this kind, needing no books to point things out to them.

Mühlhausen Divi Blasiikirche report, before 21 February 1708

Disposition der neüen *reparatur* des Orgelwercks *ad D*: *Blasii.*

1. Muss der Mangel des Windes durch drey neue tüchtige Bälge ersezet werden, so da dem Oberwercke, Rück*positive* und neüem Brustwercke genüge thun.

2. Die 4 alten bälge so da vorhanden, müssen mit stärkererm Winde zu den neüen 32 Fuss Untersaze und denen übrigen *Bass* Stimmen *aptir*et werden.

3. Die alten *Bass* Windladen, müssen alle ausgenommen, und von neüen mit einer solchen Windführung versehen werden, damit mann eine einzige Stimme alleine, und denn alle Stimmen zugleich ohne Veränderung des Windes könne gebrauchen, welches vormahln noch nie auff diese Arth hat geschelhen können, und doch höchstnöthig ist.

4. Folget der 32 Fuss *SubBass* oder so genandter Untersatz von Holz, welcher dem ganzen Wercke die beste *gravität* giebet. Dieser muss nun eine eigene Windlade haben.

5. Muss der *Posaunen Bass* mit neüen und grösern *corporibus* versehen, und die Mundstückte viel anders eingerichtet werden, damit solcher eine viel bessere *gravität* von sich geben kan.

6. Das von denen Herrn Eingepfarten begehrte neüe Glockenspiel ins *Pedal*, bestehend in 26 Glocken à 4 Fuss-thon; Welche Glocken die Herrn Eingepfarten auff ihre kosten schon anschaffen werden, und der Orgelmacher solche hernachmahls gangbahr machen wird.

Was anlanget das Ober*manual*, so wird in selbiges anstatt der *Trompette* (so da heraus genommen wirdt) ein

7. *Fagotto* 16 Fussthon eingebracht, welcher zu allerhandt neüen *inventionibus* dienlich, und in die *Music* sehr *delicat* klinget. Ferner anstatt des *Gemshorns* (so gleichfalls heraus genommen wirdt) kömmet eine

8. *VioldiGamba* 8 Fuss, so da mit dem im Rück*positive* vorhandenem *Salicinal* 4 Fuss *admirabel concordiren* wirdt.

Item anstatt der *Quinta* 3 Fuss, (so da gleichfalls heraus genommen wirdt,) könte eine

9. *Nassat* 3 Fuss eingerücket werden.

Die übrigen Stimmen in Ober*Manuale* so vorhanden, können bleiben wie auch das ganze Rück*positiv*, indem doch solche bey der *reparatur* von neüem durchstimmet werden.

10. Was denn hauptsächlich anlanget das neüe Brust *positiv*gen, so könten in selbiges folgende Stimmen kommen – als:

Im gesichte 3 *Principalia*, nahmentlich:

1. *Quinta.* 3 Fuss ⎫
2. *Octava.* 2 Fuss ⎬ Von guthem 14 löthigem Zinn.
3. *Schalemoy* 8 Fuss ⎭
4. *Mixtur.* 3fach.
5. *Tertia*, mit welcher mann durch zuziehung einiger anderer Stimmen eine vollkommene schöne *Sesquialteram* zu wege bringen kan.
6. *Fleute douce.* 4 Fuss und leztens ein
7. Stillgedackt 8 Fuss, so da vollkommen zur *Music accordiert*, und so es von guthem Holze gemacht wird, viel besser als ein *Metalli*nes Gedackt klingen muss.

11. Zwischen dieses Brust*positiv*es und OberWerckes *manual*en muss eine *Copula* seyn.

Und schliesslichen muss bey nebst durchstimmung des ganzen Werckes, der *Tremulant* in seine richtig wehende *mensur* gebracht werden.

(*Dok* 1 pp152–3)

Disposition for new repairs to the organ of Divi Blasii

1. The lack of wind must be made good by three new efficient bellows, to give enough to the *Oberwerk*, the *Rückpositiv* and the new *Brustwerk*.
2. The four old bellows now there must be made suitable, with stronger wind, for the new 32′ Untersatz and the other bass stops.
3. The old bass windchests must all be taken out and newly provided with such ducting that one could play a single stop alone and then all of the stops together without any variation in the wind – something that has never been possible previously, though it is very necessary.
4. There follows the 32′ Subbass or so-called Untersatz of wood, which gives the best *Gravität* to the whole organ. This must now have its own chest.
5. The Posaunenbass must be provided with new and larger resonators, and the reeds [mouthpieces] contrived very differently so that of themselves they can give a much better *Gravität*.
6. The new Glockenspiel in the pedal (consisting of 26 bells at 4′ pitch) desired by the parishioners [is to be added]; which bells the parishioners will acquire at their own expense, and the organ-builder will subsequently make them playable.

As concerns the *Oberwerk*, here, instead of the Trompete (which will be taken out) will be placed:

7. A Fagott 16′, which is serviceable for all kinds of new musical ideas [*inventionibus*] and sounds very pleasing in ensemble music. Furthermore, instead of the Gemshorn (which will also be taken out) should come:
8. a VioldiGamba 8′, such as will agree admirably with the Salicional 4′ in the *Rückpositiv*. Similarly, instead of the Quinta 3′ which will also be taken out
9. a Nassat 3′ can be inserted.

The other stops already to hand in the *Oberwerk* can stay, as too the whole *Rückpositiv*, although these will be thoroughly tuned as from new in the course of the repair.

10. As concerns in particular the little *Brustwerk*, the following stops could be found there – thus:

in the case-front three *Principalia*, namely

1 Quinte 3′
2 Octava 2′ } of good 87.5% tin
3 Schalemoy
4 Mixtur III
5 Tertia, with which one can bring about a perfect and beautiful Sesquialtera by drawing some other stops with it
6 Fleute douce 4′, and lastly a
7 Stillgedackt 8′, as suits ensemble music completely, and if it is made of good wood, [it] must sound much better than a metal Gedackt.

11. Between this *Brustpositiv* and *Oberwerk* keyboards there must be a coupler.

And finally as well as the thorough tuning of the whole organ, the Tremulant must be brought into its correct rate of flutter.

In general, the Mühlhausen project accords closely with Werckmeister's recommendations on organ-renovation: the organist should decide what exactly needs replacing (e.g. which chests and bellows), he should specify all the defects and not generalize about them, and he should explain what can be kept and in the case of new bellows specify what is required of them. Certain details of wording and construction also resemble Werckmeister's. Thus Werckmeister's phrase is 'Mangel am Winde' (1698 p26); one new bellows for each chest follows his advice on the same page; separate bellows for pedal, *ibid* p51; adequate wind for big pipes, p32; specifying whether new chests are needed, p60; 'Windführungen' adequate for varying numbers of stops from one to *plenum*, p27; stopped 32′ rank of wood, p52;

spelling out of metal alloy, p57; keeping ranks separate for the Sesquialtera, p74; the term 'Mensur' for the Tremulant's flutter, p37. Particularly characteristic stops in J. S. Bach's scheme also recall Werckmeister's stoplist, p50: the 32′, Posaune, Violdigamba, Fagott, Gedackte Quinte, Tertia, *Gelinde/stille Gedackt*, Mixtur III and the term 'sesquialtera' for a combination of separate stops (Werckmeister's ch.30).

Other details in the Mühlhausen project may well have been newer or more individual. Thus the *Gravität* required for both Subbass and Posaune seems to have been developing as an ideal only then – cf. the two 32′ ranks at Eisenach, the larger shallots and stronger tongues of the Posaune 16′ at Freiberg Cathedral in 1719 (only a few years after Silbermann's completion of it – Dähnert 1962 p11), Kuhnau's request for a 32′ reed instead of 16′ at Merseburg (*ibid*) and Trost's 'wider and more pompous' oak Posaune ('leather lined') for the rebuild at Altenburg in 1733 (Löffler 1932). While the stops in the new *Brustwerk* are mostly conventional enough to be found in Werckmeister's stoplist, the Schalmei in the case-front promises more than Werckmeister's *Bw* Regal and was apparently a kind of replacement for the old *Ow* Trompete – which had no place in the *pleno* and was better giving its space to the Fagott. J. F. Walther too thought Wagner's Fagott 16′ at Berlin Garnisonkirche good for running basses and ensemble music, but that was twenty years later; it is not clear how advanced J. S. Bach was in such ideas, particularly in an organ of modest size (for a note on *bicinia* in this connection, see chapter 18). Preferring a Viola da Gamba to a Gemshorn may be merely a matter of renaming (because of the quality of the old stop?) but it certainly looks as if the young composer wanted some degree of string tone in his Viola + Salicional combination, to the detriment of a more classical buildup on a wide 8′ rank (Zavarsky 1975). The Viola was common in Thuringia, but it is uncertain where he could have known the Salicional, although in catholic areas (Bohemia, Silesia) it was indeed most often 4′ (as too at Görlitz, reported on by Boxberg 1704); probably both were to be of metal, respectively conical and cylindrical. For Werckmeister, the Nassat was in addition to regular quints, not replacing them, and though it is perhaps an overstatement to see such a change as part of a general 'darkening of organ tone' typical of J. S. Bach (Zavarsky 1977), the change is suggestive. A wooden Gedackt, like the Fagott, implies an interesting priority for continuo stops, and the remark that it sounded 'much better than a metal Gedackt' must be aimed at such music.* 'Fleute douce', rather than Werckmeister's traditional flutes, may suggest that the composer was already moving towards a liking for the imitative stops. That the *Rückpositiv* 'can stay' may have been significant, since Werckmeister already noted that people 'do not willingly put up with them today' ('heutiges Tages dieselben nicht gern leiden will', p51). No doubt there was a shove-coupler *Rp/Hw* – hence the need to specify the *Bw/Hw* coupler, which may well have been less common. The idea of being able to couple all three manuals – which would be possible so long as II/III was not a shove-coupler requiring the II/I to be disconnected – seems not to have come from Werckmeister (though his reference to wire couplers on p38 is ambiguous) and may again reflect tendencies to thicken the *organo pleno*. Finally, the Glockenspiel, which may never have been added: there

---

* And is one with which it is possible to agree.

seems to have been one at Eisenach and one tried out later at Weimar, a device with which a clever organist can do 'fine things', according to Adlung ('schöne Sachen': 1768 1 p103).

Halle Liebfrauenkirche report, 1 May 1716

Nach dem es dem Hochlöblichen *Collegio Mariano* der Stadt Halle uns Endes-Unter-schriebene in Schrifften zu ersuchen beliebet, dass wir vorgestern, alss den nunmehr ver-wichenen 29sten *Aprilis*, allhier erscheinen, und das durch Gottes Gnade und zu seiner Ehre von dem Orgelmacher, Herrn Christoff *Cuncio* in der Kirche zur lieben Frauen aufferbaute neüe grosse Orgel Werck in allen Stücken *perlustrir*en, untersuchen, und was wir darinne vor tichtig oder untichtig befinden würden, auffzeichnen, auch sonsten unsere *Censur* darüber ertheilen möchten; So haben wir der Hochgeneigten *Reqvisition* und der zu unsrer *Exper-ience* und *Dexterité* getragenen guten *Confidence* zu schuldigster Folge im obgedachten *Termino* uns allhier eingefunden, und nach nochmahliger an uns geschehenen Hohen mündlichen Erfoderung die Untersuchung solches neüen Orgel Werckes in besagter Kirche in Gottes Nahmen vorgenommen. Da wir denn (1) die Balgen Kammer beqvehm genug zu denen Bälgen und vor das üble Wetter wohl verwahret befunden, doch aber auch dabey wahr genommen, dass weil das Fenster gegen Abend gehet, die Bälge der allzu grossen Sonnen Hize *exponir*et seyn müssen, dass also ein Vorhang oder sonsten ein andrer Schirm wieder die Sonne ausser der Zeit des Gebrauches dieses Orgel Werckes wird nöthig seyn.
Was zum (2) die Bälge selbst betrifft, derer Zehen an der Zahl sind, (ungeachtet der Meister im *Contract* nur 9 versprochen, vielleicht weil er gemeinet, *qvod superflua non noceant*, und dass *par numerus* dem *impari* zum Wohlstande derer beyden einander gegenüber befind-lichen Anlagen der Bälge vorzuziehen sey,) so möchten sie zwar die hiezu erfoderte Grösse und Fleiss des Meisters noch endlich zeigen, doch hat der Wind in der von uns *applicir*ten Wind Wage den *liqvorem* noch nicht auff den sonsten bey dergleichen starcken Wercken erfoderten, und an anderen im Winde tichtigen Wercken befundenen 35sten biss 40sten, sondern nur etwa biss an den 2 oder 33sten *Gradum* treiben wollen: Dahero man auch bey *Tractir*ung des Hauptwerckes einiges Schwancken der Bälge wahr genommen;
Jedoch ist dieses noch wohl zu erdulten, wenn nur nicht das Oberwerck im mittlern *Clavier* schwanckete, welches sonsten unter die Haupt *Defecte* gezehlet wird.
Sonsten aber ist uns (3) an denen Windladen kein *vitium visibile* vorgekommen, sie haben auch die Probe ausgehalten, dass bey denen auff einmahl nieder gedruckten *Clavibus* so wohl des *Manuals* alss *Pedals* kein unanständiges Durchstechen ausser etwas weniges im mittlern *Manual*, welches sonsten von nicht alzu feste eingeschraubten Stöcken herrühret, und leichte *corrigir*et werden kan sich hat mercken lassen. Man hat auch unter denen *Ventil*en nicht etwa gedoppelte oder 3fache Federn, womit die üblen Meister sonsten das Gehäule verhindern wollen, sondern alle einfach angetroffen: Bey welcher Beschaffenheit denn das *Clavier* sich noch ziemlich beqvehm *tractir*en lassen solte; Nichts desto weniger will es noch nöthig seyn, dass es etwas leichter gemachtet, und dennoch das hurtige Zurücke Prallen der *Claviere* nicht verhindert, viel weniger dadurch einiges Heülen verursacet werde: wie es denn auch der Meister in diesen Stand zu bringen versprochen hat.
Was (4). das Eingebäude anbetrifft, so wäre freilich ein weitrer Raum darzu zu wünschen gewesen, dass man nicht alles so tichte zusammen hätte sezen dürffen, und man beqvehmer zu allem kommen können.
Im übrigen finden sich (5) alle die im *Contract specific*irte Stimmen, und zwar auch aus der jenigen *Materia* verfertiget, deren daselbst gedacht wird, ausser, dass an statt des *specificir-*ten *metall*enen 16füssigen Gemshorn *Bass*es ein hölzerner 32füssiger Untersaz oder *Sub Bass* geliefert worden. Durch welche Grösse der Pfeiffen der Abgang des *Metall*es wohl dürffte ersezet seyn.
Ferner sind über dem *Contract* folgende verfertigte dienliche Stimmen dazu gekommen, nehmlich

Spizflöte	2 Fuss	
Qvinta	3 Fuss	
Octava	2 Fuss	von *Metall*.
Nachthorn	4 Fuss	
Qvinta offen	6 Fuss	

Dagegen ist aussen geblieben

der *Fagott Bass* von Zinn	8 Fuss
Gedackt von *Metall*	4 Fuss
Waldflöte von *detto*	2 Fuss
Rohr Flöte	12 Fuss von *detto*.

Ingleichen hat er vor 2 Zweyfache *Cimbaln* 2 dreyfache geliefert. Und wie man (6) es lässet dahin gestellet seyn, wie mit der *Legir*ung des *Metall*es sey verfahren worden, allermassen denn leichte zu sehen, (und es auch fast gewöhnlich) dass man zu denen Stimmen, welche nicht in das Gesichte fallen, nicht so wohl das Bley alss vielmehr das Zinn gesparet; Also hätten in diesem Wercke die bleche derer *Corporum* der Pfeiffen etwas dicker seyn können oder sollen.

Die in der *Facciata* sich *præsenti*rende Pfeiffen solten zwar mit einem hellen Lichte spielen, und wird auch vermuthlich das meiste von gutem Zinne daran seyn gewendet worden; Allein dass sie dergleichen nicht thun, muss die Schuld nicht dem Meister, sondern dem auff sie fallenden Rauche bey gemessen werden.

Hingegen ist ihm zu *imputi*ren, wenn der Klang sonderlich der grossen Pfeiffen sich nicht deütlich vernehmen lässet, wenn es an der gehörigen guten *Intonation* mangelt: wie denn dergleichen *Defect* sich auch allhier an unterschiedenen solchen *Corporibus*, unter andern im *Sub-* und Posaunen *Bass* von 32 Fuss, wie auch in übrigen Rohrwercken herfür gethan; doch hat Herr *Cuncius*, gleich wie er noch hin und wieder das Werck, welches wir in allen 3 *Clavier*en noch ziemlich unrein befunden, reiner zu stimmen, und nach der von ihm uns ein-mahl gezeigten noch *passabl*en guten *Temperatur* einzurichten ver | sprochen, auch an der *disideri*rten bessern *Intonation* einiger Pfeiffen zu derselben *Correctur* sich *obligi*ret: welches zwar besser vor der *Examination* hätte geschehen können, allermassen wir alle die jenigen Stücke, die noch fehlen, nehmlich die

Copul,

2 *Tremulan*ten,

2 Sterne

eine lauffende Sonne auss dem

Ober *Positiv*, und

den Vogel Gesang

zu gleich hätten in Augenschein nehmen können.

Dieses ist nun, was wir unten beniehmte unsrer Schuldigkeit gemäss und der Wahrheit zu steüer bey diesem Wercke errinnern sollen. Im übrigen wünschen wir, dass es dem Aller-Höchsten zu Ehren, und zu sonderbahrem Ruhme Derer HochEdlen Herrn *Patron*en auch der ganzen werthen Stadt im guten Friede und Ruhe zur heiligen Auffmunterung und Andacht sich jeder Zeit wohl hören lassen und lange Jahre beständig dauren möge. Halle am Tage *Philippi Jacobi* 1716.

Johann Kuhnau, *mpp*

Christian Friedrich Rolle

Joh: Sebast: *Bach*

(*Dok* 1 pp157–9)

Since it has pleased the honourable *Collegium* of St Mary to ask in writing us the under-signed to appear here the day before yesterday (that is, 29 April last), and to investigate and examine in all parts the new, large organ in the Liebfrauenkirche erected through God's grace and in his honour by the organ-builder Herr Christoff Cuncius, and to indicate whatever we might find efficient or inefficient in it and in other respects too to impart our judgment: so we hav'e found ourselves here on the appointed day very indebted to this gracious order and to the good confidence held in our experience and expertise, and according to a further demand made of us by word of mouth have undertaken the examination of the new organ in the said church. As, then, we (1) have found the bellows room comfortable enough for the bellows and well protected against the bad weather, yet we made note that because the window faces west the bellows would be exposed to the excessive heat of the sun, so that a curtain or some other kind of protection against the sun will be necessary outside the time when this organ is in use.

As regards (2) the bellows themselves, which number ten (irrespective of the fact that the builder promised only nine in the contract, perhaps because he thought that too much does no harm,* and that an even number was to be preferred to an uneven, for the well-being of the two rows of bellows located opposite each other), so they might still prove that the speci-fied size and the builder's diligence were both adequate, if it were not that the wind pushed the liquid in the wind-gauge applied by us not to the 35th or 40th *Grad* otherwise required in organs of similar power, and indeed found in other organs which are efficiently winded, but only to about the 32nd or 33rd *Grad*; consequently, some wavering in the bellows was noted when the *Hauptwerk* is played.

Nevertheless, this could well be tolerated if only the *Oberwerk* (middle manual) did not waver, which otherwise counts amongst the main defects.

Apart from this, however, we observe (3) no visible fault in the windchests; they also endured the test in which [all?] the keys of both manual and pedal were pressed down at one and the same time, without any improper running of wind being noticeable except for a little in the middle manual (which comes from the upper board's not being screwed in perfectly tight, and which can easily be corrected). Under the pallets the springs have not been doubled or trebled, with which poor builders wish to prevent ciphering, but all are single, through which circumstance the keyboard should be rather comfortable to depress; yet it will be no less necessary to make the keyboard somewhat lighter, but without hindering the quick return of the keys, still less thereby causing any ciphering.

As for (4) the internal arrangements, it is indeed to be wished that there had been more room, so that it had not been necessary to place everything so close together, and one could have got at everything more conveniently.

In other respects there are to be found (5) all the stops specified in the contract, and indeed prepared from the materials intended for them, except that instead of the specified metal Gemshorn Bass 16′ a wooden Untersatz or Subbass 32′ has been provided, through the size of whose pipes the absence of metal may well have been made good.

Furthermore, over and above the contract the following finished and serviceable stops have been added, namely

Spitzflöte	2′	
Quinta	3′	
Octava	2′	of metal
Nachthorn	4′	
Open Quinta	6′	

On the other hand have been left out:

Fagott Bass [pedal] of tin	8′
Gedackt of metal	4′
Waldflöte of metal	2′
Rohr Flöte of metal	12′ [pedal]

Similarly, he has provided two III-rank Cimbeln instead of two II-rank. And (6) though one may leave it undecided how the alloying of metal was dealt with, in every way, it is easy to see (as is virtually customary) that those stops not in the case-front have had more tin saved than lead; so too in this organ the metal sheets for the pipe-resonators should or could have been somewhat thicker.

---

* The original phrase (a classical allusion by Kuhnau?) recalls that of Schütz in his *Symphoniae sacrae III* (Dresden 1650) concerning adequate figuring of continuo basses: 'abundans cautela non nocet'.

The pipes standing in the front of the case should sparkle brilliantly, and most of the good tin has presumably been employed for that; that they do not quite do this must be blamed not on the builder but on the smoke falling on them.

On the other hand it is to be imputed to him if the sound (particularly of the larger pipes) does not let itself be heard clearly, [i.e.] if something of the good voicing required is lacking; this defect is prominent in various pipes, amongst others those of the Subbass and Posaunenbass 32′, as also of other reeds. But as well as promising to tune the organ (which we found rather out of tune in all three manuals) more exactly here and there, and to regulate it according to the tolerably good temperament he showed us, Herr Cuncius has undertaken to improve the voicing of the pipes as their correction may require – something that might better have happened before the examination, as too if we had been able to cast our eye over those parts that are still missing, namely the

coupler [manual?]

2 Tremulants

2 Stars

a turning sun [operating] from the

upper manual, and

the Vogelgesang.

This is now what we, named below, ought to report concerning this organ, according to our obligation and for the sake of truth. For the rest, we wish that it may be heard well each time and that it may last for many years, to the honour of the Most High, to the particular fame of its most honourable Patrons, and to the whole worthy city, in good peace and tranquillity, towards a pious incitement and devotion.

Halle, on the feast of St Philip and St James 1716 [1 May 1716]

Johann Kuhnau *mpp* [his hand]

Christian Friedrich Rolle

Joh: Sebast: Bach

Werckmeister recommends careful, unhurried testing (1698 pp38–9) – and Halle seems to have taken three days. Further suggestions include the submitting of a report to church officials who will examine the builder (as here – see *Dok* II pp59–61 and Werckmeister p69); inspection of the bellows-chamber (pp2–3), not least against the heat of the sun; testing by wind-gauge (p4), checking the size of bellows (p26) and pressure by means of *liquorem* (p64), noting the pressure (35° – 40° desirable: p64) and whether there is any *Schwanken* in the bellows (p23).* The wavering in the Halle *Ow* could have several causes, but it was probably due to insufficient wind (pp27–9). Werckmeister also speaks of visible defects ('vitium . . . quoad visum': pp26, 10) and recommends the test of pressing down all the keys (p22). The examiners use Werckmeister's term *durchstechen* for 'running' (p13) and suggest correcting the fault by a method in line with his explanations (p19); they test for double or treble springs on his advice (pp10–11) but do not presume to give the builder advice for lightening action (p16), though they do warn of ciphering if it is made too light, as does Werckmeister (p21). They also pay regard to Werckmeister's warnings about pipes placed too close together (p4), about easy access (p13), about the materials specified in the contract (p57), and about the thickness and tin content of the pipe-metal (pp4–5, 67). They probably did not need Werck-

---

* Kuhnau's report of 1714 on Silbermann's organ in Freiberg Cathedral makes similar points about such details as the curtain protecting the bellows, the wind-pressure (41° and 46°) and the arm laid on the keys to test ciphering (Müller 1982 pp420–3). This report by a well-known expert, on an important organ, may well have become a model for later examinations, such as that at the Freiberg Jakobikirche in 1718 or Rochlitz in 1727 (Müller 1982 pp426–8, 440–1). Or perhaps examiners went back to Werckmeister for the plan and terminology of organ reports?

meister's advice on faults of voicing, especially of large pipes (pp32, 52), but they follow him in recommending its immediate improvement (p71) by the builder then present (p39), who should also find a good tuning system and be able to leave the organ perfectly in tune throughout (pp30–2). Finally theorist and examiners agree in seeing such an examination as taking place 'for the truth's sake' ('wegen der lieben Wahrheit': p68).

Several features of the report, not least its language, may suggest that it was the work of Kuhnau, a trained lawyer, but presumably all three examiners agreed on its findings. They accepted some wavering in the *Hw* but not in the *Ow*, which must therefore imply a question of degree: 'flexible wind' in the former instance, 'shaking' in the latter? They thought the action somewhat heavy, without distinguishing between manuals, though Silbermann remarked at Naumburg in 1746 that no organist would wish to claim that he should be able to play the *Hw*, *Ow* and *Bw* keyboards with equal lightness (*Dok* II p431). They do not comment on the additional or substitute stops, though with these changes the organ's emphases had been rather altered. Complaining about the thickness of the pipe-metal was of course of no practical purpose at this stage, though it did attest to the examining committee's acquaintance with examiners' duties. Presumably on their advice, Cuncius undertook to 'introduce *Kammerton* into the organ' (see below), but this can hardly have referred to the whole organ: introducing *Kammerton* must have meant either lowering by one pipe the pitch of a Gedackt (or two or three pipes?) or providing one manual (*Bw*?) with a transposing device. The latter would imply a more or less equal temperament, however, and the temperament is unclear: did the examiners prefer a different temperament from Cuncius's original? Was a *passable* temperament merely one that they could 'pass' (approve) or one that allowed passing (*passus*) into many keys?* Does 'passably good temperament' mean that Cuncius's scale was new to the examiners, and that it was the same as the scale proposed by Werckmeister in 1691? It is difficult to see how information in such detail can be gleaned from the Halle report, from which it seems merely that the organ had been neither voiced nor tuned well enough for the examination and that the builder undertook to correct both.

Action following the report was as follows:

Nachdem die neue Orgel von 3. *Musicis* und *Organi*sten, Herrn Bachen, Herrn *Cuno*en und Herrn Rollen drey Tage nacheinander *examini*ret und untersucht, den 1. *Maij* durch eine Predigt und schöne *Musique* dem grossen Gott vor die darzu verliehne Genade öffentlich danckgesaget, von denen Herrn *Musicis* auch ein Bericht schrifftlich dem *Collegio* eingelieffert worden, ist in gegenwart Herrn *Cuncii* und derer Herren *Examinatorum item* des *Organi*sten Herrn Kirchhoffs der Bericht verlesen, und über jeden Punct *conferi*ret worden. *quoad* 2.) Durch Verfertigung eines anderweitigen Canals oder Gegenführung verspricht Herr *Cuncius* das Schwancken des Oberwerckes im mittlern *clavier* abzustellen, welches die Herren *examinatores approbi*ren.
3.) Durch Verfertigung und anziehung einer vorizo noch ermangelnden Schraube verspricht Herr *Cuncius* dem 3. *Defect* abzuhelffen *item* es so einzurichten, dass die *clavi*ere leichter *tracti*ret werden können.

* Probably the former, in view of Silbermann's use of the term *passable* for the Naumburg bellows in 1746 (*Dok* II p430), and the use of the same term in reports signed by J. G. Pisendel and others for Silbermann's organs at the Dresden Frauenkirche (1736) and Zittau Johanniskirche (1741 – Müller 1982 pp449, 457–8).

Die *intonation* derer pfeiffen im 32. füssigen *sub-* und Posaunen Bass verspricht Herr *Cuncius* zu *corrigi*ren.

Weil nun, wenn er diesen allem versprochener massen abhilfft, das *Collegium* damit zufrieden, auch Herrn *Cuncio*, wenn er das ganze Pfeiffwerck neu absaubern und wieder fein *poli*ren wird, ein besonderes *soulagement* dafür zu geben verspricht, so ist übrigens ihme versprochen | die Zimbeln so an 2. Sternen kommen sollen, zu kauffen. Die sperr *ventile* erkleret er sich in der Orgel zulassen, auch auss freyem willen noch den Cammer Thon in die Orgel zu bringen. (*Dok* II pp60–1)

After the new organ was examined and inspected for three consecutive days by three musicians and organists, Herr Bach, Herr Kuhnau and Herr Rolle, a public thanksgiving to almighty God for the grace granted thereto was offered 1 May with a sermon and beautiful music, and a written report delivered to the *Collegium*, the report was read in the presence of Herr Cuncius, the examiners and the organist Herr Kirchhoff, and discussion was made on each point.

Concerning item 2 [in the report: see above, p146]: Through the preparation of another [= second?] trunk or conduit Herr Cuncius promises to remedy the wavering of the *Oberwerk* (middle manual), which the examiners approve.

Concerning item 3: Through the preparation and tightening-up of a screw heretofore malfunctioning, Herr Cuncius promises to remedy the third defect, i.e. so adjusting it that the keyboards can be played more lightly.

Herr Cuncius promises to correct the voicing of the pipes in the 32′ Subbass and Posaunenbass.

Because the *Collegium* would then be satisfied if he remedied these things completely as promised, it promises in its turn to give Herr Cuncius a special allowance if he will clean the whole pipework anew and give it a fine polish again; in addition he is promised payment for the bells which should go with the stars. He declares himself ready to concede the Sperrventils and also of his own will to introduce *Kammerton* into the organ.

Leipzig Paulinerkirche report, 17 December 1717

Da auf Verlangen Ihrer HochEdlen *Magnificenz* Herrn *D.* Rechenbergs, der Zeit *Rectoris Magnifici* bey der Hochlöblichen *Academie* zu Leipzig der Untersuchung des theils neu verfertigten, theils *repori*rten *Orgel*wercks in der *Pauliner* Kirche auf mich genommen, so habe solches nach Möglichkeit bewerckstelliget, die etwanigen *defecta remarqui*ret und überhaupt vom gantzen Orgelbau folgendes ausfertigen wollen, als:

1.) Die gantze *Structur* anlangend, ist freylich nicht zu läugnen, dass solche sehr enge gefast, und daher schwerlich iedem Stücke beyzukommen, so sich etwan mit der Zeit einiges zu *repari*ren finden solte, solches *excusi*ret nun Herr Scheibe als Verfertiger schon berührter Orgel damit, dass vors erste das Orgelgehäusse von ihme nicht verfertiget, und er also, so gut es immer sich hätte vollen thun lassen, mit dem Eingebäude nach selbigen sich richten müssen, vors andere man Ihme den noch verlangten Raum, um die *Structur commod*er einzurichten, gar nicht gestatten wollen.

2.) Die gewöhnlichen Haupt*partes* einer Orgel, als Windladen, Bälge, Pfeiffen, Wellen-Breter und übrigen Stücke sind mit gutem Fleisse verfertiget, und ist dabey nichts zu errinnern, als dass der Wind durchgehends *æqual*er gemacht werden muss, damit dem etwanigen Windstossen abgeholfen werden möge, die Wellen Breter solten zwar in Rahmen gefasset seyn, um alles Geheule bey schlimmen Witterungen zu vermeiden, da Herr Scheibe aber nach seiner Arth solche mit Tafeln verfertiget, und dabey versichert, dass solche eben das thäten, was die mit Rahmen sonst thun müsten, so hat man solches *passi*ren lassen.

3.) Die in der *Disposition* so wohl, als sämtlichen *Contract*en berührten Stücke sind so wohl *qualitate* als *quantitate* befindlich, ausser 2 Rohrwercke, nehmlich Schallmey 4. Fuss und

Cornet 2. Fuss, welche vermöge eines Hochlöblichen *Collegii* Befehl haben unterbleiben müssen, an derer Statt aber die *Octava* 2. Fuss im Brustwerck, und dann die Hohlflöte 2. Fuss im Hinterwerck beygebracht worden.

4.) Die etwanigen *defecta*, so sich wegen *der inæqualitate* der *Intonation* gezeiget, müssen und können so fort von dem Orgelmacher verbessert werden, als nehmlichen, dass die tiefesten Pfeiffen im *Posau*nen und Trompeten-*Bass* nicht so grass und blatterend ansprechen, sondern einen reinen und *firmen* Thon angeben und behalten, und dann die übrigen Pfeifen so *inaequal*, fleissig *corrigi*ret und zur Gleichheit gebracht werden, welches denn vermittelst nochmahliger Durchstimmung des gantzen Wercks und zwar bey besserer Witterung, als vorietzo, gar füglich geschehen kan.

5.) Die *Tracti*rung des Wercks sollte zwar etwas leichter seyn und die *Clavi*re nicht so tief fallen, weilen aber vermittelst der gar zu engen *Structur* solches nicht anders hat seyn können, so muss man dissfalls es gelten lassen, iedoch ist es noch so zu spielen, dass man eines Stecken Bleibens im Spielen sich nicht zu befürchten.

6.) Weilen auch der Orgelmacher eine neue BrustWindlade noch über die *Contract*e hat verfertigen müssen, indem die alte Windlade, so statt der neuen hat kommen sollen, vors erste mit einem *Fundament* Brete, und also falsch und verwerflich; zweytens auch in solcher nach der alten Art die kurtze *Octave* noch befindlich, und die übrigen *Claves* so noch fehlen, nicht haben angebracht werden, und dadurch alle 3. *Clavi*ere zur Gleichheit kommen können, sondern vielmehr eine *deformitè* verursacht hätten, so ist höchstnöthig gewessen, dass eine neue verfertiget, die besorgenden baldigen *Defecta* vermieden, und eine schöne *conformitè* beybehalten worden: sind also ohne mein Erinnern dem Orgelmacher die über die *Contract*e noch neu verfertigten Stücke zu verguten, und er also schadloss zu halten.

Weiln auch der Orgelmacher mich ersuchet Einem Hochlöblichen *Collegio* vorstellig zu machen, wie dass man solche Stücke so ihme nicht ver*accordi*ret, als nehmlich die Bildhauer-Arbeit, das Vergulden, *item* die *Espeç*en, so der Herr Vetter *pro inspectione* bekommen, und was etwa sonst noch seyn möchte, zur Bezahlung anrechnen wollen, und er doch solches nicht schuldig zu thun, auch sonst niemahls gebräuchlich gewessen (Er sich sonst wohl besser würde *prospici*ret haben) so lässet er gantz gehorsamst bitten ihn dieserwegen gleichfals in keine Unkosten zu bringen.

Nun kan schliesslichen nicht ohnerinnert lässen, dass 1.) das Fenster, so weit es nehmlich hinter der Orgel in die Höhe steiget vermittelst einer kleinen Mauer, oder eines starck eisernen Bleches von inwendig verwahret, und dadurch der noch mehr zu besorgende Wetter-Schade verhütet werden möchte. 2.) ist gewöhnlich und höchstnöthig, dass der Orgelmacher ein Jahr wenigstens die Gewähre leiste, um die etwa sich noch ereignenden Mängel völlig abzuthun, welches er auch willigst über sich nehmen dürfte, daferne man ihme nur zu baldigster und völligster *Satisfaction* seiner noch über die *Contract*e aufgewendeten Kosten beförderlich sein würde.

Dieses wäre also dasienige, so bey Untersuchung der Orgel zu *remarqui*ren vor nöthig gefunden, mich fernerhin Ihrer HochEdlen *Magnificenz* dem Herrn *D.* Rechenberg, und sämtlichen Hochlöblichen *Collegio* zu allen möglichen gefälligen Diensten bestens *recommendi*rend und verharrend

Dero gehorsamst-ergebenster *Joh: Seb: Bach.* Hochfürstlich Anhalt-Cöthenscher Capellmeister. etc.

Leipzig. den 17. *Decembr. anno* 1717.

(*Dok* 1 pp163–5)

Since at the desire of Your Noble Magnificence Dr Rechenberg (at this time *rector magnificus* of the Worshipful University of Leipzig) [I have] taken on myself to examine the partly new, partly repaired organ in the Paulinerkirche, so I have effected this as best I could, noting any defects and generally trying to draw up the following concerning the whole organ, namely:

(1) As far as the whole structure is concerned, it is indeed not to be denied that it is very narrowly confined and thus that it is difficult to reach each part should there be, as time

passes, something to repair; Herr Scheibe, as builder of the said organ, excuses this first because the organ case was not made by him (and so he had to manage with the internal structure as well as it would ever let itself be managed), and secondly because in no way was he allowed the desired space to make the structure more convenient.

(2) The usual main parts of an organ, such as chests, bellows, pipes, rollerboards and other pieces, are well and industriously made, and nothing is to be called attention to there except that the wind must be made more steady throughout so that the occasional jerkiness may be remedied. [Also] the rollerboards should be held tight in frames, in order to avoid ciphering in bad weather; however, as Herr Scheibe has made the boards with tables [i.e. joined and panelled?] according to his own method and so assures [us] that this achieves exactly what otherwise must be done with frames, this has been allowed to pass.

(3) The parts listed in the *Disposition* as well as in all contracts are there both in quality and in quantity, except two [pedal?] reeds (namely Schallmey 4' and Cornet 2'), which had to be left out to conform with an order of the Worshipful *Collegium*, but in their place were added the Octava 2' in the *Brustwerk* and then the Hohlflöte 2' in the *Hinterwerk*.

(4) The several defects which show themselves through the unevenness of the voicing must and can be improved by the builder immediately, namely the lowest pipes in Posaunenbass and Trompetenbass should not speak so coarsely and rattlingly but should give and maintain a pure and firm tone [note?]; and then the rest of the pipework, now so uneven, should be carefully corrected and made uniform – something that can conveniently be done the next time the whole organ is tuned right through, and indeed in better weather than recently.

(5) The action of the organ should certainly be somewhat lighter, and the keyfall should be shallower, but because this cannot be otherwise on account of the far too tight construction, one must let this go; in any case, it is still playable enough for one to have no fear of sticking while playing.

(6) Because the organ-builder has also had to make a new *Brustwerk* chest additional to the contract, since the old chest (which should have been there instead of the new one) [had] in the first place been fixed up with a table (and [was] thus warped and false), and in the second was provided with the short octave in the old manner (and thus lacked the other keys not installed, which would have given the three manuals a *déformité* rather than uniformity [?]); so it had become very necessary to make a new [chest], to avoid the defects which would soon have been troublesome, and to keep a fine *conformité* [which is necessary between manuals]. So without a reminder from me the builder is to be compensated for parts newly made over and above the contract, i.e. he should not lose by it.

Because the organ-builder has also asked me to point out to the Worshipful *Collegium* that an attempt has been made to reckon to his account items not agreed with him (as namely the carving work, the gilding, the fees received by Herr Vetter for his inspection, and whatever else may arise) and that he has no obligation for these things (nor has it ever been customary, or he would no doubt have estimated better), he very respectfully begs not to be left out of pocket on this account.

Finally, it cannot be left unnoticed that (1) the window – that is, so far as it rises up behind the organ – might be made good on the inside by means of a little wall or strong sheet of iron to avoid still more worrying damage from the weather. (2) It is usual and very necessary that the organ-builder give a guarantee for at least one year, in order to deal completely with any faults that may arise, which he would also be very willing to take on so long only as he was favourably treated with regard to a very prompt and full satisfaction for the cost he incurred over and above the contract.

These would be the points found necessary for reporting in [my] examination of the organ, recommending myself warmly for all possible service to Your Most Noble Magnificence Dr Rechenberg and the whole Worshipful *Collegium* in the future, and remaining your most obedient and humble

Joh: Seb: Bach, Capellmeister to the Prince of Anhalt–Cöthen, etc

Leipzig, 17 December 1717

While many details of the report agreed with Werckmeister's points outlined above for Mühlhausen and Halle, there are some new points. Scheibe's complaint about the location recalls Werckmeister's advice (1698 p39) that the builder should be consulted, by way of anticipating possible faults developing in the future, on the siting of organs. The use of '*æqualer*' for the wind also recalls Werckmeister (p42), as does Scheibe's assurance that he can achieve stability of rollerboard without frames (of the kind described by Werckmeister p15?). While the voicing is one of the minor defects found at organ-testing and should generally be tidied up immediately (pp69–71), special attention must be paid the reeds which do tend to rattle in the bass (pp36–7). While it may not be owing to Werckmeister's advice that J. S. Bach mentions tuning in better weather (cf. pp31, 33), both the comments on action-weight and keyfall (p16) and Bach's note that the construction permitted no improvement may allude to Werckmeister's suggestions for (e.g.) adjustment devices on the roller-arms. Similarly, explaining carefully and thus approving Scheibe's reasons for making a new *Brustwerk* chest could reflect Werckmeister's remarks in ch.24 that the adviser should check the need for any new work of this kind. The details of the *Bw* construction (i.e. that the old one had a table) also suggest that the examiner was in agreement with Werckmeister, since the latter reported that the best builders of the day (1698) no longer made tables, which often bring 'inconvenience' in any organ ('Ungelegenheit', p19).

Bach's recommending an extra sum for the builder – as also seems to be the case in the Zschortau inspection of 1746 (see below) – illustrates the point made by C. P. E. Bach in a letter to Forkel:

> Hatte ein Orgelbauer rechtschaffen gearbeitet, und Schaden bey seinem Bau, so bewegte er die Patronen zum Nachschuss (*Dok* III p284)

> If an organ-builder worked conscientiously and made a loss on his work, he stirred the patrons to make the additional payment

Perhaps this was very unusual, for Werckmeister speaks only in general terms of an organ-builder's receiving a bonus ('*Discretion*') for good work (1698 p71), though he does recommend a banquet on the organ's successful examination (as for Bach and the others at Naumburg in 1746). As far as concerns the final recommendations at the Paulinerkirche, the protective walling-up of the window recalls advice given at Halle the year before, while the desire for a guarantee reflects Werckmeister's taking it as understood that any new organ has one (pp33, 75), and that the examination period is the time in which to deal with all minor defects (p71).

Other details also imply that these circumstances were unusual. Rather than sign with Silbermann for an entirely new organ, the university contracted Scheibe for a rebuild, evidently in the old, unenlarged case now moved from the south gallery to the west end. That Bach was (or so it seems) only fourth choice as the examiner certainly suggests that organists closer to Leipzig (see above, p129) had declined to be involved in an unsatisfactory rebuild. The omission of Schallmey 4' and Cornet 2' may well have been regretted by him (Dähnert 1970 pp29–30): Scheibe could not make these ranks because the *Collegium* allowed him to make no enlargement to the case.* Silbermann also specified 'long complete octaves' in the bass throughout (Flade 1926 p50), but it is strange that Scheibe should have claimed an extra sum

* The extra 2' ranks on the smaller chests meant no major alteration.

for the larger *Bw* chest – was this not anticipated? Having paid Scheibe little less than what Silbermann had asked for a completely new organ (Dähnert 1980 pp183–4), the university also seems to have laid to Scheibe's charge work normally contracted for separately, including the interim report of D. Vetter, who may well have been instrumental in Scheibe's having the contract (Schering 1926 pp318–19). In criticizing the key-action, it is possible that J. S. Bach was aware of Silbermann's claim in 1710 to make the Freiberg keys almost as easy as those of a clavichord, or at least of Kuhnau's good opinion of the Freiberg action in his report of 1714 (in Flade 1926 pp53, 55).

Zschortau report, 7 August 1746

Demnach der Hochwohlgebohrne Herr, Herr Heinrich August Sahrer von Sahr, Erb- Lehn- und GerichtsHerr auf Zschortau und Biesen, als Hochansehnlicher Kirchen-*Patronus* der Kirche zu Zschortau, mich Endesbenannten ersuchet, das in besagter Kirche von Herrn Johann Scheiben aus Leipzig neu erbauete Orgelwerck zu durchgehen, und zu *examini*ren; Und ich dann dasselbe, in Beyseyn Hochgedachten Herrn von Sahr von Stück zu Stück genau durchgegangen, *probir*et, und gegen den mir vorgelegten, zwischen denen Herren *Inspectoribus*, und Herrn Scheiben untern 30. *Junii* 1744. errichteten *Original Contract* fleissig gehalten, darbey aber befunden habe, dass nicht allein dem *Contract* in allen und ieden Stücken ein Genüge geschehen, alles tüchtig, fleissig und wohl erbauet, und ausser einigen kleinen Mängeln, denen iedoch Herr Scheibe bey der Probe *in continenti* abge-holffen, nirgends ein Haupt*defect* verhanden, sondern auch über den *Contract* folgende Stimmen, als

1.) *Qvinta Thön* ⎫ .... 16. *Fus*
2.) *Viola di Gamba* ⎬ von Holtz .... 8. *Fus*
3/ *Fleute-Travers* ⎭ .... 4. *Fus*.
4/ *Super Octava*, von Metall 1. *Fus*.
5/ Ein Angehänge zum *Manual*
   und *Pedal*

allesamt tüchtig und gut ge- und befunden worden seyn; Als habe auff Verlangen zu Steuer der Wahrheit, ein solches zu des Herrn Verfertigers Ruhm, vermittelst meiner eigenhändigen Unterschrifft und beygedruckten Petzschafft hierdurch bezeugen wollen;
Datum Zschortau, den 7. *August*. 1746.
Joh: Sebast: Bach. Königlich Pohln. u. Churfürstlich Sächsischer Hoff*Compositeur*
(*Dok* 1 pp168–9)

Since the Right Honourable lord, Herr Heinrich August Sahrer von Sahr, Lord of the Manor, Liege Lord and Magistrate of Zschortau and Biesen, as eminent Patron of the Church of Zschortau, requested of me, the undersigned, that I go through and examine the organ newly built in the said church by Herr Johann Scheibe of Leipzig; and I then went through and tested the same meticulously piece by piece in the presence of the said Honour- able Herr von Sahr, carefully bearing in mind the original contract made between the Inspectors and Herr Scheibe dated 30 June 1744 and laid before me; in doing so, however, I have found not only a sufficiency achieved in all and every part according to the contract, everything made skilfully, diligently and well, and apart from a few small faults (which however Herr Scheibe dealt with as we went along during the examination) no actual major defect, but even the following stops above the contract, namely

1 Quinta Thön 16' ⎫
2 Viola di Gambe 8' ⎬ of wood
3 Fleute-Travers 4' ⎭
4 Super Octava 1', of metal
5 a pulldown from pedal to manual

were all found and deemed to be well and soundly made; so by request I have wished to testify the same, in respect to truth and to the renown of the builder, by means of my own signature and affixed seal.

Given at Zschortau, 7 August 1746

Joh: Sebast: Bach

Royal Polish and Electoral Saxon Court Composer

Of the briefer reports made by J. S. Bach (Erfurt 1716, Störmthal 1723, Naumburg 1746), that at Zschortau is typical and is too general for much detail to emerge. As at Störmthal (*Dok* II pp127–8), the organ was the concern of the *Herr* of the district, and as advised by Werckmeister (p2) the contract was made available at the examination and the faults were distinguished as between minor (corrected immediately) and major (none). The additions were unusually important and may suggest collaboration between Scheibe and Bach. Thus the (single) manual received a 16′ stop (resulting in a quite different *pleno*), a string stop and an imitative flute;* as at Störmthal, the coupler was additional, but unlike Störmthal (optional *Windkoppel*)† the pedal keys pull down the manual automatically. Pulldowns seem necessarily to suggest a simpler mode of playing, not for seventeenth-century *points d'orgue* in this case but for hymns, chorales and free pieces in which the orientation of the bass line produces a texture with great gaps between bass and tenor.

It seems from contemporary remarks on J. S. Bach's examination of another Scheibe organ (see above, p137) and on his report on an organ by Hildebrandt (Naumburg 1746) that the composer was less painstaking in his examining of Hildebrandt than of Scheibe. Forkel naturally claimed that he had been impartial, but the fact that the *Obituary* itself called the Scheibe examination 'perhaps one of the severest ever made' (*Dok* II p88) whereas at Naumburg the local organist was not at all satisfied (*Dok* II pp429–31) makes this questionable. On the other hand, Hildebrandt may well have been a better maker of mechanisms and was probably a more musical voicer, judging by any comparison that can be made between Zschortau and Störmthal today.

18. Registration

Registering the organ works of J. S. Bach can be understood in terms of the organs he knew, the stops implied in a certain genre or specified in actual pieces, and the nature of *organo pleno*. There is also the special question of changing manuals in the ritornello movements. The present chapter is concerned with the second of these: stops implied or specified.

a

The famous remarks made in the *Obituary* were later amplified to build up a more complete picture:

---

* Now a traverso, unlike the fipple flute at Mühlhausen.

† *Windkoppel*: an extra row of pallets for the pedal in the *Hw* chest, but in a separate pallet-box to which the wind was admitted or not, at the choice of the player.

Er verstund . . . die Art die Orgeln zu handhaben, die Stimmen derselben auf das geschickteste mit einander zu vereinigen, und jede Stimme, nach ihrer Eigenschaft hören zu lassen, in der grössten Vollkommenheit (*Dok* III p88).

He understood the art of handling the organ, of uniting the stops together in the most clever way, and of allowing each stop to be heard according to its own nature in the greatest perfection.

Niemand konnte besser, als er, Dispositionen zu neuen Orgel angeben, und beurtheilen (*ibid*).

No one knew better than he how to draw up and judge stoplists for new organs.

Das Registriren bey den Orgeln wuste niemand so gut, wie er. Oft erschracken die Organisten, wenn er auf ihren Orgeln spielen wollte, u. nach seiner Art die Register anzog, indem sie glaubten es könnte unmöglich so, wie er wollte, gut klingen, hörten hernach aber hernach einen *Effect*, worüber sie erstaunten. Diese Wissenschaften sind mit ihm abgestorben (C. P. E. Bach, letter to Forkel c1774: *Dok* III p284).

No one understood so well as he the registering of organs. Often organists were terrified when he wished to play on their organs and drew the stops in his manner, since they believed it could not possibly sound well in the way he wanted; but little by little they heard an effect that amazed them. These sciences died out with him.*

In all three, C. P. E. Bach was at pains to claim his father's uniqueness ('no one knew better . . . '), implying that his father taught himself by observation and that organists of that time and since were conservative or unimaginative. A conclusion must also be that his father's improvisations and/or compositions were more imaginatively registered than was usual, and were thus exceptional.

The posthumous hero-worship makes it difficult to be clear what precisely C. P E. Bach meant. Forkel (1802 ch.IV) certainly did not know and, in a gloss on the foregoing passage, tried to explain it in terms of independent contrapuntal lines:

Diese ihm eigene Art zu registriren war eine Folge seiner genauen Kenntniss des Orgelbaues, so wie aller einzelnen Stimmen. Er hatte sich frühe gewöhnt, jeder einzelnen Orgelstimme eine ihrer Eigenschaft angemessene Melodie zu geben, und dieses führte ihn zu neuen Verbindungen dieser Stimme, auf welche er ausserdem nie verfallen seyn würde.

This kind of registering peculiar to him was a consequence of his exact knowledge of organ-building and similarly of all single stops. Early on he had become used to giving each stop a melody suited to its nature, and this led him towards new combinations of these stops which he would otherwise never have hit upon.

The phrase 'jeder einzelnen Orgelstimme eine ihrer Eigenschaft' suggests that Forkel was using C. P. E. Bach's words as a starting-point; but his expanding on them to depict J. S. Bach as looking for melodic colour – i.e. specific (solo) stops for a specific type of melody – smacks more of the organ ethos of 1800 than that of 1725; the only possible relevance to J. S. Bach might be that Forkel had an idea of how de Grigny was played and registered, or at least had got to know Bedos's treatise and what it said about French ingenuity.

There have been various attempts to specify what C. P. E. Bach meant, of which Klotz's suggestions (1975 p388) are the most reasoned: that J. S. Bach strengthened

* Last sentence added in the margin (David/Mendel p276).

a cantus-firmus line not with Zimbel etc (as in Scheidt, or as for the pedal at 'Te Martyrum' in Buxtehude's Te deum BUXWV 218) but with Silbermann's high mutations (e.g. 8.2⅔.1.1⅗), that he accompanied a cantus firmus with unusual colours like reed or 8.2 flutes, that he used reeds against high mutations when the lines are very different (e.g. BWV 768.v), that he used reeds for accompaniment against strong flue cantus firmus (e.g. BWV 658). Such suggestions are possible but pay too much heed to C. P. E. Bach's remarks, which may well have been based (with whatever motive) on his father's knowledge of or response to French colours. At most they suggest only that J. S. Bach 'was extraordinarily imaginative in selecting colourful combinations' (Stauffer 1981). Perhaps trios such as the Six Sonatas, when played on the church organ, kept the French 8' manual colours (reed and Cornet/Sesquialtera contrast) but deferred to German fashion in regarding the pedal as a 16' continuo line (with a 'Double Bass stop', in the later words of Kollmann – *Dok* III p582). Moreover, since the left hand of the Six Sonatas remains above tenor c (see Vol. I p9, two references), there is nothing to prevent its playing more comfortably an octave lower with 4' stops; this would accord with several registrations for chorale-trios in Kauffmann's *Harmonische Seelenlust* (1733) and would not be contradicted by the part-writing in trios by the circle of younger composers under Bach's influence. Forkel's reference to the exceptional use of single stops for trios ('Gebrauch einzelner Register, etwa in einem Trio etc. eine Ausnahme': 1802 ch.IV) could be taken for or against such theories. While the Frenchness of Silbermann's unbuilt scheme for the Paulinerkirche, Leipzig (1710) should not be exaggerated, nor J. S. Bach's music of that period seen as so very French as to allow us to call the Pauliner organ 'eine spezifische Bachorgel' (Klotz 1980 p397), there may well have been enough French elements in Bach's registration to have made contemporaries think it unusual. Certainly at least one Bach pupil knew both French and new-German tastes: J. F. Agricola described both *tierce en taille* (with pedal 16' and, in the tierce hand, optional 16' flute) and the new 8' colours (Gedackt + Vugara + Quintadena + Holhflöte – in Marpurg 1758 p505), such as would have been feasible on the Bach-approved organ at Naumburg in 1746.*

But that in general any posthumous praise has to be read with circumspection may be suggested by a later remark about W. F. Bach:

> Der Natur der Orgel hat er sich ganz bemächtiget; sein Registerverständnis hat ihm noch niemand nachgemacht. Er mischt die Register, ohne sein Spiel nur einen Augenblick zu unterbrechen, – wie der Mahler seine Farben auf der Pallette; und bringt dadurch ein bewundernswürdiges Ganzes hervor (Schubart 1806 p90).

> He had made himself master of the organ's nature; no one has yet imitated him in his understanding of the stops. He mixes them without interrupting his playing for even a moment – as the painter does his colours on the palette – and thereby produces a wonderful whole.

Posthumous hero-worship reduces even technicalities to a common factor.

b

The changing of stops in the course of a piece is also implied here and there, but the situation is not clear. If the exact dating of all the registrations in the D minor Concerto

---

* H. Löffler (1928) already pointed out the possibility that J. S. Bach used reeds *versus* flues in the French manner.

BWV 596.i were known for certain (see Vol. I pp313–14), it would still not imply whether they indicate an afterthought, a change of attitude, a specifying of what was anyway implicit, or a free option.* Some have thought that the stop-changes – or, rather, stop-additions – in BWV 596.i were possible for the organist himself to make (Harmon 1971 pp265–6; Kloppers 1966 p290), others that the passage 'amounts to proof that Bach had assistants to work the stops' (Emery 1962). Certainly the registration in BWV 596.i is a model of clarity (Klotz 1975 p385), but that it was achieved with the help of a registrant must remain unlikely in the absence of any evidence that such a concert-like approach existed at that period.† For one thing, it cannot be assumed that it was an ideal of the period (as it is now) to play continuously, with no gap between phrases bigger than a 'breath' or comma; the possibility that such gaps holding up the flow were acceptable or even conventional also bears on the question of manual-changing in the maturer works (see below, chapter 20). In the case of the earlier works, perfect sense in a movement of several sections can frequently be made by changing or adding stops as a new section begins: any of the praeludia (e.g. D major BWV 532) can be approached in this way. Less obviously, perhaps, but quite as likely, in sectional fugues such as the Legrenzi BWV 574 or the Canzona BWV 588 each of the sections can be marked by stops being added. There may have to be something of a break made between sections in BWV 574 as the player builds up from an Italianate opening (Prinzipal 8') to a German close (*organo pleno* including pedal reeds), but in no way does this violate the style-allusion, the structure, the *figurae* or even the notation of the piece in any of its variants.

The sources of BWV 593.i (Vol. I pp289, 298) and of BWV 720 (Vol. II p263) are not reliable enough for one to be sure whether the marks for *pleno* or for colour-stops imply changing the stops in the course of the piece. 'For 3 manuals' in copies of BWV 720 rather suggests setting up three manuals and using them without changes. Hertel's advice in 1666 that *Rp* stops should be near the player's right hand (i.e. not behind his back) so that they can be drawn while the left hand plays the bass (Schünemann 1922 p341) refers to continuo-playing in motets etc in which fewer or more voices take part, as does his direction to add a stop when the *tutti* sings. But it certainly suggests stop-changing in at least one kind of music, as (indirectly) does Adlung's remark that two manuals are better for continuo than one, since

> wo ein Clavier ist, da muss der Organist die Register gar oft im Ziehen verändern (1768 I p171)
>
> where there is one manual [only], the organist must very often vary the stops by pulling them . . .

though accompaniments in 1768 may not indicate solo registrations in 1700. But over the whole period, registrations for chorale accompaniments were changed from verse to verse, as is implied by chorale-versets (interludes) from Scheidt to Buxtehude and by later remarks of Adlung that in chorales 'one likes to change stops diligently' ('pflegt man mit den Registern fleissig abzuwechseln': 1768 I p172). The various choices of stops depended on the strength of the congregation, the nature of the hymn, its *Affekt*, the place, etc. *Abwechseln* is a less ambiguous term than *verändern*.

---

* There is also the question of the specifying of *Bw* in the first movement, *Rp* in the last. Perhaps *Rp* was merely an inexact term for second manual (Keller 1948 p18), like the *f/p* marks in the third movement. There are other possibilities: reasons could be conjectured for the transcriber wanting three manuals; perhaps either *Bw* or *Rp* signs were added at different times, etc. See also a remark on p127 above.

† Keller's idea that crosses marked in one copy (P 801) of Vincent Lübeck's D minor Praeludium were indications 'for the registrants' (Peters edn 4437) has been shown to be unfounded (K. Beckmann in B & H edn 6673, p69)

Such remarks on basso continuo and accompaniment seem better evidence for stop-changing than the references to builders' bringing stop-levers more conveniently to hand, as when Schnitger rebuilt the Flensburg organ in 1707–9 with conveniently designed and easily reached stop-knobs 'to make variation' ('umb Veränderung zu machen': Fock 1974 p166) or when J. F. Agricola noted that Silbermann's 48 stop-knobs at Freiberg Cathedral (1710)

> sich gar leicht und bequem ziehen lassen, ohne dass sich der Organist von seiner Stelle bewegen darf (in Adlung 1768 1p228).

> allowed themselves to be drawn very easily and conveniently, without the organist having to move from his seat.

Neither of these remarks must necessarily be a reference to stop-changing in the course of a piece. Similarly, Agricola's remarks on J. S. Bach's liking for short keys for changing manuals easily (see below, p225) do not necessarily suggest changing during a piece, much less that one hand could play on two manuals as is sometimes suggested (Löffler 1928). Nor, in the nature of things, do rests in larger works show that J. S. Bach changed manual or stop at such points (*ibid*), though this would agree with what is supposed of earlier traditions.* That Adlung in defining 'Ventil' (1768 1p152) makes no mention of the uses of ventils in registration (i.e. for preparing chests or parts of chests beforehand) suggests that they were not yet used for such purpose. Yet the account in 1840 of the organist Schneider improvising on the Silbermann organ in the Dresden Sophienkirche shows that organists did not find it physically difficult to change stops when they wanted to:

> It was the work of one hand to draw and close the stops which were wanted by the play of his imagination: a matter, of course, in which he could receive no help [from a registrant]. But he ministered to himself with such a wonderful promptness and agility of finger, that the changes of hand from the keyboard to the register were never felt. [All was] subtly . . . combined and alternated (Chorley 1841 iii p172).

> [Of interludes between verses:] The artful and unexpected [*sic*] management of the stops, so as to produce every variety of *crescendo* and *diminuendo*, entirely precluded the occupation of the swell (*ibid* p175).

While it is clear that tastes in organ music had changed by the 1830s, it is to be noted that Chorley's remarks related to an original Silbermann organ.

c

The registration of the chorale BWV 600 (see Vol. II p18) for Trompete 8′ and Prinzipal 8′ is certainly there to clarify the notation and to show the relationship between the two written canonic voices, but in that case 'Trompete 8″' means that the canon is notated at 8′ pitch, and not than an 8′ *stop* is necessarily required. The copy of de Grigny's organ-book (belonging to much the same period as BWV 600) had three staves but also left pedal themes on the middle staff requiring a rubric; the registration for BWV 600 is a comparable rubric for Weimar, where the pedal could well have played Cornett 4′ an octave lower (Klotz 1969). In the chorale BWV 608, the pedal canonic cantus firmus implies 4′ stop without saying so, recalling the high solos in Scheidt notated at sounding pitch.

---

* Thus it would only be interesting conjecture to suppose that the rests and the break in texture at the coda of the D minor Fugue BWV 538 indicated additional stops (for an *ff* close) on the analogy of (e.g.) the added trumpets and timpani at the end of 'et in terra pax' in the B minor Mass.

d

The colourful registrations of Kauffmann (1733) and Gronau (d. 1747) are of uncertain relevance to J. S. Bach; they were possible only on large organs and were conceived for the *Affekte* of expressive organ-chorale playing. Gronau worked with doublings in both manual and pedal (8.8.4, 8.4.4, 16.16, 16.8.8), and as with Mattheson he found it necessary in a large church to thicken cantus-firmus registrations (e.g. *Rp* 8.8.8.4.4.2.8).* He seems not to have required a change of stops in a movement, though two or even three manuals are used. If the repertories and registrations of the north (Mattheson in Hamburg, Gronau in Danzig) are of only marginal relevance to J. S. Bach, the suggestions made by Kauffmann (Leipzig 1733), J. F. Walther (Berlin 1727) and H. G. Trost (Altenburg 1733) are closer, though they too were designed for particular organs and for the tastes of a new period – hence the need to publish their descriptions. For various kinds of figurative chorales, Kauffmann had imaginative colours (e.g. Fagott 16′ + Quintadena 8′ + Spitzflöte 2′), solo mixtures (Vox humana 8′ + Gemshorn 8′ or Spillflöte 4′ or Principal 4′), accompaniments (Rohrflöte 16′ + Principal 8′) and a general liking for manual 16′ tone. For bass cantus firmus, reeds and flues are mixed (e.g. Violon 16′ + Trompete 8′ + Nachthorn 4′ + Kornett 2′), which could suggest either lingering traditions or an unrefined ear. H. F. Quehl (1734) based much on 8′ and 4′, whereas the more exotic Gronau did the same only for *Affekt* (e.g. 'Zion klagt mit Angst' with *I* 8.4.8, *II* 8.8.8, *Ped* 16.16.8), as perhaps was also the purpose of the 'several 8′ stops' played together by Altnickol at Naumburg (report of 1753 – Dähnert 1962 p114).

   J. F. Walther, working with the Wagner organs in Berlin, mixed the flutes (16′ to 1′) or auxiliaries (Viola, Spitzflöte etc) in variations and thought the Salicional 8′ + Fugara 4′ good for running basses or arpeggios. G. H. Trost was more in the Thuringian tradition, recommending Sesquialtera both in the *organo pleno* and for *Veränderungen*, liking imitative flutes of various kinds (including overblowing flutes), gentle stopped Nasards, leathered Posaune 16′ and imitative string stops (Violon 16′, Viola 8′ – Löffler 1932). The nature of these sources (Trost, Walther) suggests that the new organs of *c*1725 required such guides to be published; their style is less technical, more descriptive of tone, more geared to the achieving of variety and *Affekt* than earlier monographs such as Werckmeister's on the rebuilt organ of Gröningen (1705). Habits in *c*1715 are much more difficult to establish, and the frequent references to Adlung, Mattheson, Kauffmann, Gronau, Quehl, Walther and Trost found today quite disguise the fact that they have very dubious relevance to at least the music of Bach's Weimar period. With such a chorale as 'Schmücke dich' BWV 654, the big question which is still not answerable is: How far did the early-nineteenth-century attitudes to it (see Schumann's remark in Vol. II p139) reflect tastes in *c*1715? Were original registrations more 'objective' than is suggested by Mendelssohn's later remarks (in a letter to his sister Fanny of 6 October 1831) that he had found the correct stops for it (8.4 flutes in the left hand – a touching effect such as they had both heard in Berlin – with a solo reed for the cantus firmus)?† Did such music always compel organists to seek 'touching'

---

* Perhaps J. S. Bach's heavier scoring of cantus-firmus melodies in the cantatas for Leipzig (a bigger church than Weimar) offers a parallel to Gronau's registration? Though the sources are not at all conclusive, this may also be the case with Weimar cantatas revised at Leipzig (BWV 80, 161, 172, 185).

† That Mendelssohn, then in Munich, speaks of the 'distant vocal' effect of his solo combination of mellow Oboe 8′ + soft Clarion 4′ + Viola might suggest that he had found a Swell or Echo manual, something quite alien to Thuringia in 1715.

registrations for it? Was Griepenkerl speaking for 1715 as well as 1844 when he advised that stops be chosen to harmonize with the 'spirit and sense' of the piece concerned ('Geist und Sinn': Peters I p. iii)? Or did the sarabande-like details of BWV 654 bring with them a more conventional *Affekt* – that of the gentle sarabande – more objective, requiring no more an atmospheric registration than (e.g.) 'O Mensch bewein' BWV 622 would receive if played on one manual with a single 8' Gedackt?

It is difficult to believe that early works such as BWV 720 were treated to pietist expressiveness, for though it may only be a question of degree, J. G. Walther's registrations for this chorale are simpler and more modest than those which Gronau specified for his own setting. For example, Gronau suggested the complete thunderous pedal of 16.16.16.16.8.8.8.8.4.4.3.2.Mixtur + 32' reed for the line 'if the world were full of the devil'. That J. G. Walther's registration for BWV 720 was part of an unbroken tradition is also suggested by Adlung's recommendation for imaginative realization of an organ continuo, which coincides with the registration for BWV 720: an 8' or 16' Fagott for the left hand, a deeper bass support in the pedal and a right-hand solo or *traverso* part played on the Sesquialtera (1783 p588).* The Mühlhausen scheme makes it clear that the Sesquialtera was a basic effect at that period, though in his 1710 scheme for the Paulinerkirche, Leipzig, Silbermann was already claiming that his (frenchified) Cornet v would make no cackling of the kind found in that area (Flade 1926 p92), which may well be a reference to Saxon–Thuringian Sesquialteras.

e

If, as Adlung claimed, many organists of his period played the prelude before the service or cantata with no subtle registration and 'nothing other than the storming of the full organ' ('nichts, als das Toben des vollen Werks': Adlung 1768 p590), then simple, careful registrations would have left their mark. Kauffmann's were meant to be encouraging. No doubt organists did sometimes do inappropriate things, like add the drum stops etc to the Te Deum (Niedt III p46), but in various ways Mattheson suggests that at least in Hamburg registration was an admired art. Weckmann went there as a student to learn 'playing and registering the stops' ('Spielen und Registriren der Orgelstimmen': Mattheson 1740 p395), and as a young organist, H. H. Lüders had competed for a post with a more experienced rival who

> in Anziehung und Wahl der Orgel-Register, behülfflich seyn wollte (*ibid* p173)
>
> wished to be helpful in the drawing and choosing of the organ-stops

– which certainly suggests the occasional use of a registrant. It is not even out of the question that when C. P. E. Bach made the remarks on his father's registration in the *Obituary* he had in mind Mattheson's praise of J. Praetorius published in the well-known *Ehrenpforte* only a few years earlier:

---

* Adlung even notes that though such solos may be called *Traverse*, he knows that most believe the only organ effect of this kind is by means of the Sesquialtera; so the Fagott/Sesquialtera contrast is clear. The cues in the cantata BWV 161 and in one version of the opening chorus of the *St Matthew Passion* show further uses for the Sesquialtera.

An hohen Festtagen spielte er zwar freudig; aber zu Busliedern war er sonderlich aufgelegt, und wuste die Stimmen so zu gebrauchen, dass sie ihre natürliche Eigenschafften behielten, und man nicht allein das Spielen, sondern auch die Orgel rühmen muste (*ibid* p330).

On high feast-days he played very cheerfully; but for penitential hymns he was on particularly good form, and knew how to use the stops in such a way that they realized their natural properties, and one had to praise not only the playing but also the organ.

Whatever this may suggest about the *Obituary*, it certainly implies that the more meditative organ chorales received the more interesting registrations; it also implies a different technique from the mere mixing of reeds and flues so liked by *c*1750.

Particularly appropriate to the Saxon–Thuringian organ are the remarks made by Werckmeister, since he held a special position in that area: the only major theorist *c*1700, one who was apparently much quoted and who was, judging from Adlung, still very influential half a century later. For his rules against doubling stops of the same pitch, see chapter 19. His interest in the Sesquialtera led him to include a long discussion of the etymology of the term in the *Orgelprobe* of 1698, but he declined to give rules for 'drawing' and changing the stops' ('die Stimmen . . . ziehen und verwechseln': p71) for reasons typical of the period around 1700:

weil aber ein jeder, so sonst ein gesundes Gehör hat, wohl vernehmen wird, wie sich eines gegen das andere ausnimmet, so achte solches für unnötig (p71) . . .
ein gut Gehör thut hiebey das beste . . . nicht jede Manier auff alle Veränderung der Stimmen sich wohl schicket, darum ist ein gut Musicalisches *Judicium* und Gehör hierin das beste Mittel (pp72–3).

because everyone who has a healthy ear will easily hear how one [stop] goes well with another, so I think such [rules] unnecessary . . .
a good ear serves best in this matter . . . not every way of varying the stops is very suitable, therefore a good musical judgment and ear are the best means for it.

Werckmeister's 50-stop model specification concentrates on the principal, flute and reed choruses, with few colour stops and solo effects, compared to the smaller organs of Arnstadt, Mühlhausen and Weimar.

f

Assuming that J. S. Bach was responsible for the registration signs in the *Schübler Chorales*, Forkel thought that

Bey einigen derselben kann man sehen, wie Bach im Registriren von der gewöhnlichen Art abging (1802 ch.ix)

in some of them one can see how in registration Bach departed from customary practice . . .

instancing BWV 646, with its pitch indications (*I* 8', *II* 16' and *Ped* 4') together with pedal cantus firmus. However, such a disposition was by nature old-fashioned rather than strikingly inventive, giving the left hand the basso-continuo part (see Vol. II pp114–15) – perhaps with an 8' or other rank for definition, as in Adlung (1783 p587) – and keeping the pedal at the 4' level. F. W. Marpurg used a similar layout for one of his organ-chorale canons (Fellerer 1932 p85), and C. D. Graff specifies a pedal '4 fus Ton' in a chorale in Krebs's BB Mus MS 12010.

Nevertheless, such pedal solos gradually passed out of fashion during J. S. Bach's period: for a project at Naumburg in 1743, H. G. Trost left out 4' and 2' pedal reeds in his plan since they were 'no longer fashionable or usual' ('nicht mehr Mode noch usuell': Klotz 1933 p228). No doubt 4' pedal stops were thought not as pointless as certain others: A. C. Kuntzen in 1757 was against any 2' in the pedal, and even the Lüneburg Johanniskirche Kornett 2' was 'no longer in use' in 1766 ('nicht mehr . . . in Gebrauch': quoted in Frotscher 1934–5 II pp970ff). Kauffmann used both 4' and 2' liberally, but only in addition to lower ranks (see also J. F. Walther, 1727), whereas it is thought to have been due to J. S. Bach's influence that Hildebrandt made pedal 4' and 2' ranks (the 2' was alone, without 4', at Hettstedt in 1748 – Dähnert 1962 pp119, 151). A question still not answered is: Were 4' (or 2') pedal reeds played without 8' and/or 16' stops before the period when J. F. Walther and Kauffmann both registered them with such stops to bring out a chorale? If the answer is Yes, were these authors only specifying what had become habitual in Saxony–Brandenburg? Or are they referring to bass cantus firmus only, not tenor or alto?

Kauffmann also used 16' Fagott (with other and higher ranks depending on the liveliness of line) for the left-hand parts in *bicinia*. That is, he strengthened the musical allusion of such pieces to the sung basso-continuo aria on which they are based. Both J. S. Bach's careful adoption of the style (Italian *bicinium*-aria) and his remarks on the Fagott at Mühlhausen (see above, p142) make such a registration very likely for such pieces as BWV 711, 768.i etc.* It is clear from L. Compenius's remarks on his stoplist for the Erfurt Predigerkirche in 1650 that already at that date a (pedal) Fagott 16' was included for the sake of 'quiet ensemble playing' ('zur stillen Musik': Bal 1981 p57).

---

19. *Organo pleno*

The two main questions here are: For what kind of music was *organo pleno* used? and What exactly does *organo pleno* mean? Of the two, the second is the more difficult to answer with certainty.

It may be correct to see the northern European organ as having achieved two main choruses by the sixteenth century: the 'Mixture-plenum' and the 'Reed-plenum', each associated with a certain manual (main and secondary; Klotz 1978 pp7ff). The first was the combination, by then already traditional, of Principals and Mixtures: the natural development of the *Blockwerk*. The second was less regular in content, purpose and location: a group of stops which in smaller organs (or those of southern areas such as the Rhineland) were often distributed over the manuals without a clear system. Although the theory has often been stated that J. S. Bach worked with both kinds of *organo pleno* and registered certain works for 'Mixture-plenum' and 'Reed-plenum' (Klotz 1975 pp380–91), there is no demarca-

---

* In the English anthems of William Croft (1678–1727), similar 'arias' sometimes have the organ left-hand part registered '2 Diapasons upon the left hand'; the continuo figures seem to have been realized on a softer manual and in any case more discreetly than in basso-continuo arias as normally played today.

tion in any northern European organ type so clearly corresponding to this contrast as the Parisian *plein jeu* and *grand jeu*. Nor is it anything more than interesting speculation to suppose that J. S. Bach intended a quasi-Parisian alternation of the two in any of his works.* Stops making up the 'Reed-plenum' (reed, tierce, flute mutation) were and remained primarily for solo purposes until principal-scaled tierce-mixtures became fashionable here and there in the eighteenth century.†

It can scarcely be doubted that *organo pleno* in copies made both by the composer and by copyists meant the flue chorus, the 'Mixture-plenum', the *plein jeu*, deriving like the Italian *repieno* from medieval organ design, and like it not originally intended for counterpoint in the sense of later three- to five-part fugues. One builder from Saxony (K. Eckstein – Klotz 1978 p16) already defined it in 1576 as follows:

> . . . zum gantzen werkh soll das Principal, Octaf, Getackht, Quinthen, Mixtur und Zimbel gezogen werden.

> for *organo pleno* Principal, Octave, Gedackt, Quints, Mixture and Zimbel should be drawn.

Among the next generation of central German builders, Esaias Compenius confirmed the two basic features of the *organo pleno*: that it contained principals only ('do not include Gedackt stops in the *pleno*') and that its music was not contrapuntal ('play slow chordal passages, not quick coloratura' – Blume 1936 p21). Whether or not stopped ranks were included in the *organo pleno* must have depended on regional variety in voicing and wind-raising, for Werckmeister is quite emphatic:

> doch kann ich für die Einfältigen und *Incipienten*, zu erinnern keinen Umbtrit nehmen, dass man 2. *Aequal*-Stimmen, so nicht aus einem *Fundament* gearbeitet, nicht gerne zugleich ziehet; Denn ob schon dieselben so *accurat* zusammen gestimmet sind, so wollen sich doch die *Proportiones*, was die weite [!] der Pfeiffen betrifft, nicht wohl vertragen, so kann man auch die *Differens* in der *Aequalität* am ersten vernehmen, worzu denn ein ungleicher Wind viel helffen kann (1698 pp71–2).

> but for the inexpert and beginner, however, I can make the point straight away that one does not like to draw together two stops of the same [8'] pitch if they are not made to the

---

* Such as *grand/plein/grand* for the sections of the D major Prelude BWV 532 or *plein/grand/plein* in BWV 572. Though Klotz hinted at the comparison in several publications up to and including his 1975 book , only in Klotz 1980 does he compare in detail J. S. Bach's proposed new manual at Mühlhausen in 1707 with particular Parisian stoplists. But if all such comparisons derive ultimately from the remark in Williams 1966 p146 that the Mühlhausen third manual was 'more in the manner of R. Clicquot than A. Schnitger', it is right to say that at that period I had not grasped the significance of the Parisian 4' being a principal (not a Flute) and the reed being a cylindrical Cromorne (not conical Schalmei): these differences alone make any similarity between Mülhausen and Paris purely theoretical.
† E.g. the organs in Mark Brandenburg by Joachim Wagner (*c*1720–1750 – the main *Hw* Mixture); or the main chorus Mixture as described by J. F. Agricola (in Marpurg 1758 III p492): C = 15.19.22.24.26.29; or both chorus Mixtures at Altenburg Schlosskapelle (H. G. Trost 1735–9, thought to have been praised by J. S. Bach in 1739 – see *Dok* II pp368–9). E. Zavarsky (1977) has argued that because the pure thirds of a tierce rank were flatter than the tempered thirds of the scale, builders widened pipe-scales and gave them narrower mouths, smaller windways and a darker sound, banishing them from the *pleno*. But this seems not to agree with extant Thuringian–Saxon organs of the 1720s and 1730s; rather, as G. A. Sorge pointed out in 1744, the tierce ranks work well in the three upper octaves (see Lange 1973 p24). In the Silbermann temperament, the eight good thirds are only slightly sharp.

same scale; for however accurately they may be tuned together, the proportions as far as the width of the pipes is concerned will not agree, so one will immediately hear the difference in their unison tone, to which an uneven wind can add much.

Several things are unclear in Werckmeister's remarks: whether 'equal stops' means at any pitch (2 × 16′, 2 × 4′?), whether '*Fundament*' means pipe-scale (and thus whether 'so nicht' implies that ranks of the same scale may be doubled, as Adlung surmised (1768 1 p170)), whether '*Proportiones*' and 'weite der Pfeiffen' (another term for pipe-scale?) imply that he is speaking only of extreme differences of scale, and whether the last phrase means that uneven wind ameliorates the disparity of tone or aggravates it. But it is important to reach some understanding of Werckmeister's words since they are directly relevant in period and area to the earlier part of J. S. Bach's output. Moreover, later writers such as Niedt and Mattheson dealt carefully with the same point:

> Der Lehr-Begierige bemercke nur noch hiebey überhaupt, dass in den Orgel-Wercken keine *aequal* Stimmen, die von gleicher Gröbe sind, und deren die eine ein Schnarr-Werck, die andere aber ein Pfeiffen-Werck ist, zusammen angezogen werden müssen: denn sie nimmer rein klingen, sondern werden allezeit falsch seyn und starck schweben.§
> § Es war hier, zum Exempel, verboten, ein *Principal* 8 Fuss, mit dem Gedact 8 Fuss, zusammen zu ziehen, welches sich, (wenn sie reine stimmen) endlich noch wohl zur Noth vertragen könte, weil es Register sind, die fest stehen, und sich nicht verstimmen . . . wenn noch 2 oder 3 Neben-Stimmen, unterschiedener Grösse, dabey sind, die selbige vermitteln, und wird absonderlich im *Pedal*, Gross-Posaun 32 und *Principal* 32, *item*, Posaun 16 und *Principal* 16, so dann ferner *Octava* 8 und Trommete 8, *Octava* 4 und Schallmey 4 Fuss, alles auf einmahl angezogen, und mit ein paar *Mixtur*en *temperiret*, wenn man im vollen Werck arbeiten will. Dass also diese Regul auch ihre *Exceptiones* hat, und mit Unterscheid zu verstehen ist, wenn es heist: dass *Sub*-Bass oder Unter-Satz 16 Fuss, mit dem Posaunen-Bass 16 Fuss nicht zusammen klinge. Wenn man sie alleine gebrauchen wolte, absonderlich im *Manual*, so würden *aequal*-Stimmen einen schlechten *effect* thun; sind aber andere Register daneben, von 4, 8 und 2 Fuss, so kann man gar wohl 2 *aequal*-Stimmen mit einander gebrauchen. Nur die Schnarr-wercke und Pfeiffen von einander gelassen; ausser im *Pedal*, zum vollen *Wercke*.
> (Niedt/Mattheson II p116: main text by Niedt, footnote by Mattheson)

> Let him who is anxious to learn note herewith only the general point that in organs no 'equal' stops of the same size – of which one is a reed, but the other a flue – must be drawn together; for they never sound pure but will always be false and tremble [beat] noticeably.§
> § It is forbidden here, for example, to draw together a Principal 8′ and the Gedackt 8′, which after all can agree well together at a pinch (if they are tuned well), because there are stops which do remain steady and do not go out of tune . . . when indeed two or three additional stops of various scale are there they adjust with each other [?] and will do so particularly in the pedal (Posaune 32′ and Principal 32′, Posaune 16′ and Principal 16′, and further Octave 8′ and Trompete 8′, Octave 4′ and Schalmei 4′ – all drawn together, tempered with a few Mixtures, when one wishes to work in *organo pleno*). This rule too has its exceptions and is to be understood with discrimination when it says that Subbass or Untersatz 16′ [i.e. stopped 16′?] should not sound together with the Posaune 16′. If one wishes to draw them alone, particularly on the manual, 'equal' stops would have a bad effect; but if other stops are added, of 4′, 8′, and 2′, then one can certainly use two 'equal' stops with one another. Only the [equal] reeds and flues should be kept separate, except in the pedal in *organo pleno*.

Adlung (1768 1 pp168–9) took up both Niedt and Werckmeister (whose reasoning he too thought defective), noted the exception already specified by Mattheson, and claimed that wenn der Zufall des Windes stark genug ist, und die Bälge gross und wohl gemacht sind; so halt ich von dieser Regel nichts, sondern ich ziehe ohne Bedenken solche äquale Register zusammen.

when the current of wind is strong enough, and the bellows are large and well made, I take no notice of this rule but draw such equal stops together without giving it a thought.

Both Mattheson and Adlung referred elsewhere to what seems to have become a growing taste for doubling stops, but the questions are: Do the bellows and channel construction typical of c1700–25 make Adlung's remarks irrelevant to much of the Bach period? and Do J. S. Bach's well-known demands for good bellows imply that he too was moving towards Adlung's viewpoint?

The answer to the first is probably Yes, for Adlung himself noted (*op cit* p169) that some organs do have insufficient wind for such purposes,* and said in his earlier book that on his own organ in Erfurt, the Sesquialtera would almost stop speaking if 16.8.8 or 16.8.8.8 were drawn with it (1783 p591). The answer to the second is probably No, since Werckmeister too was anxious to have 'good' bellows and obviously regarded the new provision for wind on the old Gröningen organ as a great improvement (1705 *passim*). Nor were J. S. Bach's requirements for suitable bellows and chests at Mühlhausen in 1707 and Halle in 1716 (see chapter 17, above) stated for the sake of thick registration. Moreover, that bellows of the 1730s too were inadequate by later-eighteenth-century standards is clear enough from remarks by Abt Vogler:

so muss ich hier doch diese Erfahrung öffentlich bekannt machen, dass ich noch sehr wenige Orgeln in Europa angetroffen habe, die nicht windstössig sind, selbst die weltberühmte Orgel in Haarlem in Holland nicht ausgenommen; denn ich durfte nicht wagen, einen vorzüglichen orgelmässigen Vortrag mit ganzem Werk, wo die Harmonie im Diskant anhält, und das 32füssige Pedal einen laufende *Basso continuo* vorstellt, auszuführen, ohne dass sie anfing nach Wind zu schnappen, und ein, dem Ohr unerträgliches Zittern und Tremulieren entstand (*AMZ* 3 (1800) col. 525).

so here I must make publicly known this experience, that I have come across very few organs in Europe that are not wind-shaky, even the world-famous organ in Haarlem (Holland) not excepted; for I dared not risk playing an excellently idiomatic piece for *organo pleno* (where the accompaniment was in the treble and a running bass was introduced in the 32′ pedal) without its beginning to snatch at the wind and without a trembling and wavering (intolerable to the ear) being the result.

It can only be conjectured where along the line from Werckmeister to Vogler the *Orgelbüchlein* and *Clavierübung III* fell (presumably at two different points); but Vogler's remarks suggest at least either that *organo pleno* on a German organ of the 1730s required certain kinds of music (i.e. not with a running bass) or that *organo pleno* of that period was not a total *tutti*.

Both the organs of Thuringia–Saxony and the remarks of contemporary writers (e.g. Mattheson 1739 p467) leave it without doubt that the *organo pleno* meant flue-chorus only. The only questions are: Which flue stops were included? and How

---

* It is significant that the one example he cites of an old organ able to take combined registrations (Görlitz, by E. Casparini, 1697–1703) had a special chest construction, and its advocate (C. L. Boxberg, *Beschreibung*, Görlitz 1704) made a point of contradicting the 'rule'. This was the organ said to have been criticized by J. S. Bach for its heavy action (*Dok* II p389–90).

fixed or standardized was the *pleno*? In his general remarks in the *Orgelprobe* Werckmeister implies that the big *pleno* was of this order:

Hw   Principals 16.8.4.3.2.Mixtures
Ped   ditto (but with 16' reed?)

and Mattheson, in the footnote to Niedt quoted above, advises that

Wo kleine wercke sind, und grosse Gemeinen, da nimmt man bey Gelegenheit alles mit.

Where the organs are small and congregations large, one includes everything the builder happens to have provided [?].

Although Mattheson is quoted far too freely today in many aspects of Bach studies, this remark is interesting in its implication: that he is referring to congregational accompaniment, i.e. non-contrapuntal music – like the full-organ effect referred to by Niedt (II p120):

Etliche machen auch nur im *Discant* einen Lauff, und fallen alsobald mit den vollen Wercke ein: welches auch recht gut ins Gehör fällt, damit es nicht immer einerley Leyer bleibe.

Some also make a run in the treble only, joining immediately in *organo pleno* [for the big chords following]: which too strikes the ear very effectively, so long as it does not drone on in the same way for ever.

These remarks relate to the improvising of praeludia already described (see chapter 13). Primarily, it is for these two kinds of music – accompaniment and homophonic praeludia – that Mattheson gave his much-quoted directions for the *organo pleno*, saying that 'there belong to the full organ' ('es gehören zum vollen Werk': 1739 p467) the Principals, Sorduns (= Bourdons), Salicionals or Salicets, Rauschpfeiffen, Octaves, Quints, Mixtures, Scharffen, Quintatön ranks, Zimbels, Nasat, Tierces, Sesquialteras, Superoctaves and pedal (but not manual) Posaune. But he too notes that if the congregation is not large the *pleno* should be reduced (*ibid* p471). Whatever the implications for later registrations, it should not escape attention that Mattheson says 'there belong to the full organ' the following stops, not that 'full organ consists of' or 'is built on' them, as often loosely paraphrased elsewhere (Williams 1966 p143, Stauffer 1980 p160). That is to say, he was listing the stops that might be drawn, not those that must be (or even were normally?) drawn.

Adlung (1768 I p169) makes a similar listing, insisting on stops which both brighten the chorus and give depth of tone. A *volles Werk* merely of

Gedackt 16' + Principal 8' + Mixtur 4' (VI/VIII/x)

without Sesquialtera, Rauschpfeife, Quinte, Scharp, Oktave 4' and 2' is going to be unsatisfactory because it would not have 'eine so völlige und starke Harmonie' ('so complete and strong a harmony' – *ibid* p170). As his footnote shows, he is speaking particularly against Werckmeister and those who (still?) agree with his argument. More importantly, Adlung too makes no claim that such an *organo pleno* is fixed or obligatory, stating early on in the discussion:

Will man es nicht allzustark haben: so lasse man etwas weg, was man will (*ibid* p168).

If one wants to have it not too strong one leaves something out, whatever one wishes.

By 1758, J. F. Agricola too was advocating a big *organo pleno* of all Principals and Mixtures plus reeds 16.8.4 if in tune, plus coupler to a lesser *pleno*, though with no flute except 16′ (Agricola 1758 p502). But such advice should not be quoted out of context. Four details suggest that this *pleno* was no mere blanket of sound: it was at its best in *Vollstimmigkeit* (music in many parts, full chords, etc); it was appropriate only when 'the greatest strength' was required; for fugues the French were probably correct to use a reed chorus (*ibid* p504); and in any case

> Die Alten pflegten ihre Mixturen vielfacher zu machen als die Neuern

> the old builders liked to give their Mixtures more ranks than recent builders do.

J. F. Walther in his description of the Wagner organ in the Berlin Garnisonkirche (1727) also admitted Tierce and Cornet to the *pleno*, but that is no evidence that *tuttis* with so little omitted were used for counterpoint. Agricola describes the pieces suitable for a big *pleno* as those 'not only slow but fast' – does this imply that in 1758 organists were still unused to a fast, full *tutti* (including reeds and Cornet) sustained for more than a brief section? Were organs by then being built for playing such music in the way that those of Silbermann were not? Have the new big registration styles implied by Mattheson and Adlung anything to do with either prelude or fugue as developed by J. S. Bach, i.e. after the old praeludium evolved to ritornello preludes and long-limbed fugues?

Silbermann may well have paid little regard to changing musical fashions; or perhaps Saxony was behind other areas. Either way, it is striking that at Naumburg in 1746 he countered the organist's complaints that Hildebrandt's bellows

> im Spielen so geschwinde miteinander lauffen, besonders in vollen Werke (*Dok* II p429)

> collapse so quickly when the organ is played, especially in *organo pleno*

by pointing out that

> das hier angegebene Stossen, Rücken, gleiche lauffen, wenn mit dem vollen Werk gespielet wird, und geschwinde Fallen, sind ordentliche Eigenschafften *passabler* Bälge. Der Herr Organist Kluge hat also dieses nicht verstanden.

> the jolting, jerking and immediate outflow claimed here when the full organ is played, and the quick falls [of the bellows], are ordinary properties of passable bellows. The organist Herr Kluge has therefore not understood this.

Silbermann was protecting himself and J. S. Bach from the accusation that they had been hasty in approving the new Naumburg organ, and went on to claim that he had watched the bellows as the *Herr Capell-Meister* played the full organ and had not found the wind inadequate (*Dok* I p174). It rather appears that J. S. Bach was more selective in his choice of stops, and/or that he played music more suitable for a *pleno* – or at least that he and Silbermann had different expectations about *organo pleno* and what to play with it from those of the church's organist, who tested it by 'frequent repetition of full chords' ('mit vollen Griffe offte repetiret': *Dok* II p429).

On the one hand, then, it is clear that the *organo pleno* could and no doubt did gradually include more stops, but on the other that it was not rigidly fixed and was not used indiscriminately in all kinds of music. The German *organo pleno* of c1700 was never as closely bound to convention as the French *plein jeu*, which was in any case a highly selective registration. The massive or total *pleno* must have appealed to the simpler homophonies and fashionable contrasts required of organs in *c*1760; but in *c*1725 it was at most associated with certain praeludium effects, certain chorale-preludes and certain accompaniments in those churches where the congregation was indeed accompanied. As well as Mattheson, the Leipzigers spoke of a congregational *tutti*:

> man ziehet die Mixtur zum vollen Werke, damit es bey einer starken Gemeinde, in den Chorälen, wegen Menge der vielen Pfeifen, durchschneidet (Mizler 1743 II.iv pp10-11)

> one draws the Mixture for full organ so that when the congregation is big it is penetrating in the chorales, on account of the crowd of pipes . . .

> um die Kirchen besser auszufüllen, und die Gemeine zu unterstützen, Mixturen, Quinten- und Terzregister mit angebracht werden (Scheibe 1745 preface).

> in order better to fill out the church and to support the congregation, Mixtures, Quints and Tierces are brought in.

Even this use may reflect a gradual but unmistakable crudifying of sensibilities, corresponding to the organ's being used more and more as a matter of course for accompanying the congregation. The Brunswick–Lüneburg directive of 1709 specified that in churches where there were organs (!) the organist should play gently enough for one to hear the congregation (Rietschel 1893 p60). In the same tradition of tactful and varied accompaniment, J. S. Bach would have had to agree, had he accepted the Halle terms in 1713, to introduce the hymns slowly, without decoration, on the Principal, varying the stops for each verse etc (see chapter 5 above) – evidently a necessary warning against too loud or too monotonous a style of accompaniment.

When therefore Werckmeister declines to discuss registration, directing the organist to use his ears (see above, p161), he is saying more than he appears to be. Even Scheibe, writing in Hamburg and belonging to the period when more and more advice was published, recommends a fine fugue to adorn an improvised prelude* and says of it only that

> solches insgemein mit dem vollen Werke geschiehet (1745 p159).

> such happens generally with *organo pleno*.

He is therefore speaking not as categorically as at first may appear. For one thing, there is the case of music in minor keys: Niedt warned against using Mixtures in such music before ascertaining whether (particularly in a *pleno* with Tierce ranks?) clashes of major and minor thirds would result (1717 p46). Mizler claimed that sensible organists ('verständige Organisten') would avoid any Tierce ranks in minor keys (1743 p54). Then, while it is true that Adlung agrees with Scheibe:

> beym Anfange und Beschluss des Gottesdienstes lässt es besser mit dem vollen Werke zu spielen (1768 I p172)

> At the beginning and close of the service it is better to play with the full organ

the unanswered question is still At what point in the century did the chief service in St Thomas, Leipzig begin to be introduced and/or played out with organ music?

---

* Was this unfamiliar in Hamburg but familiar to the Leipziger Scheibe?

That there was a choice of *organo pleno* registrations for at least the shorter fugues (chorale-fughettas) is clear from Kauffmann's *Harmonische Seelenlust* (Leipzig 1733), where the options are:

for Ex. 59:

    Principals 8′ and 4′, or
    Gedackt 8′ and Principal 4′, or
    das volle Werk

for Ex. 60:

    Trompete 8′, Principal 8′ and Octav 4′, or
    das volle Werk

Ex. 59   Kauffmann, 'Ein feste Burg'

Ex. 60   Kauffmann, 'In dich habe ich gehoffet, Herr'

The *organo pleno* or *volles Werk* recommended by Kauffmann here and in certain *quasi stile antico* settings (cf. J. S. Bach's direction for the E flat Fugue BWV 552) can scarcely be understood in Mattheson's sense, i.e. something like 16.16.8.8.8.4. 4.3.3.2.2.II.II.III.Mixtures etc. On the other hand, the large organs for which he was writing could scarcely have had as their only *pleno* a discreet 8.4.3.2. There must have been a range of meanings for the term.

    Pleno or chorus registrations also involve the secondary manuals, obviously on a reduced scale. Such fugal sections as the passage marked 'Rückpositiv scharff' in Vincent Lübeck's E major Praeludium (b75 in *Schmahls Orgeltabulaturen*, BB 40295) presumably require a *petit plein jeu*. The marking is very useful, suggesting as it does that the secondary manual *pleno* could be used for relief, providing the fugal style is not richly worked with hidden tenor entries etc. D. Gronau, though he gave registrations for a large instrument on which doubling ranks must have been usual, also suggested *forte* combinations that must have served as kinds of *pleno* (Frotscher 1934–5 II p1031):

    Ow+Bw Principal 16′ + Octava 8′ + Flauto octava 4′ + Sedecima 1′ + Fagotto 16′ + Regal 8′

    Rp Principal 8′ + Flauto allemanda 8′ + Octava 4′ + Flauto 4′ + Salicetto 4′ + Flageolette 2′

Similar combinations were possible on the newer organs of Saxony–Thuringia by the 1720s. If the E flat Prelude and Fugue BWV 552 cannot easily be seen in terms of Mattheson's or Marpurg's *organo pleno*, how much less so can the chorales BWV 651, 661 and 667! It would certainly fall in with any cyclic nature of 'The Seventeen' to have such pieces registered more loudly than the others, especially in view of the pedal cantus firmus (complete with reed),* but BWV 651 is altogether too long and its form too intricate for any *pleno* less sensitive than Werckmeister's. In theory, BWV 651 could have a *plein jeu* and BWV 667 a *grand jeu* (Klotz 1969 pp116–17), but there is only uncertain evidence that the *grand jeu* was ever seen as such in Germany,† and the pedal cantus firmus of BWV 667 certainly implies pedal reed below *plein jeu*.‡ Niedt (in a remark not commented upon by Mattheson) speaks of the organist's prelude before the cantata being 'with full organ or otherwise strong stops' ('mit dem vollen Wercke, oder sonst starcken Registern': II p102), and it is difficult to imagine such alternatives as being beyond the choice of the organist. Adlung, in his less strongly assertive *Anleitung*, suggests that German organists were inclined to follow rules (in particular Werckmeister's directive against doubling equal pitches) because they were rules – for example, not drawing Posaune and Subbass together because the rule says so, not because the wind was insufficient (1783 p592). But, like Werckmeister, he also encouraged them to use their ears, leaving out stops that add neither lustre nor gravity. For the *pleno* on his own organ he drew

> Principal + Octaves + Mixtur + Cymbel + Sesquialter (p585)

But many stops need much wind, and the bellows must be worked more energetically, which is to their detriment. On the other hand, he is speaking for the 1750s when he justifies doubling equal pitches etc by asking

> was würde uns die Weitläuftigkeit der neuern Werke nützen, wenn uns die Hände gebunden wären, die Stärke nach Gefallen zu mehren oder zu mindern (*ibid* p594)

> what would the capaciousness of recent organs profit us if our hands were tied so that we could not increase or lessen the volume as we wished?

Evidently Werckmeister still had great influence. Nevertheless, as Griepenkerl observed in 1844, *organo pleno* cannot mean 'all stops' drawn for all pieces so labelled; players should 'sacrifice power for clarity' (Peters I p. iii). Players today, generally relying on notation to tell them what to think, should consider whether labelling a prelude or fugue 'organo pleno' was meant to do more than alert the original players merely to the category of the piece in hand, i.e. indicating that it was not a solo-stop chorale or a two-manual trio. Such 'alerting' must have become necessary as the scope of organ music grew wider and its forms became more varied by 1725.

* Hence too the 'original' registration for the 'early' version of the chorale BWV 665?
† That J. G. Walther, despite his indebtedness to Brossard, was apparently ignorant of the significance of the terms *grand jeu* and *plein jeu* (*Lexicon*, 'Jeu') argues that at least one of the Weimar organists (both of whom may have made copies of de Grigny's *Livre*) is unlikely to have understood the basic differences. If Walther did not, can one imagine that Bach did?
‡ The rubric 'in organo pleno con pedale doppio' of the chorale BWV 686 also implies pedal reed(s), of which the upper is a smooth, penetrating cantus firmus, the lower an agile, less prominent bass. The last verse of Weckmann's 'Es ist das Heil' offers a close parallel: chorale in (pedal) tenor, manual *im vollen Werck*. See also p250 below.

20. Two Manuals

The use of two keyboards is so much a part of the musical nature of J. S. Bach's trios and concertos and many of his chorales that he specifies their use by including 'à 2 Clav' in many of his titles (even that of the early BWV 739) and sometimes, if the hand moves from one manual to the other, makes it clear by cues (words or broken note-beamings). The specification of two manuals is less straightforward in certain *Orgelbüchlein* chorales, because as a rule their use is not essential and may result from second thoughts or changed intentions on the composer's part; it has yet to be shown whether such rubrics date from the earliest phase of the album or from (e.g.) the moment at which the title-page was written. More problematic still is the use of two manuals in the preludes, toccatas, fugues, passacaglia etc, where with the exception of BWV 552.i and 538.i they are never specified and never cued in the basic sources.

The late-nineteenth- and early-twentieth-century editions, such as Bridge/Higgs c1885, Straube 1913 and Widor/Schweitzer 1912, suggested changes of manual much as any edition of piano music over the previous century had suggested fingering and phrasing. Only during the last two or three decades has there emerged a different approach, still only partial though enthusiastically adopted by younger players. This changed view has been expressed as confidently as the older organists expressed theirs. Thus fugues are to be played without break on one manual, since 'in the eighteenth century firm conventions reigned'; a constant *organo pleno* was conventional, and directions to the player were 'therefore superfluous' (Musch 1974 p268). Theorists are quoted to show that fugues belong to *organo pleno* categories; cantata fugues are identified as having 'no dynamic change' (BWV 38 – *ibid* p275). Similarly, playing preludes and related genres on one manual without change 'reflects and fulfills' an 'aesthetic convention', namely that 'a composition should embody only one affect', according to the theorists and their 'doctrine of the affections' (Stauffer 1980 p171). Lists can be made of Bach pieces which 'utilize a *plenum* sound throughout' (*ibid*), such as the Third Brandenburg Concerto. On the other hand, a moderating voice is sometimes heard pointing out that vocal and instrumental works generally *support* the principle of manual-change in fugues (Klotz 1975 p393).

Any familiarity with registration practices makes it clear that both preludes and fugues are *organo pleno* pieces (e.g. Emery 1962), though it is usually less clear what that involves. It would be part of any case against changing manuals in a prelude or fugue that a *pleno* does not include all the stops (and thus is less fatiguing to the ear); that a *pleno* on an organ of 1700–50 was different in important respects from the *pleno* on most later organs (and accordingly was less tiring); and that an unbroken *pleno* sound lasting some time was known in other kinds of music, both for organ (e.g. the chorale BWV 651) and for other instruments (e.g. the harpsichord toccatas). The third of these is unreliable as evidence, since a player committed to the idea that episodes require a change of manual could no doubt treat BWV 651 in the same way; nor can comparisons with other media be by nature conclusive, since (e.g.) full harpsichord is different in kind from full organ, and even if it were not, 'examples only illustrate, they do not prove'. In any case, it is clear that an orchestral *tutti* of the kind sustained throughout the Third Brandenburg has a naturally varied dynamic that an organ *pleno* lacks. That a modern *pleno* is more likely than an older one to tire the ear is impossible to prove, begging too many questions about the historical reliability of old organs. But there is certainly no reason to think *pleno* means *tutti* or even *fortissimo*.

The history of Bach performance since 1750 has not yet been traced in detail, and it is not clear how typically Mendelssohn was representing eighteenth-century practice or early-nineteenth-century practice, or indeed his own practice in other organ works, when in 1837 he played the A minor Fugue BWV 543 in London and changed the manuals in the way described by E. J. Hopkins (quoted in Bridge/ Higgs 1887, preface):

> He played the episode commencing in [b50] on the swell organ, returning to the great organ when the pedal part re-enters [in b95 2nd half] but transferring the E in the treble (an inverted dominant pedal) to the great organ a bar before the other parts [b94 2nd half?] with fine effect.

It was presumably in order to gain contrast and relief – rather than, say, to underline the symmetry of the fugue* – that the Novello edition made suggestions for manual-changing in so many of the preludes and fugues.† The thinking player of today finds that 'contrast and relief' are less necessary on well-restored old organs and on the better new organs; in addition, he can find theoretical evidence of the kind already referred to that proves the conceptual unity of fugues; and in the preludes, 'A and B themes are usually structurally interlocked in such a way that any change is unnatural and artificial' (Kloppers 1976 pp63–4). But arguments based on sound and on form could equally be brought to support Mendelssohn's approach to BWV 543.ii, since he played 'with fine effect' and underlined the symmetry of the movement.

Hopkins does not report on whether Mendelssohn added stops for the final pedal and manual solos in the A minor Fugue; but as with the fugues of earlier composers the sectional nature of some works certainly makes it possible to add stops without offending Adlung's directive not to draw stops while the keys are being played (1758 p506). Such sectional movements, where adding stops is useful, are:

coda (postlude) in fugues BWV 531, 535, 543, 549, 561, 565, 575, 576
clearcut sections in fugues BWV 552, 574, 588
clearcut sections in preludes BWV 532, 535, 535a, 550, 551, 561, 565, 569 (?), 571, 572

Such codas or sections are more marked and less integrated than others in which the adding of stops is more disruptive and to some degree anachronistic:

fugues BWV 532, 539, 541, 547, 564, 566, 582
preludes BWV 531, 543, 564

---

* Each section then has about 50 bars in the case of BWV 543.
† And did so by means of tactful footnotes that barely affected its *Urtext*. It is a limitation of much non-English Bach scholarship in recent years to have paid the old Novello edition so little attention.

The gaps in older praeludia (of Scheidemann, Buxtehude and others) invite stop-changing;* there can be no doubt about this, any more than (alas) there is any direct evidence for it. It can even be safely supposed that in such chorale-fantasias as Bruhns's 'Nun komm' the sections were separated by a bigger gap (rest) than the score in P 802 suggests, in order for the player to change manuals and/or stops. In the case of J. S. Bach there is already a more marked continuity in such chorales as BWV 720 and 739, enough to make changing stops more difficult than changing manuals. Whatever the authenticity or even the purpose of the manual-changes in BWV 739 as they are now known, it would not be mistreating the work to interpret it *ad lib*, playing any section on either manual chorus, right or left hand:

Hw	pleno to 2′
Rp	pleno to Mixture?
Ped	reed 8′ (+ flue 16′ and 4′?)

In such movements as the D major Prelude BWV 532, there is no evidence either way as to whether 'adding stops' means the same as 'changing manuals': the registrations of the D minor Concerto BWV 596.i could support either conclusion, and the issue is not crucial in such cases. Where it is crucial is in the remaining body of the preludes and fugues, namely the great mature movements cast in one or another rounded form whose alternating sections have so often been marked, in performances in this century, by alternating manuals.

Of such rounded movements, the G minor Fantasia BWV 542 has been allowed as a possible two-manual movement on the grounds that there is a clear change of style between the two main themes (Kloppers 1976), despite there being no copy that contains cues or shows in note-groupings† that a change is required (Emery 1962). More to the point, however, is that BWV 542.i happens to allow manual-changes not because its sections are different in style but because rests between them make them relatively clearcut. No argument from 'style' can of itself say whether the player should return to the main manual in (e.g.) bars 31, 35 or even 44. The B minor Prelude BWV 544 shows a marked change in style between themes but has no convenient rests and no split note-groupings:‡ does that mean that there is no change of manual? If it is argued that the change of 'style' in BWV 542 is more marked than in BWV 544, could that not be offered as a better reason for changing in BWV 544 since the two themes of BWV 542 are already different enough to need no second sound-quality?

In the case of rounded-form fugues, the arguments centre on similar unknowns. For example, at b28 of the B minor Fugue BWV 544 (Ex. 61(i)) the changes of texture have been held to require no change of manual for the tenor theme, on

---

* This could also be true of earlier music that seems to be less sectional. Scheidt's 'Fantasia super Ich ruf' zu dir' (*Tabulatura nova* I, Hamburg 1624) could easily be interpreted in such a way that (following the composer's directions at the end of Part III) the chorale lines as they occur are picked out on a solo registration, with stops changed and at least some sections marked or 'brought out'.

† I.e. the beaming of quavers or semiquavers in such a way as to show a break in continuity and thus change of manual (as clearly marked in the engraved Italian Concerto BWV 971.i).

‡ As Stauffer notes (1980 p168), it even looks as if in b17 the composer connected up a group originally split. How important or how useful *fair* copies (autograph) are in this respect, however, is an open question; was the older copy from which the fair copy was made characterized by such groupings? In any case, are such groupings characteristic of performance copies rather than fair copies made for archival purposes?

Ex. 61   (i) BWV 544.ii

(ii) BWV 593.i

the grounds that if the composer had wanted manual-change he would have indicated it in some way, as he did elsewhere (Emery 1962). But this argument certainly cannot be supported by a comparison with b16 of the A minor Concerto BWV 593.i (Ex. 61(ii)): either the stemming of that bar is impossible to play, or it has to be modified (as in *NBA* IV/8 p17) so that the change to *Rückpositiv* leaves the cadence uncompleted by *Hauptwerk* (this would be the case however reliable the sources of BWV 593). Similarly, any different stemming for b28 of the B minor Fugue (i.e. changing to second manual for the second quaver instead of the first) leaves the fugue subject incomplete on the second manual. In other words, notation can be unreliable as evidence in this matter, for even if the composer did want a change of manual in BWV 544.ii b28 he could not write the notes in any other way than he did (e.g. by double-stemming the tenor f♯) without making them appear to be literally impossible to play.

If the composer intended certain mature preludes and fugues to be played with alternate manuals, why do no sources cue the alternations? The indications in BWV 552.i are for the echo phrases only, and because it was given a 'full-dress' form (fair-copied, engraved and then published) the piece gives the player unambiguous help as far as echoes are concerned, though it leaves any other changing of manuals unspecified. But putative echo phrases in the two chorale-partita movements BWV 766.ii and 767.ii, as well as in the two D minor Fugues BWV 539 and 565, are ambiguous – that is to say, sources either do not mark the echo passages or do so without certain authority. Yet on the analogy of BWV 552.i such echo passages – e.g. the short half-bar phrases in bb49–52 and 71–6 of BWV 539.ii, marked neither in any source nor in the composer's fair copy of the solo violin sonata concerned (P 967) – are certainly permissible, if only optional. Perhaps the *piano* markings of BWV 552.i even suggest that organists would not otherwise have found the echoes obvious; more likely, however, is that as a published work it deliberately helped the organist by marking them. Why it would not go on to specify second manual for the episodes or the new themes of the movement is discussed below (p183).

The indications in BWV 538.i are necessary not so much for the form of the movement as for its type: a concerto-grosso-like use of material on two manuals which frequently cross. However, crossing parts in some other pieces (the published Canon at the Seventh in BWV 769 and the autograph chorale BWV 617) are not marked for two manuals, although they both presumably need them. Perhaps these omissions were mistakes. But it cannot be argued that since two manuals are almost always indicated for works in which the two hands cross frequently, works in which the hands do not cross do not require two manuals. The reason for indicating two manuals in a title or rubric is that they *have* to be used. They are not optional, or part of the rhetoric of the piece; they are necessary for the player to play the notes at all.

In other repertories of organ music, the absence of cues for change of manual cannot be taken as indicating what the composer intended, expected or allowed.* For example, in Bruhns's E minor Praeludium (Möller MS), the fugue closes before its coda–postlude as in Ex. 62. Quite apart from its similarity in principle to echo

Ex. 62   Bruhns, Praeludium in E minor

phrases in violin sonatas, operas etc, is it not at least optional for the player to make three steps: *Hw, Rp, Bw*? If so, the naive broken-chord passage earlier in the same praeludium could also be broken up, as shown in Vol. I p219. Here it would be a question of a player's pleasure in playing (*Spielfreudigkeit*) and in playing with the instrument.

Even allowing for the fact that the bigger churches which had three-manual organs are likely also to have the kind of ensemble music that required the organist to play basso continuo (hence the *Brustwerk* in most instances after c1650?), it is striking how rarely the three manuals are specified in organ music. In the works of J. S. Bach, the directions in neither BWV 720 nor 596 are entirely reliable as they stand. Certainly for such chorales as BWV 720 an imaginative changing of manuals may have been traditional, as for the Bruhns Praeludium above. In 1657, the pro-

* Similarly, that only some later copies of the harpsichord toccatas specify changes of volume can also be taken as evidence not merely that they 'reflect an attempt to update the work' (Stauffer 1980 pp170–1) but that they record past practice in a period then unfamiliar with tradition. The 'emptiness' of earlier sources such as the Möller MS if anything supports this possibility.

spective organ-builder for the Weimar Schlosskapelle (Ludwig Compenius)* suggested three manuals for such an organ in such a place as follows:

> Zu solchen Werck Könten Wol 3 Claviere gearbeitet werden, Weil die Organisten Kunst bey etlichen hoch gestiegen im coral Spielen, aber es Kan auch wohl bey zweyen bleiben (Schneider 1937 p74).

> in such an organ three manuals could well be furnished, because with several manuals the organist's art can rise to great heights in chorale-playing [?], although such can also be the case with two.

Whatever Compenius means exactly, it is clear that chorales were open to varied treatment. Using three manuals for the E flat Prelude BWV 552 would be a different matter: changes of tone corresponding to the form would make the different themes explicit and thus would mark the ritornello structure. Whether or not that can ever be shown to have been the composer's wish, it would be a use of three manuals to break up a far more continuous movement than the chorales (chorale-fantasias?) that Ludwig Compenius had in mind.

When in chorales two manuals are used *in alternation* for both hands, the contrast can bring out the hymn melody itself, as in J. M. Bach's setting of 'Allein Gott in der Höh''. A similar use of two manuals was asked for by J. G. Walther in his published Prelude and Fugue of 1741 and was recommended by C. Raupach, who played each section of the chorale in plain style, on a different manual, after preluding on it (Mattheson 1739 pp474–5). Changing or using two manuals in chorales, however, always arises in respect to the given melody; more to the point is Adlung's more general advice:

> Beym Anfange und Beschluss des Gottesdienstes lässt es besser mit dem vollen Werke zu spielen. Präambuliret man aber auf etwas; so kann es . . . durch eine gemeine Fantasie geschehen, und da kann man das volle Werk nehmen; aber auch zur Abwechselung zuweilen stille klingende Register ziehen . . . (1768 I p172)

> At the beginning and close of the service it is better to play with the *organo pleno*. If one is preambling on something, however, it can be effected . . . with the usual [kind of] fantasia, and here one can take *organo pleno*, or else draw soft-sounding stops from time to time in alternating fashion . . .

which may well reflect older practice, like Scheibe's remarks:

> man durch eine geschickte Abwechselung der Claviere die Aufmerksamkeit seiner Zuhörer nicht wenig erhalten kann (1745 p427).

> one can hold his listeners' attention not a little by cleverly alternating the manuals.

For versatility in (e.g.) basso-continuo playing, Adlung recommended that every organ, however small, should have two manuals (1768 I pp182–3), and Praetorius long before him had said much the same (1619 pp116, 138).

It has frequently been pointed out that the two manuals used for the D minor Toccata BWV 538 do not mark the formal organization of the movement so much as the dialogue technique of the material itself. That is, manual-changes in the way they are introduced by many players into (e.g.) the G minor Fantasia BWV 542 would not, if applied to BWV 538.i, bring out the dialoguing itself. In general, the

---

* The finished organ was that added to and rebuilt in 1707, 1713–14 etc (see above, pp124ff).

dialogue technique of BWV 538.i is not unlike that in certain chorale-fantasias of older composers (e.g. Buxtehude's 'Nun freut euch' and Lübeck's 'Ich ruf zu dir' in P 802), but Klotz is surely right to claim BWV 538.i as a not quite straightforward dialogue (1975 p391): the *Positiv* section from b13 is more the solo exposition of a concerto, that from b78 more like the crossing of parts typical of an organ trio.* Nevertheless, the 'dialectic character' of BWV 538.i is clear enough and is in the manner of the old vocal duets/dialogues rather than the old scoring for double choir – i.e., the two voices contrast and interlock conversationally rather than polarize in two masses pitted against each other. In his *Lexicon* (Leipzig 1732, 'Dialogo'), Walther briefly refers to both techniques, remarking that works for two choirs

> . . . so Gesprächs-weise *alternir*en. Die organisten *imitir*en dergleichen Umwechsel-ungen auch auf die Orgeln, wenn sie mehr als ein Clavier haben

> . . . so alternate in a conversational manner. Organists imitate exchanges of this sort on organs, too, if they have more than one manual.

What he seems to be referring to is more the type of chorale by J. M. Bach (see above, p176) than the subtle interchange of BWV 538.i.†

If Walther was referring only to chorales (like Kauffmann's settings) or concertos (like his own transcriptions), the multi-limbed preludes and fugues of J. S. Bach are no nearer elucidation. Even the Passacaglia cannot be shown to be without problems, and its many copyists usually specified neither two manuals nor *organo pleno*. But if it can ever be shown that J. S. Bach's scores represent a 'composer's ideal', offering the player various ways to play the work, it must be here in BWV 582. Its very shape is not obvious (see Vol. I pp263–4), and the old chaconne tradition was not one that required many stop-changes, much less a sense of climax. Niedt's chaconne example runs through as many variations as the composer/player wishes but passes to a climax–postlude of the kind attached to the fugue BWV 549 – i.e., it itself does not increase in tension. Moreover, there are real questions about the purpose of the Passacaglia (see Vol. I pp253ff) which make the registration of it particularly speculative. Its very length does raise a simple question: while Raison's little *passecaille* was played on one manual, is BWV 582 to have no contrast or change? If French organ fugues or the harpsichord fugues of *The 48* kept to one manual, do not the bigger and sectional organ fugues of Bach suggest a change? Would a violin not introduce differences in tone and playing-style for the episode of a long fugue such as the one in the C major Violin Sonata BWV 1005.ii? If shorter preludes like the C major BWV 545 and G major BWV 541 do not require a change, would not the longer ones such as BWV 544, 546 and 548?

The biggest single problem of changing manuals in the mature preludes and fugues is not that the sources do not suggest it, nor that theorists of the time seem not to expect it, nor that theorists of today can marshal reasons against it, but that in most cases it is very awkward to return to the original manual. Stop- or manual-changing in a Buxtehude praeludium is easy if the player allows himself little

---

* Whether or not the copyist of BWV 538 in LM 4839e had any authority for labelling the piece 'pleno a 2 Clav.' (*NBA* IV/5–6 *KB* p375) and what he may have meant by it are unanswerable questions.
† But Mattheson thought Walther's observation 'a very fitting remark' ('eine recht artige Anmerkung' – 1739 p220) since it suggested that rhetoric or sound-speech (*Klang-Rede*) belonged also to wordless instrumental music; see also above, p71.

breaks; was an organist of J. S. Bach's generation likely to forgo such conventions because he was moving towards newer ideals of length, organization, integration? If adding stops for the postlude of the C major Fugue BWV 564 is disruptive (compared with, say, BWV 531), does this suggest that there is to be no change of tone? Or, on the contrary, are the changes of manual more evenly spaced in BWV 564 and thus more integrated? In that case, how are the changes of manual actually to be made? The episodes do seem possible on second manual: first one hand and then the other can pass to a different manual at bars 43, 53 (together), 78 (together? – the cadence is incomplete, as in the Concerto BWV 593.i b16), 100 (ditto), 115 (as 43), 123 (ditto). Despite what was said above (p158), does Agricola's observation that J. S. Bach liked short keys (because they made it easier to move from one manual to another) refer to such changing of manuals?*

There seem to be three steps in the argument:

> neither prelude nor fugue of BWV 531 requires any change of manual until (at the earliest) the coda of the fugue;

> both prelude and fugue of BWV 564 could be broken up on two manuals, the first in dialogue form, the second as an episodic fugue (framing an *arioso* movement that certainly needs two manuals);

> in neither the prelude nor the fugue in E minor BWV 548 is the use of two, three or four manuals easy, obligatory or even clearly possible – but the length and form of both could of themselves suggest it.†

Each of these three works stands for a fairly distinct type.‡ The problem of how to return (and sometimes how to move to the other manual in the first place) is most severe in the third of these. The longer fugues are certainly not as concerto-like as (e.g.) Handel's concerto fugues (Dalton 1966), and the return to the main manual in (e.g.) BWV 544.ii b59 is somewhat arbitrary in that at the 'correct' moment for a return no line can continue without disruption. The same could be said of the B minor Prelude BWV 544. Every organist knows that in the symmetrical and highly organized C minor Prelude BWV 546, a manual-change is plausible at the close of the first section (b25), but that no effortless or unproblematic return before the *da capo* of that section at b120 is possible, except perhaps briefly at bb49–52. There things result from using two manuals here: the two would have to have a comparable *pleno* for the pedal to suit either; there is an abruptness in the two returns; and overall, the second manual would then predominate.# The difficulty with this question is that there is no evidence to say that those three things were out of the question around 1725. Do we now make false assumptions in all three of those areas? How can we know? All that can be said is that the nature of organs as known justifies the first and last, while an analysis of the movement rather confirms the second (i.e. the thematic return at b120 is abrupt in any case – see Vol. I p150). But is there no evidence for moving to and from manuals in such big movements?

---

* Not conclusively, of course. But few changes for the right hand in such chorales as 'Nun komm' BWV 659 seem to require the easiness or immediacy implied by Agricola, whereas running fugues do.

† Players can find ways to use four manuals in the prelude and certainly three in the fugue. Two can be used for clarity: e.g., in the fugal episode from b60 each hand can play its own manual and so gain clarity without losing the acciaccatura flavour referred to in Vol. I p168.

‡ According to Klotz (1969a), the preludes and fugues BWV 533, 534, 541, 545 and 550 and the fugues BWV 540.ii and 546.ii not only need no change but were written at Weimar for *plein* or *grand jeu*. This is not out of the question; but see above, pp126, 163.

As it would, for example, if two manuals were used for the fugue in the Ouverture of the D major Partita for Harpsichord BWV 828.

The composer did give clear changes of manual for two large ritornello movements which to some extent correspond respectively to an organ prelude and fugue, namely the Italian Concerto BWV 971 (first movement) and the Ouverture or 'B minor Partita' BWV 831 (part of first movement), published as *Clavierübung II* in 1735. Both indicate manual-changing for major constructions in which a ritornello principle produces clear sections. Ritornello movements – whether fugues, preludes or concerto movements – have much in common, and the reason why Bach did not mark Vivaldi's tutti/solo contrasts in his transcription of BWV 596.ii (a fugue) by changes of manual is not that a fugue cannot have a change of tone – frequently claimed as the reason – but that the movement is far too unified, requires pedal throughout and in any case is not very long. It is otherwise with the two harpsichord movements:

Italian Concerto BWV 971.i

Manuals are distributed as follows:

> Manual I for both hands in main sections A_1 A_2 A_3 A_4 A_1
> Manual I for rh (*forte*) above Manual II for lh (*piano*) in the episodes B C_1 D C_2
> Manual II for short echo passages in A_2

The changes of manual have three particular characteristics: the rh is confirmed *f* when the lh changes to *p* in the episodes, a brace or bracket shows that more than one voice-part is on a certain manual, and the note-groupings always show the moment of change: Ex. 63. Changes are therefore made unambiguously. But such

Ex. 63   BWV 971.i

unambiguousness is not typical of keyboard sources in general (e.g. the copy in P 802 of Buxtehude's 'Nun freut') and suggests that *Clavierübung II* was presenting the buyer with an instructive model. Such a 'model' in manual-changing was not different in its own way from model registrations in exactly contemporary published material such as Kauffmann's *Harmonische Seelenlust* (Leipzig 1733). Such publications are indicators of what was possible, perhaps customary, in ideal circumstances,* and it is no more reasonable to argue that without such clear marking of manual-changes players would not make them than it is that without such clear specification of stops organists would not draw them.

B minor Ouverture BWV 831.i

Manuals are distributed in the fugue as follows:

> Manual I for both hands in sections involving fugal entries:
> A_1 (exposition) A_2 (1st middle entries) A_3 (incomplete return to A_1)
> A_4 (more complete return to A_1)
> Manual II for both hands in episodes B_1 B_2 C

Formally, this movement has much in common with BWV 971.i, and their methods of making the manual-changes are the same. Particularly instructive is the passage linking episode B_2 to entry A_3, for here the new fugal material of A_3 is brought in *forte* one part at a time, not without technical difficulty: Ex. 64. In neither move-

Ex. 64   BWV 831.i

b88

ment are the changes as difficult either for the eye or the hand as they would be in (e.g.) the C minor Prelude BWV 546, but at least part of this problem is notational. As BWV 831.i is a 'published model', the first note of b89 is cut short in the right hand to make the change possible; but a change of manual at b85 of the C minor Prelude is possible if the player shortens the g′ in much the same way – something not very licentious or irresponsible: Ex. 65. A similar kind of treatment would make clear three other moments of manual-change in BWV 546.i: Ex. 66. The return at b97, however, remains impossible: Ex. 67. The sources are agreed on this passage, and it certainly looks as if they and/or the composer gave no option for changing manuals here. The possibilities at b97 therefore are:

* For example, on the analogy of the French Overture fugue, manuals could be changed in four of the preludes of the English Suites (BWV 807, 808, 809, 810) and perhaps in one long episode in the opening fugues of the Partitas in D minor and E minor (BWV 828, 830), with or without entries being picked out on Manual I. That BWV 828 and 830 were published without directions for manual-changing does not invalidate the general point made here: *Clavierübung II* on its title-page was making an issue of the use of two manuals, whilst *Clavierübung I* was not.

Ex. 65 BWV 546.i

Ex. 66 BWV 546.i

Ex. 67 BWV 546.i

the notation is treated to an 'unacceptable' amount of licence (e.g., the first two or three notes of the alto are ignored);

the musical flow is treated to an 'unacceptable' break (e.g., both hands jump on the first beat);

lh only changes in b97, rh in b100; or rh plays on two manuals at the end of b96;

there is no change of manual until it is convenient (e.g. b100 or b105), i.e. not in accordance with the change of theme;

there is no change of manual anywhere.

It is true that throughout such discussions – for which BWV 546.i is merely one example – the last possibility will always remain. But the point is that it cannot be supported by certain arguments – for example, that the notation as it has come down to us makes it look out of the question, or that the pedal is unsuitable for accompanying the 'softer' manual (this ignores the nature of a two-manual *pleno*), or that it was an 'aesthetic convention' for a movement to have only one *Affekt*.*
Throughout any discussion of changes of manual in the preludes and fugues of J. S. Bach, evidence can be assembled on either side, but the question arises at all only because players (subject no doubt to changing tastes) have raised it: neither notation nor a knowledge of contemporary theory would have done so. In fact, it is possible that logic and a sense of formal contrast could at times result in more frequent manual-changing than has ever been favoured by most players. For example, the D minor Fugue BWV 538 could (not least in view of its prelude) be distributed on two equal manuals corresponding to its most striking themes, i.e. the *subject itself* and the *codetta-episode material*, heard first in b15 but regularly, even exhaustively, afterwards. Manuals could be changed without too great a violence to the notation, and the player merely has to find a feasible note on which to change, often staggering it between the hands:

1	15	18	26	29	36	57/8	67/8	81	88	101	115	130	138
Hw	Pos	Hw	Pos	Hw	Pos	Hw	Pos	Hw	Pos	Hw	Pos	Hw	Pos

167	178	188	194	203	211	last 4 bars
Hw	Pos	Hw	Pos	Hw	Pos	rh Hw, lh Pos

No source even hints at such a thing, which in any case offends what is now seen as the essential uniformity of such fugues. But the point would be that what is obligatory for the prelude remains optional for the fugue, whether it were such a novel dialogue approach or the more conventional variety between entries and episodes. Obviously, the final bars of the fugue could be played on two manuals, though no copy says so; but that such a strict fugue closes with such an 'unfugal' figure makes it at least possible that certain players, on certain suitable instruments, might have taken the option.

That options were at least sometimes given the player is clear from a further printed Bach source usually ignored by organists, namely the so-called *Clavier-übung IV* (*Goldberg Variations*). Here there are three kinds of rubric:

---

* As the Italian Concerto and B minor Ouverture movements show, a movement may have conceptually one identity, perceptually two. In any case, there never was a 'doctrine of single *Affekt*': this is an invention of retrospective musicology (one that looks more to theorists than to composers), and it certainly cannot be taken as a premise for any argument against changing manuals.

'a 2 clav.' – for movements in which hands cross a great deal, often of a virtuoso character, sometimes solo-with-accompaniment

'a 1 clav.' – for movements in which hands rarely if ever cross

'a 1 ô vero 2 clav.' – for movements in which the crossings are such as to be feasible on one manual

Although, as short binary movements, the *Variations* do not bear on the question of manual-changes in fugal and non-fugal ritornello movements, the rubrics do confirm three important principles: that the engraved fair copies give help of a kind not to be expected in manuscript copies ('a 1 clav.' is unique to this volume), that two manuals are specified only when the notes are literally unplayable otherwise (whether melodic or contrapuntal), and that where the notes are manageable without crossing the player has an option.

One powerful argument against manual-changing is the negative evidence supplied by the E flat Prelude: although it was published (and thus presented with care and clarity), is cast in multi-limbed form, very comfortably allows the likely manual-changes, and actually specifies *piano* echoes, it still gives the organist no direction for manual- or stop-changing other than for the echoes. But this too can be countered: not specifying a second manual* leaves both prelude and fugue open to both kinds of purchasers of *Clavierübung III* (i.e. organists with one manual for the so-called 'Lesser Catechism' chorales, and those with two for the 'Greater'); moments at which manual-changing is musically feasible are left easy to manage; and the fugue likewise has no indications, although its sectional shape and change-over points make manual-changing equally feasible. The most powerful single argument for changing manuals is that an unbroken *pleno* is not only unpleasant in itself but contradicts the nature of other long movements in the music of the period, in which contrast and variety are natural. But this too can be countered: *organo pleno* is unlikely to mean *tutti*; the *pleno* sound of 1725 may have offered the ear fewer problems than a later *pleno*; and 'natural variety' is relative and changes from period to period. Arguments are balanced on both sides, and there is no easy answer; but close study of the two harpsichord movements can cast light on those arguments and on the way complex movements can, if required, produce colour and contrast.

---

21. Temperament Questions

The copious (and still growing) literature on the subject of temperament makes it possible to concentrate here on a few questions of particular relevance to J. S. Bach's organ music: What were the temperaments preferred by him? and Did they change in the course of his life as a composer?

Buxtehude was known to have given his approval to Werckmeister's tunings (expressed in his poem prefacing Werckmeister's *Harmonologia musica*, Quedlinburg 1702), and from that it has been argued that

---

* The echoes can be managed by pushing in stops. Also, Niedt (1721 p57) suggests playing short echo passages at 4′ to the *forte* 8′, so an organist may not have required a second manual even for echoes.

at 20 years of age, Bach came to Lübeck and met Buxtehude to hear his organ music performed in Werckmeister's tuning (Kellner 1980 p40).

Although there is no evidence for this, the influence of Werckmeister on Buxtehude, J. G. Walther (his pupil) and J. S. Bach (see chapter 17) is plausible because he offered a new tuning to supplant the meantone tuning that, at least in theory, had prevailed in German churches. While it must be true that the good composers were always more inventive than even the cleverest theorists,* several passages in ch.32 of Werckmeister's *Orgelprobe* (1681/1698) suggest that meantone or 'Praetorian' temperament was still the most influential, and that he still felt it necessary to suggest some simple modifications. These included tempering the fifths c–g–d–a–e just flat enough to make the third c–e tolerably sharp, and tuning d♯ flatter to make a better third with f♯ and a better fifth with g♯. Such simple modifications were only rule of thumb, however; Werckmeister's aim in advising builders to find 'a good adequate temperament' ('eine gute zulängliche Temperatur' – pp79ff) or a system that was 'wohl temperiret' (a term already found on the title-page of the 1681 edition) was to enable players to transpose into remoter keys if they wished and to modulate to them if they could. For such purposes, the thirds most used should be better than the others – i.e., there was as yet no question of equality:

> d♭–f, g♭–b♭ and a♭–c were sharp by a full comma
> 'Werckmeister III' had no bad wolf, but some thirds were larger than those of equal temperament (B♭ major, A♭ major, F minor)
> eight fifths (of remoter keys) were pure, four a quarter-comma flat (c–g, g–d, d–a, b–f♯); thirds of remoter keys were large (e–g♯, b♭–d, b–d♯, e♭–g, d♭–f)

The common keys had 'limpid' triads but also had the 'least keenly inflected leading notes' (M. Lindley, 'Temperaments', *The New Grove*); the peripheral tonalities sounded 'Pythagorean'. Keys therefore had distinct characters, and all were playable – the peripheral ones 'not good and not bad but acceptable' (Rasch 1983). F minor, however, included the third g♯–c one comma sharp which Werckmeister accepted on the grounds that it was seldom used (on the use of this key for BWV 639 etc, see below).

An assumption made by Werckmeister, and later by Kirnberger,† was that C major was a kind of centre to the circle of all the keys. Even in 1511, Schlick had tempered every note in his octave with a view to some thirds being less sharp than others; those thirds too (c–e, f–a, g–b) centred on the same keys, and even the g♯/a♭ was given a mean value to make it versatile. It was to avoid 'being bound to a single key when tuning' ('wenn man sich an keinen Modum in Stimmen will binden lassen') that Werckmeister proposed what must be equal temperament (*Musicalische Temperatur*, 1691, p75), but elsewhere he argued against this, wishing to tune at least the naturals purer (*Hypomnemata musica*, Quedlinburg 1697, p36).

---

* Perhaps because his work on temperaments is not marked by any very intimate understanding of the problems, Kirnberger claimed that not a single work of J. S. Bach, C. P. E. Bach, Handel or Graun could be transposed without becoming deformed and impracticable (*Dok* III p201), despite the fact that as an experienced copyist he must have known a great deal about the unreliability of manuscript copies. Did he not know that the systems he advocated would make it difficult to play both versions of (e.g.) the Praeludium BWV 549.i or of the Fugue BWV 542.ii?

† Whose revised scheme was for a pure third divided into four tempered fifths (c–g–d–a–e) with the remaining fifths left pure.

Such pragmatism, for Schlick to Kirnberger, contrasts sharply not only with the mathematics enjoyed by theorists but with the practice of many seventeenth-century musicians for whom D minor was the *tous primus* or first key, requiring good triads in its tonic and related keys. Such cadences as Ex. 68, found from at least Byrd to Scheidemann, make best sense in a temperament in which the sharp third e–g♯ is followed by the pure third f–a (both fifths are meantone). Exactly what

Ex. 68

this temperament might be, however, is open to several interpretations; perhaps different builders and organists achieved the characteristic effects of such cadences in different ways as builders and organists of today might do. The problem of following any theorist too closely is that the writer on temperament, like all theorists, has preoccupations not necessarily borne out in the music of the better composers, which has its own harmonic characteristics. Is the D minor required by composers as a kind of 'first key', before the eighteenth-century collections (*Ariadne musica*, *Well-tempered Clavier* etc) left C major as the first-amongst-equals, properly satisfied by Werckmeister III or any other popular temperament? One particularly characteristic progression of the Monteverdi period – Ex. 69 – stretches specifically across the usable keys (E major to G minor). Such cadences and progressions were associated with certain keys and were not normally found in

Ex. 69   Monteverdi, *Orfeo*, Act II

others. There must be vestiges of such habits in J. S. Bach. For example, the sharp leading-note of E minor may have been the reason why he so rarely closed any E minor movement in the tonic minor, instead sharpening the final G and thus *softening* the D♯–G♮ contrast of a minor perfect cadence.* But perhaps organists – at least those in protestant Europe, less bound by any vocal associations that *tonus primus*, *secundus* etc may have had – were by nature inclined to see C major as a central key. Perhaps the circulating temperaments, in which all keys are more or less playable and for which Werckmeister, Neidhardt and Marpurg juggled their commas, are to be seen as furthering the instrumental–diatonic cause to the detriment of the vocal–modal.

Although it may be overbold to claim all appearances of such remote keys as E major and F♯ minor in the works of Buxtehude to be the result 'probably of transpositions made by later copyists' (Billeter 1979 p17), it certainly would be more than the sources could confirm to assume that the E major of BWV 566 or the F minor of BWV 534 were J. S. Bach's original keys for those pieces. Yet elsewhere in the organ works such keys do appear. Do they, and the chromatic/enharmonic movement of the G minor Fantasia BWV 542, suggest equal temperament? If it is true that some pieces as we know them do contain triads 'in remote keys that would have been dreadfully dissonant in any sort of tuning except equal temperament' (Barbour 1951 p196), what is the explanation? – that Bach was always inclined to equal temperament, that on the contrary he only gradually became inclined towards it, that none of the pieces centred in or modulating to remote keys can be proved to be in their 'original' key, that he experimented without regard to practicability? Or is it, rather, that *some* degree of inequality enhances in particular those pieces 'in remote keys'?

The following points can be made about this problem:

a

The F minor of BWV 639, 658 and 689 is unquestionably authentic, and the possibility that harpsichords were more easily tuned and re-tuned does not explain BWV 639 and 658, though it conceivably could BWV 689. The first piece implies that the Weimar tuning was an irregular system† (assuming that the chorale was played there); but since it is a trio – unique in the *Orgelbüchlein* – any harshness produced by its tonic triads would not have been quite so pronounced. In contrast to BWV 639, the chromatic treatment in such *Orgelbüchlein* movements as BWV 614 is much more traditional: chromatic fourths in D minor (*passus duriusculus ex tono primo*) are characteristic of much earlier music, though worked more imaginatively here. It is possible, therefore, that a specific effect was aimed at in BWV 639, a 'modern' trio of particular melancholy, not in principle so different from Zachow's 'Ach Herr, mich armen Sünder' in E♭ (BB 40037). Whether BWV 658 was written in F minor (rather than the A minor of the melody as found in BWV 73 – see Vol. II p148) in order to stay within a practicable organ compass cannot be known,

---

* That is, there may be more at stake in such cadences than the conventional *tierce de picardie*.
† Kirnberger III left key-characteristics highly differentiated and has been supposed – on no good evidence – to be the Weimar temperament (Eck 1981 pp16–17). That its third C–E is pure, however, has been seen as a reason why Kirnberger III is not the ideal temperament for *The 48*, since according to a statement by Marpurg (1776 p213) the composer recommended that all the thirds are large (*Dok* III p304).

but its F minor and A♭ harmonies are unambiguous, in no way disguised or 'softened' by careful part-writing. Even if the work were shown to be a transcription from a cantata movement, the questions about F minor would remain, unless a further conjecture (that F minor was an 'unwanted' key, reluctantly accepted etc) could ever be shown to be justified. If the so-called early version BWV 658a does belong to the Weimar years, the conclusions are similar to those for BWV 639: that the composer was experimenting in a more modern temperament but one that left the key with a melancholy *Affekt*. The so-called Leipzig version is less of a problem, for both the sets of chorales to which BWV 658 and 689 belong date from a decade which one can assume was modern in outlook. That the composer was aiming at modernity in the very opening key of *Clavierübung III* is suggested by Mattheson's remarks (1731 p244) that 'the beautiful, majestic key of E♭ major' is not 'in the head and fingers' of most organists, and that there are no toccatas and preludes, *Jahrgangs-Fugen* (chorale-fugues for the church year), or hymns in that key; nor do all organs have 'the right tuning' – at least, in Hamburg. Was BWV 552 a work that confirmed the modernity of Leipzig?*

Particularly in his early works, one must assume that J. S. Bach employed keys having certain properties which became associated with certain musical gestures. The triads of the common major keys, for example, are typical prelude material (see Vol. I pp80, 142). In irregular temperaments of the Werckmeister or Neidhardt kind, E major tended to be close to equal temperament but its related keys not: the same patterns played in E major and in F major (the best triads in Werckmeister III) would have been marked by quite different tensions. The obvious harshness of the A♭ major triad may in theory imply that its narrow fourth A♭–D♭ could be prominently featured in quiet, contemplative music, but in fact such music as BWV 622 seems to make no allowance whatsoever, positive or negative, for temperament problems: the A♭ and E♭ triads are treated without any tentativeness, except that the tessitura is low and that the composer may have deliberately avoided high thirds and fifths. (Besides, it is difficult to believe that in his maturity the composer allowed any key to be 'harsh'.) If it can be assumed that J. S. Bach composed with a view to performance, BWV 622 suggests that his tuning did favour A♭ to the detriment of G♯, whatever the usual habits of the day. It has already been suggested that the A♭ triad seems to be used particularly often, in exposed contexts, in *The 48* and so requires a better tuning than the keys of C♯ and F♯ (Barnes 1979).† In general, minor keys are less problematic, since the ear is not so sensitive to the minor third. This could help to explain why the enharmonic boldnesses in the G minor Fantasia BWV 542 (like those in the Chromatic Fantasia BWV 903 for harpsichord or opening Sinfonia of Cantata 21) begin in, pass to and return to minor keys with greater frequency than is the case with nineteenth-century enharmonicisms. Diminished sevenths are after all only superimposed minor thirds: Ex. 70. But a minor triad

---

* On the possibility that at least part of the Leipzig organ was tuned in equal temperament, see chapter 16 above (p132).

† Although Barnes's reasoning from a statistical survey of how the composer exposes intervals in his counterpoint is open to serious objection – it takes no account of the source history of the pieces, excludes the fugues, treats thirds as different from tenths, offers no objective criteria for the 'acceptability' of tempered intervals, and trusts the notation to specify whether or not a note is to be sustained – it does offer the organist a fruitful method for forming an opinion on the keys used in organ music.

Ex. 70 BWV 542.i

also includes a major third, and one that is less avoidable in four-part harmony than three-part. The opening of BWV 639 exposes that triad: does the wide spacing 'soften' it?

b

G. A. Sorge, who was the next after J. S. Bach to join Mizler's Leipzig society, described Silbermann's tuning in the 1740s fairly precisely: on the instruments he examined, it tempered the eleven fifths by one-sixth of a Pythagorean comma, left the wolf fifth sharp by almost one comma, and made the keys of A, D, G, C, F and B♭ uniformly good; E♭ and B major were still very difficult however (Lange 1972–3). Whether or not Silbermann had earlier in his career begun with pure C–G and G–D fifths (Billeter 1979 p28) – and whether or not J. S. Bach in Weimar worked with such Kirnberger-like priorities – it certainly seems that Sorge was speaking of conditions in 1748 when he wrote:

> Die Silbermannische Art zu temperiren, kan bey heutiger Praxi nicht bestehen. Dass dieses alles die lautere Wahrheit sey, ruffe ich alle unpartheyische und der Sache erfahrne *Musicos*, sonderlich den Weltberühmten Herrn Bach in Leipzig zu Zeugen . . .
> In denen 4. schlimmen *Triadibus* . . . ist ein rauhes, wildes, oder, wie Herr Capellmeister Bach in Leipzig redet, ein barbarisches Wesen enthalten . . . (*Dok* II p450)

> Silbermann's way of tempering cannot be maintained in today's practice. That this is all the absolute truth, I call as witness all impartial musicians experienced in the matter, in particular the world-famous Bach in Leipzig . . .
> In his four bad triads [C♯, F♯, A♭ and B major triads?] . . . a raw, wild or (as Capellmeister Bach in Leipzig calls it) barbaric nature is contained . . .

Also pertinent to this decade are Agricola's reports of J. S. Bach's views of Silbermann's temperament: see chapter 16. Perhaps Silbermann's temperament became increasingly difficult for J. S. Bach, in so far as he came across it. One must assume that on his Dresden visits he was careful to avoid the keys of E♭, E, B, F♯, C♯ and A♭, though one Dresden report (see chapter 7 above) says all keys were used – perhaps in major court churches the organ was tuned in a more modern manner? Why he appears so rarely to have composed in B♭ major is puzzling – perhaps more because limitations of compass meant there was no low tonic, though this would affect B minor equally. Sorge even advised on how to change Silbermann's tuning conveniently to equal temperament, pointing out that in any case Werckmeister's tuning was preferable to Silbermann's, despite its four sharp thirds, since it gave a set of eight pure fifths while Silbermann's gave none.

c

Some sources imply that temperament varied from church to church, not merely arbitrarily but at least sometimes in relation to the status of different establishments. Neidhardt twice suggested temperaments: for village, town and city (*Gäntzliche erschöpfte, mathematische Abtheilungen*, Königsberg/Leipzig 1732), and for village, town, city and court (*Sectio canonis harmonici*, Königsberg 1724); it seems that three of the temperaments progressively approached the fourth, the equal temperament thought suitable for the court – a strong hint that ideally the nature of the music performed influenced the temperament used, i.e. that the more modern or cosmopolitan the music, the closer to equal the temperament. In 'rural' temperaments, thirds and semitones were less equal (i.e., they varied more from key to key); in city and court temperaments, transposition was more feasible, e.g. when the organist had to transpose down because his pitch was higher than that of the instruments (as in Bach's Leipzig cantatas). It is clear from Werckmeister's account in *Organum Gruningense Redivivum* that by 1705 the organ in the castle chapel at Gröningen had been retuned from meantone to equal temperament to satisfy musical demands. On the other hand, Werckmeister also noted that at the court chapel of Quedlinburg, in 1677, the builder Z. Thayssner (whose case at Naumburg later housed the Hildebrandt organ approved by Silbermann and J. S. Bach) had applied the unequal temperament now called 'Werckmeister IV' (Werckmeister 1681 p36), a tuning less favourable to distant keys than 'Werckmeister III'. Perhaps it was only gradually that court chapels moved to newer idioms.* In any event, builders obviously varied in their practice: according to C. A. Sinn (1717 p116), C. Cuncius applied the tuning now called Werckmeister III several times, though he does not say where. What bearing does this have on the situation at Halle in 1716 (Cuncius organ approved in the Kuhnau/Bach/Rolle report) when the examiners noted problems with the tuning (see chapter 17 above)? Was Cuncius's attempt at this *passable* temperament an experiment, and an unsuccessful one? Did J. S. Bach not care for it at that period? Or had Cuncius merely not completed the tuning in time for the examination?

There could be many explanations of why Neidhardt's tuning of one Gedackt in the Jena organ in 1706 by means of an equally tempered monochord should have been less satisfactory to the listeners than J. N. Bach's (non-equal) tuning by ear (account in Spitta I pp135–6), but it is always possible that one reason was dissatisfaction with and reluctance to accept equal temperament for the sustained tone of organs, a reluctance found in other countries at that period.† Nevertheless, reports of this kind do not allow firm conclusions to be drawn. Even if Sorge and Agricola based their strictures of Silbermann's tuning on untypical instruments – which seems not to have been the case – it is difficult to understand how a contemporary note on the organ of Reinhardtsgrimma (built by Silbermann, 1731) could say:

* Moreover, court chapels must have set the pace for lesser churches. For example, since the very first strain of the first chorale in the Weissenfels hymnbook of 1714 closed with a chord of C♯ major ('Allein Gott in der Höh", set in A major), clearly any town or village organist using the same hymnbook had a limited choice: he could omit the third and fifth, he could play an unpleasant chord, or he could have a suitable tuning.

† That Jena may have been in the vanguard of tuning experiments is also suggested by the publication there in 1704 of J. P. Treiber's *Der accurate Organist im General-Bass*, in which two figured chorales are given (and are to be realized) in 'all keys and chords' ('durch alle Tone und Accorde'). In fact, however, twenty-two not twenty-four keys are given – F♯/G♭ major and its relative are omitted.

> die Temperierung weiss der Künstler so zu theilen dass man nicht irgendwo den schlimmen Wolf hört heulen (Dähnert 1953 p108)

> the artist knows how to distribute the temperament so that nowhere does one hear the wicked wolf howling

unless it was that village organists kept away from remote keys. A more important city church, the Johanniskirche, Zittau, had a Silbermann organ in 1741 of which a contemporary report makes a less ambiguous claim:

> ist die musicalische Temperatur passable und in allen Accorden annehmlich zu gebrauchen (Flade 1926 p93).

> the musical temperament is suitable [? allows passing or modulating?] and is usable in all chords [keys?].

But can this have been true? It would not agree with Sorge's observations on the little Silbermann in Schloss Burgk (built in 1743), thought it might have been said of Hildebrandt's organ in Naumburg, described as being in 'Neidhardt's tuning' (i.e. equal or near-equal temperament – Dähnert 1962 p115). Nevertheless, Zittau may well have had a less pronounced wolf than was often the case elsewhere, since the church itself belonged to an important city and had a large musical repertory: the kind of setting for Neidhardt's third type of temperament (see above).

Mattheson implies this too when he remarks on the tunings favoured by Silbermann and Wender in (to him) far-off Thuringia and Saxony:

> Diese Meister . . . haben sich doch zu dergleichen Neidhardtischen exacten Temperatur nicht verstehen wollen; sonder weil sie wissen, dass bey Kirchen-Musiquen die diatonische Modi, und nächst diesen die transponirten, welche nicht gar zu tieff in das Chroma fallen, die *vexatissimi Martyres* sein . . . so haben sie noch immer auf das diatonicum Genus meistens regardiret (1725 p235).

> These masters have not yet wanted to come to an understanding with this exact [uniform] temperament of Neidhardt; but because they know that in church music [cantatas?] the diatonic keys (and nearest to these the transposed keys which do not run too deep into chromaticism) are the 'martyrs most often disturbed' . . . so they have still the diatonic *genus* mostly in mind.

Moreover, fine ears (as Sorge more than once shows himself to have had) must have found equal temperament less than ideal for organs accustomed to play with wind instruments of the period, particularly trumpets, horns, oboes and flutes.

Even with a composer as modern as J. S. Bach, it is in the context of harpsichord/clavichord/chamber music, not church or organ music, that later commentators speak of his insisting on sharp major thirds (Marpurg, 1776 – *Dok* III p304) or devising fingerings to play in all twenty-four keys (Forkel 1802 ch.III). Certainly the village organist would have found the Silbermannesque temperament practicable enough by tuning as follows:

> six equally imperfect fifths (C–G–D–E–B–F♯♯) } F♯ = F♯
> six perfect fourths (C–F–B♭–E♭–G♯–C♯–F♯)

As a piece of music – wherever amongst the common keys one started – proceeded to modulate, the dominant would be the best key, the flattened supertonic the worst; 'best' and 'worst' would be relative.

The organist of today should also bear in mind the didactic or demonstrative nature of much of J. S. Bach's music before he concludes that the G minor Fantasia BWV 542 requires equal temperament, or that it could have been played only on an unusual organ or even one specially tuned,* or that it might have 'sounded tolerable' only if the usual tuning was one that made the minor-third harmonies acceptable. Like the Passacaglia, the Fantasia may have originated as a response to a genre of the period, each of them excelling its model in several respects (length in the first, chromaticism in the second), both of them demonstrating (for the composer? for a pupil?) the potential of the genre. Several practical problems in J. S. Bach arise from the later assumption that all music is composed only in order to be performed.

---

22. Harpsichord Questions

Three particular questions concerning harpsichords and the music of J. S. Bach remain only partially answered today, despite many conjectures and assertions. First, on what kind of harpsichord did the composer expect his pieces to be played? – and was it a similar kind of harpsichord for all the music (toccatas and suites, both books of *The 48*, partitas, *Clavierübung IV*, concertos, *obbligato* sonatas)? Secondly, were harpsichords used in the cantatas? – or, conversely, to what use did J. S. Bach put the harpsichords or spinets that are known to have been kept in court chapels and the larger town churches? And thirdly, were at least some of the composer's earlier keyboard works meant to be playable on both organ and harpsichord? – or, more generally, what if any is the relevance of harpsichords to the organ music of J. S. Bach? Although the three questions are not entirely separate from each other, it is the third which most obviously falls within the scope of this book.†

In the mature keyboard works of the composer, the question 'Is this harpsichord music or organ music?' arises only for those pieces the character of whose counterpoint – usually very ingenious – seems to have been the composer's preoccupation in that instance. The obvious similarity between certain passages in particular works – for example, the F major Fugue BWV 540.ii and the Italian Concerto BWV 971.iii (see Vol. I p111) – only underlines the unambiguity of the two works: neither movement as a whole could serve both instruments. In the case of those mature works conceived as 'demonstration counterpoint', the nature of that counterpoint may from time to time convince the player that either organ or harpsichord is 'better' – for example, organ for the first *contrapuncti* of the *Art of Fugue*, harpsichord for the Four Duets – since the sustained four-part writing of the former suit the organ and the sprightly two parts of the latter suit the harpsichord. But such a subjective response begs several questions, such as What is it we ask when we question whether the Four Duets are harpsichord or organ music? Did the com-

---

* 'The literature of the seventeenth and eighteenth centuries is conspicuously silent about retuning as a means of adapting to key' (Rasch 1985).
† On the harpsichords in Leipzig churches, see Schering 1941 p47; on that in the Weimar Schlosskapelle, see Jauernig 1950 p70; for regular tuning of the Leipzig church harpsichords, see Dähnert 1962 p80.

poser expect them to be played? If so, as music to be performed before listeners or rather as a means of the player 'taking in' the contrapuntal thought behind them? Even when the music can be shown to be idiomatically conceived for a keyboard instrument (such as the part-writing of the *Art of Fugue* being always in the grasp of two hands) is such a feature simply one of the disciplines or technical problems given by the composer to himself? After all, if these or any four classically conceived parts are to keep their classical conception they will remain within a certain compass, and only detailed analysis and imaginatively composed hypothetical alternatives will suggest whether in the act of composing the composer actually strove for the player's convenience at the expense of other alternatives. It is possible that such could indeed be shown to be the case with the *Art of Fugue*, as Tovey and others since have claimed. But in the nature of their sparser two-part counterpoint the Four Duets will remain more ambiguous for the modern performer who assumes that music is meant necessarily to be performed (on the implications of the word *Übung*, see Vol. II p186).

When questions of harpsichord *versus* organ are asked, two particular characteristics of keyboard music are involved: the type of figuration (range, speed, the lie of the hand) and the texture (compass, the reach of the hands, also the notation). Without doubt, the earlier keyboard music of J. S. Bach has an outlay of notes suitable to either instrument; moreover, it is far more versatile in this sense than that of many earlier composers in different traditions (e.g. de Grigny and François Couperin) where figuration and texture show different characteristic patterns in each genre. For Forkel and others after him, who knew little about either harpsichords or 'demonstration counterpoint' in the earlier eighteenth century, the question could often be answered by referring to the notation for, and the special matter of, the pedals. If a piece was notated with a bass *point d'orgue* (see BWV 561) then pedals were required; the same is true if pedals, as a kind of third hand, are needed to play some of the notes given (see BWV 563). But if the figuration is broken up, laid out with few ties even when the opportunity for them is there, then the intended instrument was either the harpsichord (i.e. pedal harpsichord for BWV 525–530) or the clavichord (pedal clavichord for BWV 582). One feature of this line of argument is that the period that found it most fertile (Forkel to Schweitzer) was also the period that produced the idea of a fixed repertory of J. S. Bach's music: it was *either* organ music *or* harpsichord music, and editions were and still are published in which the A minor Fantasia BWV 561 is called organ music and the A major fugues BWV 949 and 950 are called harpsichord music. In fact, however, the pedal points of all three works differ only in degree, and in the figuration itself the fugal section of BWV 561 would be difficult to distinguish usefully from BWV 949 and 950. As they stand, BWV 949 and 950 are different from BWV 561 only in being isolated fugues. But it is no more likely that in rigid terms BWV 561 is 'organ music' and BWV 949 and 950 'harpsichord music' than that BWV 949 and 950 once had toccata-like (organ-like) preludes and postludes which are now lost. Neither speculation is justified by the sources.

Nevertheless, the problem of such *points d'orgue* and how to play them – with or without pedals, at written or octave pitch, held or re-struck – is often acute. To begin with, BWV 561 has several held pedal points which, as transmitted by the sources, can be played by the left hand without pedals, whether on organ (as in *BG*,

Schmieder *BWV* etc) or on harpsichord (as in P 318); the three staves of modern editions make explicit what earlier notations would not. The left hand cannot so easily keep the *point d'orgue* in BWV 949, still less in BWV 950, whose sources give bass notes impossible for the left hand. The most striking example of this impossibility, and one clear from the most impeccable source, is in the A minor Fugue, *The 48* Bk 1, where the autograph fair copy (P 415) keeps a long and tied tonic *point d'orgue* at the close, with no indication of how it is to be reached. Was there a *genre-association* in J. S. Bach's mind between the pedal point and the key of A minor/major? A solution, and one most appropriate to Book 1 of *The 48* as a whole, could be to see the composer here not so much expecting a second player (Keller 1965 p103) or implying harpsichord pedals (Spitta 1 p770), but producing a 'demonstration coda' for a long fugue engaged in *rectus* and *inversus* counterpoint based on old-fashioned *figurae*. Playing the piece was a secondary consideration; the player managed as best he could to hint at the *point d'orgue*. Even if this piece should be (as Spitta claims) a fugue representing a particular youthful imitation of a particular mature Buxtehude work, such a practical problem as how to play it would not necessarily have been in the forefront of the composer's interests. The coda is certainly not playable by left hand except in the form of frequent short acciaccaturas at the bottom of spread five- to seven-part chords. Was that what the composer expected, himself being concerned only with an ideal notation?*

The problem is similar where the bass is not a *point d'orgue* but a moving line at the final coda – for example, in the C major Fugue BWV 946 where, after a *manualiter* fugue (in which bass entries are harmonized with textures more like the harpsichord's than the organ's), an extra bass part completes the closing postlude-like harmonies and results in textures that are, if played literally, closer to organ than to harpsichord. It is not surprising that characteristics of notation and figuration in J. S. Bach's earlier keyboard music should have puzzled the later copyists, leading them to add many a '*Ped*' cue for what look like held notes out of reach of the left hand (e.g. BWV 950a in P 804) or for textures that need more than two hands (e.g. BWV 532.ii, 550 and 564 in the MS Fétis 2960) or for particular moments when they thought a pedal could be added (e.g. the G major *manualiter* Toccata BWV 916 in Rinck's LM 4838: pedal cues on the copyist's own initiative?). The problem is not exclusive to J. S. Bach, of course. J. G. Walther's two sets of chorale-variations (*Musicalische Vorstellung*, Erfurt 1713) have what is clearly harpsichord figuration, although in each set the last variation cannot be played as written without pedals. Some free works (such as Reincken's Toccata in G) in which *points d'orgue* near the close suddenly require pedal do so only for the lower note of an octave *point d'orgue*: i.e., it adds nothing to the harmony and could be optional.

The possibility that pedal harpsichords were sufficiently well known to allow composers and copyists to regard them as the means of solving such difficulties

---

* Not unrelated to this problem are the long-held bass notes in recitatives, taken short universally from about c1735 but not always before that time, at least in the ambiance of J. S. Bach (despite recent assertions propagated by recordings). Notational convention (especially in fair-copy scores) left the bass notes, whether *points d'orgue* or not, written as semibreves etc, held until the note changed; by what date and in what areas did players of the various continuo instruments (organ, cello, violone, bassoon) take that note off or re-strike it as the text or the harmony seemed to them to require? Do ties, especially in the simple two-stave scores of Italian *recitativo secco* around 1700, indicate 'hold the note' or 'the bass note is unchanged here, whether sounded or not' or 'play this note as often as the singer needs harmonies for support' etc?

must be remote. Yet they did exist. Forkel (David/Mendel p311) reported that the composer used both pedal harpsichord and pedal clavichord; and it is clear from organologists between Bach and Forkel that central German makers built both pedal pulldowns and independent pedal harpsichords. It is doubtful whether Forkel can be relied on; but the independent pedal harpsichord was certainly known to one of J. S. Bach's pupils, J. C. Vogler in Weimar (with the specification 16.8.8, according to Adlung 1758 p556), and the pedal clavichord to another, H. N. Gerber in Sondershausen (according to Kinsky 1936 p161). However, it is also clear that sets of pedals (not always simple pulldowns) were known in many countries of Europe for instruments of many kinds over the whole period c1450–1800 (see references to harpsichord, virginals, spinet and clavichord *passim* in Hubbard 1965, Russell 1959 and Kinsky 1936) but that nowhere was there an established repertory for them – as well established as would be implied by considering BWV 551, 561, 563, 946, 950 etc to be pedal-harpsichord pieces. One could make a similar point about other fringe instruments (such as *Geigenwerk*, *Lautenwerk* and *claviorganum*) or about the works of other composers (such as Buxtehude of Böhm). In Germany as a whole, from at least the later sixteenth century, harpsichords more often originated in organ-builders' workshops* than was generally the case elsewhere, but this does not necessarily suggest that harpsichord pedals were better known in Germany, since organ pedals were not universal and since in any case organ-builders made other keyboard instruments for which there was no question of pedalboards (e.g. G. Silbermann's *cembali d'amour* and fortepianos).

The pedal harpsichord/clavichord is altogether too fertile a hare raised in the hunt for answers to the problem of how one is to play J. S. Bach's *manualiter* works that go beyond what two hands can do. The A minor Variations or *Aria variata* BWV 989 is one example: two good early sources give Ex. 71. Now some of these bars seem to require an exceptional stretch while others are only possible if juggled athletically. In such cases as these, is the answer more likely to have been pedal

Ex. 71   BWV 989

* For example, the harpsichord used in St Thomas, Leipzig from 1672 to 1756 was made by Ludwig Compenius, organ-maker in Halle (Schering 1936 pp61ff). Werckmeister (1698 p68) remarks on organists accepting the present of a harpsichord or clavichord from an organ-builder as a return for undeservedly favourable reports.

harpsichord, some kind of short-octave compass and/or retuned bass strings (a compass of AACDEFG–c''' is required for BWV 989), or a free interpretation of the notation? Of these, the short octave* is perhaps the most likely; but it is certainly possible, especially in view of the nature of the Andreas-Bach-Buch (a model repertory for the composer–player), that the source is an 'ideal', and that the player amends such a fair copy to play it as best he can. This would be so whether or not the piece is considered a compositional *exemplum*: a composer's carefully thought-out response (on paper) to a popular *genre*. Other characteristics of keyboard music of *c*1700 may also have been open to great licence. *Points d'orgue* written out as simple, long notes may often have been mere indicators of harmony (like the figures below some Corelli continuo basses marked *tasto solo*) rather than notes to be played literally: they showed the player what harmony was the basis of the music at that moment, not necessarily what he was to hold or what was supposed to be audible to the listener. J. S. Bach was not a composer to put the player's convenience before the clear exposition of a musical concept. How many players even now can grasp immediately what is at stake for them *as keyboardists* in the autograph fair copy of the B minor Invention BWV 801?

If notated *points d'orgue* are no indication of the instrument intended by the composer, no more is compass. That the CD–c''' compass of BWV 911–915 (six harpsichord toccatas) follows the 'usual organ compass', and the C–c''' compass of the first Toccata BWV 911 specifically that of the Weimar organ (Klotz 1975 pp377–8), is not of itself significant. First, other early works indisputably written as harpsichord music keep a similar compass, such as the Capriccio in B flat BWV 992. Secondly, as is clear from an anonymous 8.8 harpsichord now kept in Eisenach (Thuringian make of the seventeenth century?) and a quasi-Italian instrument of German make now in the Leipzig Collection, C–c''' and even CDE–c''' were also compasses known to the German harpsichord (see Henkel 1977). Thirdly, while it is true that the compass of *Clavierübung I, II* and *IV* is longer (as would in any case be expected of later music), earlier music such as the Two- and and Three-part Inventions (1722) still keep largely to C–c''', despite the FF–f''' known on (e.g.) the Harrass harpsichord now in Sondershausen, which was made before 1714 (Henkel 1977). It is also subtly argued that the toccatas BWV 912 and 914 use motifs so similar to two of the larger organ preludes (BWV 532 and 534 respectively) that a sheer comparison between the way each *genre* treats them proves the toccatas to be more suitable for harpsichord (Klotz 1975 pp377–8). This is clear enough: BWV 914 and 534 show as incontrovertibly as was likely at that period how similar motifs can produce both an idiomatic, unambiguous harpsichord work and an idiomatic, unambiguous organ work.

---

* The C♯ key plays AA, F♯ plays D, G♯ plays E? or (better) normal short-octave compass (E key = C, F♯ = D, G♯ = E) while an extra key (looking like D) plays AA? or (if G♯ is required, and if in any case the piece is assumed not to call for every available note) bass keys were retuned *ad hoc*.

The Music and Its Performance

23. Certain Details of Performance: Articulation and Legato

The performance practice of J. S. Bach's keyboard music as outlined successively by the *Obituary*, Forkel, Spitta and more recent studies can serve as a background for the player of today, but that player needs to rethink the connection between organs and their playing, music as left in the sources, and keyboard technique as known to have evolved by 1700. Evidence before 1750, as it relates to J. S. Bach, is vague. No speculation will ever make it certain why one organist (G. H. L. Schwanenberger of Brunswick) thought he must

> meine Spielart gantz anders ändern, denn es nichts zu rechnen ist (*Dok* II pp178–9)

> completely change my style of playing, for it is worth nothing

after he had heard J. S. Bach. Evidence after 1750, though frequently suggestive, relates to repertories of a different, particular kind and can often be contradictory; Bedos speaks of a 'non-legato' touch in which every note is followed by silence (directions for pinning organ–barrels for secular French music *c*1765 - *L'Art du Facteur d'Orgues* §§1418–21) while Türk speaks of a legato without silence between notes, as well as sostenuto or super-legato for broken chords (piano tutor of 1789, p355). The late-eighteenth-century liking for dictionaries and encyclopedias led the player to depend on notation and literate record more than did the composers before him, and it is not even possible always to be certain what the early terms mean. For example, the three meanings of *legato* in J. G. Walther's *Lexicon* (1732) leave what became the most important the least well explained:

> Im ersten Verstande wird es gebraucht: wenn zwo Noten mit einem halben Circul . . . bezeichnet sind . . .
> auch öffters etliche Noten . . . mit solchen Zeichen gebunden, um anzuzeigen: dass *vocaliter* nur eine Sylbe unter solche gelegt, *instrumentaliter* aber dergleichen gezogen, und mit einem Bogen-Strich *absolvirt* werden sollen.
> Im zweyten Verstande wird es gebraucht: wenn ein Componist sich vorsetzet, etwas auf gewisse Art angefangenes zu vollführen, und davon im geringsten nicht abzugehen.

> In its first meaning it is used: when two notes . . . are marked with a tie . . .
> and more often several notes are . . . bound with such a sign in order to show that in vocal music only one syllable lies under them; but in instrumental music such notes are slurred and are to be played with one bow-stroke.
> In its second meaning it is used: when a composer undertakes to finish something begun in a certain way and not to depart from it in the slightest [i.e. = a bracket covering a repeated figure or sequence?].

Walther may be making a useful point when he compares legato with motifs sung to one syllable in vocal music, but nothing more can be learnt from the *Lexicon*. Did keyboard-players know legato? Was it an exceptional effect, like string vibrato? Is he referring merely to the notational sign rather than the playing technique itself? Is legato touch always associated with the one-syllable melisma of vocal music – i.e., is its use in keyboard music merely allusive and imitative? If so, is legato an effect for a few notes, a short phrase such as could be sung to one syllable, rather than a general style? Is such an effect of smoothness – of a phrase in string music played under one bow – what J. S. Bach was aiming at when in the title-page to the Inventions he refers to their offering the player music with which to practise *cantabile* – and when he then proceeds to slur (e.g.) the D major and F minor Two-part Inventions in virtually every bar? Would the player of 1720, if not given such an indication, still have been conceiving such lines as in some degree *détaché*? In any case, what exactly do *legato* and *cantabile* mean?

Although no answers to such questions are given in Walther's *Praecepta* (1708) either, it does make some important implications about slurring, even attempting to be systematic about terminology – at a period, moreover, when he and his cousin had recently moved to Weimar (1955 edn pp34–5) and when, no doubt, they were both turning their interests to questions of style both in composition and in playing.* Of articulation dots, Walther says:

> *Punctus percutiens* . . . in den sing- oder klingenden Stücken . . . anzuzeigen, dass dergleichen Noten gestossen, und nicht geschleiffet werden sollen . . .

> The 'striking dot' in vocal or instrumental music, to show that the notes concerned are to be struck [separately] and not slid . . . [Ex. 72]

Ex. 72

Tra - hit, tra - - - hit su - a quem - que vo - lup - tas

> *Punctus serpens*, zeiget an, dass die auf folgende Art gesetze Noten sollen schleiffet werden . . .

> The 'creeping dot' shows that the notes composed in the following manner are to be slid: [Ex. 73]

Ex. 73

> Wenn . . . garzu viel Noten unter eine Sylbe sollen geleget werden, so wird das *Ligatur*-Zeichen aussen gelassen . . .

> The slur is omitted when too many notes are laid under one syllable: [Ex. 74]

Ex. 74

lau -da-te pu - e -ri, lau - da - - - - te

---

* The markedly Italianate (in particular Carissimi-like) nature of the examples Walther offers his reader may well reflect the particular interests of the young Prince Johann Ernst, known for his later importing of (and stylistic copies of) Venetian concertos.

Wenn das *Ligatur*-Zeichen in *instrumental*-stimmen über oder unter denen Noten vorkommt, so bedeutet es, dass solche Noten sollen gezogen oder geschleiffet werden . . .

When the slur appears above or below the notes in instrumental parts it means that such notes are to be bowed together or slid . . . [Ex. 75)

Ex. 75

Man findet auch in *instrumental*-stimmen, und sonderlich in denen, welche mit Bogen *tractir*et werden, das *Ligatur*-Zeichen und Puncte zugleich über oder unter denen Noten gesezet; und bedeutet alsdenn, dass solche Noten nicht allein geschleiffet und mit einem Strich *absolvir*et, sondern auch zugleich gestossen werden sollen.

One finds also in instrumental parts, and particularly in those that are played with bows, slurs and dots placed together above or below the notes; and this means that such notes are not only slid and completed with one bow but that they are to be struck [separately] at the same time: [Ex. 76].

Ex. 76

Thus slurs cover notes sung to one syllable and those played in one bow: did keyboard slurs and thus 'phrase-marks' develop from these? There are three steps, from staccato through slurred staccato to legato: is it expected that the keyboard-player, being also a singer and string-player, would interpret the several note-patterns in the ways Walther describes whether or not the slurs were written in? Vocal slurs cover not only melismas but strong–weak pairs: does this suggest that on the analogy of vocal slurs, the organist is to understand slurred groups of notes as *by nature* inclined to the strong–weak?

The rarity of slurs and dots in sources of J. S. Bach's music must reflect one or more of the following conditions or characteristics of his period and his interests: that in general touch was more *détaché* than in later periods; that *figurae* or patterns had their own conventions and did not need signs;* and that even in the autograph fair copies of the Italianate and very violin-like Six Sonatas, the greater frequency of slurs and dots tends to suggest that such were special devices or 'ornaments' applied to or for certain musical ideas. In the Sonatas the very slurring alludes to a specific style. But that there was at least a tradition of such 'ornaments' current amongst keyboard-players in that part of Germany during the first half of the eighteenth century is suggested by the use of the same terms (*gestossen, geschleiffet, gezogen*) in both J. G. Walther and C. P. E. Bach.

* Walther himself does not actually slur the snapped rhythm of Ex. 72 above, nor, as he says, the long melisma.

If there is an Italianate element in the bowing-like slurs of the Six Sonatas – the melodies and motifs of these pieces being in themselves violinistic – so there are many motifs in organ music of the early eighteenth century that have a distinctly French flavour, regardless of whether or not the composer concerned actually notated slurs. André Raison, in the preface to his *Premier Livre d'Orgue* (Paris 1688),* refers to two particularly interesting opportunities for some kind of legato playing. First, in *plein jeu* music the sustained textures conceived for an *organo pleno* registration and built on suspensions and slow-moving harmonies

> se touche fort lentement, il faut lier les Accords les uns aux autres.

> are played very slowly – one must tie the chords to each other.

Except that it cannot be 'very slow', BWV 572.ii suggests such treatment. Secondly, there are motifs that may be played slurred for melodic effect: in Ex. 77

Ex. 77   (Raison)

> il ne faut lever le re qu'apres avoir posé l'ut.

> the d″ need not be raised until after the c♯″ has been played.

What underlies this 'ornament' is the desire to convey the nuance of voices. In contrast to *la distinction* or distinct touch, G.-G. Nivers defined *le coulement* ('sliding') as the touch in which

> il ne faut pas lever les doigts si promptement . . . De touttes ces choses on doit consulter la methode de chanter, par ce qu'en ces rencontres l'Orgue doit imiter la Voix (*Livre d'Orgue*, Paris 1665).

> one need not raise the fingers so promptly . . . In all these things, one should bear in mind the way a singer would do it, for on these occasions the organ has to imitate the voice.

Although Nivers's examples (Ex. 78) may suggest a French *figura* not easily found in J. S. Bach's organ music, in fact many melodies in the gentler pieces – the tenor line of BWV 663, the soprano of BWV 656 or 622, various voices in the C minor Fantasia BWV 562 – give an opportunity for such vocal effects. Indeed, it is difficult to imagine such 'carrying of the voice' (*port de voix*) being anything but obvious to a good player or good composer of any century, and not least to German organists from Scheidemann to J. S. Bach; the melodiousness which sensitive touch of this kind leads to must be part of the beauty of playing for which such composers as Froberger or Chambonnières were noted. Moreover, the sweet expressiveness of such articulation may also be behind Schwanenberger's quoted remarks about J. S.

Ex. 78

---

* Apparently connected in some way with the Passacaglia BWV 582: see Vol. I p255.

Bach (see above, p196) and can be understood, with experience, on a suitable organ. In addition, it is obviously in the interests of 'counterpoint by articulation' that some types of theme or melodic line are more slurred than others. A good example is the chromatic fourth, so often one of the themes in a permutation fugue (see Vol. I p6). In the case of the Canzona in D minor BWV 588, it could well be part of the contrapuntal intention of the movement that the chromatic fourth be predominantly legato. Such chromatic lines, like the chromatic passages in the old German chorale-fantasias or the chromatic variations in many a partita, are obviously well marked when played legato; furthermore, it is usually easy for the alternate-foot pedalling to be smooth at such moments or in such themes (e.g. BWV 588 at bb63–4).

Legato was not only a melodic 'ornament' but had further uses in its super-legato form. When Daniel Vetter speaks as follows of a simple *brisé* technique for chorale-variations

> welche Manier gewiss eine sonderbahre Anmuth bey sich führet, wenn sie rechtschaffen und also tractiret wird, dass die Hände beständig auff dem Clavier liegen bleiben, sonderlich aber, wann in der rechten Hand mit dem kleinen Finger der Choral geführt, und man sich des Daumens fleissig bedienet, insgemein aber dieses Merckmahl behält, dass alles *douce* geschleiffet werden soll . . . (1709/1713 preface)

> which manner [of composing variations] certainly has about it a particular charm when it is played properly in such a way that the hands remain lying continuously on the keyboard, and particularly when in the right hand the chorale is carried by the little finger, and one makes good use of the thumb, in general however taking care that everything glides along [i.e. is slurred?] sweetly . . .

is he saying anything more than that in such variations as in Ex. 79 the *brisé* technique needs sustained playing, with the chorale melody held on the top? Is legato or 'super-legato' reserved for such textures, 'broken variations on the spinet and clavichord' as Vetter calls them (see Vol. II p328)? Is such legato more in the nature of the sustaining pedal of the later fortepiano than an element in phrasing?

Ex. 79   (Vetter, after Schering)

Both *brisé* and sostenuto were employed as occasional or even special effects in Saxon–Thuringian keyboard music c1700, as can be clearly seen in such works as the Vetter Variations, Kuhnau's 'Biblical Sonatas' (Leipzig 1700) and J. S. Bach's Capriccio in B flat BWV 992. Such styles are reserved for particular moments. It is not even clear from (e.g.) Kuhnau's salute to Froberger (*ibid* preface) and his allusion to *lamenti* (Sonata no. 4) whether he grasped Froberger's idiomatic sustained harpsichord lyricism, but it is possible that only from c1710 was the Saxon–Thuringian harpsichord itself beginning to be sensitively handled by makers and players alike. Perhaps the late-blooming, or never fully developed, *sensibilité* in making, voicing and composing for harpsichords in the Weimar-Leipzig area was responsible for two assertions of Forkel, that J. S. Bach preferred the clavichord and that he insisted on quilling and voicing his own harpsichords (1802 ch.III). On the other hand, the less idiomatic – i.e. the less *brisé* or sostenuto – the writing is for harpsichord, the more versatile the music becomes and the more it will suit harpsichord, clavichord or organ interchangeably.* Unfortunately, how each instrument was composed for is not usually clear from the notation: Couperin's sostenuto style for the opening of a harpsichord piece later copied into the *Klavierbüchlein für Anna Magdalena Bach* is not conveyed by the copy's notation,† a case offering parallels to the differences in notation between sources for the A major Fugue BWV 536 and 536a. Although bold assertions are made about these discrepancies – e.g. that BWV 536 came to represent how the composer actually played the notes (Zacher 1973) – the sources are of such uncertain authority that such assertions are guesswork. Similarly, there is no evidence that the sostenuto final chord of BWV 632 means that the motif is played in this way throughout the prelude, or that the final chord of BWV 564 accumulates held notes from previous bars, or that the notation of the C major Prelude BWV 545 suggests a sostenuto element that was intended but not notated in the 'earlier version' BWV 545a – musically interesting though such ideas may be (Zacher 1973).

Neither sostenuto nor *brisé* style is entirely foreign to the organ, as is clear from (e.g.) BWV 536 or 599, where the *brisé* style is integrated subtly into the four- and five-part harmonization. A 'super-legato' interpretation of leaning-note ornaments, familiar from the French harpsichord style, was illustrated by Rameau in *Pièces de Clavecin* (Paris 1724, *table*) – Ex. 80 – and Kuhnau had already remarked

Ex. 80

in *Clavierübung I* (Leipzig 1689) that the second note of such *accentus* ornaments should be 'delicately gentle' ('fein sachte'). The educated Thuringian–Saxon organist must have been aware of such things. Such references suggest one kind of touch on the keyboard that must have been known to the Naumburg organist in 1746 when he complained that the sluggish key-action produced a kind of '*accentuation*' (*Dok* II p430), i.e. an effect he did not want indiscriminately. Another contemporary of J. S. Bach, G. F. Kauffmann, remarked in the preface to *Harmonische Seelenlust* (Leipzig 1733) on differences in touch for his interline interludes in chorales:

> die Passagen, welche oben mit einem Bogen bedeckt seyn, nicht eben geschwind, wohl
> aber etwas gezogen, und gleichsam, wie mit dem Bogen auf der Violin, müssen heraus

* That Kuhnau's frontispiece shows all three instruments is of itself no more significant than is the array of instruments on contemporary French title-pages (e.g. Rameau, *Premier Livre*, Paris 1706).

† The *rondeau*, called 'Bergeries' in Couperin's Sixth Suite (*Second Livre*, c1717), was said by Daquin to be a work of Marchand except for the last couplet, which he regarded as feeble (cited in Pirro 1901). Probably the source, therefore, was not Couperin's second book, and the *Klavierbüchlein* did not change the notation?

gebracht werden; welche aber frey, und ohne solche Bogen oder Schleiffer stehen, die können so geschwind, als es die Umstände des Liedes zulassen, gemacht werden

the flourishes covered above with a curve must be performed not quickly but on the contrary somewhat drawn-out and even, as with the bow on a violin; but those which stand free, without such a curve or slur, can be done as quickly as the circumstances of the chorale allow.

From a typical passage it is difficult to see any difference in musical character between those phrases that are slurred and those that are not: the legato seems to be an 'ornament' applied freely, according to taste (Ex. 81).

Ex. 81   Kauffmann, 'Ich ruf zu dir'

[figures omitted]

The use of legato as a more general technique is more difficult to establish, although Forkel, partly drawing on C. P. E. Bach's keyboard *Versuch* and Quantz's flute *Versuch* (see *Dok* III p18), seems to have been trying to show that on all keyboard instruments the playing method of the Bachs was distinguished from that of others in having some such quality (David/Mendel 1966 pp307–8). At least, the middle path between too long a touch (keeping 'the keys down beyond their time') and too short ('as if the keys were burning hot') suggests some degree of legato, as does the *Obituary*'s claim that all the composer's fingers, including the thumb, were equally strong. The desire of the fortepiano period to see J. S. Bach as originator, autodidact and true German genius is understandable, but players will know that using the thumb does not by any means lead necessarily to a smooth legato; on the contrary, using the thumb in the counterpoint of the Inventions or *The 48* results in a *détaché* quality vital to the clarity of harpsichord and organ, particularly in the inner parts of contrapuntal music. But when Forkel discusses the 'open harmony' of the four-part chorales and uses such an example to show how J. S. Bach's organ texture differs from that of 'ordinary organists' ('getheilter Harmonie . . . gewöhn-

Ex. 82 (i)   (ii)

liche Organisten': 1802 ch.IV), is he not also implying that Ex. 82(i) is played more legato than Ex. 82 (ii)? In 1792, Gerber too spoke of J. S. Bach's 'excellent legato manner' ('vortrefliche gebundene Manier' – *Dok* III p473); but was this merely a reference to *durezza*-playing?

In the notation of J. S. Bach's organ works, four particular details suggest lines of approach: first, the implications of the few dots that are found there; secondly, the absence or presence of ties; thirdly, the probability that J. S. Bach's style of playing changed over the years; and fourthly, the care with which copies were made from about 1730 onwards.

Dots so rarely occur in any earlier source (primary or secondary copy) that it must be considered a sign of the special position held by the Six Sonatas – as Italianate sonatas written out in fair copy – that these pieces gradually admit more phrase-marks, including dots, as P 271 (autograph) and P 272 (W. F. Bach and A. M. Bach) proceed. The dots indicate not only *détaché* quavers (BWV 527.i) but also phrase-ends (BWV 530.ii in P 272), which in turn may indicate newer tendencies towards explicit phrasing after about 1730. That is, the dot marks the end of a phrase (the last note of a motif, whether actually slurred or not) and helps to make clear what motifs are conceived as distinct groups of notes. This is a way of using dots that is in principle different from the mere staccato dot familiar from later music. The staccato dot, however, does characterize the 'tendencies towards explicit phrasing after about 1730', as is suggested by the dots in the F major Toccata BWV 540 bb169–70 in the copy P 290 (C. P. E. Bach circle), for a cadence figure already heard in the movement. Presumably it was also played *détaché* on its first appearance in b81? Was C. P. E. Bach's copyist trying to show that in its emergence as a longer theme the figure became more marked, more detached (*marqué*)? – Ex. 83. Also, are the slurs in the Six Sonatas a sign that younger copyists added more as they copied? and (if so) did they do such things to remind the reader (the copyist himself in the first instance) of normal practices, or to suggest a new kind of interpretation (see Emery 1957 pp184, 187)? – reflecting a general tendency in the more

Ex. 83   BWV 540.i

empty-headed styles of the mid eighteenth century towards pernickety phrasings? If the general touch in keyboard-playing of the earlier eighteenth century was still somewhat *détaché*, then it seems the composer wrote in signs only to point out harmonic details such as appoggiaturas or accented passing-notes or *tierces coulées* or violin-like bowing-marks: Ex. 84. Since such harmonic details and such

Ex. 84

bowings do require a legato manner, is the purpose of the written-in marks not to indicate legato etc as such but to point out to the player what is happening harmonically? The distinction between these two is important, since it goes some way to explaining first why J. S. Bach is sparing with slurs and phrase-marks (bowing-marks) and secondly why it is that the younger copyists may have been using notation to different ends when they themselves added slurs.

The question is not only whether W. F. or A. M Bach had authority for adding all the slurs and dots in Ex. 85, but whether they were using slurs and dots for a dif-

Ex. 85   BWV 530.iii

ferent purpose from J. S. Bach – the slurs and dots (*détaché*? staccato? *staccatissimo*?) of a coming generation with different tastes. But the possibility that this is so should not be exaggerated: the G major Sonata is unusual – unique, even – in giving many signs that the composer too was moving towards the refined and clearly marked articulation of the mid eighteenth century. The slurs in Ex. 86(i) are in his old manner of 'harmonic slurs or bowing-marks', as suggested in the last paragraph; but the slurs in Ex. 86(ii) are more for touch, delicate shaping, refinement of detail, such as might be associated in the new chamber music of the period with violinists' bowing or flautists' tonguing.* It could certainly be thought that the

---

* This would be so whether or not one regarded the slurs of b14 and b15 as 'das Bogenvibrato der Streicher' ('the bowed vibrato of string-players' – Lohmann 1982 p191).

Ex. 86   BWV 530.i

(i)

(ii)

added slurs and dots in the third movement of this sonata (as in Ex. 86) were in keeping with the music itself (i.e. the new, rather *galant* chamber music of a violinistic cast) and hence that their composer was at least from time to time working in such nicely articulated idioms.

There still remain some questions, however. How staccato were J. S. Bach's dots? It is difficult to believe that anything more than a moderate *détaché* is required even in music of *c*1740: Ex. 87. Real staccato is not an effect for either organ or harpsi-

Ex. 87   BWV 677

chord. In the case of BWV 552.i, however, it certainly looks as if the composer intended the three themes, themselves related but contrasted (see Vol. I pp185–6), to be characterized by three quite different articulations: Ex. 88. The first of these is particularly interesting: the slurs indicate a marked dotted rhythm with a held dotted note – implying that without them the organist would have assumed they were short, as must often have been the case in French Overtures (Ex. 89). Such rests are very harpsichord-like.* The second of the BWV 552.i phrasings in Ex. 88

Ex. 88   BWV 552.i

---

* Judging by such an interpretation of slurs, the issue of whether J. S. Bach 'expected overdotting' in French rhythms is virtually irrelevant. The question is, rather, Are dotted notes played slurred or short? It should not be missed that when the dotted figures of BWV 552.i are leaping, the slur covers two beats not one.

Ex. 89   BWV 828.i

– the dots – obviously helps to distinguish the *galant* second subject from the *francese* first: the more staccato, the more *galant*, perhaps, with the bass pipes *quasi pizzicato*? The third theme of BWV 552.i, though unmarked, implies a traditional articulation in keeping with its traditional character: no legato and no marked staccato but a somewhat *détaché* manner of playing scale-patterns, perhaps pairing off the broken thirds.

Bearing in mind the kind of slurs found in (e.g.) the Six Sonatas as shown in Exx. 85 and 86, and the traditional seventeenth-century German keyboard slurs of Scheidt's *imitatio violistica* (see p217), two important questions for the player are: Did what would now be called phrase-marks grow out of – become extended forms of – string bowing-marks? and Were Scheidt's *violistica* slurs (and other short groupings suggested by 'old fingerings') typical of the first attempts at keyboard phrasing? His own description is as follows:

> Wo die Noten, wie allhier, zusammen gezogen seind, ist solches eine besondere art, gleich wie die Violisten mit dem Bogen schleiffen zu machen pflegen. Wie dann solche Manier bey fürnehmen Violisten Deutscher Nation, nicht ungebreuchlich, gibt auch auff gelindschlägigen Orgeln, Regalen, Clavicymbaln und Instrumenten, einen recht lieblichen und anmutigen *concentum*, derentwegen ich dann solche Manier mir selbsten gelieben lassen, und angewehnet.

> Where the notes, as here, are slurred together, such is a special style equal to the way viol-players like to make slide with the bow. As then such a manner, [which is] not unusual with the distinguished viol-players of Germany, also produces from organs, regals, harpsichords and spinets with easy touch a really lovely and agreeable *concentus*, so I have therefore allowed such a manner to please me and have applied it.*

If such slurs had become longer by the time of (e.g.) Leopold Mozart's *Versuch einer gründlichen Violinschule* (Augsburg 1756), where do the various kinds of melodic line in J. S. Bach's organ music fit in? It is striking that Leopold Mozart's sixteen ways of bowing a figure (ch.7) are shown by means of a phrase very like Scheidt's, and that he suggests successively longer phrases as ways of playing it, as in Ex. 90. Was J. S. Bach closer to Mozart or to Scheidt? In violin or keyboard music? Are there in any case many opportunities in J. S. Bach's organ music for the longer phrases of Mozart? – is not BWV 734 more likely to be cut up into many four-note patterns than sustained in one long line? The remarks on BWV 552.i above do not suggest that J. S. Bach in his later works moved much closer to the long phrase.† But a remark in J. G. Walther's *Praecepta* (1708) suggests not that

---

* The Latin version of the postscript says 'eaque saepissime utor', 'and make use of it very often'.

† From the point of view of the player, at least. Structural phraseology, the treatment of four-bar phrases and control over long stretches of music are not concerned in such problems of articulation.

Ex. 90

[cf. Scheidt's *imitatio violistica*]

Thuringian–Saxon organists of the period were restricted to the short, bowed groupings of notes, but merely that they did not write them in (see above, p197). If this implies that such organists were playing longer slurred phrases than their predecessors, it is possible to see the gradual changes in fingering techniques as part of the same move in about 1710 towards phrasing as it became familiar in the less contrapuntal styles of the later eighteenth century. An even use of fingers leads to the longer line.

Ties provide a second line of approach from the sources to questions of articulation. Copyists both omit ties between notes (e.g. BWV 574b in the Andreas-Bach-Buch) and add them (e.g. BWV 548.i in Mempell's manuscript Lpz MB MS 7) – omitting more often than adding. It is not only that in each case most sources show what is more correct, but that the composer seems to have distinguished carefully between a note that is suspended over to its resolution and a note that is repeated. Thus, in Ex. 91 (from BWV 548.i) the fact that the two d♯'s are accompanied by

Ex. 91   BWV 548.i

(autograph)   (copyist)

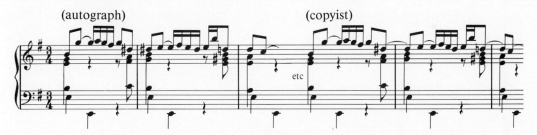

etc

detached inner parts duplicating the rhythms means that all the notes of the last quaver are detached and thus that Mempell's copyist is wrong. Such criteria are not infallible but are nevertheless suggestive. If all or most of the notes are tied – as in the massive suspensions of the Fantasia BWV 542.i – then it is clear that legato is correct: Ex. 92. But so it is equally in the Italianate idiom of the C minor Fugue BWV 574b where single parts are suspended, sometimes with the ties omitted or forgotten by the copyists. The player should appreciate that tying short notes over a strong beat has the effect of an accent followed by a diminuendo, providing the resolution is not obtrusively played; it is therefore only being true to the logic of the music in hand if the player adds ties elsewhere to imply the fall at the end of a phrase. The Toccata in D minor BWV 538.i provides good examples of the maturing

Ex. 92   BWV 542.i

Bach's attitude towards tied notes, *brisé* and (semi-) sustained chords, especially when compared with an earlier piece such as the E minor Praeludium BWV 533.i where only one section includes any tied notes at all – i.e., it is outside the *Affekt* of the others.*

Revisions or supposed revisions to earlier works provide a third line of approach to problems of articulation, though one that is very conjectural in most cases (see above, remarks on BWV 536). Perhaps J. S. Bach was reflecting a general eighteenth-century move towards a smoother touch (unless a theme was *détaché* by design) in at least a few works. Even to the eye, the 'additions' to the C major Prelude BWV 545a as they appear in the version BWV 545 add a sostenuto element that is not at all pronounced in the earlier version. But the main motif of the piece is also written more sostenuto (BWV 545a b1, BWV 545 b4), as too seems to be the case in another mature work using a similar theme, the C major Prelude, *The 48* Bk II (see Vol. I p141). Other examples can be found: a particularly instructive one is the alteration made by the composer in the G major Prelude BWV 541 (*NBA* IV/5 p148 and *KB* p679) – Ex. 93. Rather than suggesting that earlier music be interpreted in this way, however, such an example would confirm the idea that tastes in such details changed and that both styles are valid. Conversely, when in mature copies there are still so few articulation signs (e.g. the B minor Prelude and Fugue BWV 544), the

Ex. 93   BWV 541.i
'early'

'late'

* Thus it could be that the ties suggested for the fugue in *NBA* IV/5 p93 are disguising the tie-less nature both of the work as a whole (cf. the absence of ties in certain sources *ibid KB* pp388–9) and more generally for the keyboard styles that can be associated with the young Bach.

reason could well be that the composer saw them as not belonging to the idiom – a relatively conservative, 'German' organ idiom – of the piece concerned. It does look as if traditional German organ idioms, such as are represented by the third (but not the first or second) of the themes in the E flat Prelude (Ex. 88), were marked neither by particular slurrings nor by startling staccato dots.

Mature copies and engravings (the latter in particular) offer the player many important hints on slurs and dots. Slurs begin to appear as style-indicators warning the player that the movement concerned requires a touch specific to that moment. The slurs of BWV 552.i have already been commented on; a similar point could be made about the Sarabande of the G major Partita, where the slur clearly tells the player not to take off the second beat and to lean on the dotted notes: Ex. 94. In this

Ex. 94   BWV 829.iv (Sarabande)

connection, it is interesting that the *francese* fugue of the *Art of Fugue* does not have its groups slurred* but that the dotted-note countersubject to Contrapunctus II does. Slurs are also absent from the scales of the G major Partita's Praeambulum – a common enough absence, and yet perhaps significant here in that rather than being built up of long smooth scales the Praeambulum plays with scale-fragments. The distinction between these two is most important for the player. It is even possible that this Praeambulum is meant to bring out a broken-up phrasing when the lines are fingered as (conjecturally) in Ex. 95.

But slurs are found in two other interesting moments in the *Art of Fugue*. In the Canon *alla duodecima* the whole subject is slurred: some slurs are ambiguous,† but the intention – since by nature groups of *six* would be slurred – certainly seems to be

Ex. 95   BWV 829.i

* Perhaps the *francese* style by definition required dotted notes to be short and very *détaché* (see remarks on the Ouverture to the D major Partita, Ex. 89 above); but it is always possible that in the case of the *Art of Fugue* the French rhythms, being the result of the composer's revisions to a movement originally undotted (evident in the autograph P 200), were not fair-copied by the composer and thus were not finalized in notation.
† *BG* 25.i (p83) plausibly makes slurs cover all notes in a group.

Ex. 96

[or]

to make virtually the whole subject legato: Ex. 96. In the Canon *per augmenta-tionem*, slurs (looking like bowing-marks) cover chromatic phrases, both quavers and semiquavers. Does this suggest that all chromatic lines are by nature smooth? Is it not true that chromatic moments in the works of older composers (e.g. the penultimate sections of chorale-fantasias such as Buxtehude's 'Gelobet seist du' and Bruhns's 'Nun komm, der Heiden Heiland') are aptly coloured by an over-lapping legato, as too would be the chromatic-fourth countersubject to the melody of 'Das alte Jahr' BWV 614?

But such speculation is merely another demonstration of the chief problem offered by such late works as the *Art of Fugue*: does the notation express a conven-tion that was old and implicit, or establish a convention that is new and original? Earlier examples of slurring are also bound to the *figurae* in hand and do not appear arbitrary. The copies of the Passacaglia, though not autograph, usually agree to mark the new *figura* of bb104ff with a slur: Ex. 97. The reason must be

Ex. 97   BWV 582

that, despite appearances, this is the first entry in the work of a *figura* that begins on the beat and not off it (see Vol. I p260). The scale-passage from b80 could then be supposed to require a marking of the little off-beat *figurae* from which it is made (Ex. 98), though in the tact with which this is done lies the challenge to the player. It is possible that an organist of c1710 would understand that the distribution between hands implied in the notation at bb120ff leads to a marked pairing of the notes, without the legato which later organists took as read: Ex. 99.

Ex. 98   BWV 582

Ex. 99   BWV 582

Dots in the engravings offer a simpler picture. The characterization implicit in BWV 552.i has been referred to; in *Clavierübung III*, the *Musical Offering* and the *Art of Fugue* dots occur in particular for contrapuntal purposes, i.e. to mark the contrapuntal lines from each other, giving them an identity and enriching the counterpoint. The countersubject of the Ricercar *a 3*, the second half of the Canon *all'ottava*, the themes in BWV 677, 682 and 804 (and certain fugues in *The 48* Bk II) provide varied illustrations: Ex. 100. All are suggestive. The Ricercar suggests that

Ex. 100

plain countersubjects are best played *détaché et marqué*; but how far BWV 682 or 677 indicates a way to play figures that are familiar throughout the repertory (triplets in the first, a well-known phrase in the second – cf. BWV 547.ii) is very uncertain. Both pinpoint the big unknown: How far is the player justified in interpreting older music in the light of more recent notation? Arguing from the absence of indications can be pointless, and – to take one example – triplets must often have been slurred, just as they must often have been *détaché*: Ex. 101. Certainly in the

Ex. 101

earlier variation techniques it might well not have been a burning issue which way they were taken, so long as they were marked or given character in some way. The same is true of dactyl figures. But at least in one late example the absence of a *détaché* dot does suggest that the touch changes at that point: Ex. 102(i). That is to

Ex. 102 BWV 1079.i

(i)   **(ii)**

say, the countersubject crotchets are short, while the characteristic dactyl rhythm is slurred as in Ex. 102(ii). Logically, therefore, all the dactyls in the Ricercar *a 3* could be played in this way, to mark the contrapuntal identity of the different lines.* Was this the general aim of articulation for J. S. Bach?

---

24. Fingering

Closely related to the question of articulation is that of fingering, a subject which is not only better studied now than in Spitta's day but one which every player feels he understands at least in part, based on experience of the music itself. Already in the *Obituary*, the authors tried to sum up the composer's contribution (*Dok* III p88):

> Alle Finger waren bey ihm gleich geübt; Alle waren zu der feinsten Reinigkeit in der Ausführung gleich geschickt. Er hatte sich so eine bequeme Fingersetzung ausgesonnen, dass es ihm nicht schwer fiel, die grössten Schwierigkeiten mit der fliessendesten Leichtigkeit vorzutragen. Vor ihm hatten die berühmtesten Clavieristen in Deutschland und andern Ländern, dem Daumen wenig zu schaffen gemacht. Desto besser wusste er ihn zu gebrauchen.

> With him all fingers were used equally; all were adapted equally to the finest accuracy in performance. He had thought out for himself so comfortable a fingering that he did not find it hard to encompass the greatest difficulties with the most fluent ease. Before him, the most renowned keyboard-players in Germany and other countries had made little use of the thumb. All the better did he know how to use it.

On the basis of this, and referring (without acknowledgment) to further details taken from Quantz (see below, p214), Forkel devoted the whole of his ch.III and parts of ch.IV to the composer's keyboard techniques. His pupil F. C. Griepenkerl followed in his footsteps, evidently regarding C. P. E. Bach's *Versuch* as conveying his father's fingering; he also thought certain pieces had been written by J. S. Bach to further a player's fingering technique. For example, the Two-part Invention in E flat gave practice for thumb and little finger on the sharps/flats (preface to Peters edn of the Chromatic Fantasia BWV 903 in 1820). Later still, Spitta (II pp645–52) attempted to put the fingering in a context, not least in connection with François Couperin, whose method was already recommended by Marpurg in 1750 on the grounds that 'the learned Bachs' valued it (*Dok* III p4). None of these early Bach commentators, however, is free of preoccupations from his own period or area, and none is of more than marginal use in an attempt to reconstruct Bach's techniques.

Forkel not only listed the attributes – unconstrained fingers, beautiful touch, clarity and precision, new systems of fingering, all fingers equally adept, ability in all keys – but implied that the composer's facility in these respects dates from at least the Weimar years (whence the setting for Forkel's anecdote about Bach's ability to play anything at sight). It would be more characteristic of $c1800$ (as in Forkel's remarks) than of $c1750$ (as in the *Obituary*'s) to think that the composer's attributes as a player were the same throughout his life: to ensuing generations it

---

* Such arguments are not affected by the likelihood that the Ricercar *a 3* is fortepiano music (suggested by the opening tessitura, the compass to d''' as in Silbermann's pianos in Potsdam, and the swelling triplets of the episodes). No slurs or dots in Bach sources have yet been identified as evidence that he distinguished organ, harpsichord, clavichord and piano from each other in this respect.

must have become increasingly hard to distinguish between the Weimar and the Leipzig periods, especially in such technical matters as fingering. That Couperin's *L'Art de toucher le Clavecin* (1717) can scarcely have been available in Weimar while J. S. Bach was there would not affect Forkel, since he understood from C. P. E. Bach's *Versuch* that Couperin's fingering method was inferior.* In any case, the tenor of both the *Obituary* and Forkel is not only that J. S. Bach – as coming from the stock of 'honourable Thuringians satisfied with their fatherland' ('diese ehrlichen Thüringer mit ihrem Vaterlande . . . zufrieden': *Dok* III p81) – was superior to foreign players, but that his skill had come from his own abilities and from hard work assimilating what it could. But how many of the attributes listed by the *Obituary* and Forkel could have dated from the period before Leipzig? Facility in all twenty-four keys? If so, on the organ or only on the harpsichord? (The *Obituary* refers to tuning harpsichords in this connection.) With the thumb? If so, why should the *Obituary* still find it a matter worthy of comment? In order to claim the importance and originality of the composer's contribution?

Several features of the Bach technique as described in these sources were already implied in the preface to J.-P. Rameau's *Pièces de Clavecin* (Paris 1724). Just as Forkel (ch. III) speaks of all fingers bent and equally ready over the keys, so Rameau describes the positioning as follows:

> Le 1. & le 5. se trouvant sur le bord des touches, engagent à courber les autres doigts, pour qu'ils puissent se trouver également sur le bord des touches . . . on ne doit plus ni les alonger, ni les arondir d'avantage (p4)

> The first and fifth fingers, finding themselves at the [front] edge of the keys, make the other fingers curve, so that they can likewise find themselves at the edge of the keys . . . one should not then straighten nor curve them any further.

J. S. Bach is reported by Forkel and probably also by Kirnberger (*Dok* III p215) as playing with such facility that his finger-motion was slight enough to be barely perceptible – with motion only from the first joint, while the hand remained still. Rameau's advice on this matter is:

> Le mouvement des doigts se prend à leur racine . . . & jamais ailleurs . . . sans qu'aucun autre doigt, ni sans que la main fassent pour lors le moindre mouvement

> The movement of the fingers takes place at their root [first joint] and never anywhere else . . . without any other finger or the hand [as a whole] at that moment making the slightest movement.

Rameau also describes use of the thumb. Although experience teaches any player that many a Bach fugue calls for particular versatility from both thumb and fifth finger, the general points made by the *Obituary* and Forkel concerning the thumb are implied by Rameau's recommendation for it:

> Pour continuer un *roulement* plus étendu . . . il n'y a qu'à s'accoutumer à passer le 1. par-dessous tel autre doigt que l'on veut, & à passer l'un de ces autres doigts par-dessus le 1. Cette maniere est excellente, sur-tout quand il s'y rencontre des *Dièzes* ou des Bemols (p5).

> To continue a more extensive *roulement* [= fast scale passage] . . . one need only accustom oneself to passing the thumb under whichever finger one wishes, and to passing one of the other fingers above the thumb. This method is excellent, particularly when one comes across sharps and flats.

* C.P.E. Bach, however, criticized Couperin only for under-using the thumb at such moments as finger-replacement, i.e. when a finger is changed on a held note (1753 I p45).

The last remark may also hint at C. P. E. Bach's point (see below) that the thumb was more necessary for the remote keys then becoming more familiar. But while Rameau as a harmonic theorist may have been familiar to Marpurg and others, as a player and practical teacher he does not seem to have been a great influence, even on writers of the Forkel period. Yet Forkel knew enough Rameau to condemn his keyboard music as 'schoolboy *Exercitia*' (*Dok* III pp328–9), and it is possible that Rameau's prefaces had some influence on the way he and others described the Bach technique.

It was obviously in C. P. E. Bach's own interest to claim for himself a kind of apostolic succession, not least as Marpurg had also done so in his keyboard tutor (see *Dok* III p4). C. P. E. Bach's claim, supported by Kirnberger (*Dok* III pp344–5), was as follows:

> [J. S. Bach] wurde . . . genöthiget, einen weit vollkommnern Gebrauch der Finger sich auszudencken, besonders den Daumen, welcher ausser andern guten Diensten haupt-sächlich in den schweren Tonarten gantz unentbehrlich ist, so zu gebrauchen . . .
>
> Da diese neue Art der Fingersetzung so beschaffen ist, dass man damit alles mögliche zur bestimmen Zeit leicht herausbringen kann, so lege ich solche hier zum Grunde (1715 p17).
>
> [J. S. Bach] was obliged to think out a far more complete use of the fingers, and especially to make such use of the thumb, which apart from its other good services is quite indispensable, chiefly in the difficult keys . . .
>
> As this new kind of fingering is so constituted that with it one can easily bring out at the right time everything that is possible, I am taking it here as the foundation.

The last remark is concerned not with 'bringing out' parts in a contrapuntal texture but with a virtuoso control of the whole of the music – something which J. S. Bach is praised for. But it is not immediately clear why the thumb should be so par-ticularly useful 'in the difficult keys', nor for what period in his father's life such comments were useful, since presumably he did not at first play in such keys.* Turning the thumb under, as described in the *Versuch* for passages beyond five notes, is necessary in both easy and 'difficult' keys; in difficult keys the thumb is more likely to be on weaker notes (leading notes etc) if it is placed on the naturals, and it is then 4 or 5 that requires strength and versatility.

Quantz fits J. S. Bach more into the tradition of striving after more tasteful play-ing, a tradition that had motivated (better) German players since the middle of the seventeenth century. Such players were Froberger and Pachelbel as harpsichordists, Reincken, Buxtehude and Bruhns as organists (1752 p329):

> Absonderlich wurde die Kunst die Orgel zu spielen, welche man grossen Theils von den Niederländern empfangen hatte, um diese Zeit schon, von den obengenannten und einigen andern geschickten Männern, sehr weit getrieben. Endlich hat sie der bewundernswürdige Johann Sebastian Bach, in den neuern Zeiten, zu ihrer grössten Vollkommenheit gebracht.

> In particular the art of playing the organ, which had been largely received from the Netherlanders, was very much furthered at this time by those mentioned above and by some other clever men. Ultimately the admirable Johann Sebastian Bach brought it to its greatest perfection in more recent times.

---

* For the period's interest in playing in or modulating to distant keys, see notes on the Labyrinth BWV 591 in Vol. I, and below p270. In his tutor of 1750, Marpurg gave a left-hand fingering exercise passing through the twelve major keys.

Perhaps Quantz (and Forkel, copying him) was correct to see the playing of J. S. Bach as characterized by a drawing-in of the fingertips towards the player as the finger leaves the key, which he plays on the 'foremost part' (Quantz 1752 p232). C. P. E. Bach implies that this is the correct manner (1753 pp17ff), but the whole of his first chapter is devoted to explaining that

> Weil jeder neue Gedanke fast seine eigene Fingersetzung hat, so folgt, dass die heutige Art du denken, so weit sie sich von der in vorigen Zeiten unterscheidet, auch eine neue Applicatur einführen müsste.

> Because every new idea has its own fingering, so it follows that the present-day kind of musical idea, as far as it is different from that of previous times, must also introduce a new method of performance.

This sounds very much as if C. P. E. Bach saw fingering to be related to *Figuren*: that is, each *figura* has its own character and hence its own idiomatic fingering. Fingering had the nature of a set formula rather than the thorough versatility required of later players. But in any case, new fingering and touch are not applicable to the music of the Weimar period, because

> unsere Verfahren, welche sich überhaupt mehr mit der Harmonie als Melodie abgaben, spielten meistentheils vollstimmig.

> our predecessors, generally occupied more with harmony than melody, played mostly in full parts.

C. P. E. Bach implies on the one hand that such 'full-part' music as (e.g.) the Capriccio in B flat BWV 992 does not require his new fingering, and on the other that this new fingering is conceived more for melodies than for counterpoint – especially in the more distant of the twenty-four keys (*ibid*), which do not concern the organ. It can easily be imagined that J. S. Bach had exceptional skill, that he worked in all twenty-four keys at least on paper and from *c*1720 at the latest, that throughout his life he invented unusual figuration, and finally that he kept in touch with new melodic tastes of the *style galant* music for harpsichord and clavichord: nevertheless, the picture as left by his younger contemporaries cannot be regarded as necessarily valid either for his earlier keyboard music in general or for his organ music in particular.

One particular problem concerns scales. It is now generally assumed not only that fingering scales indicates general points about fingering, but that each player learns by these means how to play. C. P. E. Bach deals with the octave scales of all twenty-four keys in the first chapter of his *Versuch* and thus shows signs of the pedagogic movement that was to result in the practising of multi-octave scales by all learners of keyboard instruments over at least the last century and a half. Thus it is reasonable to assume that when he gives three different fingerings for C major they should produce a similar effect, i.e. one of even touch modified by neither phrasing nor expression: Ex. 103. But concerning the situation in 1715, three things in particular are still very uncertain: that scales as such were ever practised, that the evenness required of them in later periods was already desired at that period, and that such evenness (though it may have been easier in some keys) was characteristic of all keys. If the 12343434 fingering was meant to produce an even line by means of controlled fingers, one can imagine this as a characteristic of scales as scales, not of

Ex. 103   C. P. E. Bach, *Versuch*

music. If such a scale-like pattern occurred as a contrapuntal motif – as in the *Orgelbüchlein* chorale BWV 644 –it could well be that 3434 fingering resulted in a degree of pairing. Scales are scales, exercises are exercises, and an organ chorale that uses elements of both is less regular than either.

Even C. P. E. Bach's examples showing how the C major fingering may be applied suggest that some degree of 'interest' or 'unevenness' should be given to the phrases: Ex. 104. Had either phrase been meant to be infallibly smooth, the thumbs could have been used more, and no doubt they would have been by Czerny. Conversely, when they are used for a longer phrase, the on-beat thumb naturally produces some degree of 'grouping': Ex. 105. The slurs are conjectural; but in all

Ex. 104

Ex. 105

references to the fingerings of C. P. E. Bach or Kirnberger today, the performer should ask himself to which of J. S. Bach's work periods the remarks might have the most application, what scales have to do with music in *c*1715, whether there is a pattern of notes (*figurae*) behind the passage of music concerned, whether he is implicitly assuming that articulation results from using the weak fingers of either hand. The last is a difficult point; but in such an early instance as Ex. 106 the conjectural fingering that has been added would produce strong main beats lost in the fluent style admired at later periods. The earliest known phrasing, Scheidt's *imitatio violistica*, also emphasizes the main beats. In Ex. 107, one can suppose by

Ex. 106   J. P. Sweelinck, 'Ons Vader in hemelrijck' (Var. 3), with conjectural fingering

considering the nature of semiquaver figures that the aim of the slurs is to bring out the main beats in a context of longer phrases (previous bars) and shorter, cadential phrases (following bars). The question is therefore not so much 'What does "old fingering" suggest for such lines?' as 'Against a background of unsmooth scale-fingerings, how can the nature of the note-pattern (*figura*) be faithfully conveyed?' Although it lies outside present considerations, it may be doubted whether any approach very different from this is implied in the music of C. P. E. Bach or even of Mozart.

Ex. 107   S. Scheidt, 'Vater unser im Himmelreich' (*Vers* 9), with added slurs (bb13, 14)

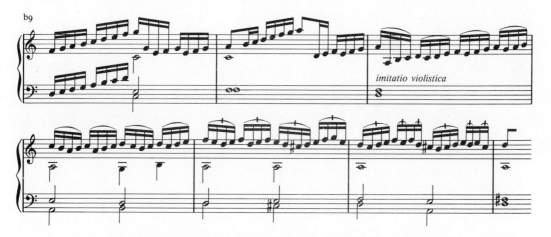

Quantz's reference to 'the Netherlanders' accords with the notion of keyboard history implied by Mattheson's reporting that Scheidemann and J. Praetorius fell within the Sweelinck tradition (1740 pp328–9). Sweelinck, it seems, had

> eine gantz eigene Fingerführung, die sonst ungewöhnlich, aber sehr gut war

> a kind of fingering all his own, otherwise unfamiliar but very good.

Scheidemann learnt how to compose according to the notion of the instrument; his pieces 'allow themselves to be played with ease' and are generally 'more cheerful and good-humoured' ('liessen sich leicht spielen . . . munter und aufgeräumt') than those of J. Praetorius, because he (Scheidemann) was a more cheerful person. Though he develops the idea no further, Mattheson has hit on the important fact that idiomatically conceived keyboard music is 'easy to play', if not in any super-ficial sense of the phrase. Had C. P. E. Bach applied his scale-fingerings to Scheide-mann's coloratura lines and capricious melodies, he would have lost much of the nature that such music had when played with earlier techniques, accurate and fluid though those lines might have become in his hands.

Exactly what those 'earlier techniques' involved is far less clear than confident assertions often made today suggest. Clues lie less in what theorists say or in what a very few manuscript sources may suggest than in the nature of the lines and pat-terns. A *suspirans*, for example, begins off the beat even in the longer phrases it leads to (see notes to the fugues BWV 540 and 733), and it would be natural to finger the lines in such a way as to show this. Almost no fingerings are given in the sources of Bach's organ music, though perhaps the occasional indication distributing certain scale-passages between the hands also helps the player to observe the patterns from which such lines are made. This distribution implies that all fingers were not used equally: Ex. 108. The authority for the signs is uncertain (e.g. Oley's

Ex. 108   BWV 535.i

P 1097 – see *NBA* IV/5–6 *KB* p449), but both of the two sources 'probably originated in Bach's household' (*ibid* p444). However one may speculate on the use of the thumb later, in bb72–3, it is difficult to see that 'the most fluent ease' (if taken to mean an unbroken smoothness) is the purpose behind distributing the hands in this manner – rather, the player must feel the notes to be paired in some or other degree. A certain rhetorical *effort* is given to the music in this way. This would be so even if players assumed that the aim of their practice or skill was to eliminate uneven playing. It is very unlikely that, for example, the opening arpeggios of the charming A major Prelude BWV 536 are meant to be played uniformly under one legato line. Unfortunately, sources do not always show the (or an) original distribution of hands in passage-work, but where they do (as in the G minor Prelude BWV 535) modern editions obviously ought to preserve it. As Ex. 95 shows, continuous lines were distributed between the two hands even in the most sophisticated music.

The question then is: Do later lines of a similar kind require a similar distribution (Ex. 109(i))? Also, have the earlier pieces known only from later sources lost any such original distribution (Ex. 109(ii))? Should such lines be divided in the

Ex. 109   **(i)** BWV 542.i

(ii) BWV 564.i (in P 803 *c*1729)

manner of BWV 535 (see above), and if so, does such division imply a broken phraseology not understood in periods when evenness and fluent ease are admired? In any case, do such examples as those in Exx. 108 and 109 imply an important, even crucial, element in early Bach fingering and that of his predecessors – namely that the German keyboard-players (not least since they were also generally string-players) thought in terms of shifting hand-positions? What was familiar to a violinist must also have been familiar to organists *c*1700: passages (especially sequences and successive *figurae*) could be fingered by a hand shifting in position, rather than changing its shape by means of a versatile thumb and small finger. If this were so, it would help to explain the changes in attitude sought or summarized by Rameau and after him C. P. E. Bach, and would confirm that during the lifetime of J. S. Bach there was a changing technique amongst players. However, the principle of hand-shifting can also be seen in mature music of J. S. Bach, such as bb162–7 in the left hand of the Ricercar *a 3* of the *Musical Offering*.*

Arguments from the absence of signs are pointless; but it is clear from the presence of signs (slurs in Ex. 110) that at certain times the player is to finger in such

Ex. 110

a way as to keep the line unbroken. Was the norm then a more broken line, with many paired notes, versatile use of fingers 3 and 4 (rh) and a *détaché* manner for most patterns? When Adlung told of J. S. Bach playing for him Marchand's suites of 1718

> nach seiner Art, das ist, sehr flüchtig und künstlich (*Dok* III p125)

> in his own way, that is, with volatility [fluency?] and artistry

or when Forkel reported that

> bey der Ausführung seiner eigenen Stücke nahm er das Tempo gewöhnlich sehr lebhaft, wusste aber ausser dieser Lebhaftigkeit noch so viele Mannigfaltigkeit in seinen Vortrag zu bringen, dass jedes Stück unter seiner Hand gleichsam wie eine Rede sprach (1802 ch.III)

> in the performance of his own pieces he usually took a very lively tempo, but in addition to this liveliness he knew how to bring into his delivery such a many-sidedness that each piece spoke under his hand exactly like a speech

they are at least implying that in his later years he varied his touch according to the style of the piece. Fingering serves such distinctions. For example, assuming that in semiquaver lines no phrased group ought to be marked with undue force, does the

---

* That a texture merely of three parts can still require such shifting is a useful reminder of the composer's prime interest in contrapuntal thought rather than in keyboard technique as such.

last bar of BWV 632 (here with notes tied not slurred) suggest that the triadic figure is phrased off the beat throughout the piece (Ex. 111)? Either way, how legato are

Ex. 111   BWV 632

the notes within the slur? Given that smooth scales (especially those that pass beyond an octave or so) belong more to the *galant* period, does Walther's fingering in P 801 for one awkward scale-line in the Albinoni Fugue BWV 951 carry the im-

Ex. 112   BWV 951

plication that the semiquavers are to be paired (Ex. 112)? Walther's fingering for some of his own music (including his copy of three movements of 'Allein Gott' published without fingerings in 1738) suggests various principles – Ex. 113:

> versatile use of thumb (i) (ii)
> but not the same finger on adjacent notes – hence the strange fingering of (iii)
> some deliberate pairing, by means of a fingering that could be easily replaced by the simpler 5432 or 4321 (iv)

From Walther's incomplete and apparently obscure fingerings (made mostly for certain copies in the MS Kö 15839), it looks as if the grouping of smaller notes in twos or fours depended on the nature of the patterns. Neither aims at smoothness.

It is, however, a great unknown of early systems whether or how far paired fingerings actually imply phrasing: does 3434 suggest Ex. 114? Or was the whole point of proficiency to smooth out irregularities? In general, the latter must have been the aim; and we may imagine a process of gradual evolution in which slurred pairs, *détaché* lines, short figures, cross-rhythms, grouped semiquavers etc merged by degrees into the long-phrased legato. Perhaps in this as in other respects the early decades of the eighteenth century made the period of greatest change.

That at least is the implication behind the difference in fingering between the *Applicatio* BWV 994 of the *Klavierbüchlein für W. F. Bach* (written or copied c1720 – *NBA* v/5 *KB* p63) and the 'modern' and more complex texture of the C major Prelude BWV 870a (in J. C. Vogler's MS P 1089). Uncertainty arises from two

Ex. 113   **(i)** 'Allein Gott' *Vers* 1

(ii) 'Allein Gott' *Vers* 2

(iii) 'Allein Gott' *Vers* 5

(iv) 'Wir glauben' *Vers* 2

Ex. 114

unanswerable questions: Does Vogler's copy represent the composer's own method? and Do the fingerings imply pairings (Ex. 115)? Such fingering for the fugue results in a broken-up semiquaver line, although a more even effect is easier for the right hand in the prelude. The awkwardness of fingering in P 1089 makes it difficult to see as authentic. For one thing, it seems generally to favour the 4 and 5 of each hand less than the composer's own fingering in the *Applicatio*, where already in the second bar the rh needs a fine command of 543 in order to play the ornament: Ex. 116. Not for the first time in theory books or tutors, this little piece gives no advice on the fingering of ornaments, which are quite the most difficult thing in the movement. Does this suggest that they were optional (played only when feasible) or that they were fingered as best one could? Either way, Vogler's fingerings do not suggest how versatile must have been Bach's use of 543, and the problem of ornaments remains. For example, a not dissimilar point arises from J. G. Preller's copy of the Canzona BWV 588, where it is unclear whether the fingering 45 (rh) – whatever its authority – indicates a change of finger on the long note or

Ex. 115 BWV 870a.i Prelude

BWV 870a.ii 'Fughetta'

Ex. 116 BWV 994

the fingering for the previous ornament (the *accent*): Ex. 117. Both the *Applicatio* and Preller's copy of the Canzona need a good 4 and 5 in both hands, however versatile the thumb needs to be for the inner lines. Judging by them both, the reports that J. S. Bach called for each finger to be reliable refers as much to the fifth finger as to the thumb.

Ex. 117 BWV 588

The *Applicatio* and the Canzona also imply *non legato* in their lines – in particular the paired fingerings (both hands), the $\frac{2}{4}$ thirds and (most suggestive of all) the consecutive 55 for discord-and-resolution (appoggiatura in the *Applicatio* b4, suspension in the Canzona bb27–8 lh). Such fingering must suggest that the notes in question are not slurred, and so must contradict the French-inspired 'sensitivity' of touch that has come to be associated with keyboard-playing in recent times. It also suggests that when the composer does call for slurred pairs of notes – as in the dragging motif in the chorale BWV 618 or *Goldberg Variation* 15 – a specific effect is wanted, one otherwise not usual. It is certainly not easy to resolve a suspension smoothly (i.e. strong–weak) by using the same finger for both notes.

While the *Applicatio* served the young W. F. Bach as a model piece for scale-like fingerings, so the G minor Praeambulum BWV 930 in the same album gives careful fingering for broken chords. Again it is clear that the 345 part of the hand must be reliable and that a 'modern' orientation around 1 or 3 is not characteristic of the composer's fingering in the period c1720: Ex. 118. In J. C. Vogler's copy of the

Ex. 118   BWV 930

C major Prelude BWV 870a, a greater variety of figuration, now scale-like, now broken chords, makes the fingering of great interest, not least as it may have implications for the C major organ Prelude BWV 545/545a. It is difficult to see quite why Vogler fingered some passages in the way he did – for instance, at points marked *

Ex. 119   BWV 870a.i

in Ex. 119. There seem to be three principles here: versatile 5 for the rh and versatile 1 for the lh; the avoidance of stretches where possible; and never using the same finger for two consecutive notes. It is striking that all three principles tend to contradict 'inevitable' phrasings. Were they fingerings for a small hand? For example, a more natural fingering for the three excerpts in Ex. 119 would be as in Ex. 120.

Ex. 120

Each of the fingerings makes possible some degree or other of articulation or phrasing implied by the motifs themselves (Ex. 121), but neither of itself necessarily leads to it. The crucial questions remain: Do the fingerings imply articula-

Ex. 121

tion; and, whether they do or not, how marked should any articulation be in such music? No answer to such questions can ever be more than conjectural; but the semiquaver lines of the C major Prelude and Fugue BWV 870a are made up so inventively from their motifs that it is impossible to believe that an even, unmarked, uninterrupted flow came naturally to players. The fact that the prelude's semiquaver lines are made up in a way quite distinct from those of the fugue is itself a reason to suppose that some distinction must have been made by the player. His playing shows the figural make-up of the movements.

In addition to what might be suggested by theorists on one hand and by the music on the other, the gradual development of keyboards with longer keys must be relevant.† The length of the natural key in front of the sharp and the length overall from front to back of the natural both have a bearing on fingering and touch, and the development of the keyboard suggests that both were smoother in 1775 than in 1675. No doubt the 'great men' heard by J. S. Bach in his youth who used the thumb only for big stretches (C. P. E. Bach – *Dok* III p23) were playing on shorter keys than were usual in 1753. J. F. Agricola reported that J. S. Bach liked 'short keys' for the reason that

† In the absence of any thorough study yet made of this detail, I have preferred not to give more or less random examples or key-lengths. As with clavichords (see J. H. van der Meer, 'The Dating of German Clavichords', *The Organ Yearbook* 6 (1975) p106), no single line of development in this respect can be traced, and yet without doubt keys generally became longer between 1675 and 1775.

kann der Spielende, wenn die Claviere kurz sind, mit viel mehr Bequemlichkeit von einem auf das andere kommen (Adlung 1768 II pp23-4)

if the keys are short the player can pass from one keyboard to another with much more comfort

– which may or may not be the same point being made by Marpurg (1758 p500 – quoting something Agricola told him?) when he claimed that Silbermann organs were 'very comfortable to play' ('zum Spielen sehr bequem'), not least because of the short keys.* Perhaps by 1768 Agricola was influenced by his French interests when he added that with short keys the organist

kann gerade sitzen bleiben, wenn er auch auf dem vierten oder gar fünften Claviere spielen will

can stay well and truly seated when he wishes to play on the fourth or even fifth manual

for playing up there was seldom if ever required by J. S. Bach. But Agricola also implies that Bach liked short keys for two other reasons: even on three-manual organs, long keys made it uncomfortable to play for any length of time on the top manual; and any organist who is 'used to correct fingering' ('einer richtigen Fingersetzung gewohnt') knows that he need not stretch out a finger straight, so why should he need long keys?†

---

25. Ornaments

Questions concerning ornaments in J. S. Bach's organ music centre on three particular areas: What is meant by a certain sign? Who wrote it? and Should ornaments be played when not notated? As far as tabulating what the theorists say (or seem to say) is concerned, the English-language reader in particular has been well served during this century. Not only have books listed the signs and given interpretation of them but every author has attempted to understand the spirit rather than the letter of the law, each pointing out in one way or another that 'contrary to widely held opinion, there are for Bach no rules that present us with easy solutions for the realization of his symbols' (Neumann 1978 p124). Like other technical areas of musical study, ornamentation is a subject that attracts a certain kind of evangelistic pedantry, and few authors have wholly escaped the tendency to overstate. Add to that the impossibility of conveying by conventional musical notation the character of any ornament played on any instrument whatsoever, and it gradually becomes clear to the player that what he must understand is the nature of his instrument and of keyboard touch. Ornaments are not abbreviations but guides

---

* The author of the note also regrets the longer keys of newer organs, but it is striking that Silbermann kept to the some dimensions over a working life of forty years: naturals c22 × 120 mm, sharps c10 × 82 mm (Dähnert 1953 p77).

† Agricola (in a footnote in Adlung 1768 II p24) also recommends that on an organ with three or more manuals the lowest manual and a half should protrude from the organ front (as at St Thomas and St Nikolai, Leipzig – after recent rebuilds?) and so make it possible for the organist to play more than a few long notes on the pedal when he is reaching forward to play on the top manual. Does this imply that on older organs the pedal barely accompanied manual III? Were third manuals traditionally associated with continuo-playing, without pedals?

towards achieving the kind of expressiveness or gesture native to the composer or *genre* in question. Similar points can be made about phrasing, articulation, rubato, registration; and in each case the notation, whatever its source, gives the player unsufficient information. However well it is done, to play an ornament on the organ only when it can be found notated in one source or another is unlikely to reflect the expectations of J. S. Bach.*

The question 'What is meant by a certain sign?' is the one that has received most attention. The composer himself, in the *Klavierbüchlein für W. F. Bach*, set out thirteen signs in a table (reproduced in *NBA* v/5) which has been taken as a basis for study (e.g. Emery 1953), related in general to d'Anglebert and Couperin (Klotz 1969a) and accused of being 'more of a hindrance than a help' (Neumann 1978 p126), but which so far has not been placed thoroughly in its context with other relevant tables. These include that in the Möller MS (one based on that in Dieupart's *Six Suittes de Clavessin*, Amsterdam *c*1702), that in the Andreas-Bach-Buch ('Marques et demonstration des agréments'), and the copy of d'Anglebert's *table* made by J. S. Bach and included with de Grigny's *Livre d'Orgue* (*Dok* III pp634–5; *NBA* v/5 *KB* p66 and 1/40 *KB* p28).† The thirteen signs, like those in the Möller MS and the Andreas-Bach-Buch, do not include the grace-note, perhaps because it is not strictly a 'sign' and may have seemed self-evident. Whether it took its value from the preceding or the following note may well have seemed of less importance than modern commentators have thought.

Among the many commentaries on the *Klavierbüchlein* table, Neumann's may well be the most influential in coming years in its claim that the ornaments in question '*may* have the shapes indicated, but not that they *must* have these shapes which . . . are often disqualified by musical evidence'. It is true that the table – which, like the others, is particularly French – has a limited purpose and relevance to the keyboard works as a whole. But its usefulness is clearer if its written-out examples are seen as abstract models – *exempla*, convenient sketches rather than literal equivalents. For example, it is significant that the *cadence* (turn) is shown on a quaver not a crotchet, insofar as it suggests an embellishment useful on a short note, the others on longer. Also, what is significant about the explanation of the *accent* is not that a crotchet so marked is always to be understood as two quavers but that the notes concerned are slurred and that their melodic character is therefore strong-weak. Such slurring, with the kind of keyboard touch it requires, is what the ornament is aiming at – it is, after all, a quicker way of writing two slurred quavers. The *accent* implies accentuation and even an overlapping of the notes.‡ Perhaps such overlapping was intended with the short–long, so-called lombardic figure in 'Vater

---

* Even Couperin's well-known remark in his *Troisième Livre* (Paris 1722) – 'il n'est point arbitraire d'y mettre tels agrémens qu'on veut . . . mes pièces doivent être exécutées comme je les ay marquées . . . sans augmentation ni diminution' – says less than it seems to at first, since it is not clear at what level he is speaking. Of players who amend his directions slightly or of players who have made no effort to follow them? Moreover, it often seems in French music that the generous signs (ornaments, bowing, registration) are also a warning against doing something else at that point.

† The de Grigny copy was evidently made from an edition of 1700, not otherwise known to have existed. Did it too incorporate d'Anglebert's *table*?

‡ In 1746 the Naumburg organist blamed an effect of '*accentuation*' on a sticking action: see above, p201. Silbermann replied that the '*accentuation*' did not mean that the keys were sticking but was due to natural reverberation (*Dok* II p430).

unser' BWV 682, or in the countless patterns throughout J. S. Bach's organ music when a fingering of 4343 leads to a natural pairing of the notes. Those frenchified movements in which *accents* or appoggiaturas – often both accented passing-notes – produce seemingly plain quaver lines, such as BWV 562.i (Ex. 122), do so only because notation is an inexpressive medium. With the correct touch, the strong–weak vocal effect or *port de voix* of such figures gives an expression and lilt very characteristic of such lines.

Ex. 122   BWV 562.i

Thus, although the table in Friedemann's *Klavierbüchlein* may have been a simple explication for a ten-year-old pupil, the ornament signs say something about touch and style. Other effects belonging to the idiomatic playing of good organ actions are not so easy to demonstrate from any table of notated ornaments. One particular question concerns trills or long mordents: certainly not all of them begin on upper notes, but the bigger questions for the player sensitive to touch are: Do trills accelerate? and Where do they stop? Three of the *Klavierbüchlein* examples suggest that they stop before the end of the note-value, with or without an appoggiatura at the beginning; the fourth example in Ex. 123 is typical of those

Ex. 123   *Klavierbüchlein für W. F. Bach*

that continue into the next note with a slide or turn. But the notation gives no clue about acceleration, particularly on longer trills. In the copies of the D minor Fugue BWV 538 the long pedal trill in bb178–83 is notated as if the written-out quavers of the first bar should continue evenly and without accelerating;* moreover, it seems from the stretto theme entering in the pedal in b184 that the trill ends in the previous bar. Another appearance of the even trill must be the chains of trills in the C

* Today's players have various conjectures about this trill; but to an organist of the period, unacquainted with nineteenth-century piano trills, it must have looked like a simple abbreviation – i.e., '*tr*' indicated 'continue in this manner'. Such a trill gives a distinct harmonic shading to what is otherwise the simplest stretto in the movement (manual octaves). Two copyists also wrote b178 not as quavers but as a *tr*, thus leaving it very unclear to their readers whether it starts or continues as quavers (*NBA* IV/5–6 *KB* p381).

minor Sonata BWV 526.i bb66–70 – to be played as demisemiquavers beginning on the main note?* It seems from Altnickol's remarks on the action of the Naumburg organ in 1753 (Dähnert 1962 p114) that he distinguished between a quick mordent or *Prall-Triller* (which he found difficult to play when all stops were drawn) and a long trill or *Trillo* (which he could play with all three manuals coupled), as if the latter were by nature slower and more even. But even in the course of a short double mordent there is scope for acceleration. Perhaps that is also implied by the change in emphasis between J. S. Bach and C. P. E. Bach when the latter (unlike the French sources that influenced his father) stated a preference for trill-shakes taking up the whole of their note: did those French 'ornamental manners' that J. F. Reichardt saw as characteristic of J. S. Bach ('zierliche Manier': *Dok* III p545) emphasize more the shorter trill and double mordent – more dashingly played than the even, conventionalized melodic decorations of the modern *galant* period?

The character of a trill cannot often be reasoned from its context, but another detail implied in the *Klavierbüchlein* is also supported from a good source: an example in *Clavierübung III* shows the long turned trill (whatever it is called in the theory books) taking up the whole value of the note – Ex. 124.† That this is a final

Ex. 124   BWV 552.ii

cf. *Explicatio* no. 8:

cadence – the last cadence of *Clavierübung III* – seems (at least now) to justify the playing of such an ornament very fully, with an accelerando or ritardando or both, and without a comma before the last chord. But insofar as such crucial aspects of ornament-playing are still not fully understood, the counting of repercussions becomes very secondary. At one important perfect cadence in *Clavierübung IV*, a similar but not identical ornament does suggest not only that there are fewer repercussions but that the ornament stops before the little anticipatory note that follows: Ex. 125. Thus neither of these cadential trills can be taken literally from the *Klavierbüchlein für W. F. Bach*; but about the playing method of both it does seem to drop a hint.

Ex. 125   BWV 988 Var. 16

* I.e. on the analogy of BWV 538.ii, and because the sign used (long continuous shake) seems to express a shimmer of sound without leaps to upper notes. The consecutive-fifths argument – that beginning with upper notes would make fifths between b68 and b69 – is theoretical. For 'shimmering' trills, see also the Organ Sonata BWV 528.ii bb38–9 and the Violin and Harpsichord Sonata BWV 1016.iv bb98–102: were these passages all originally contemporary?

† An important copy of the engraving has the initial curve of the ornament going the other way (*NBA* IV/4 *KB* p46).

If such tables are taken literally, ornaments will appear to be demisemiquavers, confirming such claims as that the *trillo* in the B minor Prelude BWV 544 bb67–8 is in the same time as the left hand (Emery 1953): Ex. 126. But is this likely? If such tables are 'abstract models', there is no specific value to the little embellishments.

Ex. 126   BWV 544.i

Keyboard-players must be wary of taking literally or prosaically an ornament which a melodic instrument would interpret more melodiously and naturally: Ex. 127. It is characteristic of a good keyboard action that any mordent or trill can shimmer and that therefore in Ex. 128 *a* is less idiomatic than *b*. Similar points can be made about any mordent or trill on a tied note, and the reasoning behind such interpretations as Ex. 129 is very obscure. What is or is not 'idiomatic' can often be subjective, but it should not be missed that in this instance the *Klavierbüchlein* supports the interpretation of Ex. 128*b*.

Both the 'shimmer' effect of trills and the 'strong–weak' effect of appoggiaturas must often, if they are to be fully expressive, suggest something much freer than note-against-note realization. Similarly, dividing the beat into multiples of two can reduce expressiveness – in Ex. 128, version *b* gives only a rough idea of the rhythm

Ex. 127   e.g. approximately

Ex. 128   BWV 527.i

Ex. 129   BWV 527.ii (Neumann 1978 p329)

an imaginative player would use. In the E flat Prelude BWV 552 b45,* it is possible to see the leaping appoggiatura as having one of several possible interpretations: Ex. 130. The player responsive to good action and a sense of melody might well feel the third of these to be nearest the intended effect, assuming that the lower note is allowed to overlap the upper. Such overlapping (here the *tierce coulée* or 'glided third')† seems also to be the point of the *accent fallend* in the chorale BWV 662: Ex. 131. But this notation cannot make clear that the dotted note is 'lazy' rather than

Ex. 130   BWV 552.i

Ex. 131   BWV 662

sprightly, and that the slurs suggest more an overlapping slide than a sharp phrasing. In practice, much of the interest given by an ornament consists in the responsive performer's shaping his touch at that point, especially in his quick recognition of an accented passing-note in its various forms. In the transcription BWV 648, b12 already shows how b23 is to be interpreted: Ex. 132. Both phrases are

Ex. 132   BWV 648

paired appoggiaturas, and it could be said that the notation of b23 clarifies the harmonic nature of the note-pattern written in simple form in b12: i.e., one articulates as in the version in b23. From this example the player can begin to see that many groups of quavers and semiquavers in J. S. Bach have this character of paired appoggiaturas, and there must be hundreds of examples for him to treat accordingly. For example, in the E minor Fugue BWV 548 b8 both hands must surely have four quavers and both groups of four quavers must be based on accented passing-notes, with all that that means for lively, paired phrasing – Ex. 133. But

Ex. 133   BWV 548.ii

* And b47 – in this instance exactly the same, since (a sign of the modernity of the movement?) there is an unusual repetition of the simple two-bar phrase.
† There is no certain evidence to show whether the grace-note falls on or slips in between the quaver beats.

why does the composer persistently write the two groups of notes differently if they mean the same thing? Not because the small notes are later additions, but because the small notes always belong to the fugal counterpoint and the four 'equal' quavers to the subject? It could be characteristic of J. S. Bach to distinguish in this way. Moreover, the fugue then demonstrates the principle of 'counterpoint by articulation': the quavers of the movement are (*a*) *détaché*, (*b*) paired and (*c*) off the beat, depending on their position in the counterpoint: Ex. 134.

Ex. 134   BWV 548.ii

Amongst the 'general rules' for ornaments that are sometimes attempted by theory books, old or new, are the rule against parallels, the rule of consistency, and the rule of imitation between parts. None of these is a very reliable guide to the player. For the first, although it has been claimed that mordents in Buxtehude often produce consecutives (Emery *MT* 1971 pp483–8), it has also been claimed that some trills must begin on the main note in order to avoid consecutives (Emery *MT* 1973 pp891–2). Similarly, the 'avoidance of parallels will almost always require shortness and often anticipation' of grace-notes (Neumann 1978 p135). Thus in the G major Sonata BWV 530.ii, the little note 'must' be taken before the beat in order to avoid open consecutive fifths (*ibid* p136): Ex. 135*a*. Moreover, in order to avoid implied octaves the slide in the same movement 'must' also precede the beat (*ibid* p221): Ex. 135*b*. Now, avoiding consecutives in harmony and counterpoint is

Ex. 135   BWV 530.ii

virtually irrelevant to ornamentation. To be aware of consecutives in these examples requires the listener to have a regard for notation and theory to an extent that is simply not justified by experience. I do not believe that the ear unaided by prejudice (or governed by the eye) hears consecutives in such examples. Moreover, if it hears them in Ex. 135*a* it is of no consequence, since the second fifth is on an accented passing-note, and the d$\sharp$' 'is the 'real' harmony: Ex. 136. Against the claim that consecutives should be avoided in such progressions stands a counter-claim, just as valid, that such progressions consciously play with the consecutive

Ex. 136

rule – i.e., that the composer is engaging in a kind of musical irony.* Neither claim reflects how conventional such progressions were during the eighteenth century. The 'rule against parallels' is valueless as a criterion. For example, the reason for taking the little note before the beat in Ex. 137*a* but on it in Ex. 137*b* has nothing to do with consecutives in the former: rather the reason lies in the melodic character and phraseology. In *a*, the little note is taken smoothly into the turning figure; in *b*, it follows a leap and thus accentuates the next beat. In *a*, the figure as a whole is legato; in *b*, the high bb′ is *détaché*. Such things belong to keyboard idiom.

Ex. 137

BWV 769.iii
a

BWV 645
b

Similarly, whether or not the pedal's small note in the B minor Prelude BWV 544 b9 is played short (Ex. 138), it is important that the previous high note is played *détaché* and the following grace-note therefore accentuated.

Ex. 138

BWV 544.i

The 'rule of consistency' – that each appearance of a theme is coloured by the same ornament – is very uncertain in J. S. Bach and can rarely be established or obeyed. In general, the composer and most copyists wrote in fewer ornaments on a returning theme as the movement progressed: one sees this already in the opening 20 bars of the autograph (P 274) of the E minor Fugue BWV 548.ii. But sources can seldom be typecast in this respect. The source for the Fugue in F minor BWV 534, far from showing less consistent use of trills as the movement progresses (Emery 1971), is nowhere consistent at all (*NBA* IV/5-6 *KB* p416). In the case of the E flat Prelude BWV 552, however, the right-hand shake at the close of the first ritornello should certainly be added at the corresponding place in the final bars (b204 soprano) – but should it in the middle ritornello (b110 tenor)? There is nothing to help the player know whether the composer assumed the addition of appoggiaturas in bb124, 126 on the analogy of bb45, 47, although the particular engraving process† (which made use of a handwritten original) suggests at least that the composer's fair copy did not contain the extra grace-notes.

---

* Another fine example occurs at the end of the Sarabande of the E minor Partita BWV 830, where in contrast to the rich harmonies of the movement as a whole, the fifths between outer parts are particularly exposed.

† The process – which involved oiling a manuscript sheet (such as the composer's fair copy) to render it transparent, turning it over, and in effect tracing through it onto the plate – is described in *Current Musicology* 17 (1975) 61–7.

The 'rule of imitation between parts' – that each line (including pedal) should have similar ornaments for the same theme – also evaporates as an easy guide, though it has more musical usefulness than the consecutive rule. German figured-bass theorists of the middle and later eighteenth century suggest that ornaments can be added to any part (Heinichen 1711, 1728), in this perhaps reflecting certain Italian influences (Williams 1970 I p40); and C. P. E. Bach recommended that the bass should imitate the melody's ornaments (1762 ch.33). But he also advised great caution in introducing appoggiaturas into the bass, which might disturb the line of harmony (*ibid* ch.40). There are very few authenticated pedal ornaments in the organ works of J. S. Bach which imitate those of the manual parts. Such fugal movements as the E minor Sonata BWV 528.iii and the E minor Fugue BWV 548.ii have no pedal ornaments – a picture confirmed by the general tendency, in both these works and elsewhere, to simplify and de-colour fugue themes in the pedal. That being so, it is puzzling that E. L. Gerber (son of a Bach pupil) should say in 1790:

> Auf dem Pedale mussten seine Füsse jedes Thema, jeden Gang, ihren Vorgängern den Händen, auf das Genaueste nach machen. Kein Vorschlag, kein Mordent, kein Prall-triller durfte fehlen, oder nur weniger nett und rund zum Gehör kommen. Er machte mit beyden Füssen zugleich lange Doppeltriller, indessen die Hände nichts weniger als müssig waren (*Dok* III p468).

> On the pedal his feet had to imitate their predecessors the hands in each theme, each passage, as precisely as possible. No appoggiatura, no inverted mordent, no mordent [short trill] was allowed to be missing or to be heard any less neat or round. With both feet he made long trills at the same time as his hands were anything but idle.

Indirectly quoting the *Obituary*, Gerber may have been only glossing the stories that were told of the composer's pedal technique, including the naturally unverifiable accounts of his improvisations. Or what he says might be an exaggeration based on (e.g.) the *lange Doppeltriller* of the D minor Fugue BWV 538 and or on the highly decorated and late manuscript versions of keyboard works copied or owned by his father. However, judging by the absence of marks in the slow movement of the first Sonata BWV 525.ii and the presence of one or two graces in BWV 544.i and 682, it is possible that J. S. Bach did move towards embellishing his pedal lines more in his later years. Was this a tendency born of changing basso-continuo habits?

Of the three questions at the head of this chapter, the two concerning sources and 'improvised' ornaments may be quickly dealt with. It is clear from the *NBA KB* volumes that the variety, even discrepancy, of ornaments in the sources has several origins: carelessness, deliberate addition and omission, differing notations of the same ornament. Although in some cases it may be correct to speak of C. P. E. Bach 'using' some of his father's ornaments and 'suppressing' others (Klotz 1969a), it is injudicious to take too orderly a view of what must often have been insignificant differences. An absence of ornaments in the copy of a work whose ornaments are highly integrated, such as the Fantasia in C minor BWV 562,* might well go with an

---

* That the composer himself wrote in a few, but only a few, slurs between small note and main note for the many appearances of the appoggiatura-coloured theme in this movement (*NBA* IV/5–6) rather argues against Neumann's attempted distinction between grace-notes with and without slurs (1978 pp125ff).

absence of other signs such as many accidentals and ties. This is the case with J. P. Kellner's copy (see *NBA* IV/5–6 *KB* p338), and it would be logical to assume not so much that he was careless at that he 'understood' all three and would have added them in a performance, unreliable though the result might have been. The presence of many and varied ornaments in a work closer to the German tradition – a good example is the sources for the D minor Toccata and Fugue BWV 538 (see *ibid* pp365, 377–81) – shows the situation more clearly. Thus some manuscripts have many signs; others have very few, even when they contain some on which most are agreed (e.g. the pedal trill in the fugue); some have particular signs (e.g. the *turn* in one later-eighteenth-century manuscript only) or effects (e.g. arpeggio line in manuscripts of Kittel, Kellner or the C. P. E. Bach circle); the simplest signs seem often to be the most arbitrary (e.g. mordents reflecting the copyist's own habits?), while there is often more agreement about more complicated ones (e.g. slides and appoggiaturas in the fugue). Early works, at least in earlier copies, preserve the richer array of simple ornaments (e.g. BWV 533/533a and 575). Throughout the composer's life there remained ambiguity or inconsistency about the lengths of such simple mordent and inverted-mordent signs (e.g. BWV 548 – see *ibid* p402), and copyists tend to blur distinctions between those simple signs (e.g. BWV 527 in its 'early version' – see Emery 1957 p84). Of the earlier copyists, J. G. Walther in particular had his own habits that may well not reflect any manuscript made by the composer (e.g. BWV 574a); and he may have added ornaments, as he occasionally did fingerings, for his own students.

That some copyists undoubtedly added their own ornaments to the source they were copying is itself evidence that German organists, during and after Bach's period, took liberties with a piece of music as they found it. Whether they were inclined to add more ornaments to pieces taken from non-autograph copies is now usually impossible to say, though the nature of copies of BWV 544 and 548 rather suggests this. Either way, if ornaments were added (or omitted) in the recopying, it can hardly be doubted that the same thing happened in performance. C. P. E. Bach only confirms what might be expected when he complains of tasteless players 'selecting' ornaments (1753 ch.2) or when he speaks of adding ornaments (*Sonaten . . . mit veränderten Reprisen*, 1760). Much depended on context and genre, especially in the middle of the century as ornaments become melodic graces in what would otherwise be plain, uncoloured melodies. Perhaps it had always been true – at least in the Italian violin concerto – that, as Scheibe wrote in 1745, slow movements of concertos were best left free of fanciful ornaments

> weil man demjenigen, welcher die Hauptstimme spielen soll, gerne Freyheit lässt, nach seiner eigenen Geschicklichkeit damit zu verfahren (1745 p633)

> because one willingly allows him who is to play the solo part freedom to proceed with it according to his own ability.

But when Birnbaum defends J. S. Bach against Scheibe's attack by pointing out that writing in all the decorations was characteristic also of the organ music of de Grigny and Du Mage (*Dok* II p304), he seems to be confusing fanciful figuration and ornamental melodies with copiously notated ornaments, which is not the same thing. The player today has to distinguish between the two: is he free to add ornaments (mordents, slides etc) and/or new figurations (melismas in slow chorale melodies, runs, broken chords etc), neither or both?

Only gradually can the player reach a climate in which to answer such questions. A study of the chorale BWV 652/652a will suggest that the sources (autograph for one, and perhaps – if one goes back far enough – autograph for the other) often mean to indicate the same ornament with different signs but at other times give an alternative that, regardless of whether or not both could be proved to be J. S. Bach's, certainly belongs to the period as a whole. General experience with binary movements or Italian *ABA* arias might suggest that on repeats in the slow movements of the Six Sonatas simple ornaments (mordents, slides, some appoggiaturas, some *tierces coulées*) could be convincingly added. In general, some simple ornaments such as trills or long mordents must often have been meant to have closing turns whether they are specified in any way or not. The same goes for beginning a trill etc with a turn or appoggiatura (see the chorales in *NBA* IV/2 *KB* pp66, 73); adding a turn or appoggiatura at the beginning is not something most editors or players since the eighteenth century have felt free to do, but such long trills as at bb87–90 in the D minor Toccata BWV 565 could well begin with a turn. The most likely places for playing unwritten ornaments – i.e. those most likely to have been added by original performers – are without doubt cadences, where shakes presumably began on whichever note was dissonant to the bass, therefore sometimes the main note* and sometimes the upper note: Ex. 139.

Ex. 139   *a*   main note   *b*   upper note

The freest quasi-improvisations in the organ works of J. S. Bach must be the interline interludes in certain chorales, which present a musical situation strikingly close to the 'embellishment on a fermata' described (in a different musical idiom) by C. P. E. Bach (1753 ch.2). That the scales, broken chords and ornaments of such interludes are still relatively restricted in vocabulary can be seen by comparing (e.g.) the chorale BWV 726 with J. G. Müthel's coloratura treatment of the melody 'Jesu, meine Freude': Ex. 140. Whoever was the composer of BWV 726, copyists rarely

Ex. 140

J. G. Müthel, 'Jesu, meine Freude' (Sietz 1935)

---

* This too can be taken to pedantic lengths. Does beginning on the upper note in Ex. 139*a* really lessen the effect of the 4–3 progression?

supply evidence for playing new figurations or embellishing the melody beyond the expressive playing of simple ornaments. Absence is not proof, but it seems from J. T. Krebs's copy of 'Ich ruf zu dir' BWV 639 – a chorale in which the melody becomes plainer in its second half – that even in such expressive music a good pupil found only simple ornaments to add, not new melismas or figurations. Perhaps J. T. Krebs could not match his teacher's inventiveness. But organists today, who after careful study can get to know much more of J. S. Bach's music than Krebs ever knew, might well reach the spirit of BWV 639 if they add an appoggiatura or two, even perhaps a spontaneous and expressive melisma.*

26. Certain Details of Performance: Finals, Fermatas and Repeats

It is a sign of the power exercised by notation that such aspects of performance as ornamentation and fingering have been much more fully treated, both at the time of this music and since, than aspects requiring a certain independence of, even indifference to, the notation† – such as touch, rubato and phrasing. Since it is clear that ultimately all such aspects of performance are related, it is useful to look at certain other details of notation.

Every player is struck by certain short final chords in the good sources, such as the C major Fugue BWV 547 (Kellner circle manuscript) or the B minor Prelude BWV 544 (autograph), where the rests have been written in so carefully as to leave the matter quite unambiguous. Three particular questions arise from such chords. First, are they meant to have a literal value? Everything in the notation of BWV 547.ii suggests so: Ex. 141. But secondly, since the abruptness of this, if played as

Ex. 141   BWV 547.ii

b66

---

* The *NBA* version of the Two- and Three-part Inventions (1972) gives an authority, inadvertently perhaps, to Gerber's ornamental signs that is problematic to the player sensitive to 'what feels right' for such very expressive music on a suitable harpsichord. Like J. T. Krebs's ornaments for BWV 639, they are mostly a matter of mordents etc which it is possible to feel as quite insensitive to the nature of the music. What is suggested by this? – that J. S. Bach himself played such simple ornaments at the period when his later pupils heard him play, that Gerber added them with neither authority nor understanding, or that like other German players Gerber did not grasp the nature of the harpsichord and its expressive ornamentation?

† It can also be argued that twentieth-century books and essays dealing with ornamentation have been far more dependent on notation and on the written remarks of undistinguished composers than they should have been, often isolating the subject from matters without an understanding of which the nature of ornamentation cannot be grasped, e.g. the qualities of the instrument concerned.

written, seems to offend musical common sense, does it do so because such common sense is an anachronism, or because the notation is implying something else as well – namely, that there must be a rallentando? That could also be the case with the short chord closing the pedal point of a much less sophisticated work, the Fantasia BWV 571, or at similar moments in other works when the pedal point is only implied, such as BWV 574 b104. The latter, however, is a good example of an 'early' cadence – one very like that at the close of many a seventeenth-century chorale-fantasia – for which a rallentando would be an anachronism, and which would be better served by a comma after the dotted note: Ex. 142. Cadences of

Ex. 142   BWV 574

these kinds are important in many an early work of J. S. Bach and require a short final, played by the right kind of *plenum*.* And thirdly, whether or not particular cadences imply rallentando and/or preparatory commas, should other major works be played with short finals, and if so, which works and why? Already in 1844 Griepenkerl warned that notes 'at the end of a section or movement need nto be played as long as notated' (Peters I p.ii), particularly if varying the length of a final can help to convey the shape and direction of a movement.† Even those players who have never been alerted to the importance of how long a final is held would in practice rarely obey the notation literally. How often is a notated semibreve-plus-fermata held for five or more beats?

The autograph notation of BWV 544.ii, which ends halfway through the bar, gives a fermata above the last chord, which is already written as a minim – Ex. 143 –

Ex. 143   BWV 544.ii

---

* Because their *plena* are not voiced with that immediacy of tone that marks the beginning and end of the pipe-speech characteristic of older organs, most instruments made since c1720 destroy the effectiveness of a succinct cadence and a short final, so that it is matter of indifference how long the final chord is held. This is not the least reason why the art of distinguishing cadence-types has been largely lost.

† For example, the short chord at the end of the B minor Prelude BWV 544 closes a section which, rondo-like, also appeared with the same short chord earlier in the movement.

but there seems no reason for playing a long chord even of two beats, still less one of three or more. A further autograph example of a full-length final is the opening chorale of the *Orgelbüchlein*; and there are other examples in this album of finals that involve either a suspension or a running-out of the chief motif: Ex. 144. But is

Ex. 144 BWV 617

such 'running-out' as good a reason as a suspension for taking a long final chord? Is it possible that 'running-out' of motifs (of which there are several striking examples in the *Orgelbüchlein*) implies a rallentando rather than a final pause? Can a 'running-out' suggest neither a rallentando nor a long final, as perhaps at the close of the C major Fugue BWV 564? Does the fermata of BWV 617 suggest both? or is it a notational convention characteristic of organ chorales in general and especially in the *Orgelbüchlein*, where the fermata generally marks the end of each line? In which case, does fermata mean 'mark this cadence as you play it by a slight release of tension'? In the curious case of the D major Fugue BWV 532.ii – where there is no real final (perfect) cadence, but merely a 'running-out' of the main motif on a very grand scale – the copyists evidently did not feel free to change the notation of the final notes: these had to remain succinct, with no fermata to say to the player 'mark the final pedal drop' etc.

The reason why BWV 547.ii and 544.i have short finals cannot be merely that they can be made 'musically convincing'. Nor can it be in BWV 547.ii that the tenor comprises (and compresses) a final entry: so does the top line of BWV 769.v, where the final suspension implies a long final chord: Ex. 145. When the final chord involves

Ex. 145 BWV 769.v

a suspension so spacious, a long final is natural. And in BWV 544.i it cannot be merely that the last bar duplicates a final already heard in a previous section (bb16–17) and therefore needs no drawing-out: the final chord of the E minor Fugue BWV 548.ii (another *tierce de picardie*)* also marks the close of a section previously

---

* Which is so normal, so much to be expected, that many copies do not give the final chord (*NBA* IV/5–6 *KB* p398); see also a remark on E minor in chapter 21.

heard, but its long final cannot be doubted, whether or not there is a fermata (see *NBA* IV/5–6 *KB* p671). It cannot be that preludes necessarily have shorter finals than fugues (though in this respect the good sources for BWV 544 and 541 are suggestive) or that earlier fugues necessarily close more succinctly than later ones: BWV 547.ii goes against both of these. Nor can it be taken for granted that the copyist understood or transmitted the intentions of the composer, particularly when they were copying earlier fugues: Kellner (?) lengthened the final of the C major Fugue BWV 564 by sustaining the *point d'orgue*, lengthening the last chord, and adding a fermata (*ibid* p691). Certainly some succinct finals were obvious to the copyist: the D major Fugue BWV 532 was usually copied without one, while the C major Prelude BWV 547 received a fermata only in P 274 (*ibid* p317), presumably reflecting not what the autograph said but what conventions the Kellner circle followed. The C major Prelude BWV 547.i, like the succinctly finished chorale BWV 736, is a compound-time movement, and it could well be that pieces in compound or triple time naturally move towards shorter finals than pieces in simple duple time: hence the short finals of BWV 536.ii, 543.ii, 541.i, 566.iv, 544.i and the quasi-ostinato BWV 569? In that case, is it reasonable to suspect that fermatas at the ends of some such movements (e.g. in some copies of the F major Toccata BWV 540.i) may be the copyist's own conventions, with or without the intention of indicating a pause?

There are other questions about final chords. First, the number of notes in the last chord of a piece often inspires doubts. The nine parts at the close of the F major Toccata may reflect the spectacular nature of the piece; but the six parts at the close of the F minor Fugue BWV 534 or the G major Fugue BWV 550 are probably one too many, and the eight notes at the end of the C major BWV 531 or the E major Prelude BWV 566.i two or three too many.* That organs (or their registration centring on Principal 8′) made thick chords feasible is clear from the end of the *Orgelbüchlein* chorale BWV 632; as with the sostenuto chords at the end of the partita movement BWV 768.iii, such effects are created motivically in setting chorale melodies and offer another way of closing a piece. It is a different matter with the 'optional' or extra notes added (at least in some copies) to final chords, even when they seem to be prepared or are (whether prepared or not) undeniably effective (e.g. both the Fantasia and the Fugue in G minor BWV 542).† In any case, it can become clear to the alerted player that the length of the final chord and number of notes in it are related and are both questionable in many a piece known only through copies; this is true of both early and later works. For example, the Fugue in C major BWV 531 and the Prelude in D minor BWV 538 should probably have both a thinner and a shorter final, as in Ex. 146. Perhaps, like the G major Concerto BWV 592, certain pieces should have no final chord, whatever the copyists say and however (as in the case of the close of the C major Toccata BWV 564) they may interpret it; an example is the prelude of the C major Praeludium BWV 531 (Ex. 147).

Secondly, the absence or presence of fermatas leads to questions not only when they occur at the ends of works (Are they over/under the last chord or over/under

---

* Big chords in earlier works are also often suspect, e.g. the sudden short, full seventh in b113 of the C minor Fugue BWV 574 (see the corresponding place in BWV 574b) – did the various copyists add it to fill in what they thought to be a gap, as too halfway through b111?

† The rather similar final of the G minor Fugue BWV 578 would also be 'undeniably effective' in seven parts, but no source gives more than four. The shape of its fermata in good sources (P 320, P 803) resembles J. S. Bach's (*NBA* IV/5–6 p546): did the composer write a short final of four-part crotchets?

Ex. 146   BWV 531.ii   BWV 538.i

Ex. 147   BWV 531.i

the double bar-line? Do they signify the close, indicate a pause or follow a meaningless convention?) but also when they occur between movements. Did the composer normally omit them when the movement ended with a half-close, as in the slow movements to the C minor and C major Sonatas in the autograph fair copy?* If so, does a fermata over/under the double bar-line of a full-close movement, as in the autograph copy of the E minor Prelude BWV 548, indicate merely that the movement is complete, or that a pause is required? Either way, do the fermata-less double-bar and short final chords at the end of the G major and B minor Preludes (BWV 541, 544) suggest that the fugue follows in exact time? If not, can it be shown that such preludes and fugues as the mature organ works or *The 48* are quite different from those preludes and fugues that form the two halves of a French Overture in which the fugue follows in strict time?† In any case, where do the earlier praeludia fit in, when the later copies confuse the question of whether the fugue is meant to follow on immediately? Since the one copyist who separated the Prelude and Fugue in G BWV 550 with a double bar-line no doubt did so without authority (see *NBA* IV/5–6 *KB* p424), does the style of such earlier works suggest that in such cases as the E major Praeludium BWV 566 each movement passes immediately to the next, irrespective of the length of the final chord and the presence‡ of fermatas? Perhaps it was the tablature tradition, rather than a different musical taste, that leaves the pause-less sequence of movements in Buxtehude's praeludia clearer.

Thirdly, do double bar-lines with repeat dots in Bach sources ever indicate anything more or other than 'repeat the enclosed section'? Relevant theorists explain them thus (e.g. Speer 1697 pp14–15), and contemporary composers use them outside binary suite movements to indicate echo-like repetition of a few bars (e.g. no. 2 of Kuhnau's *Biblische Sonaten*, Leipzig 1700). In the *Orgelbüchlein* (P 283) J. S.

---

* And in J. T. Krebs's copy of the C minor Prelude BWV 537 in P 803.

† In this respect, the E flat Prelude BWV 552 is itself a prelude and fugue, perhaps more integrated than the B minor Harpsichord Partita *ouverture* but like it passing from dotted prelude to fluent fugue without break.

‡ Particularly in the Kellner copy – see *ibid* p533.

Bach uses them both in binary movements (one or both halves repeated) and for repetition of phrases. First- and second-time bars are clear in the binary movements of the Six Sonatas (P 271), just as they are in the *Orgelbüchlein*; but it is striking that the composer does not write in fermatas when there are repeat marks or second-time bars, even to mark chorale-melody lines in the *Orgelbüchlein*. Does this suggest that binary dots (or repeat dots) indicate a repetitious form requiring the player not to mark the moment by a rallentando? Or, conversely, that fermatas are only end-signs, unnecessary when repeat dots are involved?

---

27. Pedals and Pedalling

The two main questions here are: What were pedals expected to play? and How did they play it? The two are connected, as too they are with matters arising from the notation (see chapter 28) and from the instrument (see chapter 22). Although several studies have been devoted to the subject in recent years, it is difficult to view in the round because the period concerned was more than usually transitional in its methods of building, playing, registering and composing for pedals.

When in 1743 Constantin Bellermann (not a professional musician) praised the pedal-playing of J. S. Bach thus (*Dok* II p410):

> solo pedum ministerio, digitis aut nihil, aut aliud agentibus, tam mirificum, concitatum, celerem[q]ue in Organo ecclesiastico mouet vocum concentum, ut alii digitis hoc imitari deficere videantur

> by means only of the feet – the fingers doing either nothing or something else – he sets in motion on the church organ such an admirable, exciting and lively blending of voices that others would seem incapable of imitating it with their fingers

and spoke of his solo pedal-playing at Kassel (at the organ-trial of 1732, or privately before the Prince of Hessen–Kassel?), he may well have been typifying a new trend towards reviewing organists in this way. Such praise is of a different order from many earlier references to organists, for example Mattheson's notes on Kerll (that he brought in the pedal at the end of improvisations) and Bruhns (that he accompanied himself on the violin with the feet playing an appropriate pedal stop – 1740 pp136, 26). Bellermann's anecdote of the prince giving the composer a ring for his pedal-playing – what might he have given him had he used his hands as well, asks Bellermann – may suggest, together with the phrase 'vocum concentum', that the performance included double pedal.* Perhaps this is the implication too behind the *Obituary*'s note:

> Mit seinen zweenen Füssen konnte er auf dem Pedale solche Sätze ausführen, die manchem nicht ungeschickten Clavieristen mit fünf Fingern zu machen sauer genug werden würden (*Dok* III p88).

> With his two feet he could perform such movements on the pedal that would have been troublesome enough for many a not unskilled keyboard-player to do with his fingers.

---

* Such evidence is no more questionable than the assumptions running through Bruggaier 1959 and other accounts (e.g. Geck 1968 p23) that notated organ scores prove that earlier composers must have intended double pedal parts.

This note was later repeated or embroidered by J. A. Hiller (*Dok* III p403), Gerber (*Dok* III p468) and Forkel (1802 ch.IV), who sometimes added details of their own (such as Gerber's note on pedal ornaments: see above, p233), but who did not find it necessary actually to explain what the *Obituary* meant. Was the fame of J. S. Bach's pedal-playing a reflection not merely of his skill but of changing conventions? Composers of his earlier years, though they were presumably often virtuosos, frequently left the pedal parts in their scores less unambiguously *obbligato*, while composers of his later years had for the moment lost the old tradition of playing pedal melodies. Hence it was that Forkel felt obliged to explain what a pedal cantus firmus was, or that late references to the organ works called them *Pedal-Stücke* (e.g. C. P. E. Bach's letter to Forkel of 1775, *Dok* III p291).

That earlier Bach works still showed the old, optional nature of the pedal is clear enough from such musical details as texture and layout,* and there is no reason to think the composer required that certain chorales be played in only one way. Is it possible that the (later) title-page and *p* cues in the *Orgelbüchlein* (P 283) were reflecting a change, at least in J. S. Bach's output and emphasis, towards making the pedal less optional? In any case, is not any such move towards *obbligato* pedal – not as a special device for cantus-firmus canons† or for ostinatos but as an everyday norm – a reflection of a larger and growing emphasis, that on providing a constant 16′ bass line? F. E. Niedt, who died in 1708, had already grumbled that

> es ist aber bey etlichen Organisten solche übele Gewohnheit eingerissen, dass sie, so zu reden, nicht leben noch spielen können, wenn nicht immer im *Pedal* sechzehen-füssige Stimmen mitbrummen (1721 p121).

> however, such a nasty habit has gained ground amongst various organists that they can (so to speak) neither live nor play unless 16′ stops are always growling away in the pedal.

He thought the pedal 'tortured' ('gemartert') when such growling rose to the upper end of the compass (above c′), which rather suggests that he saw that part of the pedal compass as melodic and believed that the pedal required good 16′ tone primarily when serving as a low bass (in praeludia). While neither of these is a startling idea, it is important to appreciate that Niedt was writing before the basso-continuo approach to composition and performance had entirely overtaken German organists, ‡ and that even in *tutti* orchestral works of the late seventeenth century it cannot always be assumed that the orchestra had a 16† bass line.# His remarks, therefore, speak of a 'nasty habit' that was in principle new.

---

* Since many of the earlier works are known only from copies, one cannot always trust even the layout to indicate whether or not pedals are obligatory. The D minor Canzona BWV 588, for example, far from being a unique fugal work opening with pedals, does not require them until the entry in b54, and then only because of the wide stretches that are not very different from those in non-autograph copies of other early Bach works (e.g. the *Aria variata* BWV 989). On the other hand, 'the exposed entry of the bass part' ('der exponierte Einsatz der Bassstimme') in such early works as BWV 588, 570, 563, 573 and the unattributed C minor Fantasia in the Andreas-Bach-Buch has been thought to indicate that this bass is intended for pedal (Kilian 1983 p167). Against this, however, the clear layout for BWV 573 (with 'Ped.' specified, and the lower stave largely devoted to the pedal part) suggests rather that by then (*Klavierbüchlein für Anna Magdalena Bach*, 1722) choice was less open than it had been in earlier notations. For the G minor Fantasia BWV 572, see below p268.

† The only pedal c.f. parts in the *Orgelbüchlein* are those of canons, in the Scheidt tradition: BWV 600, 608, 618, 620, 629. Amongst the chorales as a whole, Krey (1956 p51) counts thirty-seven pedal c.f. parts sanctioned in the sources, out of 131 chorales using pedal.

‡ Hence the anecdotal first part of his treatise, telling of the persistence of tablature in Germany.

Cf. J. Eppelsheim, *Das Orchester in den Werken Jean-Baptiste Lullys* (Tutzing 1961).

Ex. 148 BWV 534.i

BWV 544.i

BWV 548.i

Bruggaier must be correct to call such pedal motifs as the leaping octaves in Ex. 148 'appropriate to pedals' (1959 p168); but more specifically, these motifs are also typical of the double bass (with cello). While any distinctions between a pedal part and a double-bass part should not be exaggerated – an ostinato phrase like that in 'Wir glauben' BWV 680 could serve either – it is striking that the transcriptions of string music include more repeated notes for the pedal than is usual in original organ pieces (BWV 539.ii, 592.i, 593.iii, 596.i and even the reworked Corelli fugue BWV 579),* suggesting that some lines are more characteristic of the one than of the other. In so far as no pedal cantus firmus of J. S. Bach is expected to sound in the soprano, he may have consciously turned away from some older techniques, although his copyists seem to have felt free to arrange chorale-preludes (see notes to BWV 660b, 695a, 713) and may themselves have tacitly acknowledged such traditions. In the case of free works – at least the earlier preludes and fugues – players must often be struck by the greater difficulty of pedal parts in the fugues than in the preludes, even when the preludes include pedal solos (e.g. Praeludia in A minor BWV 543 and G major BWV 550). Does this suggest that most copyists and editors have given more to the pedal than the composer expected? Perhaps fugues (especially the earlier fugues) were left more ambiguous as a matter of convention, i.e. the organist was left to use pedals where he could. It is possible to imagine a line of development from the very sparing use of pedals in BWV 531, 533 and 549 through more optional use to the very fully *obbligato* pedal bass in BWV 538, 547, 548 etc. Or on the contrary, was it in the nature of fugues – using the pedal for integrated counterpoint rather than isolated solos – to demand a more versatile pedal technique and in the process to encourage such developments as heel-pedalling? These two possibilities may seem mutually exclusive; yet they must both be true to some extent.

Whether or not the title-page of the *Orgelbüchlein* implies a didactic element that had not originally belonged to the collection, it is clear that the composer's Weimar contemporary J. G. Walther rarely demanded from the pedal a contribution so well developed or so much expected as the norm. Moreover, the pedal parts of the *Orgelbüchlein*, though rarely virtuoso, seem to require a facility or versatility not inferior to but quite different from the traditional alternate-foot virtuosity of composers such as D. M. Gronau (Bruggaier 1959 p200): Ex. 149. The question is:

Ex. 149 D. M. Gronau, 'Ein feste Burg'

---

* Does this imply that repeated-note themes in (e.g.) the fugues of V. Lübeck are to be played by hands? If the pedal is registered at the same octave pitch as the manual, as it might well be in such traditions, does one distribute such pieces as convenient between hands and feet?

Does the primitive alternate-foot nature of such pedal solos suggest the manner still normal for playing pedals? If so, does the *Orgelbüchlein* represent a new style, a technique less bound to any 'toe-only' tradition, in the way that Book I of *The 48* required more than a 'no-thumbs' technique? Were the 'compositorial demands' in the *Orgelbüchlein* stronger than the observance of technical convenience (Zavarsky 1965)?* Or, rather, did the *Orgelbüchlein* bass line show the composer's interest in exploiting *figurae* by means of a bass line that developed a less *détaché* technique than usual? If so, does 'less *détaché*' imply using heels? Neither the *Obituary* nor any of the accounts up to Forkel that comment on J. S. Bach's use of the thumb in his manual-playing say whether he used both heel and toe in his pedal-playing, though one later source does (see below). Was this because he followed convention and had made no special point of a 'new method' when teaching such pupils as C. P. E. Bach and Agricola? If his playing was pragmatic and adaptable in this respect, why should the pupils not say so? Either way, what were the conventions?

Two kinds of evidence have been called upon in recent years to show that J. S. Bach is likely to have used heels: from theorists and from notation. D. G. Türk (1787 pp158–60) speaks of using the heel as if it were nothing new, giving some alternatives, as in Ex. 150. He also uses both heel and toe for three- and four-part

Ex. 150

△ = *foot in lower position;*   ⋀ = *foot in upper position*

chords. From such an example, it has been reasoned that since Türk was a pupil of a pupil of J. S. Bach he was giving 'a clear indication of the playing method of the Bach tradition' (Krams 1974 pp107–8). Unfortunately, not only is the link with J. S. Bach for more tenuous than such an assertion suggests, but the Bach pupil J. C. Kittel gave directions in the preface to his *Vierstimmige Choräle mit Vorspielen* (Altona 1803 – see Bal 1981 pp65–6) that do not fully agree with those of Türk. He regards toe-heel pedalling (Ex. 151: left foot for the lower octave, right for upper)

Ex. 151

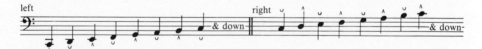

* Zavarsky makes several suggestions from a study of the still-extant Arnstadt console: toe-only pedal-ling was customary; in Arnstadt for the first time Bach practised the organ assiduously; the console has its pedalboard built not so far into the organ (i.e. not so far under the lowest manual) as is the case with modern organs; the Lübeck organs were superior, and Bach returned dissatisfied with Arnstadt; heels are feasible at Arnstadt only for moving from a sharp to a natural and for playing at either end of the flat pedalboard (sharps 115 × c36 mm, naturals 435 × c36 mm, octave width 535 mm); in the middle, only toe-pedalling is feasible, but foot-crossing is easier with such high stools. Although the history of both pedalboard and stool at Arnstadt is too uncertain for such claims, the relatively short keys and wide-spaced pedalboards of Thuringia must be considered a factor arguing against constant toe–heel pedalling or fluent passing-under of either foot. Yet the Arnstadt keys were longer than others; one Schnitger organ of the same period (Eenum, Holland, 1704) has naturals 305 mm, sharps 80 mm.

as old-fashioned and likely to damage the pedalboard. In calling this the 'second and older kind' ('zweyte und ältere Art') of pedal-playing he seems to mean both the toe–heel alternation and the division into two octaves for the feet. In other words, heels are used only if the organist is so old-fashioned as to use left foot for lower octave and right for upper:

> Die erste und vorzüglichste Art ist der abwechselnde Gebrauch beyder Füsse.

> The first and most preferable kind is the alternate use of both feet.

E. Kooiman (1980) takes this to mean that Kittel preferred toe-only pedalling throughout in alternation. Whether or not this is a correct interpretation of what Kittel says, it is puzzling that he should call toe–heel pedalling 'older', unless that means 'more primitive' in its crude division between octaves.* In any case, Kittel certainly approved of a combination of both kinds of pedalling, as Ex. 152 shows.

Ex. 152

Griepenkerl (Peters I (1844) p. ii) summarized Kittel's three techniques as (i) alternate-toe pedalling, (ii) toes and heels (left for lower octave, right for upper), and (iii) a combination of the two; but he himself showed a nineteenth-century regard for ease and convenience in suggesting that each player can choose the technique most comfortable for his physique.

Various suggestions made by J. S. Petri (Leipzig, 1782) also imply that organists needed to master several methods – a view in which he may have found support from W. F. Bach, whose friendship in Halle he claimed in the *Anleitung* (p101) and from whom he may have obtained copies of Bach cantatas after his unsuccessful candidature for the cantorate at St Thomas, Leipzig in 1755 (see *Dok* III p549). Petri thought that the division into lower and upper octaves was a failing of 'inexperienced organists' (p314) and outlined the techniques as follows, pointing out that the beginner should not be accustomed to one method only (p321):

> One foot (toe) can play several consecutive notes.

> Passing under and over requires care (left under in the lower octave, right under in the upper):† Ex. 153.

Ex. 153

> Heels can be used when suitable (Petri does not say so, but his example shows it): Ex. 154.

> The last note before a leap up should be played by the left toe; before a leap down, by the right.

* And in the need to rest one foot on the ledge while the other played everything in its own octave as best it could.

† Adlung (1758 p359) notes that the keys should be of adequate length, because 'otherwise the feet could not pass comfortably behind each other' ('die Füsse sonst nicht bequem hinter einander gehen können'). It is not clear why Krams (1974 p69) should see this as evidence for heel-pedalling.

Ex. 154

If the alternate-toe method is used to play (e.g.) a scale of A major, then foot-sliding ('Fuss-schieben', pp317–18) is necessary: i.e., right foot must slide out of the way along the key of the rising f♯, left foot along the key of the falling g♯ – Ex. 155.

Ex. 155

Alternatively, the heel may be used after semitones (c#–d left, g#–a right). Petri's examples also show that heels are necessary when pedals play in three or four parts (Ex. 156 (i)) and that heels can play appoggiaturas on semitones (Ex. 156 (ii)). Trills, long or short, are played by right/left toes in alternation. Adlung had

Ex. 156   **(i)**

(ii)

already observed, perhaps ruefully, that

> Die Zeiten ändern sich; jetzo will man mit den Füssen 2 bis 3 geschwänzte Noten tractiren, auch gut schleifen können (1758 p359).

> Times are changing: now one wants to play semiquavers and demisemiquavers with the feet, and to be able to slide [slur?] well.

Later in date even than Türk, the anonymous reviewer of M. C. G. Hering's *Kunst das Pedal zu spielen* (Leipzig 1816) in *AMZ* 18 (1816) col. 201–5 referred to J. S. Bach's heel-pedalling. After first commending the book as necessary now that the Bach school had died out,* and agreeing that exercises for pedal were indispensable, the reviewer distinguishes 'simple and natural' playing from 'combined and artful' ('einfaches und natürliches . . . zusammengesetztes und künstliches'). Under the first, Hering gives exercises for changing feet on one key and one different keys, for stepwise or leaping passages, for left under/over right and right under/over left, and for scales with alternate feet; under the second, toe and heel are changed on the same and different keys, two- and three-part chords are played with two notes in either foot, and scales are played by toe–heel pedalling. The reviewer notes:

> Zu diesen und allen folgenden Uebungen ist die besondere Vorrichtung hoher Absätze, oder besser, besonderer Ueberschuhe zum Orgelspiel mit solchen Absätzen, wie Vogler

* J. C. Kittel died in 1809.

und vormals Seb. Bach sich ihrer bedienten, zu empfehlen, ja, bey den meisten unentbehrlich.

For these and all exercises to follow, the special provision of high heels, or (better) of special overshoes for organ-playing with such heels, as Vogler and before him J. S. Bach made use of, is to be recommended; indeed, for most of the exercises they are indispensable.

In a periodical originating in Leipzig, there may have been reluctance to ascribe changes in organ technique to the credit of the showman Vogler.* Perhaps the reviewer by then could imagine Bach pedal parts to be playable in no other way; perhaps Kittel played with such heels and/or claimed that J. S. Bach did; perhaps the most that can now be said is that Kittel, who remembered Bach only as an elderly man, recalled his using such heels in the last years of his life. But two particular observations diminish the force of such late evidence: first, what was written in 1816 at Leipzig can have very little bearing on conditions in Weimar in 1716; and secondly, an anachronistic outlook is already conveyed by a reviewer who, in praising exercises for 'dexterity and certainty', implies a view of dexterity as the fruit of long practice that is far more typical of Czerny's period than of Buxtehude's. In any case, commentators do not agree. A pupil of Kittel reported him as saying that J. S. Bach used only alternate-toe pedalling; and other writers of tutors in the early nineteenth century kept the toe-pedalling technique (see Lohmann 1982 p183).

Evidence from late written sources is therefore of doubtful value. Nor is it easy to argue from the various kinds of old pedalboard how they were played, since virtually nothing is known of J. S. Bach's pedalboards and since in any case it is possible to develop an even or legato approach on many kinds of keyboard.† A third possible kind of evidence could perhaps be supplied by the musical notation.

Unfortunately, a recent attempt to use notation as an indication of pedal technique (Hisao Mabuchi 1979) only serves to raise more questions. Neither the dots in b21 (lh) of the G major Sonata BWV 530.ii nor the pedal slurs two and three bars later are the composer's: Ex. 157. Since they belong to Anna Magdalena or W. F.

Ex. 157   BWV 530.ii

Ped.

* Vogler had played three recitals in Leipzig during the Easter Fair of 1801 (two in the Nikolaikirche, one in the Paulinerkirche), but no details were given in the *AMZ* reviews of them (*AMZ* 3 (1801) col. 563).

† Nevertheless, the two original pedalboards drawn by Bruggaier (1959 pp260–1) are suggestive:

	E. Compenius (Frederiksborg, 1610)	G. Silbermann (see Dähnert 1953 p77)
length	87 mm	90–100 mm
length	430 mm	550 mm
key-breadth	26.0–26.9 mm	35 mm
total breadth	1150 mm (CDEF–d')	1110 mm (CD–c')
octave breadth (c–c')	525 mm	536 mm

Does the similarity in octave breadth (Stichmass) and ♯ length suggest that the change in ♯ length was deliberate, to facilitate crossings?

Bach, the question is: Do they make explicit what the composer left implicit, or do they express the younger generation's interest in varying the way of playing appoggiaturas – now paired notes, now staccato, now legato? In either case, the slurs in bb23–4 cannot be adduced as proof of toe–heel pedalling: Türk gave two ways of playing such semitones (see Ex. 150), each of which no doubt could be played slurred or unslurred. More reliable as an indicator is the staccato dash in b19 of the 'Pedal-Exercitium' BWV 598 – Ex. 158 – for this certainly looks like a warning not to

Ex. 158 BWV 598

play heel–toe. Unfortunately, not only is the piece of totally uncertain provenance, but its notation in the hand of C. P. E. Bach only raises the same query as the P 272 copy of the Six Sonatas, works which have virtually no pedal slurs or pedal dots in the composer's fair copy.* The printed *Clavierübung III* is probably a better indicator of the composer's own notation, where in two movements (only!) the pedal imitates the manual themes: Ex. 159. Always assuming that the engraver of

Ex. 159
BWV 552.i

BWV 552.i got b18 correct, not only is the pedal partaking of a phraseology common to the whole of the music at these points, but that music itself is in a specific style, allusive of up-to-date French rhythms (BWV 552.i) or, in the case of BWV 682, of proto-*galant* features. The more traditional movements or sections (e.g. the fugal section of BWV 552.i, or the whole of the fugue BWV 552.ii) are without signs of any kind. It therefore looks as if style-allusion required a pronounced playing method, with slurs, paired notes, *détaché* effects etc more marked than usual – cf. the staccato triplets in BWV 682, presumably something unusual.

Three further notational examples raise more general points of importance. The slurs in 'Meine Seele' BWV 648, though not present in the Schübler print, may be authentic corrections by the composer (see Wolff 1977): Ex. 160. In any case, they correspond to single syllables (melismas) in the text of the original cantata movement. Would an organist and continuo-player slur in such a manner, and if so would the organist not find it convenient to use the heel?† Secondly, while the slurs marking very clear *tierces coulées* at certain points in the pedal solos of the C major

---

* The only two examples are BWV 526.i b70 and BWV 527.iii b144 (first slur only), where the two momentary pedal solos are clearly meant to be phrased 'interestingly' (by alternate-toe pedalling?)
† Always assuming, of course, that the transcription did mean the lowest stave to be taken by the pedal.

Ex. 160   BWV 648

Toccata BWV 564 may be of doubtful authenticity,* they certainly express a musical characteristic – i.e., that the slurred dactyl figure is separated from its neighbours: Ex. 161. While in theory the same foot could play the first pair of each group, the

Ex. 161   BWV 564

slurred dactyl may well have been a convention familiar in the early eighteenth century (cf. BWV 629 and 631 in the *Orgelbüchlein*) and because it was a convention it may have demanded to be slurred even when it appeared in the pedal – which in turn would demand the use of the heel. It is certainly likely that Bach, writing pedal solos as a matter of familiar convention in toccatas (opening or closing sections of praeludia etc), should expand technical requirements and compose motifs that do seem to require the heel. Another good example is the G major Praeludium BWV 550, where the pedal solo develops a motif playable either way (alternate-foot or toe–heel): Ex. 162. Perhaps the organist is meant to have a choice, and although

Ex. 162   BWV 550.i

one can imagine toe–heel pedalling used to produce a slur as in b21 onwards, the pedal solos are so written as to exercise the technique of alternate-toe pedalling. In any case, like thumbless fingering, a rigorous alternate-toe pedalling does not of itself either prohibit slurs or necessarily encourage them. The final pedal solo of the A minor Fugue can be played entirely by alternate-toe pedalling; but the chromatic semitones off the beat (first five bars) seem better suited to *détaché*, and those on the beat (penultimate bar) to slurred pairs – the latter on the analogy of bowed basso-continuo passages in Weimar† cantatas: Ex. 163. The *figura* of b144 too could be either paired or separated; since it falls on the beat, it should perhaps be slurred as suggested in the example.

Thirdly, in the B minor Prelude BWV 544 the composer twice slurred and twice ornamented the pedal – another instance of a momentary pedal solo – Ex. 164. Why it was not so written in bb33–4 is open to much speculation (the slur in b34 is present in P 290). But the nature of both slurs in bb7–8 (little cambiata for the right foot, appoggiatura for the left) does make a smooth toe–heel and heel-toe per-

---

* Though the copy in P 801 was written *c*1729 and goes back 'directly to the autograph' (*NBA* IV/5–6 *KB* pp489, 495).

† Similar slurred semiquavers can be found in both early and mature keyboard music (e.g. Capriccio in B flat BWV 992.iii; Concerto in C major for Three Harpsichords BWV 1064.iii, episode before final ritornello).

Ex. 163   BWV 543.ii

BWV 161.ii

Ex. 164   BWV 544.i

[grace-notes ♪♫ – *NBA* IV/5–6 *KB* p487]

formance obvious. Perhaps by *c*1730 the composer was introducing up-to-date articulation marks (as in the manuals from b18) typical of the newer instrumental styles that were influencing his organ music. In the case of the more old-fashioned double pedal for the chorale BWV 686, the pedal reed conveys the cantus firmus if the right foot plays smoothly, while the left foot is more *détaché* as a moving bass; both seem to need the toe-heel technique, the right foot in particular.*

Three of these examples – BWV 648, 564 and 544 – do suggest a pragmatic approach to pedalling in which slurs, natural respectively to (i) vocal music, (ii) older styles based on individual *figurae*, and (iii) advanced instrumental music, are not only appropriate but seem in each case to indicate some use of the heel. Very likely it was also the demands made by (i) and (iii) in his popular transcriptions played at the end of the century that led Abt Vogler to publicize his then unusual virtuosity in toe-and-heel pedalling (J. H. Knecht, *Orgelschule*, Leipzig 1795). More pertinent to the music of J. S. Bach, perhaps, is the implication behind (ii) – i.e., that as an eighteenth-century composer intent on developing the earlier *figurae* beyond older techniques he was also encouraging a wider-ranging technique for the pedal part.†
But there is no reason to think that this last point constitutes evidence for frequent use of the heel. On the contrary, with such motifs as those in Ex. 165 (from the *Orgelbüchlein*) is it not rather that the alternate-foot technique (without the heel, but with an occasional leap or slide from one note to another with the same foot) suggests how naturally non-legato the hands are? Both may be considered a sophisticated version of the alternate-foot figures known to earlier composers, and only an anachronistic notion of how legato or how slurred the hands should be leads to assumptions about heel-pedalling.

* This interpretation is strictly conjectural and would contradict the view that the sound of the two pedal parts is 'completely equal' ('völlig gleich' – Wolff 1968 pp116–17); but it would be natural to a player.
† Thus the motivic counterpoint of a Bach trio results in much more difficult lines for the player than those of (e.g.) J. L. Krebs's more *galant* trios, which are much more manageable by alternate-toe techniques.

Ex. 165   BWV 643

BWV 615

An English visitor to the Sophienkirche, Dresden in the 1820s admired the

> rapidity and smoothness with which the *toeing* and *heeling* of the pedals are managed (Holmes 1828 p198)

by the organist Johann Gottlob Schneider; moreover, the

> rolling passages that were thus given by the feet with the greatest smoothness and certainty (*ibid* p208)

were in works of no less stature than the C sharp minor, F sharp minor and A flat major fugues of Book II of *The 48*. Similarly, Mendelssohn, who reported on Schneider playing the D major fugue subject from the same volume on an organ with pedals, found he could learn to do the same (as well as BWV 532.ii and 540.i) by assiduous practice – presumably in the same manner, although alas he does not say so (letter to Fanny, 3 September 1831). But such reports are part of the modern tradition of virtuoso pedal-playing and say nothing certain about Cöthen in 1720 or Leipzig in 1740.

28. Three-stave Notation

Three-stave notation, as now used for all organ music other than *manualiter*, leads to assumptions justified neither by the sources nor by what is known of performance practice. This is clear from the C minor Fugue BWV 574 and the E minor praeludium BWV 533: did the composer intend pedals to be reserved – in the convention of the day – for the fugal entries only, plus perhaps one or two other moments cued in?* Why should J. G. Preller give no pedal cues in BWV 574 (*NBA* IV/5–6 *KB* p511)? Did copyists both add and omit them, either from carelessness or following their own ideas and tastes? At what period did composers begin to have fixed requirements for the pedal? Were pedals optional in praeludia (speaking from the composers' point of view) outside their three classic uses for virtuoso solos, *points d'orgue* and fugal entries? When copyists after J. S. Bach were specific in their pedal cues, as in the toccata BWV 566 (*ibid* p532), were they reflecting practice

---

* For example, is there any authority for having the pedal play the middle episode in the E minor Fugue BWV 533 or the first episode in the C minor Fugue BWV 574? Not least for the use of pedals, there is no better instance of the greater sophistication which J. S. Bach brought to the organ fugue than that offered by a comparison between the early and late E minor Fugues BWV 533 and BWV 548.

in *c*1700 or *c*1750, or both, or neither? If the copy Am.B.544 gives no pedal cues throughout the four movements of the same toccata, is the copyist being careless or in fact more faithful to his source? If the latter, did that source reflect the custom of optional 'scoring' of the bass line – i.e., that the composer usually left it open whether or not to use pedals? In their very framing, such questions often imply an answer, and in the present instance attention will be drawn to one particular aspect, the number of staves.

Quite apart from the evidence about staves supplied by the sources and summarized in Vols. I and II, the significance of different layouts was appreciated from at least the time of J. S. Bach onwards. The composer himself seems to have meant no more by his curious term 'distinctius' for the *Orgelbüchlein* chorale BWV 633 than that it was written 'more distinctly' on three staves instead of the two used for the version BWV 634. Distinctness was the aim of the third stave also according to Türk, who in his book of 1787 quoted the closing bars of the *Canonic Variations* BWV 769, music already on three staves in its original engraving but redistributed by Türk so that the tenor appeared with the pedal part on the lowest stave (see *Dok* III p433). Bach's three staves are organ score, Türk's a kind of open score – as indeed are the four staves of Var. IV in the same engraving. At the same period as Türk, the author of the 1788 *Comparison between Handel and Bach* points out, as if with pride, that for the music of J. S. Bach three staves are used often, and indeed 'always for works with two manuals and pedal' (*Dok* III p441). Taken literally, this is true neither of the earlier sources nor of BWV 769 Var. IV, where the pedal takes the third of four staves and so runs between the two staves for the left hand. This disposition of parts in the engraving may reflect two older traditions of using open score: for clarity when parts cross (e.g. Reincken's G major Toccata, on three staves in the Andreas-Bach-Buch) and for visual immediacy, facilitating quick understanding and correct phraseology, when the parts share a particular quality.* Both these traditions leave the contribution of the pedal ambiguous; hence, presumably, the need for a pedal cue in BWV 769.iv (four staves) and for the various cues in the *Schübler Chorales* (three staves). Indeed, not only the pedal cues but several features of the *Schübler* notation provoke questions. Is it an open score or an organ score? Did the composer and/or the arranger and/or the publisher intend to leave the buyer free to distribute the staves as he wished? Or did he merely reproduce a score of the cantata arias concerned? Was the use of three staves by then conventional enough to need no cues? Are there not two ways of playing at least the first of the *Schübler Chorales*, BWV 645?

There can be little doubt that one of the interests the composer had in three famous collections of organ music in his possession was notational: the traditional German tablature of Ammerbach's *Orgel oder Instrument Tabulatur* (Leipzig 1571), the four-stave open score of Frescobaldi's *Fiori musicali (Venice* 1635) and the three-stave score of de Grigny's *Livre d'Orgue* (Paris 1699).† Adlung (1768 I p96) noted that de Grigny put a stop-registration by each stave – something unusual in Germany – and it certainly seems that various french *livres* were the first organ

---

* E.g. Buxtehude's settings of 'Mit Fried und Freud' (published in 1674) which demonstrate both inversion and invertible counterpoint.
† The sheer variety of clefs used by Frescobaldi and de Grigny – e.g. 𝄡 and 𝄢 – is interesting in the light of J. S. Bach's openness to music of other schools and contexts.

music systematically to use three five-line staves (Riedel 1960 p37), perhaps precisely because each stave was to have a different registration. But it is striking that de Grigny does not use the third stave only for pedal, using it rather for whatever is the bass line and cuing in entries from time to time, even in a movement such as *tierce en taille* where the scoring of two manuals and pedal is clear enough. This was the scoring which seems to have established the three-stave convention. Free preludes and fugues – i.e. music with no solo line that must be marked – continued to be notated mostly on two staves even when the pedal was *obbligato* and fully developed.* Thus a trio would always be notated on three staves, whether a sonata, a chorale (e.g. BWV 660a and 639, copied by J. G. Walther in P 802), or a single movement added to a two-stave prelude and fugue (e.g. BWV 545 plus 529.ii: see Kilian 1969 p19); but the criterion was not three-part counterpoint as such but the distribution on two manuals and pedal. Such too is the implication of the title-page of H. F. Quehl's *Versuch* of 1734:

> Der . . . erstere musicalische Versuch. Bestehend in Zweyen Choralen, mit unterschiedenen, theils Fugirten, theils auf zwey Clavieren und obligatem Pedal, auf drey Linien eingerichteten Variationen.

> First Musical Essay. Consisting of two Chorales, with several Variations, partly fugal, partly for two manuals and *obbligato* pedal, arranged on three staves.

In the case of three-stave copies written before the 1730s, it is important to consider whether they were so written for clarity, or to specify pedal, or to specify distribution on two manuals and pedal. The three are related but essentially different. The tradition for keeping preludes and fugues on two staves suggests that the first two reasons were less crucial than the third: it is a tradition still clear in *Clavierübung III* (BWV 552) and in manuscripts of J. L. Krebs (C major Prelude and Fugue in BB 12014/5, where pedal is clearly cued) and of the Kirnberger circle (Bruhns's G major toccata in Am.B.462 and 430, with pedal lines in red ink). In such sources, three staves are used for trios (BWV 676, etc; those of Krebs in BB Autog. JLK 5), for other pieces using two manuals at once (Bruhns's 'Nun komm'; BWV 678, 682), and for pieces using double pedal parts (section in Bruhns's G major Toccata; BWV 686). If the layout of parts allowed it, however, two staves could be used even for pieces with two manuals and pedal cantus firmus (BWV 684), though copyists such as J. G. Walther (P 802) usually used three staves for such genres,† including trio sections in pieces otherwise on two staves (e.g. J. T. Krebs's copy of BWV 720 in P 802). Walther did so not only to mark the distribution of parts on their respective keyboards but because the tradition of chorale-fantasias (e.g. by Buxtehude, Lübeck and Reincken in P 802) had established the three-stave notation when such pieces were no longer copied in tablature.

One example shows the uncertainties about such notation. In his copy of Weckmann's 'Ach wir armen Sünder' *Vers* 1 (in P 802), Walther uses the third stave both for a pedal line (marked 'p.') and to take the tenor line when there would otherwise be low leger-lines on the middle stave; but it is not known if his source authorized

---

* And written in red ink in some Kirnberger copies.
† 'O Mensch bewein'' BWV 622a must therefore have had the superscription 'for two manuals and pedal' by the time Krebs copied it in P 802, for he put it on three staves; but whether the composer originally intended that in the autograph P 283 is uncertain.

his marking the bottom line 'p.', whether it is an independent bass line (i.e. at 16′ pitch), whether the organist was meant to be free to play the piece as best he could, and how the extra part for the final bars was to be played – pedal? extra solo part?*

It remains an open question whether in this and other examples Walther (and thus other copyists) confused the third stave with the pedal stave, giving the pedal more than it should have been given in (e.g.) Buxtehude's fantasia 'Gelobet seystu Jesu Christ' and so misleading editors and players ever since. Were tablatures and early three-stave notations forms of open score leaving the player to distribute the parts as he wished? Was Walther simplifying the older northern fantasia? and if so, did he do so as a central German organist not very familiar with it or as an early-eighteenth-century organist whose ideas on registration were losing the freedom of earlier composers?† Either way, it should noted that Walther's layout of *Vers* I of Weckmann's 'Ach wir armen Sünder' in P 802 leaves the choice much more open to the organist than the modern three-stave edition, in which (however reasonable in itself the three-stave layout might be) no player would find it convenient to exchange tenor and bass parts: he *has* to play the theme in the pedal, whereas Walther gave him the choice of either doing that or playing the bass on the pedals and the tenor melody on a second manual (see Ex. 166). Vestiges of the old ambiguity – and thus of choice – are still to be seen in *Orgelbüchlein* and *Schübler* chorales.

Ex. 166   M. Weckmann, 'Ach wir armen Sünder', *Vers* I Choral im Tenor

---

* See *Matthias Weckmann: Choralbearbeitungen*, ed. W. Breig, Kassel 1979, pp. xi, 4–5, 104.

† Such 'loss of freedom' comes not only from a simpler notion of organ design (two conventional manuals in partnership, usually within the same organ case, distinct from and complementary to each other in volume and tone) but also from the idea that there is an 8′ norm: i.e., whether or not other ranks are added, manuals are based on 8′ stops. See note on the Fantasia BWV 720, Vol. II p263. As organs lost the extremes of tone and sound between *Hauptwerk*, *Rückpositiv* and *Brustwerk*, and thus the inventive and even capricious registration that this could lead to, composers and copyists wrote out or interpreted the organ chorale in conventions more amenable to 'norms'.

Additions and Corrections to Volumes I and II

In references made to Volumes I and II

'¶1' begins either with the top line of the page or, if it follows a **bold** BWV number, with the next line after that new entry;

when lines are numbered 'from bottom', footnotes are not counted.

Volume I

131a   *p5 line 2, for* (J. C. Kittel) *read* (J. C. Kittel?)

525–530   **Six Sonatas**

p9 lines 2–3: Their compass alone (neither C♯, nor d‴, etc) is characteristic of music for organ rather than for harpsichord, at least by *c*1729).

p9 lines 10–11 after inset: Both W. F. Bach and Gerber were pupils of J. S. Bach during the period when the Six Sonatas were compiled.

p9 lines 18–19 from bottom: The 'Inventions' in LM 4941 are headed 'a 2 Clav. et Pedal'.

p13 ¶3 line 2: The organ movements have such simple proportions as 1:1 in BWV 525.iii or 3:4:3 in BWV 527.i

525   *p18 line 7 from bottom, for* LM 4842 (J. C. H. Rinck *read* LM 4842a (J. C. H. Rinck?

p22 lines 4–5 after Ex. 17: There is a similar sequence of (incomplete) bass entries in another trio slow movement, the Adagio ma non troppo of the Sixth Brandenburg Concerto.

527   *p36 footnote*: This stands despite the apparent 'common sense' of such an assumption (Emery *MT* 1971 pp697–8).

529   *p45 lines 2–3*: BWV 529 was probably added to BWV 545 in the Weimar period (*NBA* IV/5–6 *KB* pp302, 307).

530   *p55 lines 8–10 after inset*: See also above on this page, comment on Vol. I p22.

531   *p57 ¶1, delete lines 1–5 and replace by* No Autograph MS; that once thought to be autograph (prelude, Washington Library of Congress ML 96.B 186) copied by C. G. Gerlach; copies in Möller MS (BB 40644), P 274 (incomplete fugue; W. N. Mey?), P 286 (18th century, from P 274?), Württemberg Landesbib. Cod. mus II.288 (prelude only; *c*1740, owned by W. H. Pachelbel),

p57 ¶2: In Cod. mus II.288 the piece is marked 'Seque l'Fuga un piu Largo'.

p57 ¶4 line 6: Reasons, not by any means conclusive, have been given for thinking BWV 531 and 549a to be J. S. Bach's 'earliest surviving free organ compositions' (Stauffer 1980 p129).

p59 1st inset line 8: The b36 entry is not cued for pedal in any source.

532

p60 ¶1 line 1: Cod. mus II.288 dated '1740'.

p60 ¶1 line 7, for (Dröbs) *read* (Dröbs?)

p60 ¶2 line 1, for 'Preludio' *read* 'Preludio . . . Clavicembalo'

p60 end ¶2, add 'Praeludium Concertato' in Cod. mus II.288.

p61 end ¶1: Nor is there any support for the idea that in 1716 the work (with its many Italianisms) was used by the composer at his opening recital on the new organ of the Liebfrauenkirche, Halle (David 1951 p38). But editors have been correct to point out how the sources suggest that prelude and fugue originated together (Peters IV; *NBA* IV/5–6 *KB* p343).

p62 line 4: The *alla breve* is not so labelled in all sources.

p63 ¶2 line 9: The *doppio* is not specified or made clear in any known source.

p63 ¶2: The fourth section as a whole looks like a development of the second section of the Sonata in D major BWV 963 (in P 804).

p65 ¶2: 'Bey dieser Fuge muss man die Füsse recht strampfeln lassen' ('with this fugue one must really kick about with the feet'), according to a note in Cod. mus II.288.

532a

p66 line 6 after inset: It would hold even were we to agree that Spitta's admiration for the shorter version is 'incomprehensible' (Lohmann B & H edn 6581 p. xi).

533

p66 ¶1 line 2, for 'Anon 18' *read* J. C. Vogler

p66 ¶1 line 5, for P 557 (Grasnick), *read* P 557 (Westphal),

p66 last 3 lines: It is still sometimes claimed that the prelude and fugue are 'related motivically' (Stauffer 1980 p129), though P 804 (Kellner circle) and the Vogler copy are good evidence that the work circulated as a separate and independent prelude and fugue, at least 'for a time' (*NBA* IV/5–6 *KB* p385).

p67 footnote, before in BG 15 *add* in some 18th-century manuscripts and

533a

p69 ¶3 line 5, for (NBA IV/6 p. vi), *read* (NBA IV/5–6 KB pp382–3, 581),

p69 line 5 from bottom: Perhaps MS 7 is copyist's work, the fugue ornaments (see *NBA* IV/5–6 *KB* p194) recalling those in Walther sources.

p69 last ¶: Nevertheless, the dispensability of the pedal in BWV 533 (no source specifies it in b19, for example – *ibid* p388) does raise questions about how the organ was used in early works of Bach.

534

p70, add to ¶1: A copy said to be by Kittel, lost after 1840 (*NBA* IV/5–6 *KB* p212).

p70 end ¶3: The same reservations apply to the conclusion that the pedal D♭ proves the work to have originated during the Weimar years (Klotz 1950 p198).

p70 footnote: For the 'cadenza', cf. the Violin Sonata BWV 1003.ii.

p71 line 12: But was G minor the original key 'of BWV 534? If this was the case, not only would the pedal line in the prelude at bb20–1 be able to continue down (breaking back in b22?), but the final allusion to the theme in the fugue (see Ex. 72 below) would not need to rise an octave in the pedal: it could have been GAB♭C♯DG. The transposition would have been made to avoid the important d‴, though the need then for a C♯ would certainly have caused problems.

535

p75 ¶1 line 4, for (Kittel), *read* (Kittel?), *and for* Kellner, *read* Kellner?,

p75 ¶1 line 5, after Go.S.26 *add* fugue only

p75 ¶2 line 2, after Schubring *add* (and P 320, 557, 1097)

p75 ¶2: Title in P 288 'Praeludium con Fuga pedaliter'. Fugue marked 'allegro' in almost all copies.

p75 ¶4 lines 4–5: The term *passaggio* often implies an alternate-hand technique carefully specified by (e.g.) P 1097 (*NBA* IV/5–6 *KB* p449).

p75 ¶4 lines 11–15: This bass theme coincides (even to the key) with a melodic phrase quoted by Mattheson (1739 p154) as an ideal sequence of narrow and wide intervals: Ex. 72a.

Ex. 72a

p75 footnote: The *BG* 15 version comes from Peters III, itself from a lost Kittel source.

p76 lines 4–5: This is true too of those variant progressions given in sources whose copyists either did not understand the enharmonic diminished-seventh sequences (abbreviated in the composer's original manuscripts) or else were following a different and perhaps authentic version of them. See music examples in *NBA* IV/5–6 *KB* pp437ff.

p76 ¶ after inset: The Capriccio in B flat BWV 992 offers some useful comparisons for fugal texture and figures.

535a

p77 ¶1: Was the Möller MS known to Kellner? – cf. Peters III.

p77 ¶2 line 3, for autograph). *read* autograph?).

p77 ¶5 (2nd ¶ in small type): Perhaps the fugue was completed on a piece of paper now lost, not necessarily in the manner of BWV 535.ii (Kilian in *NBA* IV/5–6 *KB* p583).*

---

* One possible reason for the discrepancies between BWV 535 and 535a is outlined by Stauffer (1980 pp130, 39): perhaps the composer first 'prefaced a predeliberated fugue with an improvized prelude', a cursory movement that he 'apparently dashed off at the last minute'. He then 'enlarged the Prelude to produce a more symmetrical plan', and in the process 'expanded and formalized' the parts of BWV 535a, reworking them in 535.

536   *p79 ¶2*: Title in P 804 'Praeludium . . . cum Pedale'. Mistakes in P 804 suggest that its source was in tablature (*NBA* IV/5–6 *KB* pp474–5).

536a   *p82 ¶1 line 2, after* fugue only, *add* more or less shortened,

   p82 ¶2 line 2, for (*BG* 15; *read* (Peters II;

537   *p83 end ¶1, for* (19th century) *read* ('1841' copy of P 803)

   p83 ¶1: Peters III may have used an indirect Kittel source (*NBA* IV/5–6 *KB* pp330–1).

   p85 Ex. 77: Stauffer (1980 pp83–4) points out that *A* (b1 etc) is characterized by the figure *exclamatio* (cf. Walther's reference (1732 p233) to the 'anguished cry' of the minor sixth) and *B* by the figure *suspiratio* (the slurred motif of b12 etc).

   p86 line 2 above Ex. 78, for p209), *read* p210),

538   *p88, delete ¶1 and replace by* No Autograph MS; copies in P 803 (J. G. Walther), P 1099 (J. G. Preller), later-18th-century sources (P 275, P 277, P 286, P 290, P 319 Westphal, P 416, P 596), and 19th-century (P 282, P 837, unnumbered Oxford Bodleian MS); also in sources of Kittel circle (LM 4842h L. Scholz (fugue only), LM 4839e Fischer, Lpz MB III.8.16 Dröbs); toccata only in 'Schubring MS' (*BG* 15); fugue only in (late) sources Salzburg Archiv des Domchores MN 104, Vienna Gesellschaft der Musikfreunde VII 14399 a/B, and BB 30377 (shortened). Peters III used a Kellner source from which some of these derived.

   p88 ¶2: Variety of headings in the sources: thus in P 275, *f/p* registration marks, a title 'pro Organo pleno', and the first movement headed 'Allegro'. Manual indications in P 803 'O', Positiv' and (from b31) 'R'; in other sources 'Pos.' etc. but never 'Rp' or 'Rückpositiv'.

   p92 Ex. 84: It is a pardonable exaggeration to claim that 'the single half-measure-long motive provides the melodic kernel that serves as the basis for all the ritornello and episodic material' (Stauffer 1980 p57).

   p94 lines 6–10 after Ex. 87: The free lines are anticipatory of other D minor counterpoint, in particular the semiquaver passages in the *alla francese* fugue in the *Art of Fugue* and the quaver lines in the three-part fugue of the same collection.

539   *p96 delete ¶1 and replace by* No Autograph MS; complete copy in P 517 (early 19th century) and 1st edn (Leipzig 1833, Marx); fugue only in Am.B.606 (2nd half of 18th century), P 213, P 282 (Westphal?) and later sources (e.g. P 304 c1800, Vienna Gesellschaft der Musikfreunde SBQ 11500), all probably from a common source (*NBA* IV/5–6 *KB* p360). The fugue is a transcription of a violin-sonata movement (see below).

   p96 ¶2: In P 213 and P 304, one of 'VI Fughe per il Clavicembalo' (i.e. with BWV 944, Anh.177, 886, 951a, 951) but with pedal indications.

   p96 footnote last line, for (P 286) *read* (P 268)

   p98 ¶2: The copyist of P 517 also wrote out other transcribed instrumental works including the three Concertos for Three and Four Harpsichords (*NBA* IV/5–6 *KB* p357); one can therefore imagine him as having an interest in harpsichord transcriptions generally.

Volume I

540

p103 delete ¶1 and replace by No Autograph MS; copies in P 803 (toccata copied by J. T. Krebs, fugue by J. L. Krebs), P 277, P 290, P 596 and P 287 (18th century), also 'Schubring MS' (*BG* 15); toccata only, in 18th-century (P 1009 Kittel?, P 289) and 19th-century copies (e.g. BB 30387 Dröbs, Lpz Poel 16 with an anonymous fugue); fugue only, in 18th-century (P 287, P 409, Lpz Poel 28, Lpz MB MS 3,2 J. A. G Wechmar?; BB 30377 shortened, a MS owned by Rust and described in *NBA* IV/5-6 *KB* p171) and 19th-century copies (P 282, Lpz MB III. 8.29 Dröbs). Peters III used a so-called Kellner copy.

p104 lines 8–10: This variant also found in some MSS derived from a lost Kittel source (*NBA* IV/5-6 *KB* pp405-6).

p104 end ¶1: Nevertheless, the compiling of the movements is without doubt only 'weakly vouched for' by the sources (*NBA* IV/5-6 *KB* p404).

p105 2nd inset lines 8, 12 and last, for 218 (*three times*) *read* 218/19

p105 2nd inset sections B₁, B₃, B₄: In bb204-7, 318-21, 424-7 can be found transposed B-A-C-H references, but in the nature of things a 'transposed B-A-C-H' is a contradiction in terms.

p106 lines 1–2: Mendelssohn enthused over this cadence in a letter to his sister Fanny of 3 September 1831. The same major cadence occurs in the Chromatic Fantasia BWV 903 at bb54-5 and 56-7.

p106 lines 8–11 from bottom: Much of the detail of both melody and rhythm seem to originate in Vivaldi's concertos Op III, VII etc.

p107 Ex. 98, 1st stave: That the same melodic–imitative idea also occurs in Handel's early *Dixit Dominus* (3/4 movement) may well reflect a background common to both composers.

541

p112 ¶1 line 2, for owned *read* written

p112 ¶1 line 4, for (Kittel) *read* (Kittel?)

p112 ¶1 line 5, for LM 4839 *read* LM 4839d

p112 ¶2, at end add and 'Praeludium Pedaliter'.

p112 ¶3 lines 1–5: But nothing in the sources suggests that the prelude is later than the fugue, as has been suggested (Krey 1956 p183).

last 6 lines, delete 2 sentences (from p112 'There may be') and replace by The watermark has been dated 1733 (*NBA* IV/5-6 *KB* p33): i.e., the paper was used for fair-copy or revision purposes. There must have been at least two autographs, one being that referred to by May (1974 p275) when he says that Lpz MB MS a 1, P 288 and P 595 all 'apparently depend on the Weimar autograph (now lost)'. This 'lost Weimar autograph' is now thought to be the (now lost) MS once owned by Rust (see *NBA* IV/5-6 *KB* pp427ff).

p113 lines 4–6: though the prelude and fugue of BWV 541 do have the proportion 1:1.

p113 lines 6-12: It is possible, however, that Westphal saw an autograph copy of BWV 541 complete with trio (*NBA* IV/5-6 *KB* pp427-8).

p113 inset line 1, for toccata *read* toccata or *passaggio*

p113 inset line 2, for page) *read* page; implied pedal point?)

p114 Ex. 106 extract 'a', after b12 *add* (cf. Fugue b76 etc)

p115 lines 1-2: The direction 'Vivace' seems to belong only to the revised version as known from the extant autograph MS. Does it suggest that by c1740 the composer had a livelier interpretation of old *passaggio* styles? Or perhaps that it was no longer necessarily understood that 3/4 metre implied a faster tempo for the crotchet than such 4/4 *passaggio* preludes as BWV 533.i?

542

p118 delete ¶1 and replace by No Autograph MS; copies of fugue only, in P 803 (J. T. Krebs), P 1100 (J. C. Oley), P 598 (J. F. Agricola, between 1738 and 1741), P 288 (J. P. Kellner), other 18th-century (P 290, P 203 J. S. Borsch, Lpz MB MS 4) and 19th-century sources (P 282, P 837, Lpz Poel 21, BB 38276, 'Schubring MS', etc); fugue alone in F minor in P 320 (Kittel?), P 287 (J. S. Borsch), P 204 (C. F. G. Schwenke), P 518 (c1800), P 557 (Grasnick c1820), LM 4838, Lpz Go.S.26, some of these dependent on Kittel sources; fantasia alone in Lpz MB III.8.20 (Dröbs); fantasia and fugue together in Am.B.531 (18th century, but originally separate?), P 288 (2nd half of 18th century or later, ditto), P 595 and P 924 (Grasnick); together but in reversed order in P 1071 (c1800). Published separately in different volumes by Marx (Leipzig 1833).

p118 end ¶2, add; in P 1100, 'Fuga . . . pro Organo pleno'.

p118 ¶3 lines 5-7: Only if the harmonic thought of the fantasia is not examined is it possible to see it as earlier than the fugue, as is sometimes claimed (Stauffer 1980 p110).

p118 lines 3-8 from bottom: Griepenkerl (Peters II) coupled the two on evidence he found in now unverifiable sources, but it seems doubtful that there was (ever?) an autograph copy that coupled the movements (*NBA* IV/5-6 *KB* pp455-6).

p119 ¶1 lines 7-9, delete last sentence (from 'The fugue') and read The fugue as given in *BG* 15 has been claimed as a variant form 'adapted' for a less proficient player (Keller *BJ* 1913), a conclusion argued from imperfectly understood sources, Either way, the (or an) original F minor version may have been 'relatively early' (*NBA* IV/5-6 *KB* p458).

p121 line 2, for revised form *read* putative third form

p121 lines 2-4 above Ex. 113: The *A B A B A* shape theoretically recalls the free/ strict alternation familiar from the 'north-German multisectional *Praeludium Pedaliter*' (Stauffer 1980 p85), but the difference in scale must make such analogies doubtful. However, it does seem reasonable to view the pieces as built on the following shape (Dietrich 1931): *point d'orgue* – interlude – *point d'orgue* – interlude – improvisation – interlude – improvisation.

p122 lines 6-7: A similar analogy is the Vivaldi recitative of the Concerto BWV 594.ii.

p124 lines 13–14 (quotation): Was this C. P. E. Bach's opinion (*NBA* IV/5–6 *KB* p469)?

p124 Ex. 116, delete heading of 1st extract and replace by Reincken, Fugue in G minor b56

p125 Ex. 118 2nd heading, after decorated *add* or 'improved' version (*NBA* IV/5–6 *KB* p462):

543   *p126 ¶1 line 3, for* (P 819 prelude only, *read* (P 819 Grasnick (prelude only),

p127 line 1, after Am.B.60 *add* (and P 505)

p128 line 5 above Ex. 121: Another characteristic feature is the texture in bb31–2, as in the early 'Wie schön' BWV 739 at bb69–70.

p128 2nd footnote: Two further 'errors' may have been conveyed by the copyists: should the pedal point begin in the second half of b9? and should bb19 and 21 continue the crotchet line of bb11, 13, 15 and 17?

543a   *p131 delete ¶1 and replace by* No Autograph MS; copies in P 803 (? 1st half of 18th century, ?autograph corrections in (e.g.) bb110–12 of fugue), P 288 (probably J. P. Kellner) and LM 4839g (Fischer).

544   *p132 delete ¶1 and replace by* Autograph MS (now in private possession); copies in P 891 (copied by J. P. Kellner), Am.B.60 (Berlin copyist, after 1754), 18th-century sources (Am.B.54 copy of Am.B.60, P 276, P 290) and later-18th- and early-19th-century sources (LM 4839i, P 560, Lpz MB MS 1,17 Wechmar?, Lpz Poel 24 Weigand *c*1817, BB 30380 Schwenke, P 922 Grasnick, Lpz MB III.8.21 Dröbs, LM 4720, P 925 arrangement for four hands dated 1832, P 837), some presumably from Kittel sources.

p133 delete ¶2 and replace by Two staves; titles in Autograph MS 'Praeludium in Organo pleno, pedal:' and 'Praeludium pro Organo cum pedale obligato', in Lpz Poel 24 'Praeludium et Fuga . . . pro Organo Pleno cum Pedale oblig.'

p133 line 7, for 1740 *read* 1731

p134 ¶ after inset, 2nd half of ¶: The autograph notation cannot be used as evidence for or against manual-changing: see *NBA* IV/5–6 *KB* pp38–9.

p137 line 5 above Ex. 127: The subject itself is derived, some have thought, from the penultimate bar of the prelude (Stauffer 1980 p134).

p137 lines 1–3 above Ex. 127: Such lines are familiar from other mature organ works, e.g. E flat Prelude BWV 552 bb147–8.

545   *p139 ¶1 line 2, for* 658 Kittel, *read* 658 Fischer,

p139 ¶1 line 3, for 4839 Ringk *read* 4839c Fischer

p139 ¶2 line 4, after Kellner *add* *c*1725?

p139 ¶3: In LM 4718 'Preludio con Fuga e Trio'; trio marked 'Largo' in LM 4718 and Moscheles MS.

p139 last 2 lines and p140 line 1, delete from 'the same separated' to 'fugue by Walther;' and replace by the same separated by a trio (BWV 529.ii, 40 of the 50 bars placed before the fugue by Vogler, the rest after; entirely after the fugue by Walther);

p140 last ¶: Kilian's suggested order (in *NBA* IV/5–6 *KB* pp299–303) is: an original version (perhaps made already at Arnstadt-Mühlhausen); then 545a or 545b at Weimar; then 545 + 529.ii at Weimar; finally 545 (no 529.ii) fair copy at Leipzig.

545a   *p144 delete ¶1 and replace by* No Autograph MS; copies in sources of 2nd half of 18th century (P 290 prelude only, Lpz Poel 12 – the latter once owned by Forkel, hence perhaps 545a not 545 quoted in his thematic index of 1802?) and later (P 521, fugue only).

p144 last line: Title in P 290 'Praeludium Pedaliter'.

p145 lines 3–5 after inset: Kilian's conjecture is that it represents an early version of the work from the beginning of the Weimar period (*NBA* IV/5–6 *KB* p568).

545b   *main heading*: The designation 'BWV 545b', though not an 'official' number assigned by *Schmieder BWV*, is sometimes used for this variant (e.g. by Emery).

p145 delete ¶3 lines 1–2 and replace by The chief differences between the so-called BWV 545b and BWV 545 are as follows (cf. *NBA* IV/5–6 *KB* pp143–5):

p146 lines 2–6 above Ex. 135, delete from 'line); both are the work' to '1959 p184).' and replace by line), whoever he may have been.

p146 delete lines 4–13 from bottom, from 'and a violin' to 'respectively).', and replace by or transcription by another. Did Cooke's master Pepusch (1667–1752) possess works by Bach and give them to Cooke's predecessor, Robinson (to whom Cooke attributed the work)?

p147 lines 1–2: Similarly, the clever and effective close to the prelude, simpler than BWV 545 but referring both to the theme of 545b (b1) and to the concluding harmonies of 545 (bb28–31), is certainly worthy of the composer who later wrote the closes of BWV 547 and 769.

546   *p147 ¶1 line 1, for* (Kittel) *read* (Kittel?)

p147 ¶1 line 4, for 4839e *read* 4839f

p147 delete ¶2 and replace by Two staves; typical title in P 286 'Praeludium con Fuga ex C mol. pro Organo cum Pedale obligato', in P 596 '. . . pro Organo pleno'.

p147 lines 9–10 from bottom: Nothing in the older sources suggests that BWV 546.i and ii were not originally paired.

p147 footnote: Or BWV 546.ii was coupled to the Fantasia BWV 562.i in an early version (*NBA* IV/5–6 *KB* p324) before its own fugue was begun.

p148 2nd inset: While certain of the subsidiary sections of the *B* section might be differently described (e.g., Meyer 1979 sees $A_2 = 70\text{-}8$ and $B = 78\text{-}85$), the varying note-lengths employed in the themes are clear enough. Thus, *A* moves in stages from minims to semiquavers, while the triplets of the episode *B* of bb53-70 'colour' the first bar of the next entry of *A* (so that the dotted pedal of b70 means a triplet absent from b72).

p149 line 2 after Ex. 136: or like the opening of Cantata 47 (1726).

p151 inset line 1: C. P. E. Bach's copyist 'Anon 303' marked the opening subject 'manual' in P 290 since its tessitura might have suggested pedal.

547

p154 delete ¶1 and replace by No Autograph MS; copies in P 274 (Kellner circle), Am.B.60 (Berlin copyist, after 1754), P 320 (Kittel?), Lpz Poel 32 (C. F. Penzel), LM 5056 (J. Becker *c*1779), and other good 18th-century sources (P 276, P 290, P 286 Forkel?); also sources based on 'Agricola' (Am.B.54, P 557 Grasnick) and Kittel (Lpz Go.S.26, Lpz MB MS 1,8 Wechmar), and later (P 837, Brussels II.3914, P 925).

p154 delete ¶2 and replace by Two staves; pedal in red ink in Am.B.54, Am.B.60, P 276, P 290, P 837; title in P 274 'Praeludium pro Organo pedal.', in Lpz MB MS 1,8 'Praeludium con Fuga ex C♯ pro organo pleno'.

p155 lines 6-7, for final stages . . . basic theme *read* final stage of each movement is derived from its basic theme.

p156 inset: Cf. the outline of BWV 538.i

p155 footnote last 2 lines: Compare the not dissimilar Prelude from English Suite in D minor BWV 811.

p156 inset line 13, for parts *read* sections

p156 ¶1 last 4 lines: F minor and G minor are not keys typical of C major preludes.

p159 Ex. 148: [bracket for motif *y* should include the e′]

p160 Ex. 150: [bracket for motif *y* should not include the tied-over semiquaver b]

p160 Ex. 152: [3rd note in bass should be c not e]

p162 Ex. 156: [1st bracket for motif *y* should not include the 1st d′]

548

p163 ¶1 line 3, after Anon 5 *add* (a Bach pupil? after 1730?)

p163 ¶1 line 4, for Mempell *read* Mempell?

p163 ¶1 line 5, for LM 4839, *read* LM 4839h, *and for* Forkel) *read* Forkel?)

p163 ¶1 line 9, for J. L. Weigand *read* J. G. Weigand

p164 line 2, after MB III.8.21 *add* and LM 4839h

p164 line 2: In P 274, the fugal *da capo* not written out (ends at b191).

p164 ¶2 line 21: For the sequential scales of the Prelude, cf. those of the G minor English Suite BWV 808.i.

p170 ¶2 line 5, for BWV 541.ii *read* BWV 537.ii

p170 line 8 from bottom: BWV 810 = *A B A* (approximately 40 + 80 + 40 bars).

p172 Ex. 164: Cf. a passage in the *Dialogue* from Louis Marchand's *Livre d'Orgue* (Paris *c*1700).

549

p172 ¶1 line 1, for Kittel, *read* Kittel?,

p172 ¶1 line 2, for Michel, *read* Michel 1780/90,

p172 ¶1 line 6, for further Kittel MS *read* further ?Kittel MS

p172 ¶2 line 1, after Hauser MS *add* and LM 4838

p172 last 3 lines: The near-identity of the versions suggests that he did not make the transcription himself (*NBA* IV/5–6 *KB* p319).

p174 lines 5–6 from bottom: As Musch observes (1974 pp271–2), the fugue is really *manualiter*; at the entry of the pedal it becomes more like a toccata.

p175 line 13: Is the subject derived from a motif in the prelude?

549a

p175 ¶1, add: Fugue only in a lost 'Kellner source' (Peters IV).

p175 ¶2 line 1, for Fantasia pedaliter', *read* Fantasia. Pedaliter',

p175 ¶3 lines 1–3: Hauser associated the D minor version with a different fugue, one ascribed by him to Pachelbel (Kobayashi 1973 p236).

550

p176 delete ¶1 and replace by No Autograph MS; copies in Lpz MB MS 7, 20 (J. N. Mempell?), P 287 (Michel), P 1090 (Homilius, after P 1210) and later copies (LM 4839a, Brussels Fétis 2960, Scholz MS to b62 only, Salzburg Archiv des Domchores MN 104) including those of the 19th century (P 642 etc, P 512 Grasnick, P 924 Grasnick, Lpz Go.S.318a, Oxford MS); *BG* 38 used 'old MS in Hauser's Collection' (=P 1210, 1st half of 18th century, with 'corrections' by J. S. Bach) and Dresden Sächs. Landesbib. Mus. 1 T 12 (destroyed).

p176 ¶2 line 4, after P 287 *add* , P 1210 and P 642

p176 ¶3 lines 2–3, for fugue', as is also the case in P 642; *read* fugue' (the whole section bb46–62 is lacking in P 642 and P 924);

p176 ¶3 lines 3–4: The same bars marked 'Adagio' in LM 4839a.

p176 ¶3 lines 1–7: If, however, the *whole* section bb46–62 was also absent in the Kellner copy (as in P 642 and 924 – see *NBA* IV/5–6 *KB* p421), a musical case could be made for supposing those few bars to be a later addition.

p177 line 8 from bottom: A hemiola at bb43–4, however, rather supports the idea that the perfect cadence of bb45–6 was (originally) meant to close the prelude (see the discussion of sources, above).

p177 footnote: In any case, P 1210 puts b34 down an octave.

551

p179 ¶1: 19th-century sources all based on Ringk?

p179 line 3 from bottom: Both fugues have most entries in the tenor.

p180 line 4: Section 4 is built on 3 × 12 bars (Meyer 1979).

p180 under heading 'First section', lines 1–2: Perhaps Mempell's source (cf. his title) did not yet contain these eleven bars.

p181 1st music example, add caption **Ex. 168** *in left margin*

p184 ¶1 line 1: An Autograph MS seems to be referred to by C. P. E. Bach in 1774 – see *Dok* III p277.

552 *p184 inset line 1, after 32 bars add* (2 × 16-bar sections)

p184 inset, between lines 6 and 7 add new line (*A*   129   1 bar)

p185 1st inset: In the course of the prelude *A* becomes shorter and *C* longer, while *B* remains the same length.

p188 lines 1–2: N. A. Strunck (opera-director etc in Leipzig 1696–1700, and a composer admired by J. S. Bach) also mastered counterthemes and triple-time variants; one ricercar of 1683 even has a similar theme to BWV 552.ii, which may indeed be a salute to the traditions fostered in Leipzig by such composers as Strunck. The three-section Fantasia in D by Zachow (a Leipziger) also uses a theme in three forms. Such 'resemblances' are more to the point than similarities between the common-property theme of BWV 552.ii and those of other keyboard fugues of the early eighteenth century, often noticed today.

553–560   'Eight Short Preludes and Fugues'

p192 lines 6–12 from bottom: Another such observation is that the general tessitura (to c′ in pedal, only a′ in manual) is exceptional and more typical of J. L. Krebs (Klotz 1950 p200).

p193 lines 18–22: Some proportionalism between prelude and fugue (BWV 553 2:1, BWV 554 1:1, BWV 556 2:1, BWV 559 1:3) also suggests this.

561 *p201 ¶1, for* (P 318, P 1066) *read* (P 318; P 1066 C. G. Sander)

p201 ¶2, for 'Fantasia in *read* 'Fantasia' and, by a later hand, 'in

p210 end ¶3: Lohmann (B & H edn 6583 p. xiii) sees a 'style relationship' between BWV 561 and BWV 594.

562 *p202 ¶1 line 2, for* (Kittel) *read* (Kittel?)

p202 ¶1 line 3, for BWV 546.ii *read* BWV 546.ii in an older reading

p202 delete ¶2 and replace by Two staves; headed in P 490 (similarly in other MSS) 'Fantasia pro Organo. a. 5 Vocam cum pedali obligato' (last phrase added later?), fugue 'Fuga. a 5'.

p202 ¶3 line 6, for copied out *read* amended

p202 ¶3 lines 8–9 from bottom: Early on in its life, however, the Fantasia BWV 562.i might well have been followed by the Fugue BWV 546.ii (Kilian *NBA* IV/5–6 *KB* p323).

p202 footnote: Wagener owned P 490 (*ibid KB* p109).

p203 lines 1–2: Perhaps the sheet on which the fugue was completed got separated and lost (*ibid KB* p27), which could have happened early enough for copyists to have known nothing of it.

p204 lines 4–6 above Ex. 135: Kilian calls this 'a rather superficial relationship' (*NBA* IV/5–6 *KB* p334).

563   *p206 ¶1 line 2, for* Kellner, *read* Kellner? after Andreas-Bach-Buch,

p206 ¶2, after P 804 *add* (separate fascicles – see Vol. I p350)

564   *p207 delete ¶1 lines 1–2 and replace by* No Autograph MS; copies in P 803 (1st half of 18th century, Dürr's 'Hauptkopist D' c1729?), P286 (mostly J. P. Kellner?), P 1101 (copyist of BWV 563 in P 1091), P 1102 (fugue only, 18th

p207 ¶2: 'Largo' for 2nd movement in P 1101, Brussels and Oxford.

p208 line 3: That the Adagio was a subsequent addition is not substantiated by Hauser's suggestion based on an old copy in his possession (Kobayashi 1973 p235).

p208 line 4, for (bb4–5) *read* (bb84–5)

p208 last line: B also begins in the tonic.

p209 lines 4–6: The opening gestures (especially the pauses) of BWV 564 are a tamed version of the caprice typical of some pieces by Buttstedt, presumably of much the same period and area.

p211 lines 1–3: The phrases, predominantly of six bars each, become foreshortened towards the end (Krey 1956), as can be seen in the pedal part.

p211 line 6 from bottom: I.e. dotted phrases all upbeat demisemiquavers.

p212 lines 5–6 from bottom: See *NBA* IV/5–6 *KB* pp491, 690.

565   *p214 line 4*: A similar cadence phrase in the early Cantatas 131, 71, and 4.

p214 delete ¶1 and replace by No Autograph MS; copies in P 595 (J. Ringk 1717–78) and 19th-century sources, all from Ringk? (P 924 Grasnick, P 642, Lpz MB III.8.20 Dröbs); Peters IV claimed a Kittel MS as the original source; *BG* 15 used MS in possession of Schubring. All extant sources also contain BWV 551 and 532.

p215 line 7, for (as in *NBA* IV/6) *read* (see *NBA* IV/5–6 *KB* pp520, 552)

p215 line 7 from bottom: E.g., it is placed 'before 1708' in *NBA* IV/5–6 *KB* p518.

p216 inset: For those alerted to musical figures of speech, the first thirty bars are full of *repetitio, confutatio, gradatio* and others (Albrecht 1980).

p220 lines 2–3 after *** ('*Poor sources*'): However, Ringk's copy shows signs of being based on a much older MS, one perhaps brought to his attention by Kellner (see *NBA* IV/5–6 *KB* pp201–3). It is also primarily from a score made by Ringk, dated by him 1730 (when he was aged thirteen), that we now know the Wedding Cantata BWV 202, a work of undoubted authenticity. From various copies it is also clear that Ringk knew music of Bruhns, Böhm and Buxtehude (Geck 1968).

566   *p222 ¶1 line 2, for* (Kittel), *read* (Kittel?), *and for* P 577) *read* P 557) *p222* ¶*1 line 5, for* (Kittel), *read* (Fischer),

p222 ¶*1 delete lines 7–9 and replace by* Of the E major version, P 320, P 557, the 1st edn (Leipzig 1833) and Oxford MS have first two movements only, P 504 (Grasnick) the last two; of the C major version, Oxford MS has last two movements only.

p222 ¶*2 delete line 2 and replace by* P 286 'Praeludium con Fuga [added: 'e Fantasia con'] Pedal'; in Am.B.544

p222 ¶*2 line 3, after* P 203 *add* and P 837

p222 ¶*3 lines 6–9, delete sentence and replace by* It is now assumed that the original key was E major (*NBA* IV/5-6) and that the C major version was made – perhaps by J. S. Bach (Peters III), perhaps by J. T. Krebs (*KB* p302) – in order to avoid pedal D♯ (*ibid* p525) and/or pedal notes higher than c′ (Emery 1958 p. iv), or in order to simplify the playing problems of the first pedal solo (Keller 1948 p59).

p223 Ex. 204, note to 1st stave should read avoiding C♯ and/or d♯′, e′

p223 lines 17–29: The progressions themselves are not particularly remote despite the enharmonic notation, but the passage of keys does require D♯ major to be as sweet as E major.

567   *p227 title, for* G major *read* C major

p227 line 6 from end of essay, for (1702?), *read* (1702 etc),

568   *p227 last line, for* P 515) *read* perhaps P 515).

p228 line 1: No attribution to J. S. Bach.

p228 ¶*3 lines 10–11*: The *NBA* version (as Peters) of bb1–4 and 8–11 seems to distinguish too sharply between the two pedal points. No sources suggest held notes in bb8–10, but nor do they for b3; only spacing seems (marginally) to distinguish the two, and in the interests of old toccata styles it seems reasonable to hold the pedal both in bb1–2 (only) and in bb8–9.

p228 end of essay: But the question is still unanswered: Who is the composer?

569   *p228* ¶*1 line 2, before* Brussels *add* P 1105 and

p228 ¶*1 delete last line and replace by* 4842e, Lpz MB III.8.16) perhaps based on Peters IV's lost Kittel MS.

p228 ¶*2 line 2, for* con Pedal' *read* con Pedale'

p229 last ¶: Schöneich (1947/8 pp171ff) sees the movement as built on four sections (bb1–48, 49–85, 86–116, 117–52), in some sense derived from falling scales but with a partial ostinato theme close to Buxtehude's E minor Chaconne BUXWV 160.

570   *p229* ¶*1 line 2, for* Kellner), *read* Kellner?), *and for* 30069). *read* 30069 etc.

p230 line 6: The heading reads 'di J. S. B.' according to *NBA* IV/5-6 *KB* p499.

572   *p232 line 4, for* 30386 *read* 30380

p232 ¶*3 lines 1–4*: Walther (*Lexicon* 1732) defined *gayement* as 'lustig, freudig' ('jolly, joyful').

p233 footnote: Towards the end of the Fugue BWV 564.iii (bb138ff) the copy P 286 exceptionally gives a BB 'not to be believed, since no German organ of the time of Bach had the note' (*NBA* IV/5–6 *KB* pp492, 691); but in the P 286 copy of the C major Fugue BWV 566, Kellner again writes BB (b18). Whatever it was that Kellner meant by these notes, it can hardly be still maintained that BWV 572 is 'the only instance of Bach overstepping the C boundary' (Klotz 1950 p200), not least since it is unclear who was 'overstepping' – Bach, Kellner, another copyist? Yet a further important question is: is pedal required before the third section?

573   *p238 end ¶1*: There are at least three promising sequences, after which the close is conventional, albeit melodious. Since the thirteen bars do not suggest any standard prelude shape and even end on the mediant (cf. the Pastorale BWV 590.i),* perhaps the piece is an improviser's 'prompt', a stimulus for the dedicatee, or a preface such as the composer is said to have made use of in private recitals (*Dok* II p397)?

> * The final full bar of BWV 573, i.e. the one that modulates to E minor, starts a new line in the MS; until that point, it looks as if it could have proceeded to a much more conventional dominant. Does this suggest that the piece was a model for different closes and/or different continuations?

574   *p238 delete ¶1 and replace by* No Autograph MS (MS owned by Guhr, said to be autograph in Peters IV); copies in P 247 (c1730), P 1093 (J. G. Preller), Scholz MS and sources in or after c1800 (Brussels Fétis 2960; Lpz Poel 13 and 355 (J. G. Weigand, without final section), Lpz MB MS 1,18 (W. N. Mey?)).

p238 ¶2: P 247, P 1093 and Lpz MB MS 1 (chief sources for BWV 574) have 'Fuga'.

p238 ¶3 line 3, for 575a and 575b; *read* 574a and 574b;

p239 Ex. 217: The 'Benedictus' of Palestrina's Mass *Pange lingua* has a similar theme (Schöneich 1947/8 p187) – a resemblance which underlines the originality of countersubject in BWV 574.

p239 lines 1–2: Though BWV 574 is still generally referred to as an 'arrangement' (*NBA* IV/5–6 *KB* p501).

p239 inset line 4: Is the second theme also by Legrenzi?

574a   *p240 ¶2*: Title in P 207 'Fuga a 4. Voc.'

574b   *p241 ¶1 line 2, for* (Dröbs, shortened) *read* (Dröbs, without last section)

p241 ¶2: Title in P 805 'Fuga', in Fétis 2960 'Capriccio'.

p241 ¶4 lines 1–4: Kilian's view (*NBA* IV/5–6 *KB* p501), not contradicted by the sources, is that BWV 574 'gradually' deleveloped from 574b (good contemporary MSS), while 574a 'took a special position between the two' (later MS).

575   *p242 ¶2 line 1, after* 'Fuga di Bach' *add* (in P 213 etc 'Fuga di J. S. Bach')

p242 ¶2 line 2, after Peters IV *add* but at b73 (2nd beat) in Go.S.310

p242 line 2, for (neither 'Adagio' *read* (no 'Adagio'

p242 ¶3 lines 1–2, delete parenthesis '(C. P. E. . . . p63)' *and replace by* (it is attributed to C. P. E. Bach in an English edn of 1811 – see *NBA* IV/5–6 *KB* pp272, 513)

p243 last ¶: The keeping to tonic and dominant entries only can be seen as an 'early' sign, vestige of a fugal tradition in which the young Bach was being very inventive in other respects.

577 *p245 ¶1 line 1*: The former Rust MS is by the same copyist as the Göttingen MS of BWV 535 – see *NBA* IV/5–6 *KB* p171.

p246 lines 3–5 after Ex. 221: Klotz (1950 p199) is surely right to see the theme of BWV 577 as having both manual and pedal (b57) forms.

578 *p247 ¶1*: Peters IV used a (lost) Kellner source. Hauser referred to a prelude to the fugue (Kobayashi 1973 p331).

579 *p249 ¶2*: No 'adagio' (b101) in P 804 or Lpz MB MS 1.

p251 lines 4–7 above Ex. 225: The whole section around bb80–90, with its resemblances to both prelude and fugue BWV 532, can only with great difficulty be assumed to be much later in origin than the B flat Capriccio BWV 992.

582 *p253 ¶1*: Judging by occasional octave displacements in the sources (copies), the composer's original may well have been written in tablature (Kilian 1983 pp163–4).

p253 ¶1 line 5: the former Rust MS is the same copyist as the Göttingen MS of BWV 535 – see *NBA* IV/5–6 *KB* p171.

p253 ¶2 line 2, for P 803 *read* both MSS

p253 ¶3 line 3, for by Hauser *read* owned by Hauser

p253 ¶3 line 4: Mendelssohn's programme for a recital on 6 August 1840 in St Thomas, Leipzig called it 'Passacaille (21 Variationen und Phantasies für die volle Orgel)'; were at least the first word and last four words taken (or translated) from the copy he was using? Did the oldest copies, particularly the autograph, keep the allusion to Raison in the (then unfamiliar) terminology?

p253 footnote: Perhaps Guhr's 'autograph' was in fact a copy by C. G. Meissner (Kobayashi 1973 p169)? For Hauser's copy, see *ibid* p72.

p257 line 4 from bottom: J. Schmid(t)'s chorale-variations of 1710 close with a passacaglia from which a fugato is made (see Frotscher 1934–5 II p619).

p258 ¶1 last 6 lines: Nevertheless, the term *passacaglia* is not straightforward and may relate to the theme's origin. For some Germans (e.g. Mattheson 1739 p233) the passacaglia was a non-ostinato, lively dance; 'chaconne' would have been a more suitable title for BWV 582. But Walther's *Lexicon*, following Brossard's *Dictionaire*, defines *passacaglia* in the French way, i.e. slower than a chaconne, in the minor, with a more delicate *Melodie* and a less lively *Expression*. The sources for BWV 582 use the term presumably because the composer did; and perhaps he did because he took it from Raison?

p263 ¶2 lines 4–5: The principle of intermezzo is followed by F. E. Niedt in his model *praeludium* (1721 pp122ff): the chaconne which forms part of the *praeludium* is given a *Trio* section, like a French chaconne-couplet.

583 *p266 ¶1 line 1, for* Anon 300), *read* Anon 300?), *p266 ¶2:* Also 'Trio/Adagio' in P 286.

587 *p271 ¶3 line 2, for* four movements *read* ten movements

588 *p272 ¶1 line 3, for* (J. C. Kittel), *read* (J. C. Kittel?),

p272 ¶2 line 1: The movement is *manualiter* in MS 7.

p272 line 1 after Ex. 238, after by whom *add* (Preller?)

p273 line 4, for usual 3/2 second half of *read* 3/2 second half that is usual in the

p273 end ¶1: The metamorphosis of themes and the combining of subjects – aspects of solid contrapuntal skill – were techniques applied by other composers said to have been admired by J. S. Bach, e.g. N. A. Strunck.

p274 line 3 after Ex. 241: Moreover, the double-subject 3/2 section is like the *third* section of older canzonas, e.g. Froberger's Canzona II in Lpz MB MS 51.

590 *p277 ¶1 line 2, for* two Scholz MSS *read* Scholz MS

p277 ¶1 line 3, after Bodleian MS *add* (2nd movement only)

p279 line 15 from bottom: That at least Locatelli's Op I no. 8 (published c1721) was known to J. S. Bach by c1734–5 is shown by the existence of parts for the concerto (Lpz Go.S.4) copied in Bach's hand (see Schulze 1977 p15).

p280 lines 1–3: Note too that the close on a mediant cadence resembles that of the (never completed?) Fantasia BWV 573. Were both movements originally composed as incipits for improvised continuation?

591 *p281 ¶2 line 1, for* Labyrinth. *read* Labyrünth.

p281 ¶3 lines 6–7: Heinichen (1728 pp850ff) gave several examples of two-part pieces passing through twenty-two keys and requiring harmonization. F. Suppig's MS *Labyrinthus musicus* of 1722 (now Paris Bib. Cons. de Musique Rés. F 211) contains a 'Fantasia through all twenty-four keys' which 'could be played on the harpsichord without pedal or on the organ with [it]' according to the title, also quoted by Mattheson (1722 p152); it is a piece that requires the performer either to adopt equal temperament or else to tolerate the wolf intervals in meantone tuning.

p281 ¶3 line 7, for (1715), *read* (1702 etc),

592–596 Concertos

p284 lines 5–8: See also Burney's report on a conversation with Quantz, in P. Scholes (ed.), *Dr Burney's Musical Tours in Europe* II (London 1959) p185.

592 *p290 2nd footnote:* J. F. Agricola's term for Vivaldi's four-violin Concerto Op III no. 10 arranged for four harpsichords (= BWV 1065) is 'accomodato' (*NBA* VII/6 *KB* p79).

p295 line 2: I.e. with the right hand on *Rückpositiv* in the episodes.

593 *p296 ¶1 line 2, after* sources *add* (P 1066 C. G. Sander).

p297 line 1: See also *NBA* VII/6 *KB* p89.

594 *p303* ¶*1 line 2*: P 286: same copyist as BWV 595.

595 *p309* ¶*1 line 1*: P 286: same copyist as BWV 594.

p309 ¶*2 line 1, for* Principe Giov. *read* Prencipe Giov:

p309 ¶*2 line 2, for* pedal *read* Pedal

596 *p312* ¶*1 line 2, for* middle movement written by Forkel) *read* copyists J. C. Westphal and perhaps Forkel)

p312 ¶*2*: Headed in P 289 'Concerto ex D.mol à 2 Clavier et Pedale Di J. S. Bach'.

p312 line 5 from bottom, for Until 1911, *read* From c1844 to 1911,

p313 line 11 from bottom, for rebuiling *read* rebuilding

p314 ¶*2 line 1*: The Amsterdam edition is assumed to be that known to J. S. Bach (Eller in *NBA* vii/6 *KB* p89).

598 *p319* ¶*3*: Keller, developing his idea that the composer's early music was characteristically 'stormy and exuberant', conjectures that the 'Exercitium' is an early work of 1700–3 (1937 p60).

p320 lines 1–2: This is true in principle, though as they stand the examples from BWV 598 would require transposition to be feasible on cello or violoncello piccolo.

802–805 Four Duets

p323 ¶ *'(iv)' lines 9–10*: Or four stages in the life of Jesus: crucified, risen, ascended, proclaimed (R. Birk *MuK* 46 (1976) 63–9).

p323 footnote The 77 pages of music are numbered 1–77 by the engraver(s). Very striking to the eye is the neat, separate layout of the Four Duets: each duet on one pair of facing pages.

p324 lines 2–9: There may also be hints, since the duets involve exact sequential transposition, that their composer was investigating 'the consequences of equal temperament' (Eck 1981 pp21–5).

1027a *p328* ¶*3 line 10, for* (*MGG* 1 col. 1014). *read* (*NBA* iv/5–6 *KB* p144).

1029.ii *p329* ¶*1 line 1, for* only source, *read* organ version,

p330 lines 1–4: 'It may be accepted that the source of BWV 545b was not BWV 1029.iii (note there the chord in b93) but a string trio' (Kilian in *NBA* iv/5–6 *KB* p144).

1079.v *p333* ¶*1 line 2, after* P 289 *add* (2nd half of 18th century)

Glossary

p337 line 3: However, J. G. Walther (*Lexicon* 1732, 'Brust') pointed out that this chest could be placed above the *Werk*, i.e. what is elsewhere called *Oberpositif*.

p339 line 7, after rhythmic example add (in BWV 629).

p341 after 'paraphrase technique' add new entry:
passaggio: passage-work or alternating-hand figurations (usually semiquavers) opening a prelude and establishing the key; see BWV 535a and the similar material at the close of the chorale BWV 739.

p341 delete lines 4–5 from bottom and replace by
passus duriusculus: the term ('a somewhat harsh passage' or, as a musical pun, 'a passage partly in the major' and partly minor) taken from the rhetoricians by some seventeenth-century musicians (C. Bernhard) as a label for certain musical devices including the descending chromatic.

List of Musical Sources

p346 entries 'Am.B. 45' to 'Am.B. 606': The Amalien-Bibliothek, like many libraries of its period, employed professional copyists.

p346 'Am.B. 54': The copyist is 'Anon 401' ('Anon I of the Am.B.').

p346 'Am.B. 60': MS uses red ink for the pedal part and conventionalized Italianate titles. The lost 'first part' of this source (= Am.B.59) presumably contained BWV 540, 582, 562.i, 590, 538 and 566.i,ii (in C major).

p347 lines 1–8: An anonymous Fantasia in the MS ('Fantasia ex C dis. adagio') has recently been identified as probably an early work of J. S. Bach for organ with pedals, copied here in autograph tablature (Kilian 1983).

p347 delete lines 3–4 and replace by Pachelbel, Reincken), made by ten unknown copyists between c1706 and 1710/12 (perhaps mostly J. C. Bach 1671–1721, not J. Bernhard Bach sen. as suggested in *NBA* IV/5–6 *KB* p182 but countered in *BJ* 1978 p22, nor J. Bernhard Bach jun.); provides a

p347 before 'BB 40644' add two new entries:
BB 30069: An incomplete copy of the Andreas-Bach-Buch by Grasnick (*NBA* IV/5–6 *KB* p97).
BB 30377: Late-18th- or early-19th-century album of music by J. S. Bach, Handel, J. L. Krebs and others, containing BWV 538.ii, 540.ii, 578 and four chorales.

p347 'Brussels Fétis 2960' line 3, before 913, add 914,

p347 same line, for 574, read 574b, and for 990, read 996,

p347 'LM 4838', delete entry and replace by
LM 4838: Album of free organ works made from P 320 or its Kittel source, owned and mostly written by J. C. H. Rinck; includes BUXWV 148.

p347 'LM 4839 a–i', delete entry and replace by
LM 4839a–i: Collection of nine MSS, perhaps of similar provenance to LM 4838, written mostly by M. G. Fischer.

p347 'LM 4842a–h' line 3, for (4842h); read (4842h, copied by L. Scholz);

p347 'Lpz MB MS 7': Perhaps Mempell and Preller were connected in c1750 with Kellner (*NBA* IV/5–6 *KB* p194).

p348 '*Lpz MB III. 8.21*': Like some of the other Leipzig sources, the MS passed into C. F. Becker's collection.

p348 '*Möller MS*': J. S. Bach is the youngest composer represented in both MSS; they also share their chief copyist (in Möller MS for BWV 531 and 549a).

p348 '*P 228*' line *3, for* 548.ii, *read* 548.ii; *and delete remainder of that line*

p349 line 1, for (J. P. Kellner), *read* (J. P. Kellner?),

p349 '*P 276, 277*' *delete entry and replace by*
P 276, 277: Albums copied by 'Anon 401' (copyist of Am.B.54): (i) BWV 545, 546, 547, 548, 543 and 544, apparently based on Am.B.60, of which it seems to be a copy (*NBA* IV/5-6 *KB* p51); and (ii) BWV 540, 582, 562.i., 590, 538, 566.

p349 '*P 286, 287*' line *3*: BWV 538, 594, 595 all by one copyist.

p349 '*P 288, 289*' line *4, for* 543 *read* 543a

p349 '*P 290*': Pedal in red ink.

p349 '*P 301*' *etc line 3, for* 549.i *read* 549a

p349 '*P 301*' *etc lines 4-5, delete* P 313 headed . . . Kittel'.

p349 '*P 320*' *delete entry and replace by*
P 320: Important album probably written by L. E. or J. N. Gebhardi from a Kittel source (*NBA* IV/5-6 *KB* pp174-5, 212) and including BWV 533, 549, 542.ii, 572, 592, 562.i, 131a, 546, 541, 547, 578, 535, 582, 566 and 588, and fugues in D minor by C. Flor and C. H. Graun.

p349 '*P 595*' line *2*: Ringk copies made by 1756? (cf. *NBA* IV/5-6 *KB* p201). Ringk was also the copyist of pieces by Buxtehude, Böhm, Bruhns and Goldberg in BB 30381.

p350 '*P 803*' line *5, for* 543 (*twice*) *read* 543a

p350 '*P 803*': It is often assumed (unreliably) that Walther's copies were made only while the composer was still at Weimar.

p350 '*P 837*': Pedal in red ink.

p350 '*P 1071*' line *1, after* made c1800 *add* (by A. Kühnel)

p350 '*Schubring MSS*': But the Schubring MS numbered B 115 in *NBA* IV/5-6 *KB* pp114-15 contains Schubring's own copies of BWV 533, 541, 532.ii, 578, 542.ii, 565, 540.i, 538.i, 535, 531 and 549a.

List of References

p353, entry '*Kolneder*' *should precede* '*Krause*'

Index

p358 under '*Frischmuth*', *after* MS-owner *add* in Kellner circle *p359 under 'Gleichauf', for* ?-1856, *read* 1801-56,

p359 under 'Grasnick', after in Berlin *add* drawing on MSS of Kirnberger, Kittel, etc

p359 under 'Grell', after 1800-86, *add* pupil of Zelter and M. G. Fischer,

p359 under 'Guhr', after 82, *add* 238,

p360 under 'Mey', after copyist, *add* pupil of Kellner?,

p360 under 'Pachelbel, W. H.', after preceding, *add* friend of J. G. Walther,

p361 under 'Ringk', after Kellner, *add* and organist Marienkirche, Berlin,

p361 under 'Silbermann', for J. G., *read* G.,

p362 under 'Wechmar', after copyist *add* in Kellner circle

p362 delete entry 'Westphal' and replace by
Westphal, J. C. the elder, 1727-99, Hamburg music-seller, 266
Westphal, J. C. the younger, 1733-1828, copyist associated with Forkel, pupil of
    Kittel, 66, 88, 112, 113, 269, 349

p365 under '870-93', after 32, *add* 93, 118,

Volume II

559-644 *Orgelbüchlein*

p3, delete pagehead

p3 lines 8-9 from bottom: For the term *durchführen*, cf. the Arnstadt publication of 1704 by J. P. Treiber: *Der accurate Organist im Generalbasse . . . worinne . . . die Choralen . . . durch alle Töne und Accorde . . . durchgeführt sind* ('The accurate organist in figured bass, in which the chorales are set in all keys and harmonies').

p4 inset line 13, after BWV 607 *add* (last 2½ bars on p10)

p6 lines 3-5: In *Fiori musicali*, a volume acquired by J. S. Bach at this period (1714 - see *Dok* I p269), 'alio modo' is also used in both senses.

p6 ¶2 last 6 lines, delete last sentence (from 'An early copy') and replace by An early copy, later than P 283 (but not yet shown to be copied from it), once thought to be autograph and given by Guhr to Mendelssohn (letter to Fanny Mendelssohn, 18 June 1839), is now to be found, incomplete and unnumbered, in Cracow University Library, having been formerly in the Preussische Staatsbibliothek, Berlin. Mendelssohn's title reads '26 Choralvorspiele . . .', but six pieces were given away during Mendelssohn's lifetime; the remaining twenty are BWV 614, 615, 616, 619, 618, 621, 622, 620, 623, 624, 617, 625, 626, 627, 628, 630, 629, 638, 639 and 640. This early copy may be connected with the lost MS 'P 1216', some pages of which are extant and were written in *c*1727/30 by C. G. Meissner, the so-called 'Haupt-kopist B' (Schulze 1968; Kobayashi 1973 pp168–9, 204–5; and cf. Vol. III p286 below, correction to p340).†

p6 2nd footnote line 3, for L. P. *read* L. B.

p7 inset last 2 lines: The page receiving BWV 613 was the first entirely empty page in the book (and 'O Traurigkeit' almost the next), which rather suggests that the composer set out to complete the album.

p7 lines 6–7 from bottom: The editors of *NBA* IV/1 argue that BWV 603 was the first chorale to be entered into the MS, before it was 'completely ready' as an album; then BWV 599, 600, 602 etc followed. Furthermore, they see a connection between the composer's activity with cantatas at Weimar (March 1714 – December 1716) and his putative activity with the *Orgelbüchlein*, and assume that the organ chorales were composed in the appropriate seasons to which the texts relate (Advent 1713, Advent 1714, etc). The album seems unlikely to have begun as a single operation: there are in P 283 original composing copies (*Urschriften*), care-ful fair copies (*kalligraphische Reinschriften*) and hasty fair copies (*flüchtige Reinschriften*); and the book seems to have been ruled in three stages, of which the last comprises some three quarters of the book as a whole (i.e. the latter sections containing many of the newer copies and mostly blank pages). Not least in view of all these observations, it is unlikely that the title-page, with its archaic echoes (e.g. 'anfahend', found on such earlier title-pages as Ammerbach's tablature book of 1571) and its allusive couplet, can be regarded either as reflecting the original intention of the composer or as proving that the album originated with any single intention.

p9 lines 14–17, delete last sentence of ¶ (*from 'Nor is it certain'*) *and replace by* Judging by what is known of J. H. Buttstedt's chorales (Ziller 1935 pp43ff), there seems to have been a specific Thuringian or Erfurt–Weimar tradition and hymn repertory catered for by the contents of the *Orgelbüchlein*. Recent hymns are not prominent (147 of the 165 were printed before 1650) and are mostly bunched together near the end.

p12 inset: The principle of the 'melody chorale type' of organ piece has been seen to be already present in (e.g.) Scheidt's 'Mitten in dem Leben' and Zachow's 'In dulci jubilo' (Tusler 1968 p. vii); again, the tradition seems to be Thuringian.

p13 lines 3–4 after Ex. 2: Though the soprano passing-notes were added to a melody first written in plain minims.

599

p16 lines 8–11 after Ex. 3: This metrical ambiguity may well reflect that in Luther's version, as shown in the Bapst Hymnbook of 1545 – Ex. 3a – and it could well be that J. S. Bach deliberately chose an 'antique' (quasi-Gregorian?) form for the melody in BWV 599, thus producing from its first line not a 2-bar but a 2½-bar phrase.

Ex. 3a

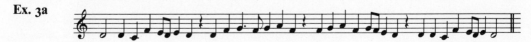

600   *p18 line above 2nd verse inset, for* in 1544 in a hymnbook *read* in 1531 (Weisse) and 1544 (Roh) in hymnbooks

p19 lines 6-8: But the 'falling motif' expressing the arrival of the Son of God may have been conventional (cf. the setting by Buttstedt).

601   *p21 delete line 2 and replace by* the song *Mein Freud möcht sich wohl mehren* in the Lochamer Liederbuch; its form in

604   *p25 ¶3 line 2, for* the Christmas *read* Notker's Christmas

606   *p29 ¶3 line 1, for* in 1539, *read* c1530,

p29 ¶3 lines 1-5: For Luther, the hymn probably had the character of a traditional dance for the Christmas manger-play.

607   *p31 line 1, after* staves *add* (pedal marked 'ped')

608   *p32 ¶2 line 2, for* 'pedal' *read* 'ped.'

p32 ¶3 line 1, for fifteenth-century *read* fourteenth- and fifteenth-century

p32 delete line after inset text and replace by Versions were known with one, three and four verses, with pure German texts, with various dialect texts, and with mariolatrous references pruned.

p33 ¶1 last 3 lines: Furthermore, the crotchets are not aligned long/short with the quaver triplets, as they are in the P 283 copy of BWV 617.

611   *p37 ¶2 line 1, for* 'Corale in Alto' *read* 'Choral in Alto.'

p37 line 2 after 1st verse, after adaptation *add* (1541)

p37 line 3 after 1st verse inset: Before the Luther period, *Hostis Herodes impie* had a different melody of its own.

p38 line 3, after Scheidemann *add* , de Grigny

p38 lines 3-4: Walther's *canone infinito gradato* derived from this melody is called 'A solis ortus cardine', like de Grigny's.

p38 Ex. 33: It appeares from P 283 that the composer first began with minim d′ and added the passing-note; moreover, the c.f. notes were first written with stems up (first 10½ bars), which rather suggests that he began with the c.f. in the 'soprano' and only then added *figurae* around it.

612   *p39 ¶2, after* staves *add* ('p' for pedal);

p40 lines 8-10 above Ex. 36: At this point *figurae* were added, so that in b3 the melody, originally ending with a minim, had to end with crotchet and rest. The final pedal point was not allowed for in the original writing-out of the cantus firmus – hence the tablature addition in the margin.

614   *p44 ¶2 lines 1-3*: Since BWV 614 is a fair copy in the autograph MS, it cannot be known whether the coloratura decorations were added to a simple cantus firmus.

p44 ¶1 lines 15-17: In Freylinghausen's hymnbooks, *Das alte Jahr* is a New Year hymn, i.e. for 1 January not 31 December.

615 *p45 ¶2 line 2, after* of any kind *add* (except 'Ped')

p45 lines 4-6 above Ex. 42: An inventory of the Leipzig bookshop Rose made in 1604 shows that Gastoldi's *Balletti a* 5 were available there (Wustmann 1909 p315, 172), and in 1607 German imitations of Gastoldi's *tricinia* were also being published.

p45 line 4 above Ex. 42, for Included *read* While the text was published

616 *p47 ¶2, after* staves *add* (and 'p')

p48 line 5: The melody may be derived (by Luther?) from an older melody.

617 *p49 ¶2, after* staves *add* and accolade for two upper voices, also 'p'

618 *p51 ¶2*: In the 'Mendelssohn MS' (cf. Vol. III pp274f above, comment on Vol. II p6) the manual parts were marked '8 Fuss' (could the pedal then be 8', 4' or 2' (Arfken 1965 pp30-2)? or did the copyist so mark the parts to show that they are played as written, and therefore that the title 'Canone alla quinta' is not quite accurate?).

p51 ¶2 line 3, after staves *add* (and 'Ped.')

619 *p53 ¶2 line 2, after* staves *add* in P 283, plus accolade in bb1, 5, 8, 9, 10 to show the two tenor lines played by left hand

620 *p54 ¶2, after* staves *add* (and 'ped.'); repeat marks for bb1-7 in P 283.

p54 ¶3: The text is assumed to be a translation of the Czech version.

p54 ¶3 line 2, for Passiontide *read* Good Friday

p56 lines 12-13 from bottom: Perhaps the pedal could be played up an octave?

620a *p57 lines 1-4 after Ex. 56*: Perhaps these bars were written on a separate sheet (now lost) in P 283. Such 'sharpening' of rhythms after a piece was completed anticipates that of the *alla francese* fugue in the *Art of Fugue*. May they even have been contemporary?

p58 last ¶ line 7: In any case, such inner parts as those of this chorale recall the texture, less fully developed perhaps, of the Italianate counterpoint in the Corelli fugue BWV 579.

622 *p59 delete ¶2 and replace by* Headed in P 283 'adagio assai' and 'á 2 Clav. & Ped', perhaps both rubrics written later than the title (but not at the same time); same headings in (e.g.) P 802; two staves in P 283, three in P 802; at end, 'adagiissimo' in P 283 (twice, above and below staves), 'più adagio' in Brussels W.12.102.

623 *p62 bottom line, after* staves *add* (and 'ped.')

625 *p66 line 1 after verse inset*: The melody has some similarities with the sequence melody *Victimae paschali laudes*.

626 *p67 ¶2, after* staves *add* (and 'p.')

627 *p69 delete ¶2 and replace by* Headed in P 283 '1. Vers' and 'Verte sequitur 2. Verse', 'Vers. 2', and 'Vers. 3'. Two staves.

628   *p71* ¶*2, after* staves *add* (and 'p.')

            p71 line 3 from bottom, *for* Latin *read* folksong

629   *p73* ¶*2*: 'a 2 Clav. & Ped.' and 'in Canone' are two phrases (written at different times?).

            p73 lines 1–3 above Ex. 79: The melody seems to have originated in older melodies both secular and sacred (e.g. the Easter antiphon *Ad monumentum venimus gementes*).

630   *p74* ¶*2, after* staves *add* (and 'ped.')

631   *p76* ¶*2, after* staves *add* (and 'p.')

632   *p79 lines 1–4 after Ex. 86*: The particular rhythmic character of the melody matches the style of the old Genevan Psalter (1562 etc).

633   *p80* ¶*3 line 1, for* L. Clausnitzer's *read* T. Clausnitzer's

634   *p82* ¶*1 line 2, after* 706.ii), *add* P 1160 (Oley, but pasted over by him?),

            p82 ¶*2 line 1*: 'in Canone alla Quinta' and 'à 2 Clav & Ped' are two phrases (written at different times?).

635   *p83* ¶*2, after* staves *add* (and 'p.')

            p85 lines 6–7: P 283 suggests that the composer first closed the piece with the pedal motif Ex. 92a, adding a ♭ to the E as an afterthought.

BWV 635

Ex. 92a

637   *p87 lines 3–4 above Ex. 97*: As the text is Meistersinger-like, so the melody is that of a Reformation battle song (Pavia, 1525).

            p88 lines 18–19 from bottom: It may escape notice because until then the piece seems to have set out to counter accepted rules on false relations etc (Budday 1977 *passim*).

638   *p89* ¶*2, after* staves *add* (and 'p.')

            p89 line 4 above Ex. 99: The melody is that of a pre-Reformation Easter song.

639   *p91 2nd footnote*: It looks as if the composer slurred each group of four when space made it convenient but shortened the slur when it did not.

            p92 lines 10–11: A meantone F minor makes three parts more feasible than four because the harmony is then thinner; conversely, a three-part chorale (exceptional in the *Orgelbüchlein*) could encourage the use of a 'difficult' key. But the use of F minor for a chorale listed as aeolian or A minor by Walther (*Lexicon* 1732 p414) and as D minor by Mattheson (1739 p162) has also been seen as evidence that J. S. Bach knew the more modern temperament now called Kirnberger I (Eck 1981 pp154–61).

640   *p93 line 7, for* fifteenth century (Terry 1921 p213). *read* fourteenth century (*Christus iam surrexit*).

p93 lines 1–2 above Ex. 104: A similar idea is used as the head motif, imitatively and melodically, in a livelier aria in E minor in Cantata 65 (1724).

641   *p94 ¶2, after* staves *add* (and 'p.')

p94 line 4 above Ex. 105: from 1588 in the hymnbooks themselves, but earlier else-where: e.g. Ammerbach's *Orgel oder Instrument Tabulatur* (Leipzig 1571). In the Genevan Psalter it was the melody to Ps. 140 or to the Ten Commandments hymn.

642   *p96 ¶2, after* staves *add* (and 'p.')

p96 ¶3 line 2, after Weissenfels *add* it was a 'local' hymn;

643   *p98 ¶2, after* staves *add* (and 'p.')

645–650   Schübler Chorales

p103 ¶ '(i) Origins': The composer's corrected copy (*Handexemplar*) added directions to BWV 645, corrected mistakes in the text, revised some details and discarded apparent corruptions in the transcription.

p103 footnote line 4, after rewriting *add* (or having someone rewrite)

p103 footnote: In two respects the *Schübler* set stands apart from the other works that Bach published in his own lifetime: this is the only publication of his transcriptions, and of all his works its date of publication is by far the most distant from its dates of composition.

p104 line 11, after (Wolff 1977a p11 *add* and *NBA* VIII/1 *KB* p109);

p106 ¶1: Many a player must feel that the pieces become harder to play as the volume proceeds.

p106 ¶2 line 11, for sehen wie *read* sehen, wie

p110 end ¶2: If the transcriber was not the composer but someone else who felt obliged to leave the key and the spacing unaltered, that choice of movements would indeed have been limited.

645   *p110 ¶3 line 1, for* 1599 *read* 1598

p112 line 1 after inset, for authenticated autograph *read* any original printed

649   *p120 lines 7–8 after Ex. 122*: Perhaps it was the greater length of the cantata version that required the 'Allegro' label?

650   *p122 line 2 after inset, for* bb2 is *read* b2 is

651–668   'The Eighteen'

p124 ¶1 line 2, for 'title-page' is *read* title-page was

p124 line 1 after inset: The present title, though old, is a later addition to P 271.

p124 ¶ '(i)' line 3, for nineteen *read* fifteen

p126 end ¶1: The Whitsuntide framework would then surround a group of general, *de tempore* and liturgical hymns, including some of those needed in every service (Gloria, sermon and Communion hymns). To that extent, BWV 651–665 thus present a kind of conglomerate or model service.

p126 last 2 lines, and p127 lines 1–2: That such movement-types are now associated with these particular composers probably reflects only the accident of which sources survive.

651   *p128 line 3*: But the melody is (like the text) older than 1524: it is related, perhaps, to that of the hymn *Adesto, sancte spiritus*.

653   *p134 line 6 from bottom, for* ausführte *read* ausführete

654   *p138 line 3 above Ex. 135*: The melody in Crüger's original form is much like that of typical Genevan Psalter tunes.

656   *p143 Ex. 144*: Mattheson (1731 p221) gives a motif similar to that in b2 as a suggestion for decorating simple lines and for improvising new right-hand melodies.

p144 line 4, for Walther's *Harmonische   read* Walther's *Harmonisches*

p144 lines 2–4 above Ex. 146: The musical point of passing the cantus firmus gradually to the bass was recognized also in Sweelinck's 'Da pacem, domine, in diebus nostris'.

660   *p154 lines 5–6*: But compare the two bass parts in the Sonata 'La Bevilaqua' in Legrenzi's Op VIII. How much Legrenzi did J. S. Bach know?

662   *p158 lines 1–2 after Ex. 162*: It was so often used presumably because of its appearance in each main service, rather than because it was one of the 'tunes that are divided throughout into two-measure phrases' (Tusler 1968 p21)?

p159 2nd inset: Also, it should not be missed that the continuo-like bass line has as its very opening phrase a version of the common and curiously melodious phrase described in Vol. II pp315–16.

665   *p164 ¶3 lines 1–3*: Hus's hymn was also published in at least one other translation (1531).

p166 line 4, for (b37 etc) *read* (b27 etc)

667   *p168 inset*: Examples of the organ chorale in two sections (fugal first half, pedal cantus firmus second half) can be found in Pachelbel's works.

p169 lines 2–4 from end of essay, delete from 'wished to reflect the change' *to* 'different times, or because he' *and so read* Walther (consciously or not) reflected

p169 end of essay: More likely, however, is that the second section was copied not by Walther but by J. T. Krebs (*NBA* IV/5–6 *KB* p189), on whose prompting can only be conjectured.

668   *p170 ¶1 line 1*: 'Anon II' (Anon 12) was not Penzel, according to Kobayashi 1973 p111.

p173 lines 4–5: But the most recent view is that BWV 668 is after all an expansion of BWV 641, made only in the late Leipzig period (*NBA* IV/I *KB*).

669–689   *Clavierübung III*

p175 ¶5 lines 1–8, delete 3 sentences from 'Two engravers' to 'and Italian Concerto).' and replace by Two engravers worked on the volume, the first for pp1–18, the second for pp56–77 and both pp19–55 (both therefore working on BWV 675, 676, 684, 687 - *NBA* IV/4 *KB* pp9–11). One engraver was Balthasar Schmid of Nuremberg, publisher of the *Goldberg Variations* (*Clavierübung IV*) and the *Canonic Variations* BWV 769. The other, perhaps J. G. Krügner senior, the Leipzig engraver of *Clavierübung I* (G. G. Butler, 'Leipziger Stecher in Bachs Original-drucken', *BJ* 66 (1980) pp14, 15), was, judging by that work, no very accomplished musician. For some of the volume the composer's fair-copy MS sheets were probably used to prepare the etched plates; hence the old claim that the St Anne Prelude etc were engraved by Bach himself. (See also above, Vol. III footnote to p232). The title-page of *Clavierübung III*, in style of writing, resembles that of *Clavierübung II*.

p175 line 2 from bottom, for höh" *read* Höh"

p175 footnote: In 1740 Mizler's translation of Fux (cf. Vol. II p183), while in preparation, was advertised at 2 Reichsthaler (Mizler 1740 p118).

p175 ¶3 line 4, for Johan *read* Johann

p175 line 9 from bottom, for Lpz BM *read* Lpz MB

p176 2nd inset line 1: Kuhnau's publication contains keyboard 'Partien'.

p176 1st footnote: Had the volume been wholly prepared in Leipzig in 1738 (rather than completed in Nuremberg in 1739) would there then have been 52 words?

p177 lines 4–8 after inset: That the composer may have expanded his original scheme while the volume was in the course of being engraved may well explain discrepancies or offer an answer to certain puzzles.

p177 ¶ '(i)': If the Leipzig engraver working on *Clavierübung III* was the same Krügner who engraved Kauffmann's wide-ranging collection of chorales *Harmonische Seelenlust* (1733), it can be imagined that Bach was in some sense influenced by it, striving perhaps to excel it.

p177 line 7 from bottom, for The *Missa* or Kyrie pieces *read* The pieces for the *Missa* (Kyrie and Gloria)

p178 line 4, for 'on *read* 'on the

p178 inset line 4, for Höh' *read* Höh"

p179 end ¶3: More than the sources warrant, but not impossible.

p180 line 11 from bottom: $3 \times 3 \times 3 = 27$: cf. the 27 books of the New Testament.

p181 lines 2–6: To those who see parallels between music and rhetoric, the three Overtures are examples of 'internal exordia' or introductions in the middle of works (U. Kirkendale *JAMS* 33 (1980) p94).

p182 line 3 up, for theorists *read* composers

p185 line 4 after inset, for before the fugue *read* before the Mass and the fugue

p186 lines 11–14 from bottom: At least one recent author has found in the chorales of this collection all kinds of numerological references to the composer's religious beliefs (Lohmann 1974), though few purely musical analyses of a less speculative kind have been made.

p186 footnote: Though Mattheson does use this term ('geübt' – 1722 p256) to refer to Reincken 'practising' organ works, as does Birnbaum ('Fleiss und Übung' – Mizler 1738 p70) referring to J. S. Bach.

669 *p189 Ex. 179*: [upper bracket should begin one note later with crotchet g′]

p189 ¶3 line 2, for this translation *read* his translation

670 *p190 footnote, for* 20–2, (alto) *read* 20–2 (alto),

677 *p200 ¶2 line 1, for* 'Fughetta *read* 'Fugetta *and for* Höh' sei Ehr'', *read* Höh sei Ehr',

680 *p206 line 1, for* used also *read* partly used

p206 lines 1–2 above Ex. 199: For a not dissimilar example of an earlier Thuringian organ chorale deriving its fugal subject and answer from the hymn melody, see Krummacher 1978 p469.

p207 line 1 above Ex. 201, for second lines *read* second line

681 *p209 line 2 after Ex. 205*: Mendelssohn seems to have known an E minor form of the melody: see his letter to his sister Fanny of 2 February 1831.

682 *p210 ¶4 lines 1–6*: For a further combination of cantus firmus and complex form, see Cantata 78.i (cantus-firmus ritornello movement plus *chaconne en rondeau*).

686 *p218 inset line 1, English text, for* have I cried *read* I cry

p218 last ¶, delete line 1 and replace by The MELODY was published with several texts in the early hymnbooks (e.g. 1524, 1530), and its melodic type (particularly the opening five notes) is common during the period; the version used

687 *p221 line above Ex. 218, for* (1715), *read* (1702 etc),

689 *p225 lines 7–8 after inset*: There are family likenesses between the codas of BWV 689, 687 and (in F minor) 658.

690–713 'Kirnberger Collection'

p226 ¶1 line 4, for in 1748. *read* in 1739–41.

p227 lines 1–3: The *44 Choraele* of J. C. Bach (1642–1703) provide model one-line fughettas, the themes sometimes including a second line; are the 'Seven Advent and Christmas fughettas' a response to this collection as the *Orgelbüchlein* may have been to other Thuringian types?

p227 ¶1 lines 17–20: Note, for example, how the fugal answer in BWV 699 preserves the flat leading-note, and how even Mattheson (1739 introduction p26) keeps the same kind of modal stretto-answer for the same theme.

690   *p228 ¶2 lines 4–7*: Cf. the three-volume *Musicalischer vorrath* (1716, 1719) by the cantor of Weissenfels and Freiberg, J. S. Beyer, who selected chorales for playing on the *Clavier* at home or school, and provided each of the ninety-seven settings with a plain figured chorale.

696   *p233 lines 2–3 after Ex. 234*: The countersubject is similarly derived from the second half of the subject in the C major Fugue in *The 48* Bk II.

697   *p234 ¶4 line 4*: And compare the inventive use of the same motif in the recitative of Cantata 91.ii.

    p234 ¶4 lines 8–12: Christmas hymns were particularly appropriate to such *Affekte* as fluttering angels' wings, judging by (e.g.) J. H. Buttstedt's settings of 'Gottes Sohn ist kommen', 'Vom Himmel kam der Engel Schaar' etc.

705   *p243 line 7, for* chorale is the subject of *read* chorale melody is subject to subdominant

    p243 lines 7–8: Such treatment lends an eighteenth-century diatonic flavour to the modal melody, the fifth line of which (here from b73) was described by Mattheson as beginning in the minor and ending in the major subdominant (1739 p384).

    p243 line 8, for soprano statement of the line. *read* authentic statement of the line (in the soprano).

707   *p244 ¶3 line 1, for* hymn *read* burial hymn

712   *p250 line 4 from bottom, for* entries or *read* entries of

714   *p254 ¶2, for* 'per Canones' *read* 'per Canonem'

715   *p255 2nd footnote*: Nevertheless, the literature still refers to these settings as 'Arnstadt chorales' (e.g. *NBA* IV/5–6 *KB* p283).

718   *p257 ¶2 line 1*: The piece is attributed to Krebs in one copy (Kobayashi 1973 p337).

    p259 last 6 lines of essay: The pedal is necessary only for the final two bars, and even these may have been governed by the same conventions as in (e.g.) the Fantasia BWV 561 (see Vol. III p192 above).

    p259 line 3 from bottom, for b35 *read* b33

    p259 last 2 lines, delete though this is less likely. *and read* onwards.

720   *p262 ¶ '(iii)' line 5, for* J. L. Albrecht *read* J. F. Agricola

    p263 inset, and lines 1–2 after inset: So nothing in this either proves or disproves the Mühlhausen association.

    p263 line 8 after inset, for were *read* was

721   *p264 line 4, for* J. Hegenwalt's *read* E. Hegenwalt's

    p265 footnote: For other examples of vocal/instrumental tremolo (Kuhnau, Boxberg etc) see also Krummacher 1978 exx.35a, 35b, 79a, 87.

722   *p266 lines 1–3 above Ex. 267*: Simpler flourishes preparing the following chord ('Zu-Lenckungen', 'linkings') were provided by H. F. Quehl for the two chorales in his *Der . . . musicalische Versuch* (1734).

725   *p269 footnote line 2, for* five times as bb53–102 *read* four times as bb63–102

727   *p271 line 1 after Ex. 268*: Mattheson (1739 p473) claimed that twenty-four different hymns were sung to this melody. Elsewhere (1731 p71) he asked how the phrygian nature of this 'bewegliche[s] Todten-Lied' ('moving death-hymn') supported the Greek idea that such a mode was inflammatory.

     p271 line 6 after Ex. 269, for bewein' *read* bewein"

     p271 line 6 from bottom, for obvously *read* obviously

733   *p276 ¶1, for* MS 525a (Oley). *read* MSS 525a (owned by Oley) and 525b (same copyist as BWV 700 in Leipzig Bach-Archiv Mus. MS 3: cf. Vol. II p237).

     p276 ¶2 line 2, for two main sources *read* Oley and Am.B.606

734   *p278 ¶3 line 1, for* Luther's *read* Ringwaldt's *and for* 1524. *read* 1582.

     p278 ¶3 line 1: Ringwaldt's hymn is ultimately based on the *Dies irae* sequence.

735   *p281 lines 1–2 above Ex. 277*: The melody seems to derive from one in the Geneva Psalter (Ps. 3).

736   *p285 line 4, for* Kauffman *read* Kauffmann

739   *p287 ¶3 line 1, for* Nikolai's hymn *read* Nicolai's *Jesuslied*

     p287 ¶3 line 1, for 1599 *read* 1598

740   *p289 line 4 after Ex. 285, for* Krebs, who is often thought to be *read* Krebs (Kobayashi 1973 p338), who may well be

     p289 lines 10–12 after Ex. 285: Luedtke (1918 p41) thought BWV 740 was a 'forestudy' for BWV 653b, but the sources of neither suggest any such relationship.

741   *p290 ¶1, before* P 1116 *add* P 1160,

748   *p294 ¶1, before* Am.B.72a *add* Am.B.72,

     p294 ¶2: The partial-canonic technique is typical of Walther (K. W. Senn *MuK* 34 (1968) p17).

749   *p294 ¶2*: Hauser attributed the piece to Telemann (Kobayashi 1973 p338).

750   *p295 line 2, for* (p 285) *read* (P 285)

759   *p297 ¶2 lines 1–3, delete sentence from* 'The attribution' *to* '(Kast 1958 p62).' *and replace by* The attribution of BWV 759 to G. A. Homilius (1714–85) in a destroyed Hauser MS (Kobayashi 1973 pp76, 162), already noted in *BG* 40, is probably confirmed by the identification of the copyist in P 1115 (Kast 1958 p62) and by the presence of the chorale in the four chief sources of Homilius's music (Feder 1958).

765   *p300 line 5, for* is an accomplished *read* is in an accomplished

766   *p301 ¶1 lines 3–4, delete from 'Scheibner MS 4' to the end of ¶ and replace by* Scheibner MS 4 (J. A. G. Wechmar? 6th movement missing) and late sources (e.g. unnumbered Oxford Bodleian MS, given by Hauser to Mendelssohn: Kobayashi 1973 p84).

        p301 lines 1–3 above Ex. 209: BWV 766 corresponds to the Darmstadt *Cantional* of 1687.

        p302 ¶1: F minor is itself an unlikely key for such organ music.

767   *p307 last 2 lines, and p308 lines 1–3*: Does the appearance of this chromatic phrase here suggest that BWV 767 is transcribed from D minor?

        p309 ¶1 last line, after late sources *add* (including unnumbered Oxford Bodleian MS (date *c*1830), P 1118).

768   *p309 line above 2nd inset, after* refrain *add* (Conrad von der Lage's *Gesangbuch*, 1681)

        p310 ¶1 and inset: The editors of *NBA* IV/1 argue that Krebs shows a first stage in the creation of the variations, one that allowed for additions; then Carpentras gives an early and cyclic form of an enlarged set; Preller alters the order; and III.8.17 gives variants in their final stages.

        p311 inset: The overall shape can also be expressed as a regular alternation between ostinato phrases and chorale lines: 3–8½–3–6½–3–9–3¼ bars.

769/769a   *p315 line 1 after subhead '769', for* her'; *read* her. per Canones. à 2 Clav: et Pedal. di J. S. Bach';

        p319 lines 6–7 after 2nd inset, for a progressive and a symmetrical *read* a symmetrical and a progressive

        p320 ¶3 lines 6–8: But did bellringers in eighteenth-century Saxony change-ring in diatonic scales? Was Terry misled by familiar English practice?

        p326 lines 1–8 after inset: The last three bars of the coda were quoted admiringly by Türk in 1787 (pp236–7).

770   *p327 lines 1–4 from bottom, and p328 line 1, delete from 'partitas of' to 'under 'Pachelbel').' and replace by* partitas of Pachelbel described by J. G. Walther (*Lexicon* 1732). Not perhaps entirely logically, Klotz states that BWV 770 cannot be the work of J. S. Bach because it requires the C♯ found only at Weimar, to which period it could not belong stylistically (1950 p197). However, H. Löffler devoted a detailed essay to the work (1923), relating the music to the text, on the assumption that it certainly was a work of J. S. Bach. The editors of *NBA* IV/1 also see it as a Bach work, with sources probably going back to a copy originating in the Thuringian period.

n.v.1   *p330 ¶4 line 3, for* 'Giovan. Sebast. Bach'. *read* 'Giovan Sebastin Bach'.

List of Musical Sources

p335 under 'Abbreviations', add
Darmstadt   Hessische Landes- und Hochschulbibliothek, Darmstadt

p336 lines 1-2, delete from 'made by' to 'J. Bernhard Bach' and replace by made by unknown copyists *c*1706–1710/12 (the chief of whom was almost certainly J. C. Bach 1671–1721; the MS has also been attributed to J. Bernhard Bach, sen. or jun. See Vol. III p272, comment on Vol. I p347.

p336 'Brussels II. 3919' delete line 2 and replace by MS probably once in Fétis's collection, corresponding in part to his

p337 line 1, for P 244 *read* P 224

p337 'LM 4983' delete from 'written probably' to 'mid 18th' and replace by copied by J. C. Bach of Gehren (Kobayashi 1983)

p337 'Möller MS' line 3, for 1705/10; *read* 1703/7;

p338 'P 448', delete entry and replace by
P 488: MS often described as J. S. Bach's earliest known autograph (*c*1705), containing BWV 739 and 764; but see Vol. II p288. The watermark is the same as that of Möller MS.

p339 line 7, for J. K. Vogler *read* J. C. Vogler

p340 line 1, after J. C. Oley *add* (BWV 716, 377, 601, 431)

p340 'P 1216' line 3, for Missing since 1945. *read* See Vol. III p275, comment on Vol. II p6. Extant are BWV 635, 636, 637 (Oxford, Bodleian) and 631a, 632 (London, private possession).

List of References

p342 'Emery 1970' line 1, for Klaviaturumgafang *read* Klaviaturumfang

p344 line 25 from bottom, for Paretorius *read* Praetorius

p345 'Weismann 1949–50' line 2, for Kalvierübung *read* Klavierübung

p345 'Williams 1979' delete entry and replace by P. Williams, 'The Musical Aims of J. S. Bach's "Clavierübung III" ' in *Source Materials and the Interpretation of Music: A Memorial Volume to Thurston Dart*, ed. I. Bent (London, 1981) 259–78

Index

p347, entry 'd'Anglebert' should precede 'Anna Amalia'

p347 under 'Bach, C. P. E.' last line, for 182, 314, *read* 182–3,

p349 under 'Hegenwal(d)t', for J., *read* E.,

p350 under 'Legrenzi', for 1636–90, *read* 1626–90,

p351 under 'Pachelbel, J.', after 329, *add* 333,

p351 under 'Scheibe', for Naumburg *read* Hamburg

p351 under 'Schmid(t)', after 175, *add* 177,

p352 under 'Türk', for Halle from 1774, *read* Halle from 1776,

p352 col. 2, for Wagner, J., *read* Wagner, J. J.,

p354 col. 2 line 2 from bottom, type broken: read 158: 66

Note on MSS Cited

For details concerning MS sources, see the 'Lists of Musical Sources' in Vol. I pp346–50, Vol. II pp335–40.

MS collections

Am.B. = Amalien-Bibliothek (Berlin, Musikbibliothek der Prinzessin Anna Amalia von Preussen), held in DSB

BB = Berlin, Deutsche Staatsbibliothek, Mus. MSS (previously Preussische Staatsbibliothek (formerly Königliche Bibliothek), Musikabteilung) – dispersed, cf. DSB and SPK

Den Haag = 's Gravenhage, Gemeente Museum

DSB = Deutsche Staatsbibliothek, Berlin (East)

Kö = Königsberg (now Kaliningrad), former Universitätsbibliothek, Mus. MSS

LM = New Haven, Connecticut, Yale University Music Library

Lpz Go.S. = Leipzig, Sammlung Manfred Gorke

Lpz MB = Leipzig, Musikbibliothek (including former Musikbibliothek Peters)

Lpz Poel = Lpz MB Poelchau Mus. MSS

P = P-signatures of BB – dispersed, partly in DSB, partly in SPK

Sp = Berlin–Charlottenburg, Hochschule für Musik Bibliothek

SPK = Staatsbibliothek Preussischer Kulturbesitz, Berlin (West)

Named MSS

Andreas-Bach-Buch = Lpz MB III.8.4
Fétis 2960 = Brussels, Bibliothèque Royale de Belgique, MS II.4093 (see Vol. I p347)
Klavierbüchlein für Anna Magdalena Bach = P 224, P225 (see Vol. II pp336–7)
Klavierbüchlein für Wilhelm Friedemann Bach = LM (see Vol. II p337)
Möller MS = BB40644

List of References

A few sources cited only once or twice in the text (where they are fully identified) are omitted from the following list.

Abbreviations

AM | *Acta musicologica*
AMZ | *Allgemeine musikalische Zeitung*
BG | *Johann Sebastian Bachs Werke*, Bach-Gesellschaft edition, 46 vols. (Leipzig, 1851–99)
B & H | Breitkopf & Härtel
BJ | *Bach-Jahrbuch*
BUXWV | G. Karstädt, *Thematisch–systematisches Verzeichnis der musikalischen Werke von Dietrich Buxtehude* (Wiesbaden, 1974)
DDT | *Denkmäler deutscher Tonkunst*
DTB | *Denkmäler der Tonkunst in Bayern*
DTÖ | *Denkmäler der Tonkunst in Österreich*
JAMS | *Journal of the American Musicological Society*
Mf | *Die Musikforschung*
MGG | *Die Musik in Geschichte und Gegenwart*, ed. F. Blume, 14 vols. (Kassel, 1949–68) plus Suppl.(Kassel, 1970–)
MT | *Musical Times*
MuK | *Musik und Kirche*
NBA | [J. S. Bach], *Neue ausgabe sämtlicher Werke*, Neue Bach-Ausgabe (Leipzig/Kassel, 1954– , in progress)
NBA KB | Neue Bach-Ausgabe, *Kritischer Bericht* (Critical Commentary)

Adlung 1758, 1783 | J. Adlung, *Anleitung zur musikalischen Gelahrtheit* (Erfurt, 1758; 2nd edn [ed. J. A. Hiller] Dresden/Leipzig, 1783)
Adlung 1768 | J. Adlung, *Musica mechanica organoedi* [ed. J. L. Albrecht & J. F. Agricola] (Berlin, 1768)
Agricola 1758 | J. F. Agricola, 'Sammlung einiger Nachrichten von berühmten Orgelwerken in Teutschland', in *Historisch-kritische Beyträge zur Aufnahme der Musik*, ed. F. W. Marpurg III (1758) 456–518
Albrecht 1980 | T. Albrecht, 'Musical Rhetoric in J. S. Bach's Organ Toccata BWV 565', *Organ Yearbook* 11 (1980) 84–94
Apel 1967 | W. Apel, *Geschichte der Orgel- und Klaviermusik bis 1700* (Kassel, 1967); English trans. H. Tischler, *The History of Keyboard Music to 1700* (Bloomington, Indiana, 1972)
Arfken 1965 | E. Arfken, 'Das Weimarer Orgelbüchlein Johann Sebastian Bachs' (unpublished diss., Göttingen, 1965)
C. P. E. Bach 1753, 1762 | C. P. E. Bach, *Versuch über die wahre Art das Clavier zu spielen*, 2 vols. (Berlin, 1753, 1762); English trans. W. J. Mitchell, *Essay on the True Art of Playing Keyboard Instruments* (London, 1949)
Bal 1981 | G. Bal, preface to facsimile edn of J. C. L. Kittel, *Der angehende praktische Organist*, 3 vols. (Erfurt, 1801–8) (Buren, 1981)

Barbour 1951 | J. M. Barbour, *Tuning and Temperament: A Historical Survey* (East Lansing, Michigan, 1951)

Barnes 1979 | J. Barnes, 'Bach's Keyboard Temperament: Internal Evidence from the *Well-Tempered Clavier*', *Early Music* 7 (1979) 236–49

Benary 1959 | P. Benary, 'Zum periodischen Prinzip bei Johann Sebastian Bach', *BJ* 46 (1959) 111–23

Bernhard 1650 | J. Müller-Blattau, *Die Kompositionslehre Heinrich Schützens in der Fassung seines Schülers Christoph Bernhard* (2nd edn Kassel, 1963); English trans. W. Hilse, 'The Treatises of Christoph Bernhard', *Music Forum* 3 (1973) 1–196

Bernsdorff-Engelbrecht | C. Bernsdorff-Engelbrecht, 'Kasseler Orgelbaugeschichte', *Acta Organologica* I (1967) 113–26

Billeter 1979 | B. Billeter, *Anweisung zum Stimmen von Tasteninstrumenten* (Kassel, 1979)

Bitter 1881 | C. H. Bitter, *Johann Sebastian Bach*, 4 vols. (2nd edn, Berlin, 1881)

Blankenburg 1961 | W. Blankenburg, 'Der gottesdienstliche Liedgesang der Gemeinde', in *Leiturgia* IV, ed. K. F. Müller & W. Blankenburg (Kassel, 1961) 601–35

Blankenburg 1965 | W. Blankenburg, 'Die Kirchenmusik in den reformierten Gebieten', in F. Blume, *Geschichte der evangelischen Kirchenmusik* (Kassel, 1965) 341–400

Blindow 1957 | M. Blindow, *Die Choralbegleitung des 18. Jahrhunderts in der evangelischen Kirche Deutschlands* (Regensburg, 1957)

Blume 1936 | F. Blume, *Michael Praetorius und Esaias Compenius: Orgeln Verdingnis* (Wolfenbüttel/Berlin, 1936)

Blume 1968 | F. Blume, 'J. S. Bach's Youth', *Musical Quarterly* 54 (1968) 1–30

Blume 1974 | F. Blume, *Protestant Church Music: A History*, rev. L. Finscher (New York, 1974)

Boxberg 1704 | C. L. Boxberg, *Ausführliche Beschreibung der Orgel zu St. Petri und Paul zu Görlitz* (Görlitz, 1704)

Braun 1972 | H. Braun, 'Eine Gegenüberstellung von Original und Bearbeitung, dargestellt an der Entlehnung eines Corellischen Fugenthemas durch J. S. Bach', *BJ* 58 (1972) 5–11

Bridge/Higgs 1887 | *The Organ Works of J. S. Bach* VIII, ed. F. Bridge & J. Higgs (London [Novello], 1887)

Bruggaier 1959 | E. Bruggaier, *Studien zur Geschichte des Orgelpedalspiels in Deutschland bis zur Zeit Johann Sebastian Bachs* (Frankfurt, 1959)

Budday 1977 | W. Budday, 'Musikalische Figuren als satztechnische Freiheiten in Bachs Orgelchoral "Durch Adams Fall ist ganz verderbt" ', *BJ* 63 (1977) 139–59

Bullivant 1959 | R. Bullivant, 'The Fugal Technique of J. S. Bach' (unpublished diss., Oxford, 1959–60)

Burney ed. Scholes | ed. P. A. Scholes, *Dr Burney's Musical Tours in Europe*, 2 vols. (London, 1959)

Chorley 1841 | H. F. Chorley, *Music and Manners in France and Germany* III (London, 1841)

Curtis 1969 | A. Curtis, *Sweelinck's Keyboard Music* (Leiden/London, 1969)

Dahlhaus 1949 | C. Dahlhaus, 'Zur Geschichte der Permutationsfuge', *BJ* 46 (1949) 95–110

Dähnert 1953 | U. Dähnert, *Die Orgeln Gottfried Silbermanns in Mitteldeutschland* (Leipzig, 1953; 2nd edn with supplement, Amsterdam, 1968)

Dähnert 1962 | U. Dähnert, *Der Orgel- und Instrumentenbauer Zacharias Hildebrandt* (Leipzig, 1962)

Dähnert 1970 | U. Dähnert, 'Johann Sebastian Bach's Ideal Organ', *Organ Yearbook* I (1970) 21–37

Dähnert 1980 | U. Dähnert, *Historische Orgeln in Sachsen* (Leipzig, 1980)

Dalton 1966 | J. Dalton, 'Bach Interpretation', *MT* 107 (1966), 341, 440, 536ff

David 1951 | W. David, *Johann Sebastian Bachs Orgeln* (Berlin, 1951)

List of References

David/Mendel 1945, 1966 | H. T. David and A. Mendel, *The Bach Reader* (New York, 1945; revised edn with supplement, 1966)

Dietrich 1929 | F. Dietrich, 'J. S. Bachs Orgelchoral und seine geschichtliche Wurzeln', *BJ* 26 (1929) 1–89

Dok I | *Bach-Dokumente* I, ed. W. Neumann & H.J. Schulze (Leipzig/Kassel, 1963)

Dok II | *Bach-Dokumente* II, ed. W. Neumann & H.J. Schulze (Leipzig/Kassel, 1969)

Dok III | *Bach-Dokumente* III, ed. H.J. Schulze (Leipzig/Kassel, 1972)

Dok IV | *Bach-Dokumente* IV, ed. W. Neumann (Leipzig/Kassel, 1979)

Dürr 1951 | A. Dürr, *Studien über die frühen Kantaten J. S. Bachs* (Leipzig, 1951)

Dürr 1977 | A. Dürr, 'Bemerkungen zu Bachs Leipziger Kantatenaufführungen', in *Bericht über die wissenschaftliche Konferenz zum III. Internationalen Bach-Fest der DDR*, ed. W. Felix (Leipzig, 1977) 165–72

Eck 1981 | C. L. Panthaleon van Eck, *J. S. Bach's Critique of Pure Music* (Culemborg, 1981)

Edler 1982 | A. Edler, *Der nordelbische Organist: Studien zu Sozialstatus, Funktion und kompositorischer Produktion eines Musikberufes von der Reformation bis zum 20. Jahrhundert* (Kassel, 1982)

Eller 1961 | R. Eller, 'Vivaldi–Dresden–Bach', *Beiträge zur Musikwissenschaft* 3 (1961) 31–48

Emery 1953 | W. Emery, *Bach's Ornaments* (London, 1953)

Emery 1957 | W. Emery, *Notes on Bach's Organ Works*, IV–V: *Six Sonatas for Two Manuals and Pedal* (London, 1957)

Emery 1962 | W. Emery, 'On the Registration of Bach's Organ Preludes and Fugues', *MT* 103 (1962) 396–8, 467–8

Emery 1971 | W. Emery, 'Is your Bach playing authentic?', *MT* 112 (1971) 483–8, 697–8, 796–7

Emery 1972 | W. Emery, 'The Bach Organ at Arnstadt', *MT* 113 (1972) 119–21

Engel 1966 | H. Engel, *Musik in Thüringen* (Cologne/Graz, 1966)

Feder 1958 | G. Feder, 'Bemerkungen über einige J. S. Bach zugeschriebene Werke', *Mf* 11 (1958) 76–82

Feder 1965 | G. Feder, 'Verfall und Restauration', in F. Blume, *Geschichte der evangelischen Kirchenmusik* (Kassel, 1965) 216–69

Fellerer 1932 | K. G. Fellerer, *Beiträge zur Choralbegleitung und Choralverarbeitung in der Orgelmusik des ausgehenden 18. und beginnenden 19. Jahrhunderts* (Leipzig/Strassburg/Zürich, 1932)

Flade 1926 | E. Flade, *Der Orgelbauer Gottfried Silbermann* (Leipzig, 1926; 2nd edn with supplement, 1953)

Fock 1974 | G. Fock, *Arp Schnitger und seine Schule* (Kassel, 1974)

Forkel 1802 | J. N. Forkel, *Ueber Johann Sebastian Bachs Leben, Kunst und Kunstwerke* (Leipzig, 1802)

Frotscher 1934–5 | G. Frotscher, *Geschichte des Orgelspiels und der Orgelkomposition*, 2 vols. (Berlin, 1934–5)

Frotscher 1935 | G. Frotscher, 'Zur Problematik der Bach-Orgel', *BJ* 32 (1935) 107–21

Geck 1968 | M. Geck, *Nicolaus Bruhns: Leben und Werk* (Cologne, 1968)

Geiringer 1966 | K. Geiringer, *Johann Sebastian Bach: The Culmination of an Era* (New York, 1966)

Gerber 1790, 1792 | E. L. Gerber, *Historisch-biographisches Lexicon der Tonkünstler* I (Leipzig, 1790), II (Leipzig, 1792)

Gojowy 1972 | D. Gojowy, 'Lied und Sonntag in Gesangbüchern der Bach-Zeit: zur Frage des "Detempore" bei Chorälen in Bachs Kantaten', *BJ* 58 (1972) 24–60

Goltzen 1956 | H. Goltzen, 'Der tägliche Gottesdienst', in *Leiturgia* III, ed. K. F. Müller & W. Blankenburg (Kassel, 1956) 99–296

Harmon 1971 | T. Harmon, *The Registration of J. S. Bach's Organ Works* (Amsterdam, 1971)

Harris 1980 | E. T. Harris, 'The Italian in Handel', *JAMS* 33 (1980) 468–500

Hawkins 1853 | J. Hawkins, *A General History of the Science and Practice of Music*, 3 vols. (new edn, London, 1853–75)

Heinichen 1728 | J. D. Heinichen, *Der General-Bass in der Composition* (Dresden, 1728)

Heinichen 1711 | J. D. Heinichen, *Neu erfundene und gründliche Anweisung zu vollkommener Erlernung des General-Basses* (Hamburg, 1711)

Henkel 1977 | H. Henkel, *Beiträge zum historischen Cembalobau* (diss., Leipzig, 1977; published Leipzig, 1979)

Hess 1774 | J. Hess, *Disposition der merkwaardigste Kerk-Orgelen* (Gouda, 1774)

Hilgenfeldt 1850 | C. L. Hilgenfeldt, *Johann Sebastian Bachs Leben, Wirken und Werke* (Leipzig, 1850)

Hisao Mabuchi 1979 | Hisao Mabuchi, 'Evidence of the Toe–Heel Pedalling in J. S. Bach's Organ Works', *Organ-Kenkyu* 7 (Tokyo, 1979) 23–8

Holmes 1828 | E. Holmes, *A Ramble among the Musicians of Germany* (London, 1828)

Hubbard 1965 | F. Hubbard, *Three Centuries of Harpsichord Making* (Cambridge, Mass., 1965)

Jauernig 1950 | R. Jauernig, 'Johann Sebastian Bach in Weimar', in *Johann Sebastian Bach in Thüringen*, ed. H. Besseler & G. Kraft (Weimar, 1950) 49–105

Kee 1982 | P. Kee, 'Die Geheimnisse von Bachs Passacaglia', *MuK* 52 (1982) 165–75, 235–44

Keller 1948 | H. Keller, *Die Orgelwerke Bachs* (Leipzig, 1948)

Keller 1965 | H. Keller, *Das wohltemperierte Klavier von Johann Sebastian Bach* (Kassel, 1965); English trans. L. Gerdine, *The Well-Tempered Clavier of Johann Sebastian Bach* (New York, 1976)

Kellner 1980 | H. A. Kellner, *The Tuning of my Harpsichord* (Frankfurt, 1980)

Kilian 1969 | D. Kilian, 'Dreisätzige Fassungen Bachscher Orgelwerke', in *Bach-Interpretationen*, ed. M. Geck (Gottingen, 1969) 12–21

Kilian 1983 | D. Kilian, 'Zu einem Bachschen Tabulaturautograph', in *Bachiana et alia Musicologica: Festschrift Alfred Dürr*, ed. W. Rehm (Kassel, 1983) 161–7

Kinsky 1936 | G. Kinsky, 'Pedalklavier oder Orgel bei Bach?', *Acta musicologica* 8 (1936) 61–72

Klein 1976 | H.-G. Klein, 'Johann Sebastian Bach. Leben und Werk: Vorbilder und Zeitgenossen', in *Johann-Sebastian Bach. Zeit. Leben. Wirken*, ed. B. Schwendowius & W. Dömling (Kassel, 1976)

Kloppers 1966 | J. Kloppers, *Die Interpretation und Wiedergabe der Orgelwerke Bachs* (Frankfurt, 1966)

Kloppers 1976 | J. Kloppers, 'A Criterion for Manual Change in the Organ Works of Bach', *Organ Yearbook* 7 (1976) 59–67

Klotz 1933 | H. Klotz, *Über die Orgelkunst der Gotik, der Renaissance und des Barock* (Kassel, 1933; 2nd, rewritten edn, Kassel, 1975)

Klotz 1950 | H. Klotz, 'Bachs Orgeln und seine Orgelmusik', *Mf* 3 (1950) 189–203

Klotz 1961 | H. Klotz, 'Die kirchliche Orgelkunst', in *Leiturgia* IV, ed. K. F. Müller & W. Blankenburg (Kassel, 1961) 786–7

Klotz 1962 | H. Klotz, 'Johann Sebastian Bach und die Orgel', *MuK* 32 (1962) 49–55

Klotz 1969 | H. Klotz, 'Originale Spielanweisungen in Bachs Orgelwerken und ihre Konsequenzen für die Interpretation', in *Bach-Interpretationen*, ed. M. Geck (Göttingen, 1969) 112–18

Klotz 1969a | H. Klotz, 'Les Critères de l'interprétation française sont-ils applicables à la musique d'orgue de J.-S. Bach?', in *L'Interprétation de la musique française aux XVIIe et XVIIIe siècles*, Colloques Internationaux de CNRS (Paris, 1969) 155–72

Klotz 1975: *see* Klotz 1933

Klotz 1978 | H. Klotz, *Pro Organo pleno: Norm und Vielfalt der Registervorschrift Joh. Seb. Bachs* (Wiesbaden, 1978)

Klotz 1980 | 'Die nordfranzösische Registrierkunst im letzten Drittel des 17. Jahrhunderts und die Orgeldisposition Gottfried Silbermanns von 1710 für die Leipziger Paulinerkirche', in *Visitatio Organorum*, ed. A. Dunning (Buren, 1980) 387–97

Kobayashi 1973 | Y. Kobayashi, *Franz Hauser und seine Bach-Handschriftensammlung* (diss., Göttingen, 1973)

Kobayashi 1983 | Y. Kobayashi, 'Der Gehrener Kantor Johann Christoph Bach (1673–1727) und seine Sammelbände mit Musik für Tasteninstrumente', in *Bachiana et alia Musicologica: Festschrift Alfred Dürr*, ed. W. Rehm (Kassel, 1983) 168–77

Kooiman 1980 | E. Kooiman, 'Pedaalapplikatuur: Kittel, Tuerk, Petri en Bach', *Het Orgel* 76 (1980) 393–402

Kraft 1950 | G. Kraft, 'Johann Sebastian Bach in Ohrdruf', in *Johann Sebastian Bach in Thüringen*, ed. H. Besseler & G. Kraft (Weimar, 1950) 25–9

Krams 1974 | P. Krams, *Wechselwirkungen zwischen Orgelkomposition und Pedalspieltechnik* (Wiesbaden, 1974)

Krey 1956 | J. Krey, 'Bachs Orgelmusik in der Weimarer Zeit' (unpublished diss., Jena, 1956)

Krummacher 1978 | F. Krummacher, *Die Choralbearbeitung in der protestantischen Figuralmusik zwischen Praetorius und Bach* (Kassel, 1978)

Kwasnik 1966 | W. Kwasnik, 'Johann Sebastian Bach als Orgelrevisor', *Instrumentenbauzeitschrift* 20 (1966) 221–3, 303–15, 340–3

Lange 1972–3 | H. K. H. Lange, 'Gottfried Silbermann's Organ Tuning', *ISO Information* 8 (1972) 543–56, 9 (1973) 647–58, 10 (1973) 721–30

Löffler 1923 | H. Löffler, 'Die Choralpartita "Ach, was soll ich Sünder machen"', *BJ* 20 (1923) 31–56

Löffler 1928 | H. Löffler, 'J. S. Bach und die Orgeln seiner Zeit', *Bericht über die dritte Tagung für deutsche Orgelkunst in Freiberg/Sachsen* (Kassel, 1928) 122–32

Löffler 1932 | H. Löffler, 'G. H. Trost und die Altenburger Schlossorgel', *MuK* 4 (1932) 171–6, 280–5

Lohmann 1974 | H. Lohmann, 'Bemerkungen zur Zahlensymbolik in der Klavier-Übung III von Johann Sebastian Bach', *Der Kirchenmusiker* 25 (1974) 55–8

Lohmann 1982 | L. Lohmann, *Studien zu Artikulationsproblemen bei den Tasteninstrumenten des 16.–18. Jahrhunderts* (Regensburg, 1982)

Luedtke 1918 | H. Luedtke, 'Sebastian Bachs Choralvorspiele', *BJ* 15 (1918) 1–96

Lux 1926 | E. Lux, 'Das Orgelwerk in St. Michaelis zu Ohrdruf', *BJ* 23 (1926) 145–55

Mahrenholz 1960 | C. Mahrenholz, 'Liturgiegeschichtliches aus dem Lande Hadeln', repr. in *Musicologica et Liturgica* (Kassel, 1960) 521–42

Mainwaring 1760 | [J. Mainwaring], *Memoirs of the Life of the Late George Frederic Handel* (London, 1760)

Marpurg 1750 | F. W. Marpurg, *Die Kunst das Klavier zu spielen* (Berlin, 1750)

Marpurg 1754/1758 | F. W. Marpurg, *Historisch-kritische Beyträge zur Aufnahme der Musik* I (Berlin, 1754), II (1756), III (1757–8), IV (1758–9), V (1760–62)

Marpurg 1761 | F. W. Marpurg, *Kritische Briefe über die Tonkunst* I (Berlin, 1760), II (1761), III (1764)

Mattheson 1713 | J. Mattheson, *Das neu-eröffnete Orchestre* (Hamburg, 1713)

Mattheson 1722/1725 | J. Mattheson, *Critica musica* I (Hamburg, 1722), II (Hamburg, 1725)

Mattheson 1731 | J. Mattheson, *Grosse General-Bass-Schule oder exemplarische Organistenprobe* (Hamburg, 1731)

Mattheson 1739 | J. Mattheson, *Der vollkommene Capellmeister* (Hamburg, 1739)

Mattheson 1740 | J. Mattheson, *Grundlage einer Ehren-Pforte* (Hamburg, 1740)

May 1974 | E. May, 'J. G. Walther and the Lost Weimar Autographs of Bach's Organ Works', in *Studies in Renaissance and Baroque Music in Honor of Arthur Mendel* (Kassel, 1974) 264–82

Meyer 1973 | U. Meyer, 'Johann Sebastian Bachs Variationenzyklus "Sei gegrüsset, Jesu gütig" (BWV 768)', *Mf* 26 (1973) 474–81

Meyer 1979 | U. Meyer, 'Zum Problem der Zahlen in Johann Sebastian Bachs Werk', *MuK* 49 (1979) 58–71

Mizler 1736/1738/1739 | L. Mizler, *(Neu eröffnete) Musikalische Bibliothek* I.i (Leipzig, 1736), I.ii (1737), I.iii (1737) I.iv–vi (1738); reprinted Leipzig, 1739

Mizler 1743 | L. Mizler, *(Neu eröffnete) Musikalische Bibliothek* II.i–ii (Leipzig, 1740), II.iii (1742), II.iv (1743); reprinted Leipzig, 1743

Mizler 1752 | L. Mizler, *Musicalische Bibliothek* III.iv (Leipzig, 1752)

Mizler 1740 | L. Mizler, *Musicalischer Staarstecher* (Leipzig, 1739–40)

Müller 1950 | K. Müller, 'Johann Sebastian Bach in Arnstadt', in *Johann Sebastian Bach in Thüringen*, ed. H. Besseler & G. Kraft (Weimar, 1950) 30–42

Müller 1982 | W. Müller, *Gottfried Silbermann: Persönlichkeit und Werk* (Leipzig, 1982)

Musch 1974 | H. Musch, 'Von der Einheit der grossen Orgelfuge Johann Sebastian Bachs', *MuK* 44 (1974) 267–79

Neumann 1978 | F. Neumann, *Ornamentation in Baroque and Post-Baroque Music: with Special Emphasis on J. S. Bach* (Princeton, 1978)

Neumann 1956 | W. Neumann, 'Zur Frage der Gesangbücher J. S. Bachs', *BJ* 42 (1956) 112–23

Niedt (Niedt/Mattheson) | F. E. Niedt, *Musicalische Handleitung* I (Hamburg, 1700; 2nd edn, 1710); II = *Handleitung zur Variation* (Hamburg, 1706; 2nd, enlarged edn by J. Mattheson, [1721]); *Musicalische Handleitung. Dritter und letzter Theil* [= III], J. Mattheson ed. (Hamburg, 1717)

Pauly 1964 | H.-J. Pauly, *Die Fuge in den Orgelwerken Dietrich Buxtehudes* (Regensburg, 1964)

Petri 1782 | J. S. Petri, *Anleitung zur praktischen Musik* (Lauban, 1767; 2nd, revised edn, Leipzig, 1782)

Pirro 1901 | A. Pirro, preface to *Pièces choisies pour l'Orgue de Louis Marchand*, ed. A. Guilmant, *Archives des Maîtres de l'Orgue* III (Paris, 1901)

Praetorius 1619 | M. Praetorius, *Syntagma musicum* III (Wolfenbüttel, 1619)

Printz 1696 | W. C. Printz, *Phrynis Mytilenaeus oder satyrischer Componist*, 3 vols. (I–II Quedlinburg, 1676–7; three vols. published as one, Dresden/Leipzig, 1696)

Quantz 1752 | J. J. Quantz, *Versuch einer Anweisung die Flöte traversiere zu spielen* (Berlin, 1752)

Rasch 1983 | R. Rasch, preface to facsimile edn of A. Werckmeister, *Musicalische Temperatur* (*1691*), forthcoming

Rasch 1985 | R. Rasch, article in volume of essays on J. S. Bach, Handel, D. Scarlatti (Cambridge, forthcoming 1985)

Riedel 1960 | F. W. Riedel, *Quellenkundliche Beiträge zur Geschichte der Musik für Tasteninstrumente in der 2. Hälfte des 17. Jahrhunderts* (Kassel, 1960)

Riedel 1968 | F. W. Riedel, 'Der Einfluss der italienischen Klaviermusik des 17. Jahrhunderts auf die Entwicklung der Musik für Tasteninstrumente in Deutschland während der ersetn Hälfte des 18. Jahrhunderts', *Analecta musicologica* 5 (1968) 18–33

Rietschel 1893 | G. Rietschel, *Die Aufgabe der Orgel im Gottesdienste bis in das 18. Jahrhundert* (Leipzig, 1893)

Russell 1959 | R. Russell, *The Harpsichord and Clavichord: An Introductory Study* (London, 1959; 2nd edn by H. Schott, 1973)

Scheibe 1745 | J. A. Scheibe, *Der critische Musikus*, 2 vols. (Hamburg, 1738–40; reprinted Leipzig, 1745)

Schering 1925 | A. Schering, 'Bach und das Symbol, insbesondere die Symbolik seines Kanons', *BJ* 22 (1925) 40–63

Schering 1926 | A. Schering, *Musikgeschichte Leipzigs,* II: *Von 1650 bis 1723* (Leipzig, 1926)

Schering 1936 | A. Schering, *Johann Sebastian Bachs Leipziger Kirchenmusik* (Leipzig, 1936)

List of References

Schering 1941 | A. Schering, *Johann Sebastian Bach und das Musikleben im 18. Jahrhundert* (Leipzig, 1941)

Schlueter 1954 | R. F. Schlueter, 'J. S. Bach and the Protestantism of his Day' (unpublished diss., Edinburgh, 1954–5)

Schmieder *BWV* | W. Schmieder, *Thematisch-systematisches Verzeichnis der musikalischen Werke von Johann Sebastian Bach* (Leipzig, 1950)

Schneider 1937 | T. Schneider, 'Die Orgelbauerfamilie Compenius', *Archiv für Musikforschung* 2 (1937) 8–76

Schöneich 1947/8 | F. Schöneich, 'Untersuchungen zur Form der Orgelpräludien und Fugen des jungen Bach' (unpublished diss., Göttingen, 1947/8)

Schrammek 1975 | W. Schrammek, 'Fragen des Orgelgebrauchs in Bachs Aufführungen der Matthäus-Passion', *BJ* 61 (1975) 114–23

Schubart 1806 | C. F. D. Schubart, *Ideen zu einer Ästhetik der Tonkunst* [ed. L. Schubart] (Wien, 1806)

Schulze 1972 | H.-J. Schulze, 'J. S. Bach's Concerto-Arrangements for Organ – Studies or Commissioned Works?', *Organ Yearbook* 3 (1972) 4–13

Schulze 1977 | H.-J. Schulze (ed.), *Katalog der Sammlung Manfred Gorke* (Leipzig, 1977)

Schünemann 1922 | G. Schünemann, 'Matthäus Hertels theoretische Schriften', *Archiv für Musikwissenschaft* 4 (1922) 336ff

Schünemann 1933 | G. Schünemann, 'J. G. Walther und H. Bokemeyer', *BJ* 30 (1933) 86–118

Seiffert 1906 | M. Seiffert, preface to *Johann Gottfried Walther: gesammelte Werke für Orgel, DDT* 16/17 (Leipzig, 1906)

Seiffert 1917 | M. Seiffert, preface to *Johann Krieger . . . gesammelte Werke für Klavier und Orgel, DDT* 30 (Leipzig, 1917)

Senn 1964 | K. W. Senn, 'Über die musikalischen Beziehungen zwischen Johann Gottfried Walther und Johann Sebastian Bach', *MuK* 34 (1968) 8–18

Serauky 1939 | W. Serauky, *Musikgeschichte der Stadt Halle* II.i (Halle/Berlin, 1939)

Sietz 1935 | R. Sietz, 'Die Orgelkompositionen des Schülerkreises um Johann Sebastian Bach', *BJ* 32 (1935) 33–96

Sinn 1717 | C. A. Sinn, *Die aus dem mathematischen Gründen richtig gestellte musikalische Temperatura* (Wernigerode, 1717)

Smets 1931 | *Orgeldispositionen. Eine Handschrift aus dem XVIII. Jahrhundert* [Dresdner MS], ed. P. Smets (Kassel, 1931)

Speer 1697 | D. Speer, *Grund-richtiger Unterricht der musicalischen Kunst* (2nd edn, Ulm, 1697)

Spitta I, II | P. Spitta, *Johann Sebastian Bach*, 2 vols. (Leipzig, 1873–9)

Stahl 1937 | W. Stahl, *Die Lübecker Abendmusiken im 17. und 18. Jahrhundert* (Kassel, 1937)

Stauffer 1980 | G. B. Stauffer, *The Organ Preludes of Johann Sebastian Bach* (Ann Arbor, Michigan, 1980)

Stauffer 1981 | G. B. Stauffer, article forthcoming in *Organ Yearbook*

Stiehl 1971 | H. A. Stiehl, *St. Thomas zu Leipzig* (2nd edn, Leipzig, 1971)

Stiller 1970 | G. Stiller, *Johann Sebastian Bach und das Leipziger gottesdienstliche Leben seiner Zeit* (Berlin, 1970)

Terry 1929 | C. S. Terry, *Johann Sebastian Bach. Eine Biographie*, German trans. A. Klengel (Leipzig, 1929)

Terry 1933 | C. S. Terry, *Bach: A Biography* (2nd edn, London, 1933)

Türk 1787 | D. G. Türk, *Von den wichtigsten Pflichten eines Organisten: ein Beytrag zur Verbesserung der musicalischen Liturgie* (Halle, 1787)

Tusler 1968 | R. L. Tusler, *The Style of J. S. Bach's Chorale Preludes* (2nd edn, New York, 1968)

Vetter 1709/1713 | D. Vetter, *Musicalische Kirch- und Hausergötzlichkeit,* 2 vols. (Leipzig, 1709–13)

Voigt 1742 | J. C. Voigt, *Gespräch von der Musik* [preface by L. Mizler] (Erfurt, 1742)

Walther 1727 | J. F. Walther, *Die in der Garnisonkirche zu Berlin befindliche neue Orgel* (Berlin, 1727)

Walther 1708 | J. G. Walther, *Praecepta der musicalischen Composition* [1708], ed. P. Benary (Leipzig, 1955)

Walther *Lexicon* | J. G. Walther, *Musicalisches Lexicon* (Leipzig, 1732)

Weismann 1956 | E. Weismann, 'Der Predigtgottesdienst und die verwandten Formen', in *Leiturgia* III, ed. K. F. Müller & W. Blankenburg (Kassel, 1956)

Werckmeister 1681/1698 | A. Werckmeister, *Orgelprobe* (Quedlinburg, 1681; 2nd, enlarged edn, *Erweiterte und verbesserte Orgelprobe*, Quedlinburg, 1698)

Werckmeister 1705 | A. Werckmeister, *Organum Gruningense Redivivum* (Quedlinburg/Aschersleben, 1705)

Werckmeister 1707 | A. Werckmeister, *Musicalische Paradoxal-Discourse* (Quedlinburg, 1707)

Werner 1902 | A. Werner, *Geschichte der Kantorei-Gesellschaften im Gebiete des ehemaligen Kurfürstentums Sachsen* (Leipzig, 1902)

Werner 1911 | A. Werner, *Städtische und fürstliche Musikpflege in Weissenfels bis zum Ende des 18. Jahrhunderts* (Leipzig, 1911)

Werner 1933 | A. Werner, *Vier, Jahrhunderte im Dienste der Kirchenmusik* (Leipzig, 1933)

Wette 1737 | G. A. Wette, *Historische Nachrichten von der berühmten Residenz-Stadt Weimar* (Weimar, 1737)

Wetzel 1961 | C. Wetzel, 'Der Träger des liturgischen Amtes', in *Leiturgia* IV, ed. K. F. Müller & W. Blankenburg (Kassel, 1961)

Williams 1966 | P. Williams, *The European Organ 1450–1850* (London, 1966)

Williams 1970 | P. Williams, *Figured Bass Accompaniment,* 2 vols. (Edinburgh, 1970)

Williams 1980 | P. Williams, *A New History of the Organ from the Greeks to the Present Day* (London, 1980)

Williams 1982 | P. Williams, article forthcoming in *BJ* 68

Witt *Cantional* | C. F. Witt[e], *Psalmodia sacra oder andächtige und schöne Gesänge* (Gotha, 1715)

Wolff 1968 | C. Wolff, *Der Stile antico in der Musik Johann Sebastian Bachs* (Wiesbaden, 1968)

Wolff 1977 | C. Wolff, 'Bachs Handexemplar der Schübler-Choräle', *BJ* 63 (1977) 120–9

Wustmann 1909 | R. Wustmann, *Musikgeschichte Leipzigs,* I: *Bis zur Mitte des 17. Jahrhunderts* (Leipzig/Berlin, 1909)

Zacher 1973 | G. Zacher, 'Über eine vergessene Tradition des Legatospiels', *MuK* 43 (1973) 166–71

Zavarsky 1965 | E. Zavarsky, 'Zum Pedalspiel des jungen Johann Sebastian Bach', *Mf* 18 (1965) 370–8

Zavarsky 1975 | E. Zavarsky, 'J. S. Bachs Entwurf für den Umbau der Orgel in der Kirche Divi Blasii und das Klangideal der Zeit', in *Bach-Studien 5,* ed R. Eller & H.-J. Schulze (Leipzig, 1975) 83–92

Zavarsky 1977 | E. Zavarsky, 'Die temperierte Stimmung, Bachs Klangideal der Orgel und die Entwicklungstendenzen der Zeit', in *Bericht über die wissenschaftliche Konferenz zum III. Internationalen Bach-Fest der DDR,* ed. W. Felix (Leipzig, 1977) 141–5

Ziller 1935 | E. Ziller, *Der Erfurter Organist Johann Heinrich Buttstädt (1666–1727)* (Halle, 1935)

Index of Names

An organist's appointments include his last major post; 'author' denotes a twentieth-century author. The Additions and Corrections on pp255–86 are indexed selectively.

Adlung, J., 1699–1762, organist at Erfurt Prediger-kirche from 1728, 18, 23, 24, 26, 31, 32, 46, 51, 57, 59, 94, 98, 118, 119, 122–3, 124–5, 128, 130, 133–4, 137, 139, 144, 157–61, 164–8, 170, 172, 176, 194, 219, 225, 245, 246, 252

Agricola, J. F., 1720–74, pupil of J. S. Bach (his continuo-player c1738–41), court composer in Berlin from 1751, 59, 64, 98, 99, 117–18, 128, 130–1, 156, 158, 163, 167, 178, 188–9, 224–5, 243, 260, 263, 270, 283

Ahle, J. G., 1651–1706, predecessor of J. S. Bach at Mühlhausen, 37–8

Alain, M.-C., author, 100

Alberti, J. F., 1642–1710, pupil in Leipzig of W. Fabricius, court organist at Merseburg, 94, 98

Albinoni, T., 1651–1750, Venetian composer, 96, 102, 111

Albrecht, J. L., 1732–69?, cantor at Mühlhausen Marienkirche from 1758, editor of Adlung 1768, 124, 283

Albrecht, T., author, 266

Albrici, V., 1631–96, Roman composer at Dresden from 1654, teacher (?) of Kuhnau, 98

Altni(c)kol, J. C., 1719–59, pupil from 1744 and son-in-law from 1749 of J. S. Bach, organist at Naumburg from 1748, 33, 137, 159, 228

Ammerbach, E. N., c1530–97, organist at Leipzig Thomaskirche from 1561, 252, 275, 279

d'Anglebert, J. H., c1635–91, Parisian composer, 226

Anton Güntler, Reichsgraf von Schwarzburg, 1653–1716, 35

Apel, W., author, 48, 68, 109

Arfken, E., author, 277

Aristotle, 69

Armsdorff, A., 1670–99, organist in Erfurt, 56

Bach, A. M., 1701–60, second wife of J. S. Bach (1721), 78, 203–4 (for *Klavierbüchlein* see BWV Index p306 below)

Bach, C. P. E., 1714–88, fifth child of J. S. Bach, by 1740 musician to Frederick II at Potsdam, 1767 succeeded Telemann at the Hamburg Johanneum, 51, 94, 98, 108, 139, 152, 155, 160, 184, 198, 202, 203, 212–17, 224, 228, 233, 234–5, 242, 243, 248, 263, 265, 268

Bach, J. Bernhard sen., 1676–1749, son of J. Egidius Bach, organist in Erfurt from 1695, Eisenach from 1703, teacher of J. G. Walther, 272, 286

Bach, J. Bernhard jun., 1700–43, nephew and pupil

of J. S. Bach, organist in Ohrdruf, 272, 286

Bach, J. C., 1642–1703, cousin of J. S. Bach's father, organist at Eisenach Georgenkirche from 1665, 16, 24–5, 108, 110, 111, 123, 139, 282

Bach, J. C., 1671–1721, brother of J. S. Bach, organist in Erfurt and in Ohrdruf from 1690, 272, 286

Bach, J. C., 1673–1727, cantor in Erfurt from 1695 and in Gehren from 1698, 286

Bach, J. G. B., 1715–39, sixth child of J. S. Bach, organist in Mühlhausen 1735, Sangerhausen 1737, then Jena, 23, 43, 134

Bach, J. L., 1695–1773, son of J. S. Bach's cousin, pupil 1715–17, cantor at Lahm from 1718, 134

Bach, J. M., 1648–94, brother of J. C. Bach (1642–1703), organist in Gehran, 24–5, 55, 176, 177

Bach, J. N., 1669–1753, son of J. C. Bach (1642–1703), organist in Jena from 1696, 31, 189

Bach, W. F., 1710–84, second child of J. S. Bach, organist at Dresden Sophienkirche 1733, Halle Liebfrauenkirche 1746, from 1774 in Berlin, 33, 42, 52, 95, 135, 203–4, 245, 255 (for *Klavierbüchlein* see BWV Index p306 below)

Bal, G., author, 46, 162, 244

Barbour, J. M., author, 186

Barnes, J., author, 187

Battiferri, L., 1600/10–c1682, pupil of Frescobaldi, at Ferrara with Legrenzi, 95

Becker, C. F., 1804–77, successor to Dröbs at Leipzig Peterskirche, 273

Becker, J., 1726–1804, copyist, 263

Becker, N., 18th-cent. organ-builder in Mühlhausen (former assistant to Stertzing?), 134

Beckmann, K., author, 157

Bedos de Celles, Dom J. F., 1706–79, French Benedictine organ-builder and theorist, 51, 155, 196

Bellermann, C., 1696–1758, *rector* in Hanover from 1743, 54, 241

Benda, F., 1709–86, Bohemian composer, 108

Bendeler, J. P., 1654–1709, godson of Werck-meister, appts in Quedlinburg from 1681, 140

Bernhard, C., 1627–92, 'pupil' of Schütz, kapell-meister at Dresden from 1681, 23, 68, 83, 272

Bernsdorff-Engelbrecht, C., author, 134

Beyer, J. S., 1668–1744, cantor in Freiberg, 283

Billeter, B., author, 186, 188

Birk, R., author, 271

Birnbaum, J. A., 1702–48, *Dozent* of rhetoric in Leipzig from 1721, 53, 98, 234, 282

Index of BWV Works Cited (Volume III)

Title Index of BWV Numbers in Volumes I-III

The wording and form of titles are as they appear in the first (or only) BWV number referred to. Cantatas and plain chorale harmonizations are not indexed here.

'Ach bleib bei uns, Herr Jesu Christ' BWV 649
'Ach Gott und Herr' BWV 692, 693, 714
'Ach Gott, vom Himmel sieh' darein' BWV 741
'Ach Herr, mich armen Sünder' BWV 742
'Ach, was ist doch unser Leben' BWV 743
'Ach, was soll ich Sünder machen' BWV 770
'Ach wie nichtig, ach wie flüchtig' BWV 644
Advent and Christmas fughettas: see BWV 696–699, 701, 703, 704
'Albinoni Fugues' BWV 950, 951
Allabreve BWV 589
'Alle Menschen müssen sterben' BWV 643
'Allein Gott in der Höh' sei Ehr'' BWV 662, 663, 664, 675, 676, 677, 711, 715, 716, 717, 771
'An Wasserflüssen Babylon' BWV 653
'Applicatio' BWV 994
'Aria ' BWV 587
Aria variata BWV 989
Art of Fugue BWV 1080
'Auf meinen lieben Gott' BWV 646, 744
'Aus der Tiefe rufe ich' BWV 745
'Aus tieffer Noth schrey ich zu dir' BWV 686, 687

B minor Mass BWV 232
Brandenburg Concertos BWV 1046–1051

'Canzona' BWV 588
Capriccio 'on the departure of a beloved brother' BWV 992
chorale partitas BWV 766–768, 770, 771
'Christ, der du bist der helle Tag' BWV 766
'Christ ist erstanden' BWV 627, 746
'Christ lag in Todesbanden' ' BWV 625, 695, 718
'Christ, unser Herr, zum Jordan kam' BWV 684, 685
'Christe, aller Welt Trost' BWV 670, 673
'Christe, du Lamm Gottes' BWV 619
Christmas Oratorio BWV 248
'Christum wir sollen loben schon' BWV 611, 696
'Christus, der uns selig macht' BWV 620, 747
Chromatic Fantasia BWV 903
Clavierübung I: BWV 825–830
Clavierübung II: BWV 971, 831
Clavierübung III BWV 552, 669–689, 802–805
Clavierübung IV: BWV 988
Concertos for Harpsichord BWV 1052–1058
Concertos for Three and Four Harpsichords BWV 1063–1065
concerto transcriptions for organ BWV 592–596
'Corelli Fugue' BWV 579

'Da Jesu an dem Kreuze stund' BWV 621
'Das alte Jahr vergangen ist' BWV 614
'Das Jesulein soll doch mein Trost' BWV 702
'Der Tag, der ist so freudenreich' BWV 605, 719